GCSE
Combined Science
Biology
The Complete Course for Edexcel

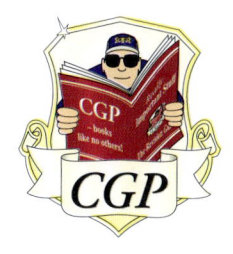

How to get your free Online Edition

Go to **cgpbooks.co.uk/extras** and enter this code...

2540 3588 1906 9743

This code will only work once. If someone has used this book before you, they may have already claimed the Online Edition.

Published by CGP

From original material by Paddy Gannon.

Editors:
Alex Billings, Mary Falkner, Emily Forsberg, Sarah Pattison, Hayley Thompson.

ISBN: 978 1 78294 813 1

With thanks to Katherine Faudemer, Rachel Kordan and Claire Plowman for the proofreading.
With thanks to Jan Greenway for the copyright research.

Printed by Elanders Ltd, Newcastle upon Tyne.
Clipart from Corel®

Text, design, layout and original illustrations © Coordination Group Publications Ltd. (CGP) 2017

All rights reserved.

Photocopying more than one chapter of this book is not permitted. Extra copies are available from CGP.
0800 1712 712 • www.cgpbooks.co.uk

Contents

Introduction
How to use this book i

Working Scientifically
1. The Scientific Method 2
2. Scientific Applications and Issues 5
3. Limitations of Science 6
4. Risks and Hazards 7
5. Designing Investigations 9
6. Collecting Data 12
7. Processing Data 14
8. Graphs and Charts 16
9. Units 19
10. Conclusions and Evaluations 21

Topic 1 — Key Concepts in Biology

Topic 1a — Cells and Microscopy
1. Cell Structure 23
2. Specialised Cells 26
3. Microscopy 28
Exam-style Questions 35

Topic 1b — Biological Molecules and Transport in Cells
1. Enzymes 36
2. Investigating Enzymatic Reactions 39
3. Enzymes in Breakdown and Synthesis 41
4. Transport in Cells 43
5. Investigating Osmosis in Plant Cells 47
Exam-style Questions 51

Topic 2 — Cells and Control

Topic 2a — Cell Division and Stem Cells
1. Mitosis 53
2. Cell Division and Growth 57
3. Stem Cells 59
Exam-style Questions 63

Topic 2b — Nervous Control
1. The Nervous System 64
2. Synapses and Reflexes 67
Exam-style Questions 71

Topic 3 — Genetics

Topic 3a — Reproduction, DNA and Protein Synthesis
1. Sexual Reproduction and Meiosis 72
2. DNA 75
Exam-style Questions 79

Topic 3b — Genetic Diagrams and Inheritance
1. Genes and Alleles 80
2. Genetic Diagrams and Family Pedigrees 81
3. Sex Determination 87
4. Variation 89
5. The Human Genome Project 92
Exam-style Questions 95

Topic 4 — Natural Selection and Genetic Modification

Topic 4a — Natural Selection and Evolution
1. Natural Selection and Evidence for Evolution   97
2. Evidence for Human Evolution — Fossils   100
3. Evidence for Human Evolution — Stone Tools   103
4. Classification   105

Exam-style Questions   **108**

Topic 4b — Genetic Modification
1. Selective Breeding   109
2. Genetic Engineering   111

Exam-style Questions   **114**

Topic 5 — Health, Disease and the Development of Medicines

Topic 5a — Health and Disease
1. Introduction to Health and Disease   115
2. Communicable Diseases   116

Exam-style Questions   **122**

Topic 5b — Fighting Disease
1. Defences Against Disease   123
2. Memory Lymphocytes and Immunisation   125
3. Developing Drugs   127
4. Antibiotics   131

Exam-style Questions   **133**

Topic 5c — Non-Communicable Diseases
1. Risk Factors for Non-Communicable Diseases   135
2. Measures of Obesity   138
3. Treating Cardiovascular Disease   140

Exam-style Questions   **145**

Topic 6 — Plant Structures and Their Functions
1. Photosynthesis   146
2. Limiting Factors in Photosynthesis   148
3. Investigating the Rate of Photosynthesis   152
4. The Inverse Square Law   154
5. Transport in Plants   155
6. Transpiration and Stomata   158

Exam-style Questions   **163**

Topic 7 — Animal Coordination, Control and Homeostasis

Topic 7a — Hormones and Fertility
1. Hormones   165
2. Adrenaline and Thyroxine   168
3. The Menstrual Cycle   170
4. Controlling Fertility   174

Exam-style Questions   **177**

Topic 7b — Homeostasis
1. Homeostasis   178
2. Controlling Blood Glucose   179

Exam-style Questions   **185**

Topic 8 — Exchange and Transport in Animals
1. Exchange of Materials   186
2. The Alveoli   189
3. Circulatory System — The Blood   191
4. Circulatory System — The Blood Vessels   193
5. Circulatory System — The Heart   195
6. Respiration   199
7. Investigating Respiration   202

Exam-style Questions   **207**

Topic 9 — Ecosystems and Material Cycles

Topic 9a — Ecosystems and Biodiversity

1. Ecosystems and Interactions Between Organisms — 209
2. Abiotic and Biotic Factors — 212
3. Investigating Ecosystems — 214
4. Human Impacts on Biodiversity — 218

Exam-style Questions — 222

Topic 9b — Material Cycles

1. The Carbon Cycle — 224
2. The Water Cycle — 226
3. The Nitrogen Cycle — 229

Exam-style Questions — 232

Practical Skills

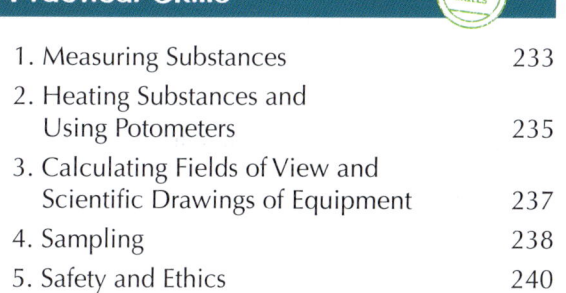

1. Measuring Substances — 233
2. Heating Substances and Using Potometers — 235
3. Calculating Fields of View and Scientific Drawings of Equipment — 237
4. Sampling — 238
5. Safety and Ethics — 240

Maths Skills

1. Calculations — 241
2. Algebra — 245
3. Graphs — 246

Exam Help

1. The Exams — 249
2. Exam Technique — 250
3. Question Types — 251

Reference

Answers — 254
Glossary — 273
Acknowledgements — 280
Index — 281

How to use this book

Learning Objectives
- These tell you exactly what you need to learn, or be able to do, for the exam.
- There's a specification reference at the bottom that links to the Edexcel specification.

Examples
These are here to help you understand the theory.

Working Scientifically
- Working Scientifically is a big part of GCSE Combined Science. There's a whole section on it at the front of the book.
- Working Scientifically is also covered throughout this book wherever you see this symbol.

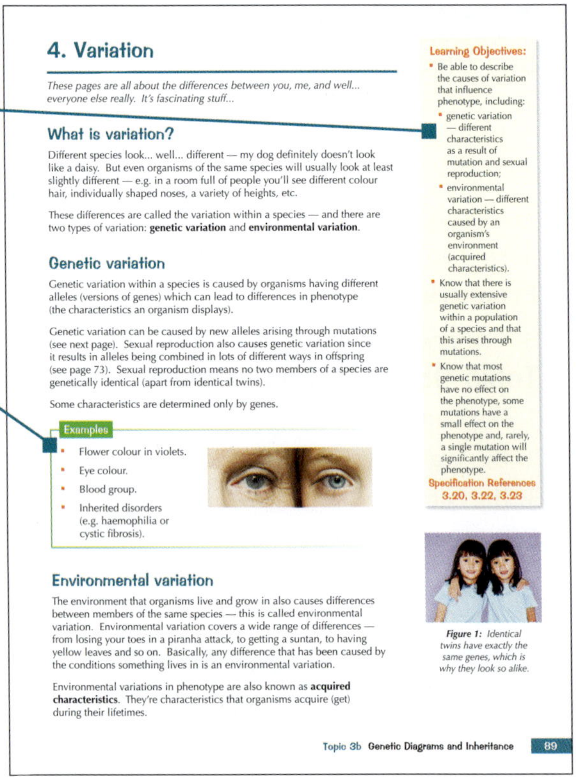

Core Practicals
There are some Core Practicals that you'll be expected to do throughout your course. You need to know all about them for the exams. They're all marked with stamps like this.

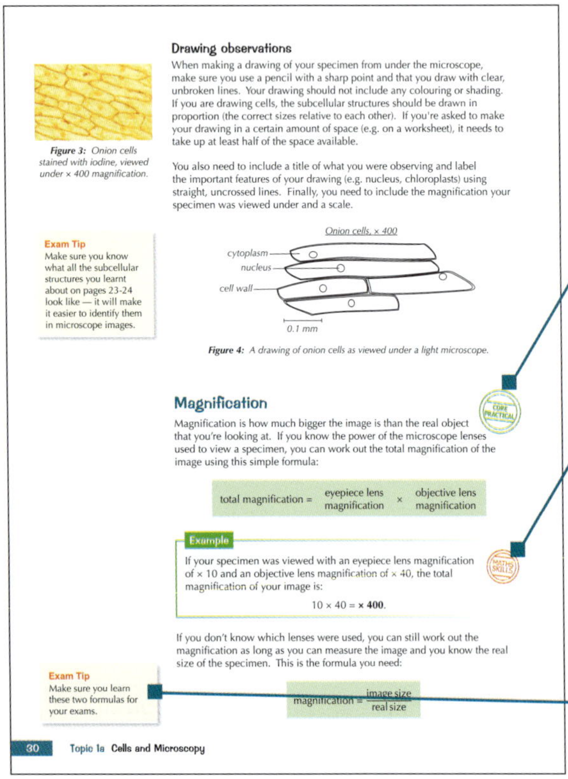

Maths Skills
- There's a range of maths skills you could be expected to apply in your exams. The section on pages 241-248 is packed with plenty of maths that you'll need to be familiar with.
- Examples that show these maths skills in action are marked up with this symbol.

Tips and Exam Tips
- There are tips throughout this book to help you understand the theory.
- There are also exam tips to help you with answering exam questions.

Higher Exam Material

- Some of the material in this book will only come up in the exam if you're sitting the higher exam papers.
- This material is clearly marked with boxes that look like this:

  Higher **H** **Q1**

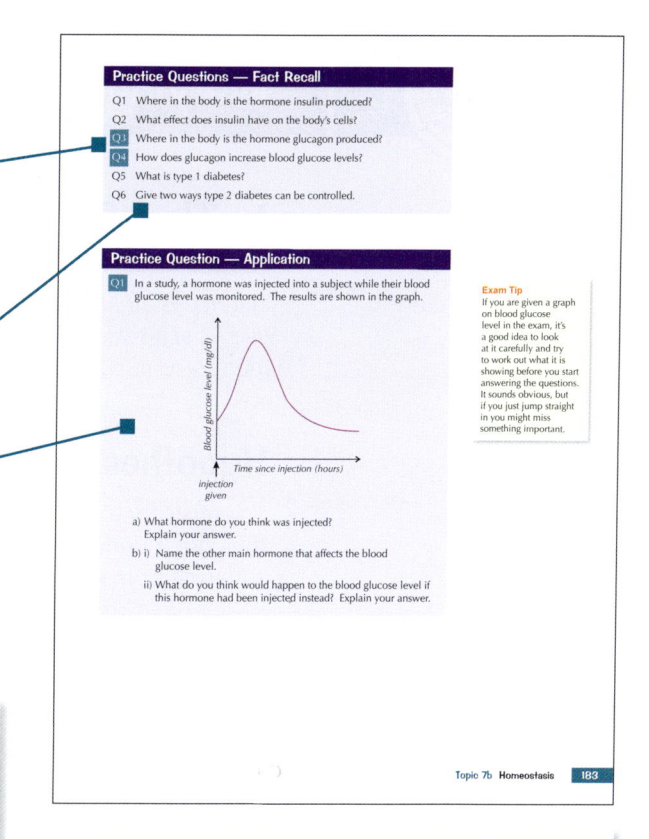

Practice Questions

- Fact recall questions test that you know the facts needed for your biology exams.
- Annoyingly, the examiners also expect you to be able to apply your knowledge to new situations — application questions give you plenty of practice at doing this.
- All the answers are in the back of the book.

Practical Skills

There's also a whole section on pages 233-240 with extra details on practical skills you'll be expected to use in the Core Practicals, and apply knowledge of in the exams.

Practice Questions — Fact Recall
Q1 Where in the body is the hormone insulin produced?
Q2 What effect does insulin have on the body's cells?
Q3 Where in the body is the hormone glucagon produced?
Q4 How does glucagon increase blood glucose levels?
Q5 What is type 1 diabetes?
Q6 Give two ways type 2 diabetes can be controlled.

Practice Question — Application
Q1 In a study, a hormone was injected into a subject while their blood glucose level was monitored. The results are shown in the graph.

Exam Tip
If you are given a graph on blood glucose level in the exam, it's a good idea to look at it carefully and try to work out what it is showing before you start answering the questions. It sounds obvious, but if you just jump straight in you might miss something important.

a) What hormone do you think was injected? Explain your answer.
b) i) Name the other main hormone that affects the blood glucose level.
   ii) What do you think would happen to the blood glucose level if this hormone had been injected instead? Explain your answer.

Topic 7b Homeostasis 183

Topic Checklist

Each topic has a checklist at the end with boxes that let you tick off what you've learnt.

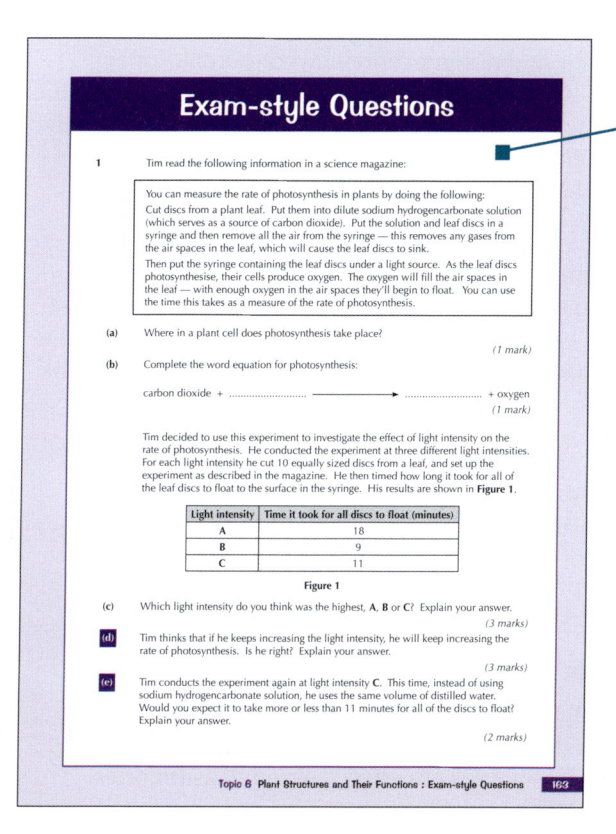

Exam-style Questions

- Practising exam-style questions is really important — this book has some at the end of every topic to test you.
- They're the same style as the ones you'll get in the real exams.
- All the answers are in the back of the book, along with a mark scheme to show you how you get the marks.
- Higher-only questions are marked like this: **1** **(a)** **(i)**

Glossary

There's a glossary at the back of the book full of definitions you need to know for the exam, plus loads of other useful words.

Exam Help

There's a section at the back of the book stuffed full of things to help you with the exams.

Working Scientifically

1. The Scientific Method

Science is all about finding things out and learning things about the world we live in. This section is all about the scientific process — how a scientist's initial idea turns into a theory that is accepted by the wider scientific community.

Hypotheses

Scientists try to explain things. Everything. They start by observing something they don't understand — it could be anything, e.g. planets in the sky, a person suffering from an illness, what matter is made of... anything.

Then, they come up with a **hypothesis** — a possible explanation for what they've observed. (Scientists can also sometimes form a model — a description or a representation of what's physically going on — see page 3).

The next step is to test whether the hypothesis might be right or not. This involves making a **prediction** based on the hypothesis and testing it by gathering evidence (i.e. data) from investigations. If evidence from experiments backs up a prediction, you're a step closer to figuring out if the hypothesis is true.

Tip: Investigations include lab experiments and studies.

Testing a hypothesis

Normally, scientists share their findings in peer-reviewed journals, or at conferences. **Peer-review** is where other scientists check results and scientific explanations to make sure they're 'scientific' (e.g. that experiments have been done in a sensible way) before they're published. It helps to detect false claims, but it doesn't mean that findings are correct — just that they're not wrong in any obvious way.

Once other scientists have found out about a hypothesis, they'll start basing their own predictions on it and carry out their own experiments. They'll also try to reproduce the original experiments to check the results — and if all the experiments in the world back up the hypothesis, then scientists start to think the hypothesis is true.

However, if a scientist somewhere in the world does an experiment that doesn't fit with the hypothesis (and other scientists can reproduce these results), then the hypothesis is in trouble. When this happens, scientists have to come up with a new hypothesis (maybe a modification of the old hypothesis, or maybe a completely new one).

Tip: Sometimes it can take a really long time for a hypothesis to be accepted.

Accepting a hypothesis

If pretty much every scientist in the world believes a hypothesis to be true because experiments back it up, then it usually goes in the textbooks for students to learn. Accepted hypotheses are often referred to as **theories**.

Our currently accepted theories are the ones that have survived this 'trial by evidence' — they've been tested many, many times over the years and survived (while the less good ones have been ditched). However... they never, never become hard and fast, totally indisputable fact. You can never know... it'd only take one odd, totally inexplicable result, and the hypothesising and testing would start all over again.

Example

Over time scientists have come up with different hypotheses about how illnesses are caused:

- Hundreds of years ago, we thought demons caused illness.
- Then we thought it was caused by 'bad blood' (and treated it with leeches).
- Now we've collected more evidence, we know that illnesses that can be spread between people are due to microorganisms.

Figure 1: Historical artwork of a woman using leeches to treat disease.

Models

Models are used to describe or display how an object or system behaves in reality. They're often based on evidence collected from experiments, and should be able to accurately predict what will happen in other, similar experiments. There are different types of models that scientists can use to describe the world around them. Here are just a few:

- A **descriptive model** describes what's happening in a certain situation, without explaining why. It won't necessarily include details that could be used to predict the outcome of a different scenario. For example, a graph showing the measured rate of an enzyme-catalysed reaction at different temperatures would be a descriptive model.

- A **representational model** is a simplified description or picture of what's going on in real life. It can be used to explain observations and make predictions. E.g. the lock and key model of enzyme action is a simplified way of showing how enzymes work see pages 36-37). It can be used to explain why enzymes only catalyse particular reactions.

- **Spatial models** are used to analyse the way that data is arranged within a physical space. For example, a spatial model could be used to look for relationships between the distribution of a species and physical aspects of its environment.

- **Computational models** use computers to make simulations of complex real-life processes, such as climate change. They're used when there are a lot of different variables (factors that change) to consider, and because you can easily change their design to take into account new data.

- **Mathematical models** can be used to describe the relationship between variables in numerical form (e.g. as an equation), and therefore predict outcomes of a scenario. For example, an equation can be written to predict how quickly molecules will diffuse into cells based on factors such as how large they are. On a larger scale, a mathematical model can be used to predict the way that a disease might spread through a population, e.g. by estimating the number of people that will become infected with the disease based on the number of people that are currently infected.

Tip: Like hypotheses, models have to be tested before they're accepted by other scientists. You can test models by using them to make a prediction, and then carrying out an investigation to see whether the evidence matches the prediction.

Tip: Mathematical models are made using patterns found in data and also using information about known relationships between variables.

Tip: Like hypotheses, models are constantly being revised and modified, based on new data.

All models have limitations on what they can explain or predict. Climate change models have several limitations — for example, it's hard to take into account all the biological and chemical processes that influence climate. It can also be difficult to include regional variations in climate.

Communicating results

Some scientific discoveries show that people should change their habits, or they might provide ideas that could be developed into new technology. So scientists need to tell the world about their discoveries.

> **Example**
>
> Gene technologies make use of discoveries that scientists have made about genes and DNA. Some of these technologies are used in genetic engineering, to produce genetically modified crops. Information about these crops needs to be communicated to farmers who might benefit from growing them, and to the general public so they can make informed decisions about the food they buy and eat.

Tip: New scientific discoveries are usually communicated to the public in the news or via the internet. They might be communicated to governments and large organisations via reports or meetings.

Reports about scientific discoveries in the media (e.g. newspapers or television) aren't peer-reviewed. This means that, even though news stories are often based on data that has been peer-reviewed, the data might be presented in a way that is over-simplified or inaccurate, leaving it open to misinterpretation.

It's important that the evidence isn't presented in a **biased** way. This can sometimes happen when people want to make a point, e.g. they overemphasise a relationship in the data. (Sometimes without knowing they're doing it.) There are all sorts of reasons why people might want to do this.

Tip: If you're reading an article about a new scientific discovery, always think about how the study was carried out. It may be that the sample size was very small, and so the results aren't representative of the whole situation (see page 11 for more on sample sizes).

> **Examples**
>
> - They want to keep the organisation or company that's funding the research happy. (If the results aren't what they'd like they might not give them any more money to fund further research.)
> - Governments might want to persuade voters, other governments or journalists to agree with their policies about a certain issue.
> - Companies might want to 'big up' their products, or make impressive safety claims.
> - Environmental campaigners might want to persuade people to behave differently.

Tip: An example of bias is a newspaper article describing details of data supporting an idea without giving any of the evidence against it.

There's also a risk that if an investigation is done by a team of highly-regarded scientists it'll be taken more seriously than evidence from less well known scientists. But having experience, authority or a fancy qualification doesn't necessarily mean the evidence is good — the only way to tell is to look at the evidence scientifically (e.g. is it repeatable, valid, etc. — see page 9).

2. Scientific Applications and Issues

New scientific discoveries can lead to exciting new ways of using science in our everyday lives. Unfortunately, these developments may also come with social, economic, environmental or personal problems that need to be considered.

Using scientific developments

Lots of scientific developments go on to have useful applications.

Examples

- When it was discovered that penicillin acted as an antibiotic, drugs were developed that used penicillin to treat bacterial infections.
- As scientists have investigated the role of reproductive hormones in the body, treatments that use these hormones have been developed to allow women to become pregnant who wouldn't be able to otherwise.

Tip: There's lots more about antibiotics on page 131.

Issues created by science

Scientific developments (e.g. new technologies or new advice) can create issues. For example, they could create political issues, which could lead to developments being ignored, or governments being slow to act if they think responding to the developments could affect their popularity with voters.

Example

Some governments were pretty slow to accept the fact that human activities are causing global warming, despite all the evidence. This is because accepting it means they've got to do something about it, which costs money and could hurt their economy. This could lose them a lot of votes.

Scientific developments can cause a whole host of other issues too.

Examples

- Economic issues: Society can't always afford to do things scientists recommend (e.g. investing heavily in alternative energy sources) without cutting back elsewhere.
- Social issues: Decisions based on scientific evidence affect people — e.g. should junk food be taxed more highly (to encourage people to be healthy)? Should alcohol be banned (to prevent health problems)? Would the effect on people's lifestyles be acceptable?
- Environmental issues: Human activity often affects the natural environment — e.g. genetically modified crops may help us produce more food, but some people think they could cause environmental problems.
- Personal issues: Some decisions will affect individuals. For example, someone might support alternative energy, but object if a wind farm is built next to their house.

Figure 1: Solar farms can be used to generate 'clean' electricity, but some people think that the money needed to invest in them should be spent elsewhere.

Working Scientifically

3. Limitations of Science

Science has taught us an awful lot about the world we live in and how things work — but science doesn't have the answer for everything.

Questions science hasn't answered yet

We don't understand everything. And we never will. We'll find out more, for sure — as more hypotheses are suggested, and more experiments are done. But there'll always be stuff we don't know.

> **Examples**
> - Today we don't know as much as we'd like about the impacts of global warming. How much will sea levels rise? And to what extent will weather patterns change?
> - We also don't know anywhere near as much as we'd like about the universe. Are there other life forms out there? And what is the universe made of?

Figure 1: *Global warming could cause weather patterns to change — which may result in longer, hotter droughts in some areas.*

In order to answer scientific questions, scientists need data to provide evidence for their hypotheses. Some questions can't be answered yet because the data can't currently be collected, or because there's not enough data to support a theory. But eventually, as we get more evidence, we probably will be able to answer these questions once and for all. By then there'll be loads of new questions to answer though.

Questions science can't answer

There are some questions that all the experiments in the world won't help us answer — for example, the "should we be doing this at all?" type questions.

> **Example**
>
> Think about new drugs which can be taken to boost your 'brain power'.
> - Some people think they're good as they could improve concentration or memory. New drugs could let people think in ways beyond the powers of normal brains.
> - Other people say they're bad — they could give you an unfair advantage in exams. And people might be pressured into taking them so that they could work more effectively, and for longer hours.

Tip: Some experiments have to be approved by ethics committees before scientists are allowed to carry them out. This stops scientists from getting wrapped up in whether they can do something, before anyone stops to think about whether they should do it.

The question of whether something is morally or ethically right or wrong can't be answered by more experiments — there is no "right" or "wrong" answer. The best we can do is get a consensus from society — a judgement that most people are more or less happy to live by. Science can provide more information to help people make this judgement, and the judgement might change over time. But in the end it's up to people and their consciences.

4. Risks and Hazards

A lot of things we do could cause us harm. But some things are more hazardous than they at first seem, whereas other things are less hazardous. This may sound confusing, but it'll all become clear...

What are risks and hazards?

A **hazard** is something that could potentially cause harm. All hazards have a **risk** attached to them — this is the chance that the hazard will cause harm.

The risks of some things seem pretty obvious, or we've known about them for a while, like the risk of causing acid rain by polluting the atmosphere, or of having a car accident when you're travelling in a car.

New technology arising from scientific advances can bring new risks. These risks need to be thought about alongside the potential benefits of the technology, in order to make a decision about whether it should be made available to the general public.

> **Example**
>
> Radiotherapy is a cancer treatment that uses radiation to kill cancer cells. However, radiation itself carries a risk of causing cancer in the patient.
>
> The risk of cancer caused by radiotherapy has to be weighed against the risk of the existing cancer that needs to be treated.
>
> In most cases, the risk from the original cancer far outweighs the risk from radiotherapy, which is why it is available to be used as a treatment.

Tip: The application of a new technology can change over time if new risks are discovered. For example, radiation was widely used as a medical treatment before it was known that it can cause cancer. These days, its use as a treatment is a lot more limited and techniques have been improved to reduce the risk.

Estimating risk

You can estimate the risk based on how many times something happens in a big sample (e.g. 100 000 people) over a given period (e.g. a year). For example, you could assess the risk of a driver crashing by recording how many people in a group of 100 000 drivers crashed their cars over a year.

To make a decision about an activity that involves a hazardous event, we don't just need to take into account the chance of the event causing harm, but also how serious the consequences would be if it did.

The general rule is that, if an activity involves a hazard that's very likely to cause harm, with serious consequences if it does, that activity is considered high-risk.

> **Example 1**
>
> If you go for a walk, you may sprain an ankle. But most sprains recover within a few weeks if they're rested, so going for a walk would be considered a low-risk activity.

> **Example 2**
>
> If you go skiing, you may fall and break a bone. This would take many weeks to heal, and may cause further complications later on in life. So skiing would be considered higher risk than walking.

Perceptions of risk

Not all risks have the same consequences, e.g. if you chop veg with a sharp knife you risk cutting your finger, but if you go scuba-diving you risk death. You're much more likely to cut your finger during half an hour of chopping than to die during half an hour of scuba-diving. But most people are happier to accept a higher probability of an accident if the consequences are short-lived and fairly minor.

People tend to be more willing to accept a risk if they choose to do something (e.g. go scuba diving), compared to having the risk imposed on them (e.g. having a nuclear power station built next door).

Tip: Risks people choose to take are called 'voluntary risks'. Risks that people are forced to take are called 'imposed risks'.

People's perception of risk (how risky they think something is) isn't always accurate. They tend to view familiar activities as low-risk and unfamiliar activities as high-risk — even if that's not the case. For example, cycling on roads is often high-risk, but many people are happy to do it because it's a familiar activity. Air travel is actually pretty safe, but a lot of people perceive it as high-risk. People may over-estimate the risk of things with long-term or invisible effects.

Reducing risk in investigations

Part of planning an investigation is making sure that it's safe. To make sure your experiment is safe you must identify all the **hazards**. Hazards include:

- Microorganisms: e.g. some bacteria can make you ill.
- Chemicals: e.g. sulfuric acid can burn your skin and alcohols catch fire easily.
- Fire: e.g. an unattended Bunsen burner is a fire hazard.
- Electricity: e.g. faulty electrical equipment could give you a shock.

Tip: You can find out about potential hazards by looking in textbooks, doing some internet research, or asking your teacher.

Once you've identified the hazards you might encounter, you should think of ways of reducing the risks from the hazards.

> **Examples**
>
> - If you're working with sulfuric acid, wear gloves and safety goggles. This will reduce the risk of the acid coming into contact with your skin and eyes.
> - If you're using a Bunsen burner, stand it on a heat-proof mat. This will reduce the risk of starting a fire.

Figure 1: Scientists wearing safety goggles to protect their eyes during an experiment.

5. Designing Investigations

To be a good scientist you need to know how to design a good experiment.

Making predictions from a hypothesis

Scientists observe things and come up with hypotheses to explain them. To decide whether a **hypothesis** might be correct, you need to do an investigation to gather evidence, which will help support or disprove the hypothesis. The first step is to use the hypothesis to come up with a **prediction** — a statement about what you think will happen that you can test.

> **Example**
>
> If your hypothesis is "increasing the temperature will increase the rate of an enzyme-controlled reaction", then your prediction might be "an enzyme-controlled reaction carried out at 40 °C will be faster than the same enzyme-controlled reaction carried out at 20 °C".

Once a scientist has come up with a prediction, they'll design an investigation to see if there are patterns or relationships between two variables. For example, to see if there's a pattern or relationship between the variables 'temperature' and 'time taken for enzyme-controlled reaction to finish'.

Tip: A variable is just something in the experiment that can change.

Repeatable and reproducible results

Results need to be **repeatable** and **reproducible**. Repeatable means that if the same person does an experiment again using the same methods and equipment, they'll get similar results. Reproducible means that if someone else does the experiment, or a different method or piece of equipment is used, the results will be similar. Data that's repeatable and reproducible is **reliable** and scientists are more likely to have confidence in it.

> **Example**
>
> In 1998, a scientist claimed to have found a link between the MMR vaccine (for measles, mumps and rubella) and autism. This meant many parents stopped their children from being vaccinated, leading to a rise in the number of children catching measles. However, the results have never been reproduced. Health authorities have now concluded that the vaccine is safe.

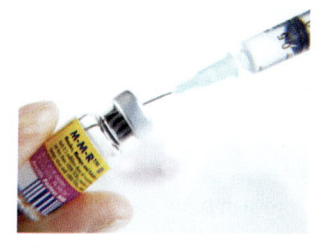

Figure 1: The MMR vaccine.

Ensuring the test is valid

Valid results are repeatable, reproducible and answer the original question.

> **Example**
>
> **Do power lines cause cancer?** — Some studies have found that children who live near overhead power lines are more likely to develop cancer. What they'd actually found was a **correlation** (relationship) between the variables "presence of power lines" and "incidence of cancer". They found that as one changed, so did the other.
>
> But this data isn't enough to say that the power lines cause cancer, as there might be other explanations. For example, power lines are often near busy roads, so the areas tested could contain different levels of pollution. As the studies don't show a definite link they don't answer the original question.

Tip: Peer review (see page 2) is used to make sure that results are valid before they're published.

Tip: See page 18 for more on correlation.

Working Scientifically

Ensuring it's a fair test

Tip: For the results of an investigation to be valid the investigation must be a fair test.

In a lab experiment you usually change one variable and measure how it affects another variable. To make it a fair test, everything else that could affect the results should stay the same (otherwise you can't tell if the thing you're changing is causing the results or not — the data won't be valid).

> **Example**
>
> You might change only the temperature of an enzyme-controlled reaction and measure how it affects the rate of reaction. You need to keep the pH the same, otherwise you won't know if any change in the rate of reaction is caused by the change in temperature, or the change in pH.

The variable you change is called the **independent variable**. The variable you measure when you change the independent variable is called the **dependent variable**. The variables that you keep the same are called **control variables**.

> **Example**
>
> In the enzyme-controlled reaction example above, temperature is the independent variable, the rate of the reaction is the dependent variable and the control variables are pH, volume and concentration of reactants, etc.

Control experiments and control groups

Tip: Control experiments let you see what happens when you don't change anything at all.

To make sure no other factors are affecting the results, you often include a **control experiment** — an experiment that's kept under the same conditions as the rest of the investigation, but doesn't have anything done to it.

> **Example**
>
> You can investigate antibiotic resistance in bacteria by growing cultures of bacteria on agar plates, then adding paper discs soaked in antibiotic.
>
> If the bacteria are resistant to the antibiotic they will continue to grow. If they aren't resistant a clear patch will appear around the disc where they have died or haven't grown.
>
> A disc that isn't soaked in antibiotic is included to act as a control. This makes sure any result is down to the antibiotic, not the presence of a paper disc.
>
> *Agar plate · Discs soaked in antibiotic · Bacteria · Zone of dead bacteria · Control disc*
>
> **Figure 2:** An investigation into antibiotic resistance.

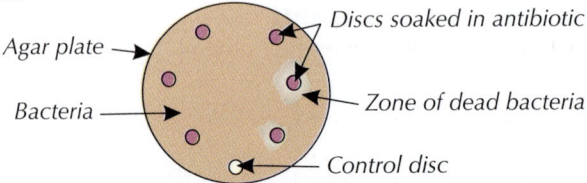

Tip: A study is an investigation that doesn't take place in a lab.

It's important that a study is a fair test, just like a lab experiment. It's a lot trickier to control the variables in a study than it is in a lab experiment though. Sometimes you can't control them all, but you can use a **control group** to help. This is a group of whatever you're studying (people, plants, lemmings, etc.) that's kept under the same conditions as the group in the experiment, but doesn't have anything done to it.

> **Example**
>
> If you're studying the effect of pesticides on crop growth, pesticide is applied to one field but not to another field (the control field). Both fields are planted with the same crop, and are in the same area (so they get the same weather conditions).
>
> The control field is there to try and account for variables like the weather, which don't stay the same all the time, but could affect the results.

Tip: A pesticide is a chemical that can be used to kill insects.

Sample size

Data based on small samples isn't as good as data based on large samples. A sample should be representative of the whole population (i.e. it should share as many of the various characteristics in the population as possible) — a small sample can't do that as well.

The bigger the sample size the better, but scientists have to be realistic when choosing how big.

Tip: It's hard to spot anomalous results (see p.13) if your sample size is too small.

> **Example**
>
> If you were studying how lifestyle affects people's weight it'd be great to study everyone in the UK (a huge sample), but it'd take ages and cost a bomb. Studying a thousand people with a mixture of ages, gender and race would be more realistic.

Tip: Samples should be selected randomly. There's an example of how to do this on page 239.

Trial runs

It's a good idea to do a **trial run** (a quick version of your experiment) before you do the proper experiment. Trial runs are used to figure out the range (the upper and lower limits) of independent variable values used in the proper experiment. If you don't get a change in the dependent variable at the upper values in the trial run, you might narrow the range in the proper experiment. But if you still get a big change at the upper values you might increase the range.

Tip: If you don't have time to do a trial run, you could always look at the data other people have got doing a similar experiment and use a range and interval values similar to theirs.

> **Example**
>
> For an experiment into the rate of an enzyme-controlled reaction, you might do a trial run with a temperature range of 10-50 °C. If there was no reaction at the upper end (e.g. 40-50 °C), you might narrow the range to 10-40 °C for the proper experiment.

Trial runs can be used to figure out the appropriate intervals (gaps) between the values too. The intervals can't be too small (otherwise the experiment would take ages), or too big (otherwise you might miss something).

> **Example**
>
> If using 1 °C intervals doesn't give much change in the rate of reaction each time, you might use 5 °C intervals instead, e.g. 10, 15, 20, 25, 30, 35, 40 °C.

Trial runs can also help you figure out whether or not your experiment is repeatable — e.g. if you repeat your experiment three times and the results are all similar, the experiment is repeatable.

Tip: If your repeat results are consistent, you can say your results are repeatable.

6. Collecting Data

Once you've designed your experiment, you need to get on and do it. Here's a guide to making sure the results you collect are good.

Getting good quality results

When you do an experiment you want your results to be **repeatable**, **reproducible** and as **accurate** and **precise** as possible.

> **Tip:** Sometimes, you can work out what result you should get at the end of an experiment (the theoretical result) by doing a bit of maths. If your experiment is accurate there shouldn't be much difference between the theoretical result and the result you actually get.

To check repeatability you need to repeat the readings and check that the results are similar — you should repeat each reading at least three times. To make sure your results are reproducible you can cross check them by taking a second set of readings with another instrument (or a different observer).

Your data also needs to be accurate. Really accurate results are those that are really close to the true answer. The accuracy of your results usually depends on your method — you need to make sure you're measuring the right thing and that you don't miss anything that should be included in the measurements. For example, estimating the amount of gas released from a reaction by counting the bubbles isn't very accurate because you might miss some of the bubbles and they might have different volumes. It's more accurate to measure the volume of gas released using a gas syringe (see p.234).

Your data also needs to be precise. Precise results are ones where the data is all really close to the mean (average) of your repeated results (i.e. not spread out).

> **Tip:** For more on means see page 14.

> **Example**
>
> Look at the data in this table. Data set 1 is more precise than data set 2 because all the data in set 1 is really close to the mean, whereas the data in set 2 is more spread out.
>
> | Repeat | Data set 1 | Data set 2 |
> |---|---|---|
> | 1 | 12 | 11 |
> | 2 | 14 | 17 |
> | 3 | 13 | 14 |
> | Mean | 13 | 14 |

Choosing the right equipment

When doing an experiment, you need to make sure you're using the right equipment for the job. The measuring equipment you use has to be sensitive enough to measure the changes you're looking for.

> **Example**
>
> If you need to measure changes of 1 cm^3 you need to use a measuring cylinder that can measure in 1 cm^3 steps — it'd be no good trying with one that only measures 10 cm^3 steps, it wouldn't be sensitive enough.

Figure 1: *Different types of glassware used for measuring — make sure you choose the right one before you start an experiment.*

The smallest change a measuring instrument can detect is called its **resolution**. For example, some mass balances have a resolution of 1 g, some have a resolution of 0.1 g, and some are even more sensitive.

Working Scientifically

Also, equipment needs to be **calibrated** by measuring a known value. If there's a difference between the measured and known value, you can use this to correct the inaccuracy of the equipment.

> **Example**
> If a known mass is put on a mass balance, but the reading is a different value, you know that the mass balance has not been calibrated properly.

Tip: Calibration is a way of making sure that a measuring device is measuring things accurately — you get it to measure something you know has a certain value and set the device to say that amount.

Errors

Random errors

The results of an experiment will always vary a bit due to **random errors** — unpredictable differences caused by things like human errors in measuring.

> **Example**
> Errors made when reading from a measuring cylinder are random. You have to estimate or round the level when it's between two marks — so sometimes your figure will be a bit above the real one, and sometimes a bit below.

You can reduce the effect of random errors by taking repeat readings and finding the mean. This will make your results more precise.

Systematic errors

If a measurement is wrong by the same amount every time, it's called a **systematic error**.

> **Example**
> If you measured from the very end of your ruler instead of from the 0 cm mark every time, all your measurements would be a bit small.

Tip: If there's no systematic error, then doing repeats and calculating a mean can make your results more accurate.

Just to make things more complicated, if a systematic error is caused by using equipment that isn't zeroed properly it's called a **zero error**. You can compensate for some of these errors if you know about them though.

> **Example**
> If a mass balance always reads 1 gram before you put anything on it, all your measurements will be 1 gram too heavy. This is a zero error. You can compensate for this by subtracting 1 gram from all your results.

Tip: Repeating the experiment in the exact same way and calculating a mean won't correct a systematic error.

Anomalous results

Sometimes you get a result that doesn't seem to fit in with the rest at all. These results are called **anomalous results** (or outliers).

> **Example**
> Look at the data in this table. The entry that has been circled is an anomalous result because it's much larger than any of the other data values.
>
> | Experiment | A | B | C | D | E | F |
> |---|---|---|---|---|---|---|
> | Rate of reaction (cm³/s) | 10.5 | 11.2 | 10.8 | (85.4) | 10.6 | 11.1 |

Tip: There are lots of reasons why you might get an anomalous result, but usually they're due to human error rather than anything crazy happening in the experiment.

You should investigate anomalous results and try to work out what happened. If you can work out what happened (e.g. you measured something totally wrong) you can ignore them when processing your results.

Working Scientifically

7. Processing Data

Once you've collected some data, you might need to process it.

Organising data

It's really important that your data is organised. Tables are dead useful for organising data. When you draw a table use a ruler, make sure each column has a heading (including the units) and keep it neat and tidy.

Tip: If you're recording your data as decimals, make sure you give each value to the same number of decimal places.

Person	Reaction time (s)
1	0.22
2	0.17

Figure 1: Table showing the time taken to react to a stimulus for two people.

Processing your data

When you've collected data from an experiment, it's useful to summarise it using a few handy-to-use figures.

Tip: Annoyingly, it's difficult to see any patterns or relationships in detail just from a table. You need to use some kind of graph or chart for that (see pages 16-18).

Mean and range

When you've done repeats of an experiment you should always calculate the **mean** (a type of average). To do this add together all the data values and divide by the total number of values in the sample.

You might also need to calculate the **range** (how spread out the data is). To do this find the largest number and subtract the smallest number from it.

Example

Look at the data in the table below. The mean and range of the data for each test tube has been calculated.

Test tube	Repeat (g) 1	2	3	Mean (g)	Range (g)
A	28	36	32	(28 + 36 + 32) ÷ 3 = 32	36 − 28 = 8
B	47	52	60	(47 + 52 + 60) ÷ 3 = 53	60 − 47 = 13

Median and mode

There are two more types of average, other than the mean, that you might need to calculate. These are the **median** and the **mode**.

- To calculate the median, put all your data in numerical order — the median is the middle value.
- The number that appears most often in a data set is the mode.

Tip: You should ignore anomalous results when calculating the mean, range, median or mode — see page 13 for more on anomalous results.

Example

The results of a study investigating how many minutes it took for people's heart rates to return to resting after sprinting 100 m are shown below:

3, 6, 5, 4, 6, 4, 6, 5, 7

First put the data in numerical order: 3, 4, 4, 5, 5, 6, 6, 6, 7

There are 9 values, so the median is the 5th number, which is **5**.

6 comes up 3 times. None of the other numbers come up more than twice. So the mode is **6**.

Tip: If you have an even number of values, the median is halfway between the middle two values.

Uncertainty

When you repeat a measurement, you often get a slightly different figure each time you do it due to random error. This means that each result has some **uncertainty** to it. The measurements you make will also have some uncertainty in them due to limits in the resolution of the equipment you use. This all means that the mean of a set of results will also have some uncertainty to it. Here's how to calculate the uncertainty of a mean result:

$$\text{uncertainty} = \text{range} \div 2$$

The larger the range, the less precise your results are and the more uncertainty there will be in your results. Uncertainties are shown using the '±' symbol.

Tip: There's more about errors on page 13.

Example

The table below shows the results of a respiration experiment to determine the volume of carbon dioxide produced.

Repeat	1	2	3	mean
Volume of CO_2 produced (cm^3)	20.2	19.8	20.0	20.0

1. The range is: $20.2 - 19.8 = 0.4$ cm^3
2. So the uncertainty of the mean is: range ÷ 2 = 0.4 ÷ 2 = 0.2 cm^3. You'd write this as **20.0 ± 0.2 cm^3**

Tip: Since uncertainty affects precision, you'll need to think about it when you come to evaluating your results (see page 22).

Measuring a greater amount of something helps to reduce uncertainty. For example, in a rate of reaction experiment, measuring the amount of product formed over a longer period compared to a shorter period will reduce the percentage uncertainty in your results.

Rounding to significant figures

The first significant figure (s.f) of a number is the first digit that isn't a zero. The second, third and fourth significant figures follow on immediately after the first (even if they're zeros). When you're processing your data you may well want to round any really long numbers to a certain number of significant figures.

Exam Tip
If a question asks you to give your answer to a certain number of significant figures, make sure you do this, or you might not get all the marks.

Example

0.6874976 rounds to **0.69** to **2 s.f.** and to **0.687** to **3 s.f.**

When you're doing calculations using measurements given to a certain number of significant figures, you should try to give your answer to the lowest number of significant figures that was used in the calculation. If your calculation has multiple steps, only round the final answer, or it won't be as accurate.

Tip: Remember to write down how many significant figures you've rounded to after your answer.

Example

For the calculation: $1.2 \div 1.85 = 0.648648648...$

1.2 is given to 2 significant figures. 1.85 is given to 3 significant figures. So the answer should be given to 2 significant figures. Round the final significant figure (0.6<u>4</u>8) up to 5: $1.2 \div 1.85 = $ **0.65 (2 s.f.)**

Tip: When rounding a number, if the next digit after the last significant figure you're looking at is less than 5 you should round it <u>down</u>, and if it's 5 or more you should round it <u>up</u>.

The lowest number of significant figures in the calculation is used because the fewer digits a measurement has, the less accurate it is. Your answer can only be as accurate as the least accurate measurement in the calculation.

Working Scientifically | 15

8. Graphs and Charts

It can often be easier to see trends in data by plotting a graph or chart of your results, rather than by looking at numbers in a table.

Plotting your data on a graph or chart

One of the best ways to present your data after you've processed it is to plot your results on a graph or chart. There are lots of different types you can use.

Bar charts

Bar charts can be used to show categoric, discrete or continuous data.

- **Categoric** data comes in distinct categories, e.g. blood group, eye colour.
- **Discrete** data can only take certain values, with no in-between value, e.g. number of people is discrete because you can't have half a person.
- **Continuous** data is numerical data that can have any value within a range, e.g. length, volume, temperature.

There are some golden rules you need to follow for drawing bar charts:

- Draw it nice and big (covering at least two-thirds of the graph paper).
- Make sure all the bars are the same width.
- If the data is categoric or discrete, include gaps between the bars. If the data is continuous, the bars should be touching.
- Label both axes and remember to include the units.
- If you've got more than one set of data include a key.
- Give your chart a title explaining what it is showing.

Have a look at Figure 1 for an example of a pretty decent bar chart.

Tip: These golden rules will make sure that your bar chart is clear, easy to read and easy to understand if someone else looks at it.

Exam Tip
You could be asked to read a value from a bar chart in the exam. An easy way to do this is to line up a ruler with the top of the bar and follow it across to the *y*-axis (the vertical axis). If there are two sets of data, make sure you use the key to help you identify which bar you need to read the value from.

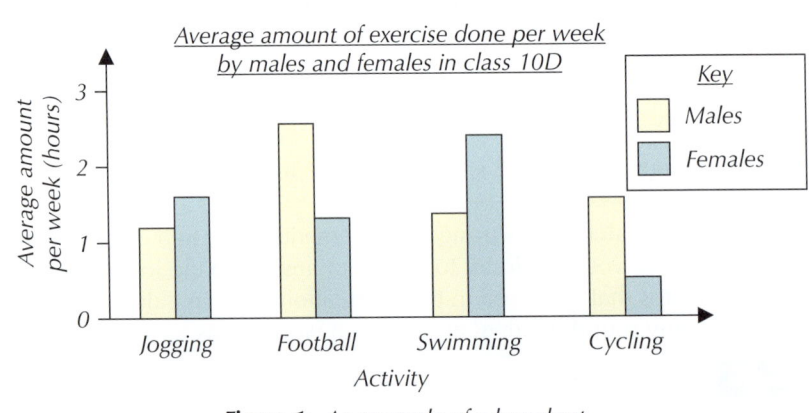

Figure 1: An example of a bar chart.

Histograms

Histograms are a useful way of displaying frequency data when the independent variable is **continuous** and the data is grouped together in classes (see next page). Histograms may look like bar charts, but it's the area of the bars that represents the frequency (rather than the height) so the bars can be different widths. The height of each bar is called the frequency density.

Tip: Frequency is just the number of times that something occurs.

Height of tomato plants

The frequency density is plotted on the y-axis.

The width of each bar is the class width — the bars can be different widths.

The area of each bar is the frequency of the class — the class with the largest area has the highest frequency.

The independent variable is plotted on the x-axis.

There are no spaces between the bars.

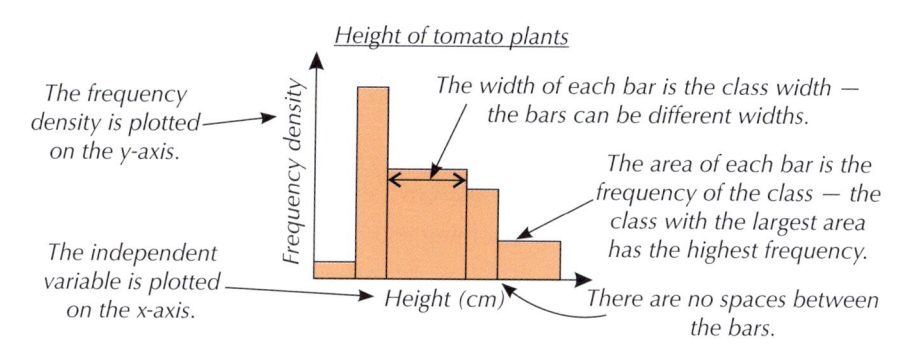

Figure 2: *An example of a histogram.*

Tip: Don't be fooled by the height of the bars in a histogram — the tallest bar doesn't always belong to the class with the greatest frequency.

Tip: If all the classes are the same width, you can just plot frequency on the y-axis, e.g.

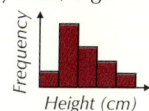

This type of graph is called a frequency diagram.

You calculate the frequency density using this formula:

$$\text{frequency density} = \text{frequency} \div \text{class width}$$

Example

The table on the right shows the results of a study into variation in pea plant height. The heights of the plants were grouped into four classes.

Height of pea plant (cm)	Frequency
$0 \leq x < 5$	5
$5 \leq x < 10$	14
$10 \leq x < 15$	11
$15 \leq x < 30$	3

Tip: This continuous data has been split into classes. $0 \leq x < 5$ means the data in the class is more than or equal to 0 and less than 5.

1. To draw a histogram of the data, you first need to work out the width of each class. Write the class width in a new column.

Class width
5 − 0 = **5**
10 − 5 = **5**
15 − 10 = **5**
30 − 15 = **15**

Tip: The table in the example is a frequency table — it shows how many plants are in each height category.

2. Use the formula above to calculate the frequency density for each class. Add a new column to your table for the frequency density.

Frequency density
5 ÷ 5 = **1**
14 ÷ 5 = **2.8**
11 ÷ 5 = **2.2**
3 ÷ 15 = **0.2**

Tip: You might have to round the frequency density — if so, choose a sensible number of decimal places that will be possible to plot using your graph's scale.

3. Work out a suitable scale for each axis, then plot the histogram. It should look something like this:

Frequency density goes on the y-axis. (So the height of the bars is the frequency density.)

The width of each bar is the class width.

Make sure the bars are touching.

Height (the independent variable) goes on the x-axis.

Tip: The width of the whole histogram shows the range of results (how spread out they are).

Tip: You can calculate the frequency of a class from a histogram by rearranging the formula: frequency = frequency density × class width.

Working Scientifically 17

Plotting points

If both the independent and dependent variables are **continuous** you should plot points on a graph to display the data. Here are the golden rules for plotting points on graphs:

- Draw it nice and big (covering at least two-thirds of the graph paper).
- Put the independent variable (the thing you change) on the x-axis (the horizontal one).
- Put the dependent variable (the thing you measure) on the y-axis (the vertical one).
- Label both axes and remember to include the units.
- To plot the points, use a sharp pencil and make a neat little cross.
- Don't join the dots up. If you're asked to draw a line of best fit (or a curve of best fit if your points make a curve), try to draw the line through or as near to as many points as possible, ignoring anomalous results.
- If you've got more than one set of data include a key.
- Give your graph a title explaining what it is showing.

Exam Tip
You could be asked to plot points for a graph in your exam. If so, make sure you follow the golden rules or you could end up losing marks.

Tip: Use the biggest data values you've got to draw a sensible scale on your axes. Here, the highest rate of reaction is 22 cm³/s, so it makes sense to label the y-axis up to 25 cm³/s.

Tip: If you're not in an exam, you can use a computer to plot a graph and draw the line of best fit for you.

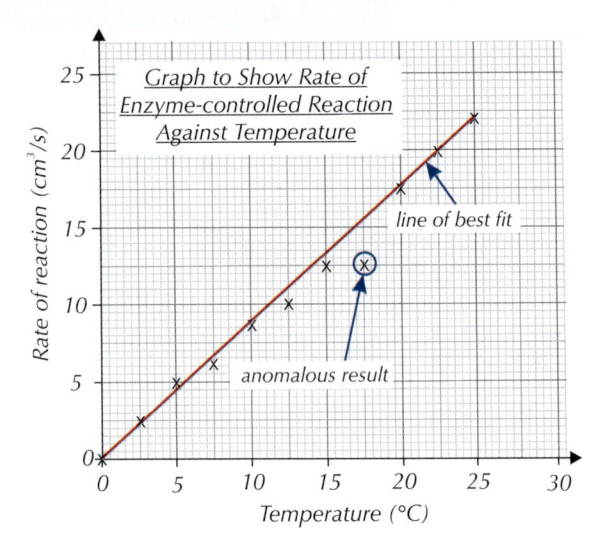

Graph to Show Rate of Enzyme-controlled Reaction Against Temperature

Figure 3: *An example of a graph with a line of best fit.*

Correlations

Graphs are used to show the relationship between two variables. Data can show three different types of **correlation** (relationship):

Tip: Just because two variables are correlated doesn't mean that the change in one is causing the change in the other. There might be other factors involved, or it may just be down to chance — see pages 21-22 for more.

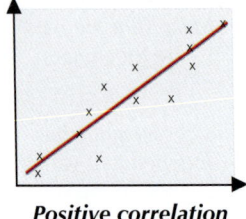

Positive correlation
As one variable increases the other increases.

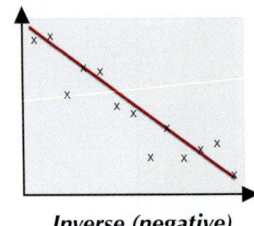

Inverse (negative) correlation
As one variable increases the other decreases.

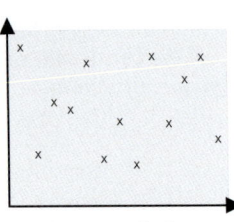

No correlation
There's no relationship between the two variables.

Working Scientifically

9. Units

Using the correct units is important when you're drawing graphs or calculating values with a formula. Otherwise your numbers don't really mean anything.

SI units

Lots of different units can be used to describe the same quantity. For example, volume can be given in terms of cubic feet, cubic metres, litres or pints. It would be quite confusing if different scientists used different units to define quantities, as it would be hard to compare people's data. To stop this happening, scientists have come up with a set of standard units, called **SI units**, that all scientists use to measure their data. Figure 1 shows some SI units you'll see in biology:

Quantity	SI Base Unit
mass	kilogram, kg
length	metre, m
time	second, s

Tip: SI stands for 'Système International', which is French for 'international system'.

Figure 1: *Some common SI base units used in biology.*

Scaling prefixes

Quantities come in a huge range of sizes. For example, the volume of a swimming pool might be around 2 000 000 000 cm^3, while the volume of a cup is around 250 cm^3. To make the size of numbers more manageable, larger or smaller units are used. Figure 2 shows the prefixes which can be used in front of units (e.g. metres) to make them bigger or smaller:

prefix	tera (T)	giga (G)	mega (M)	kilo (k)	deci (d)	centi (c)	milli (m)	micro (μ)	nano (n)
multiple of unit	10^{12}	10^9	1 000 000 (10^6)	1000	0.1	0.01	0.001	0.000001 (10^{-6})	10^{-9}

Figure 2: *Scaling prefixes used with units.*

These prefixes are called scaling prefixes and they tell you how much bigger or smaller a unit is than the base unit. So one kilometre is one thousand metres.

Converting between units

To swap from one unit to another, all you need to know is what number you have to divide or multiply by to get from the original unit to the new unit — this is called the conversion factor and is equal to the number of times the smaller unit goes into the larger unit.

- To go from a bigger unit to a smaller unit, you multiply by the conversion factor.
- To go from a smaller unit to a bigger unit, you divide by the conversion factor.

Tip: If you're going from a smaller unit to a larger unit, your number should get smaller. If you're going from a larger unit to a smaller unit, your number should get larger. This is a handy way to check you've done the conversion correctly.

Working Scientifically

Here are some conversions that are particularly useful for biology:

- Mass can have units of kg and g.

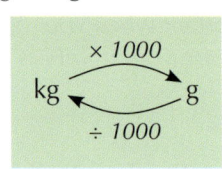

$$kg \xrightleftharpoons[\div 1000]{\times 1000} g$$

- Length can have lots of units, including mm, μm and nm.

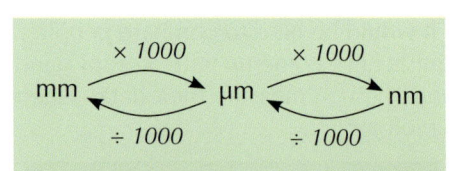

$$mm \xrightleftharpoons[\div 1000]{\times 1000} \mu m \xrightleftharpoons[\div 1000]{\times 1000} nm$$

Exam Tip
Being familiar with these common conversions could save you time when it comes to doing calculations in the exams.

- Time can have units of min and s.

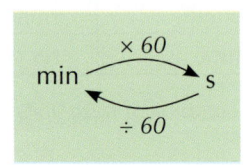

$$min \xrightleftharpoons[\div 60]{\times 60} s$$

- Volume can have units of m^3, dm^3 and cm^3.

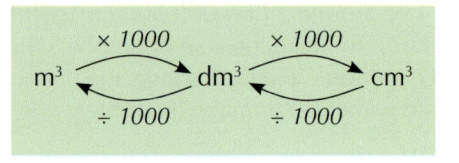

$$m^3 \xrightleftharpoons[\div 1000]{\times 1000} dm^3 \xrightleftharpoons[\div 1000]{\times 1000} cm^3$$

Tip: Volume is also often given in L (litres) or ml (millilitres). To convert, you'll need to remember that 1 ml = 1 cm^3 and so 1 L = 1000 cm^3.

Examples

- To go from dm^3 to cm^3, you'd multiply by the conversion factor (which is 1000).

    2 dm^3 is equal to 2 × 1000 = **2000 cm^3**

- To go from grams to kilograms, you'd divide by the conversion factor (which is 1000).

    3400 g is equal to 3400 ÷ 1000 = **3.4 kg**

Exam Tip
As well as rates of reaction, you'll be expected to calculate things like rate of water uptake (see p.159).

Tip: The units of time might be different, e.g. they could be in minutes, hours or days.

Units of rate

Rate is a measure of how much something changes over time. For example, a rate of reaction measures how quickly reactants are changed into products. The units of rate are 'units of the quantity that changes / units of time'.

Example

For an enzyme-controlled reaction that releases a gas as a product (measured in cm^3), the units of rate might be cm^3/s. This can also be written as cm^3 s^{-1}. Both mean 'centimetres cubed per second'.

20 Working Scientifically

10. Conclusions and Evaluations

So... you've planned and carried out an amazing experiment, got your data and have processed and presented it in a sensible way. Now it's time to figure out what your data actually tells you, and how much you can trust what it says.

How to draw conclusions

Drawing conclusions might seem pretty straightforward — you just look at your data and say what pattern or relationship you see between the dependent and independent variables.

But you've got to be really careful that your conclusion matches the data you've got and doesn't go any further. You also need to be able to use your results to justify your conclusion (i.e. back up your conclusion with some specific data).

When writing a conclusion you need to refer back to the original hypothesis and say whether the data supports it or not.

> **Example**
>
> The table shows the heights of pea plant seedlings grown for three weeks with different fertilisers.
>
> | Fertiliser | Mean growth (mm) |
> |---|---|
> | A | 13.5 |
> | B | 19.5 |
> | No fertiliser | 5.5 |
>
> You could conclude that fertiliser B makes pea plant seedlings grow taller over a three week period than fertiliser A.
>
> The justification for this conclusion is that over the three week period, fertiliser B made pea plants grow 6 mm more on average than fertiliser A.
>
> You can't conclude that fertiliser B makes any other type of plant grow taller than fertiliser A — the results could be totally different.
>
> The hypothesis for this experiment might have been that adding fertiliser would increase the growth of plants and that different types of fertiliser would affect growth by different amounts. The data supports this hypothesis.

Figure 1: *A pea plant seedling.*

Correlation and causation

If two things are correlated (i.e. there's a relationship between them) it doesn't necessarily mean that a change in one variable is causing the change in the other — this is really important, don't forget it. There are three possible reasons for a correlation:

1. Chance

Even though it might seem a bit weird, it's possible that two things show a correlation in a study purely because of chance.

> **Example**
>
> One study might find a correlation between the number of people with breathing problems and the distance they live from a cement factory. But other scientists don't get a correlation when they investigate it — the results of the first study are just a fluke.

Tip: Graphs can be useful for seeing whether two variables are correlated (see page 18).

Tip: Causation just means one thing is causing another.

Working Scientifically

Tip: Lots of things are correlated without being directly related. E.g. the level of carbon dioxide (CO_2) in the atmosphere and the amount of obesity have both increased over the last 100 years, but that doesn't mean increased atmospheric CO_2 is causing people to become obese.

2. They're linked by a third variable

A lot of the time it may look as if a change in one variable is causing a change in the other, but it isn't — a third variable links the two things.

> **Example**
>
> There's a correlation between water temperature and shark attacks. This isn't because warm water makes sharks crazy. Instead, they're linked by a third variable — the number of people swimming (more people swim when the water's hotter, and with more people in the water shark attacks increase).

3. Causation

Sometimes a change in one variable does cause a change in the other.

> **Example**
>
> There's a correlation between smoking and lung cancer.
> This is because chemicals in tobacco smoke cause lung cancer.

You can only conclude that a correlation is due to a cause if you've controlled all the variables that could be affecting the result. (For the smoking example, this would include age and exposure to other things that cause cancer.)

Evaluation

An evaluation is a critical analysis of the whole investigation. Here you need to comment on the following points about your experiment and the data you gathered:

- **The method:** Was it valid? Did you control all the other variables to make it a fair test?

- **The quality of your results:** Was there enough evidence to reach a valid conclusion? Were the results repeatable, reproducible, accurate and precise?

Tip: When you're commenting on the quality of your results, think about things like whether you took enough repeats and whether other people's results were similar to your own.

- **Anomalous results:** Were any of the results anomalous? If there were none then say so. If there were any, try to explain them — were they caused by errors in measurement? Were there any other variables that could have affected the results? You should comment on the level of uncertainty in your results too.

Once you've thought about these points you can decide how much confidence you have in your conclusion. For example, if your results are repeatable, reproducible, accurate and precise and they back up your conclusion then you can have a high degree of confidence in your conclusion.

Tip: When suggesting improvements to the investigation, always make sure that you say why you think this would make the results better.

You can also suggest any changes to the method that would improve the quality of the results, so that you could have more confidence in your conclusion. For example, you might suggest changing the way you controlled a variable, or increasing the number of measurements you took. Taking more measurements at narrower intervals could give you a more accurate result.

You could also make more predictions based on your conclusion, then further experiments could be carried out to test them.

Working Scientifically

Topic 1a   Cells and Microscopy

1. Cell Structure

All living things are made of cells — they're the building blocks of every organism on the planet. But different organisms have different cell structures...

Prokaryotes and eukaryotes

Cells can be either **prokaryotic** or **eukaryotic**. Eukaryotic cells are complex and include all animal and plant cells. Prokaryotic cells are smaller and simpler, e.g. bacteria (see next page).

Eukaryotes are organisms that are made up of eukaryotic cells. A **prokaryote** is a prokaryotic cell (it's a single-celled organism).

Both eukaryotic and prokaryotic cells contain various cell parts called **subcellular structures**.

Animal cells

Most animal cells have the following subcellular structures — make sure you know them all. The parts are labelled in Figure 2.

- **Nucleus** — contains genetic material that controls the activities of the cell. Genetic material is arranged into chromosomes (see p.53).
- **Cytoplasm** — a gel-like substance where most of the chemical reactions happen. It contains enzymes (see p.36) that control these chemical reactions.
- **Cell membrane** — holds the cell together and controls what goes in and out.
- **Mitochondria** — these are where most of the reactions for aerobic respiration take place (see p.199). Respiration transfers energy that the cell needs to work.
- **Ribosomes** — these are involved in protein synthesis (making proteins).

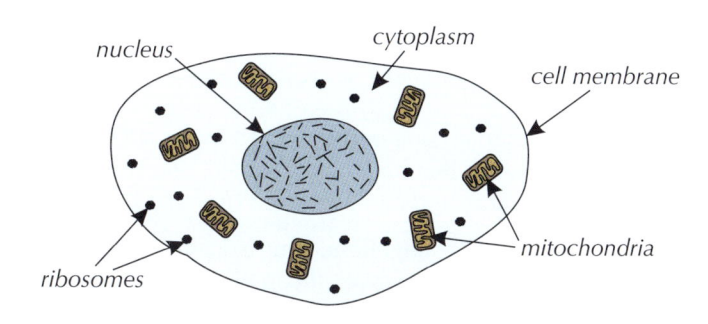

Figure 2: The structure of a typical animal cell.

Learning Objective:
- Be able to explain how the subcellular structures of eukaryotic and prokaryotic cells are related to their functions, including:
  - the nucleus, cell membrane, mitochondria and ribosomes in animal cells;
  - the nucleus, cell membrane, cell wall, chloroplasts, mitochondria, vacuole and ribosomes in plant cells;
  - chromosomal DNA, plasmid DNA, cell membrane, ribosomes and flagella in bacteria.

Specification Reference 1.1

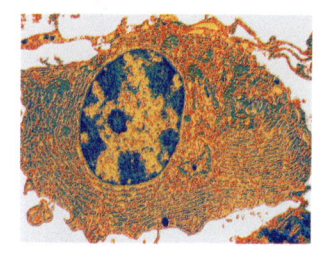

Figure 1: A human cell seen under a microscope — the blue and yellow oval is the nucleus.

Tip: A nucleus isn't really blue and yellow. The image in Figure 1 would have been made in black and white — colour has been artificially added to make it easier to see.

Tip: The diagrams on this page and the previous one all show 'typical' cells.
In reality the structure of a cell varies according to what job it does, so most cells won't look exactly like these.

Plant cells

Plant cells usually have all the bits that animal cells have, plus a few extra:

- **Cell wall** — a rigid structure made of cellulose. It supports and strengthens the cell.
- **Large vacuole** — contains cell sap, a weak solution of sugar and salts. It maintains the internal pressure to support the cell.
- **Chloroplasts** — these are where photosynthesis occurs, which makes food for the plant (see page 146). They contain a green substance called **chlorophyll**, which absorbs the light needed for photosynthesis.

The subcellular structures of a typical plant cell are shown in Figure 4.

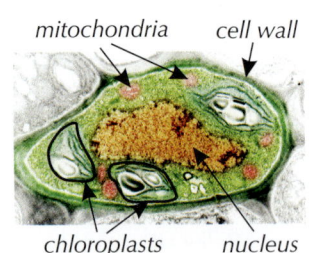

Figure 3: A cross-section of a plant cell seen under a microscope.

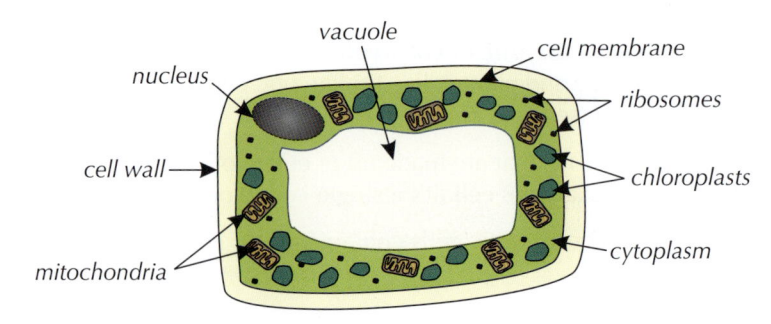

Figure 4: The structure of a typical plant cell.

Bacterial cells

Bacteria are prokaryotes. A bacterial cell has cytoplasm, containing ribosomes, and a cell membrane surrounded by a cell wall.

The cell doesn't have a 'true' nucleus — instead it has a single circular strand of chromosomal DNA that floats freely in the cytoplasm (see Figure 5). This controls the cell's activities and replication.

Tip: Bacterial cells don't contain any chloroplasts or mitochondria.

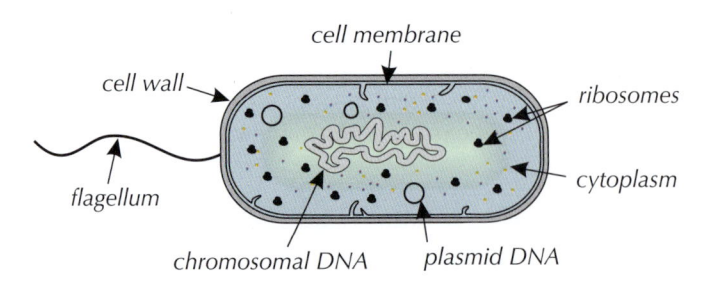

Figure 5: The structure of a typical bacterial cell.

Bacterial cells may also contain one or more small loops of DNA called **plasmids**. These aren't part of the main chromosome. Plasmids contain genes for things like drug resistance, and can be passed between bacteria.

Tip: The plural of flagellum is flagella. Some bacteria have more than one flagellum.

Some bacterial cells also have a **flagellum**. This is a long hair-like structure that rotates to make the bacterium move. It can be used to move the bacterium away from harmful substances like toxins and towards beneficial things like nutrients or oxygen.

Practice Questions — Fact Recall

Q1 Which part of an animal cell controls its activity?

Q2 Where in a cell do most of the reactions involved in aerobic respiration take place?

Q3 What are the ribosomes needed for in a cell?

Q4 a) Name three structures that a plant cell usually has, that an animal cell doesn't.

b) Describe the functions of each of the structures you named in part a).

Q5 What is a plasmid?

Q6 a) What is a flagellum?

b) Give two things that a bacterium might use its flagellum for.

Exam Tip
You need to learn the functions of the subcellular structures, not just their names.

Practice Questions — Application

Q1 The table below contains some information about a typical fungal cell. Fungal cells are eukaryotic. They share some similarities with animal and plant cells but are different to both.

Tip: Fungal cells make up fungi. Fungi include things like mushrooms and yeast.

Contains a nucleus	✓
Contains mitochondria	✓
Contains chloroplasts	✗
Has a cell membrane	✓
Has a cell wall	✓

a) Using the information in the table, give one way in which a fungal cell is similar to an animal cell, but different to a plant cell.

b) Using the information in the table, give one way in which a fungal cell is similar to a plant cell, but different to an animal cell.

Topic 1a Cells and Microscopy

Learning Objectives:
- Be able to describe how specialised cells are adapted to their function, including:
  - sperm cells, and how the acrosome, haploid nucleus, mitochondria and tail make them adapted to their function;
  - egg cells and how nutrients in the cytoplasm, the haploid nucleus and changes in the cell membrane after fertilisation make them adapted to their function;
  - ciliated epithelial cells.

Specification Reference 1.2

2. Specialised Cells

Multicellular organisms contain lots of different types of cells — each type does a different job. A cell's structure is related to the job it does, so cell structure can vary.

What is a specialised cell?

A specialised cell is one that performs a specific function. Most cells in an organism are specialised. A cell's structure (e.g. its shape and the parts it contains) helps it to carry out its function — so depending on what job it does, a specialised cell can look very different to the cells you saw on pages 23-24.

You need to learn how the structures of three particular types of specialised cell — **sperm cells**, **egg cells** and **ciliated epithelial cells** — make them adapted to their function.

Sperm cells and egg cells

Sperm cells and egg cells are specialised cells. They are adapted to carry out their functions in sexual reproduction.

During sexual reproduction, the nucleus of an egg cell fuses with the nucleus of a sperm cell to create a fertilised egg (see Figure 1) which then develops into an embryo.

Tip: There's more on sexual reproduction on pages 72-73.

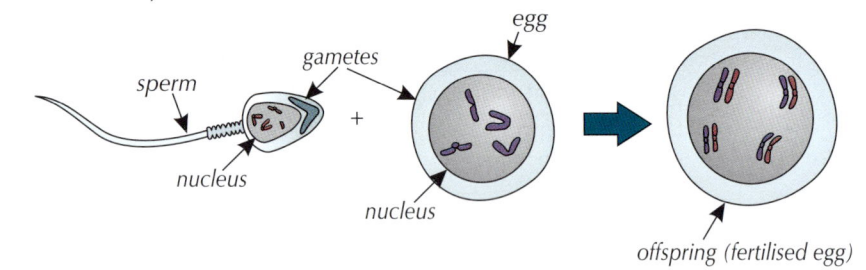

Figure 1: Diagram showing fertilisation.

Adaptations of a sperm cell

The function of a sperm is to transport the male DNA to the female DNA in the egg. As a result, a sperm cell has a long tail so it can swim to the egg. It also has lots of mitochondria in its middle section to provide the energy needed to swim this distance. The **acrosome** at the front of the sperm's 'head', stores the enzymes the sperm needs to digest its way through the membrane of the egg cell. A sperm cell also contains a haploid nucleus — there's more on this on the next page. The structure of a sperm cell is shown by Figures 2 and 3.

Tip: Mitochondria (see p.23) provide energy through aerobic respiration (see p.199).

Figure 2: A microscope image of a sperm cell. It's easy to see the long tail.

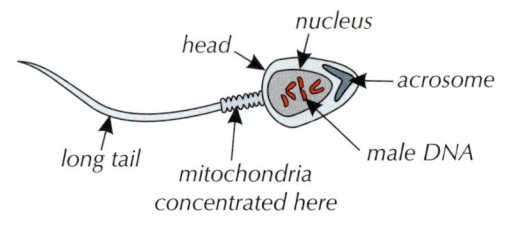

Figure 3: A sperm cell.

Topic 1a Cells and Microscopy

Adaptations of an egg cell

The main functions of an egg are to carry the female DNA and to nourish the developing embryo in the early stages. To enable it to do this, it contains nutrients in the cytoplasm to feed the embryo. It also has a haploid nucleus (see below). Straight after fertilisation, its membrane changes structure to stop any more sperm getting in. This makes sure the offspring end up with the right amount of DNA.

Haploid nuclei

A sperm cell and an egg cell both have what's called a '**haploid**' nucleus — this is a nucleus that contains half the number of chromosomes that's in a normal body cell. For example, a human sperm cell and a human egg cell each contain 23 chromosomes. A normal human body cell contains 46 chromosomes. This is important as it means that when a sperm cell nucleus combines with an egg cell nucleus at fertilisation, the resulting cell will have the right number of chromosomes.

Tip: The plural of nucleus is nuclei.

Tip: Chromosomes are long coiled up molecules of DNA — the genetic material of a cell. There's more on chromosomes on p.53.

Ciliated epithelial cells

Epithelial cells line the surfaces of organs. Some of them have **cilia** (hair-like structures) on the top surface of the cell (see Figures 4 and 5).

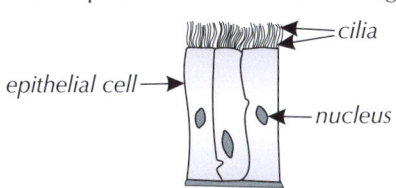

Figure 4: Ciliated epithelial cells.

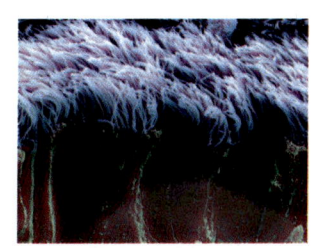

Figure 5: A microscope image showing ciliated epithelial cells in the airways. The cilia (shown in blue here) are on top of the cells.

The function of these ciliated epithelial cells is to move substances — the cilia beat to move substances in one direction, along the surface of the tissue.

> **Example**
> The lining of the airways contains lots of ciliated epithelial cells. These help to move mucus (and all of the particles from the air that it has trapped) up to the throat so it can be swallowed and doesn't reach the lungs.

Practice Questions — Fact Recall

Q1 The head of a sperm cell contains enzymes that can digest through the membrane of an egg cell. Name the subcellular structure in which these enzymes are stored.

Q2 Give two functions of an egg cell.

Q3 Give two ways in which an egg cell is adapted to help make sure an embryo ends up with the correct amount of DNA.

Practice Question — Application

Q1 Suggest why ciliated epithelial cells usually contain large numbers of mitochondria.

Exam Tip
In the exams, you might get asked to suggest how a specialised cell that you've not come across before is adapted to its function. If so, don't panic — just apply what you've learnt about the specialised cells here, as well as your knowledge of subcellular structures.

Topic 1a Cells and Microscopy

Learning Objectives:

- Be able to explain how changes in microscope technology, including electron microscopy, have enabled us to see cell structures with more clarity and detail than in the past and increased our understanding of the role of subcellular structures.
- Be able to investigate biological specimens using microscopes, including labelled scientific drawings from observations and magnification calculations. (Core Practical)
- **H** Be able to carry out calculations with numbers written in standard form.
- Be able to demonstrate an understanding of the relationship between quantitative units in relation to cells, including: milli (10^{-3}), micro (10^{-6}), nano (10^{-9}) and pico (10^{-12}).
- Be able to demonstrate an understanding of number, size and scale, including the use of estimations and explain when they should be used.

Specification References 1.3 – 1.6

Tip: Make sure you carry out a risk assessment so that you're aware of any hazards, particularly for any stains you're using, before you start preparing your slide.

3. Microscopy

Microscopy is the study of very small objects (such as cells) using an instrument called a microscope. It's an essential part of biology, really.

Microscopes

Microscopes let us see things that we can't see with the naked eye, such as individual cells and their subcellular structures. The microscopy techniques we can use have developed over the years as technology and knowledge have improved. The two types of microscope you need to know about are:

Light microscopes

Light microscopes were invented in the 1590s. They use light and lenses to form an image of a specimen and magnify it (make it look bigger). They let us see individual cells and large subcellular structures, like nuclei and chloroplasts. They can also be used to study living cells.

Electron microscopes

Electron microscopes were invented in the 1930s. They use electrons instead of light to form an image. They have a much higher **magnification** than light microscopes. They also have a higher **resolution**. Resolution is the ability to distinguish between two points, so a higher resolution gives a sharper, clearer image.

Electron microscopes let us see much smaller things in more detail, like the internal structure of mitochondria and chloroplasts. They even let us see tinier things like ribosomes and plasmids. This has given us a greater understanding of how cells work and of the role of subcellular structures within cells. However, electron microscopes can't be used to view living cells.

Using a light microscope

You need to know the ins and outs of using a light microscope, including how to prepare your specimen, how to focus the microscope and how to make accurate drawings of what you observe.

Preparing a slide

If you want to look at a specimen (e.g. plant or animal cells) under a light microscope, you need to put it on a microscope slide first. A slide is a strip of clear glass or plastic onto which the specimen is mounted. For example, here's how to prepare a slide to view onion cells:

1. Add a drop of water to the middle of a clean slide. This will secure the specimen in place.

2. Cut up an onion and separate it out into layers. Use tweezers to peel off some epidermal tissue from the bottom of one of the layers.

3. Using the tweezers, place the epidermal tissue into the water on the slide.

4. Add a drop of iodine solution. Iodine solution is a stain. Stains are used to add colour to objects in a cell, making them easier to see. Different stains can be used to highlight different things. E.g. methylene blue can be used to stain DNA and eosin can be used to stain the cytoplasm.

5. Place a cover slip (a square of thin, transparent plastic or glass) upright on the slide, next to the water droplet. Then, holding it at an angle with a mounted needle, carefully lower it so it covers the specimen. Try not to get any air bubbles under there — they'll obstruct your view of the specimen. Steps 1-5 are shown in Figure 1.

Tip: In light microscopes, the beam of light passes through the object being viewed — so the specimen needs to be thin enough to let light through it (like onion epidermal tissue). An image is produced because some parts of the object absorb more light than others. If the object being viewed is completely transparent, the whole thing looks white because the light rays just pass straight through. To get round this, stains are used to highlight parts of the object, making them more visible.

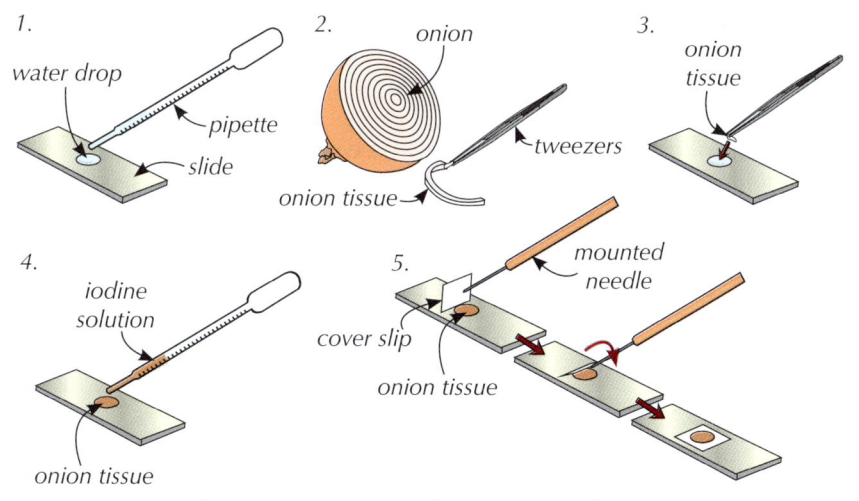

Figure 1: Preparation of a microscope slide.

Observing the specimen

You need to know how to set up and use a light microscope (see Figure 2) to observe your prepared slide:

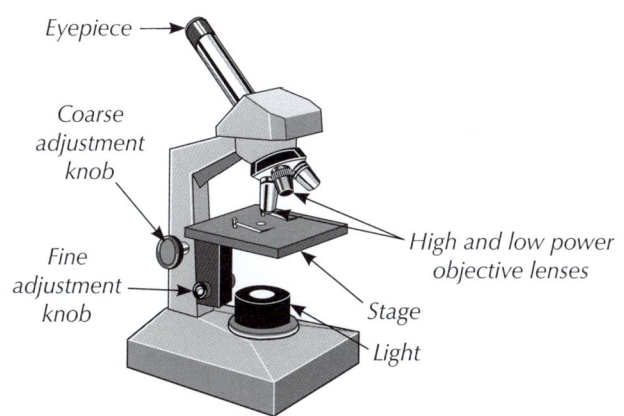

Figure 2: A light microscope.

1. Start by clipping the slide you've prepared onto the stage.
2. Select the lowest-powered objective lens (i.e. the one that produces the lowest magnification).
3. Use the coarse adjustment knob to move the stage up to just below the objective lens.
4. Look down the eyepiece. Use the coarse adjustment knob to move the stage downwards until the image is roughly in focus.
5. Adjust the focus with the fine adjustment knob, until you get a clear image of what's on the slide.
6. If you need to see the slide with greater magnification, swap to a higher-powered objective lens and refocus.

Tip: Don't use the eyepiece while you're moving the stage up with the coarse adjustment knob, as you could cause the lens and stage to collide.

Tip: Before focusing on your specimen, you can measure the field of view (the circular area that's visible under the microscope). This will allow you to estimate the size of your specimen. See page 237 for how to do this.

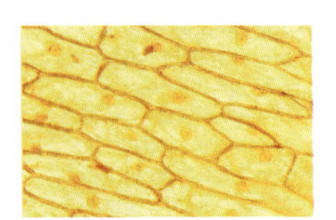

Figure 3: Onion cells stained with iodine, viewed under × 400 magnification.

Drawing observations

When making a drawing of your specimen from under the microscope, make sure you use a pencil with a sharp point and that you draw with clear, unbroken lines. Your drawing should not include any colouring or shading. If you are drawing cells, the subcellular structures should be drawn in proportion (the correct sizes relative to each other). If you're asked to make your drawing in a certain amount of space (e.g. on a worksheet), it needs to take up at least half of the space available.

You also need to include a title of what you were observing and label the important features of your drawing (e.g. nucleus, chloroplasts) using straight, uncrossed lines. Finally, you need to include the magnification your specimen was viewed under and a scale.

Exam Tip
Make sure you know what all the subcellular structures you learnt about on pages 23-24 look like — it will make it easier to identify them in microscope images.

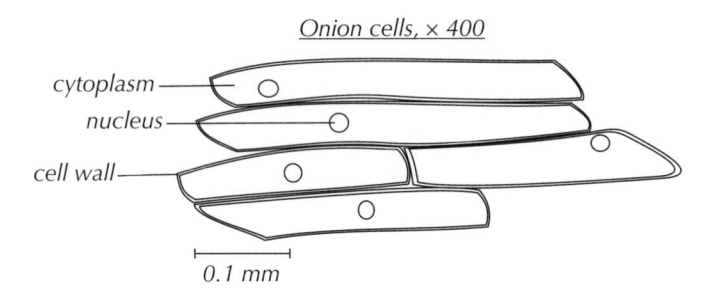

Figure 4: A drawing of onion cells as viewed under a light microscope.

Magnification

Magnification is how much bigger the image is than the real object that you're looking at. If you know the power of the microscope lenses used to view a specimen, you can work out the total magnification of the image using this simple formula:

$$\text{total magnification} = \text{eyepiece lens magnification} \times \text{objective lens magnification}$$

Example

If your specimen was viewed with an eyepiece lens magnification of × 10 and an objective lens magnification of × 40, the total magnification of your image is:

$$10 \times 40 = \times\, 400.$$

If you don't know which lenses were used, you can still work out the magnification as long as you can measure the image and you know the real size of the specimen. This is the formula you need:

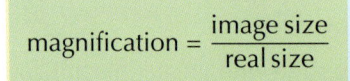

Exam Tip
Make sure you learn these two formulas for your exams.

$$\text{magnification} = \frac{\text{image size}}{\text{real size}}$$

Topic 1a Cells and Microscopy

Example

If you have a magnified image that's 2 mm wide and your specimen is 0.02 mm wide the magnification is:

$$\text{magnification} = \frac{\text{image size}}{\text{real size}}$$

$$= \frac{2}{0.02} = \times 100$$

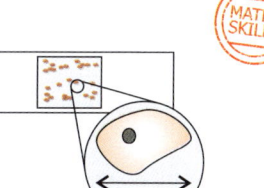

Tip: Both the image size and the real size should have the same units. If they don't, you'll need to convert them first (see next page).

If you want to work out the image size or the real size of the object, you have to rearrange the equation.

Example

Calculating image size

If your specimen is 0.3 mm wide and the magnification of the microscope is × 50, then the size of the image is:

$$\text{image size} = \text{magnification} \times \text{real size}$$
$$= 50 \times 0.3 = \mathbf{15\ mm}$$

Calculating the real size of an object

If you have a magnified image that's 10 mm wide and the magnification is × 400, then the real size of the specimen you're looking at is:

$$\text{real size} = \frac{\text{image size}}{\text{magnification}} = \frac{10}{400} = \mathbf{0.025\ mm}$$

Exam Tip
If you find rearranging formulas hard you can use a formula triangle to help:

(Image size / Magnification × Real size)

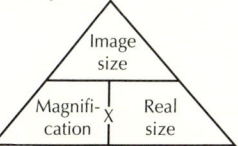

All you do is put your finger over the one you want and read off the formula. E.g. if you want the real size of the object, you put your finger over that and it leaves behind image size ÷ magnification.

Microscopes are used to look at tiny objects, so it's sometimes useful to write the real size of a specimen in standard form. This is where you change very big or small numbers with lots of zeros into something more manageable, e.g. 0.000017 can be written 1.7×10^{-5}. If you're sitting a higher paper, you might need to carry out magnification calculations that involve standard form.

Example — Higher

A specimen is 5×10^{-3} mm wide. A magnified image of the specimen is 2 mm wide. Calculate the magnification it was viewed under.

If you've got a scientific calculator, you can put standard form numbers into it using the 'EXP' or the or the '×10^x' button. So to enter 5×10^{-3}, press 5, then 'EXP' or '×10^x', then −3. The calculation is:

$$\text{magnification} = \frac{\text{image size}}{\text{real size}} = \frac{2}{5 \times 10^{-3}} = \mathbf{\times 400}$$

With an ordinary calculator, you'll need to write the values out in full. The power of 10 is negative, so 5×10^{-3} must be a small number (less than 1). The power is −3, so the decimal point moves 3 places:

$$0005.0 \times 10^{-3} \longrightarrow 0.005$$

The calculation is: $\frac{2}{0.005} = \mathbf{\times 400}$

Tip: There's more on using standard form on pages 241-242.

Topic 1a Cells and Microscopy

Converting between units

When you're calculating magnification you need to make sure that all measurements have the same units, e.g. all in millimetres. When dealing with microscopes these units can get pretty tiny. The table below shows the units you need to know and how to convert between them:

Tip: There's more on converting units on pages 19-20.

Unit	In standard form
Millimetre (mm)	$\times 10^{-3}$ m
Micrometre (μm)	$\times 10^{-6}$ m
Nanometre (nm)	$\times 10^{-9}$ m
Picometre (pm)	$\times 10^{-12}$ m

To convert: × 1000 (down) / ÷ 1000 (up)

Tip: So 1 pm = 0.000000000001 m. (That's tiny!)

Examples

- To convert from a smaller unit to a bigger unit you have to divide. So to convert 5 micrometres to millimetres you divide 5 by 1000. 5 ÷ 1000 = **0.005 mm**

- To go from a bigger unit to a smaller unit you have to multiply. So to convert 0.025 micrometres to nanometres you multiply 0.025 by 1000. 0.025 × 1000 = **25 nm**

- If you have a specimen that's 5 μm wide and an image that's 5 mm wide, you need to put both measurements in the same units before you can work out the magnification using the formula:

  5 mm = 5 × 1000 = 5000 μm

  $$\text{magnification} = \frac{\text{image size}}{\text{real size}} = \frac{5000}{5} = \times\, 1000$$

Tip: It doesn't matter which units you choose to convert to. In the calculation on the right, if you converted 5 μm to mm (5 ÷ 1000 = 0.005 μm) instead, you'd get the same answer of × 1000 magnification.

Estimating size and area of cell structures

You can estimate the size of a subcellular structure by comparing its size to that of the cell.

Tip: Estimates can come in handy if you don't have a small enough scale to measure something accurately.

Example

Figure 5 shows a cheek cell.

Estimate the width of the nucleus of the cell.

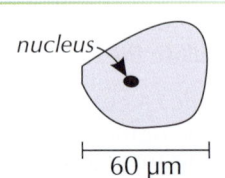

Figure 5: Cheek cell with scale. (60 μm)

1. Estimate the number of times that the nucleus could fit across the width of the cell.

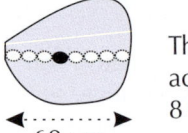

   The nucleus would fit across the cell about 8 times. (60 μm)

2. Divide the width of the cell by the number of times the nucleus would fit across it.

   width of nucleus = 60 μm ÷ 8 = **7.5 μm**

Tip: You can estimate the size of a cell by comparing its size to the size of the field of view. See page 237.

You can estimate the area of a subcellular structure by comparing it to a regular shape.

> **Example**
>
> Figure 6 shows a diagram of a mitochondrion measured under an electron microscope. 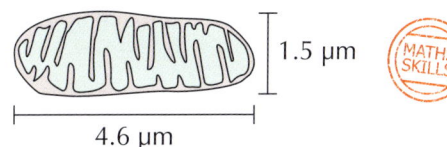
>
> **Figure 6:** A mitochondrion.
>
> The shape of the mitochondrion is close to that of a rectangle.
>
> So to estimate its area, use the formula for the area of a rectangle:
> area = length × width
>
> Area = 4.6 µm × 1.5 µm = **6.9 µm²**

Exam Tip
In the exam, you could be given a photomicrograph (a picture taken down a light microscope) of a cell and its subcellular structures rather than a diagram. You can estimate the size of the subcellular structures in a photomicrograph in the same way.

Tip: Don't forget to include the units of area in your answer.

Estimating can also help you to check that your answer is correct. To estimate an answer, round the numbers so you can do the maths in your head.

> **Example**
>
> Say you know the real size of a specimen is 21.5 µm and the image size is 9800 µm. To get an estimate of the magnification used, round both numbers to 1 significant figure (see p.15) and do 10 000 ÷ 20 = × 500.

Practice Questions — Fact Recall

Q1 Why can an electron microscope be used to look at smaller objects than a light microscope?

Q2 Why are stains used when preparing microscope slides?

Q3 Describe the steps you would take to obtain a clear image of a specimen on a microscope slide.

Q4 What is 1 nanometre in metres? Give your answer in standard form.

Practice Questions — Application

Q1 Calculate the total magnification of an image viewed with a × 15 eyepiece lens and a × 40 objective lens.

Q2 A bacterial cell is 0.002 mm long. A magnified image of the cell is 18 mm long. What is the magnification of the image?

Q3 A plant cell is 0.08 mm wide. It is examined under a × 400 microscope lens. Calculate the width of the magnified image.

Q4 A specimen is observed under × 1500 magnification. The magnified image is 10.5 mm wide. What is the real width of the specimen? Give your answer in µm.

Q5 A ribosome is 2×10^{-5} mm wide. In an electron microscope image, it is 900 µm wide. What is the magnification of the image?

Tip: If it helps you to work out what size you're looking for, you could draw a diagram of what the question is describing. So for Q2 it might be like this:

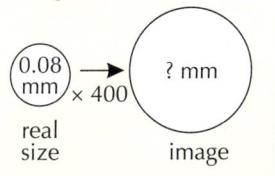

0.08 mm (real size) × 400 → ? mm (image)

Topic 1a Cells and Microscopy

Topic 1a Checklist — Make sure you know...

Cell Structure

☐ That animal and plant cells are eukaryotic cells, which make up eukaryotic organisms, and that bacterial cells are prokaryotic cells.

☐ That most animal cells have: a nucleus (which contains the genetic material that controls the activities of a cell), cytoplasm (where most chemical reactions happen), a cell membrane (which controls what goes in and out of the cell), mitochondria (where most of the reactions for aerobic respiration happen), and ribosomes (which are involved in protein synthesis).

☐ That a typical plant cell has all the same parts as an animal cell, plus a cell wall made of cellulose (which supports and strengthens the cell) a large vacuole containing cell sap (which maintains the internal pressure of the cell) and chloroplasts (where photosynthesis occurs).

☐ That a bacterial cell has ribosomes, a cell membrane and a cell wall, and that its genetic material is a single loop of chromosomal DNA found in the cytoplasm (rather than in a nucleus) and potentially one or more plasmids (small rings of DNA). It may also have a flagellum (which rotates to move the cell).

Specialised Cells

☐ That specialised cells are adapted to carry out their functions, and that their adaptations include things like their shape and their subcellular structures.

☐ That the function of a sperm cell is to carry the male DNA to the female DNA during sexual reproduction and how the sperm cell's tail, mitochondria, acrosome and haploid nucleus help it to do this.

☐ That the function of an egg cell is to carry the female DNA during sexual reproduction and to nourish the developing embryo in its early stages, and how nutrients in its cytoplasm, changes to the cell membrane after fertilisation and a haploid nucleus help the egg cell to do this.

☐ That ciliated epithelial cells have cilia (hair-like structures) which beat to move substances along the surface of the epithelial cells.

Microscopy

☐ That microscopy techniques have developed over time due to improving technology.

☐ That electron microscopes can produce images with a higher magnification and resolution than light microscopes, which has allowed us to see subcellular structures in more detail and increased our understanding of their roles.

☐ How to prepare a slide containing a biological specimen and use a light microscope to observe it, how to produce a scientific drawing of your observations, and how to use the formulas: total magnification = eyepiece lens magnification × objective lens magnification <u>and</u> magnification = image size ÷ real size (Core Practical).

☐ The relationship between the units millimetres (1×10^{-3} m), micrometres (1×10^{-6} m), nanometres (1×10^{-9} m) and picometres (1×10^{-12} m) and how to convert between these units.

☐ [H] How to carry out magnification calculations with numbers written in standard form.

☐ How estimations can be used when working with cells and why they might be used.

Exam-style Questions

1   **Figure 1** shows a palisade cell from a plant.

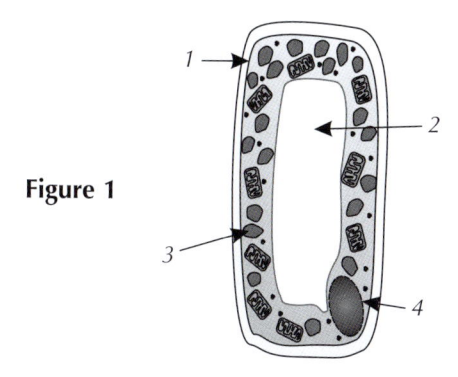

Figure 1

(a)   Look at the structures labelled 1-4 in **Figure 1**.
Which of the following options gives the correct labels for these structures?

   A   1 — vacuole, 2 — nucleus, 3 — chloroplast, 4 — cell membrane
   B   1 — nucleus, 2 — chloroplast, 3 — cell membrane, 4 — vacuole
   C   1 — cell membrane, 2 — vacuole, 3 — chloroplast, 4 — nucleus
   D   1 — cell membrane, 2 — nucleus, 3 — chloroplast, 4 — vacuole

(1 mark)

(b)   Is a palisade cell an example of a eukaryotic cell or a prokaryotic cell?
Give a reason for your answer that refers to the cell's structure.

(1 mark)

(c)   Palisade cells are specialised cells. They are the main site of photosynthesis in a plant and are found grouped together near the top of a leaf.
Suggest **one** subcellular structure that is found in greater numbers in a palisade cell than in other plant cells.

(1 mark)

2   **Figure 2** is a scale drawing of sperm cell viewed under a light microscope.

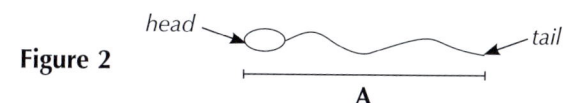

Figure 2

(a)   How does the sperm cell's tail make the cell well adapted to its function?

(1 mark)

A is the image length. The real length of the sperm cell is 55 μm.

(b)   Calculate the magnification that the sperm cell was viewed under.

(3 marks)

(c)   Use **Figure 2** to estimate the length of the sperm cell's head.

(2 marks)

Topic 1b — Biological Molecules and Transport in Cells

Learning Objectives:
- Be able to explain the mechanism of enzyme action including the active site and enzyme specificity.
- Be able to explain how enzymes can be denatured due to changes in the shape of the active site.
- Be able to explain the effects of temperature, substrate concentration and pH on enzyme activity.

Specification References 1.7 – 1.9

1. Enzymes

Enzymes are essential. There are loads of different types in the body. They play an important role in speeding up chemical reactions in your insides.

Enzymes

Living things have thousands of different chemical reactions going on inside them all the time — most are useful (you need them to stay alive) but some aren't. The useful reactions need to be carefully controlled — to get the right amounts of substances.

You can usually make a reaction happen more quickly by raising the temperature. This would speed up the useful reactions but also the unwanted ones too... not good. There's also a limit to how far you can raise the temperature inside a living creature before its cells start getting damaged.

So... living things produce enzymes that act as **biological catalysts**. Enzymes reduce the need for high temperatures and we only have enzymes to speed up the useful chemical reactions in the body.

> A **catalyst** is a substance which increases the speed of a reaction, without being changed or used up in the reaction.

Enzymes are all large proteins and all proteins are made up of chains of amino acids. These chains are folded into unique shapes, which enzymes need to do their jobs (see below).

Active sites

Chemical reactions usually involve things either being split apart or joined together. Every enzyme has an **active site** with a unique shape that fits onto the substance involved in a reaction. Enzymes are really picky — they usually only catalyse one specific reaction. This is because, for the enzyme to work, the substrate has to fit into its active site. If the substrate doesn't match the enzyme's active site, then the reaction won't be catalysed.

Tip: The substance that an enzyme acts on is called the substrate.

Tip: Enzymes are said to have a "high specificity" for their substrate.

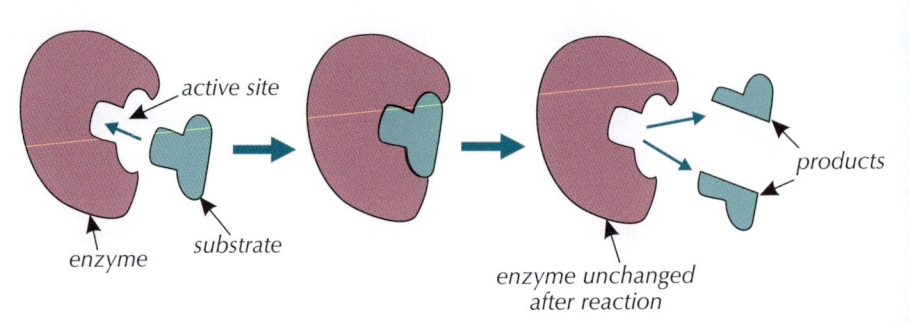

Figure 1: Diagram to show how an enzyme works.

Figure 1 (on the previous page) shows the 'lock and key' model of enzyme action. It is so called because the substrate fits into the enzyme like a key fits into a lock.

Optimum conditions for enzymes

Enzymes need the right conditions, such as the right temperature, substrate concentration and pH for them to work best — these are called optimum conditions.

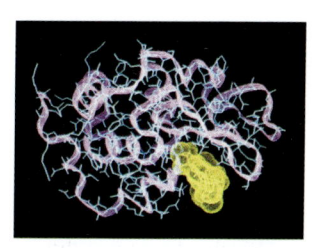

Figure 2: Computer model of an enzyme bound to a substrate (yellow).

Temperature

Changing the temperature changes the rate of an enzyme-catalysed reaction. As with any reaction, a higher temperature increases the rate at first. But if it gets too hot, some of the bonds holding the enzyme together break. This changes the shape of the enzyme's active site, so the substrate won't fit any more. The enzyme is said to be **denatured**.

Therefore enzymes have a temperature at which they are most active — this is called the optimum temperature (see Figure 3). Enzymes in the human body normally work best at around 37 °C.

Tip: Increasing the temperature increases the rate of a reaction because the reactants have more energy, so they move about more, and collide with each other more often.

Tip: As well as having different optimum temperatures, enzymes denature at different temperatures too. Most human enzymes denature at around 45 °C.

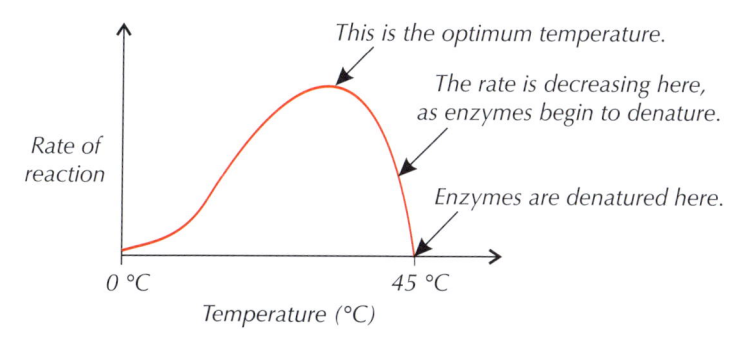

Figure 3: Graph to show how temperature affects enzyme action.

Substrate concentration

Substrate concentration also affects the rate of reaction — the higher the substrate concentration, the faster the reaction. This is because it's more likely that the enzyme will meet up and react with a substrate molecule.

This is only true up to a point though. After that, there are so many substrate molecules that the enzymes have about as much as they can cope with (all the active sites are full), and adding more makes no difference (see Figure 4).

Tip: The active site can only catalyse one reaction at a time. Once all of the active sites are full, increasing the amount of substrate has no effect on the rate — there are no available enzymes to catalyse further reactions. The point where increasing the substrate concentration has no effect on the rate will depend on the number of enzymes around.

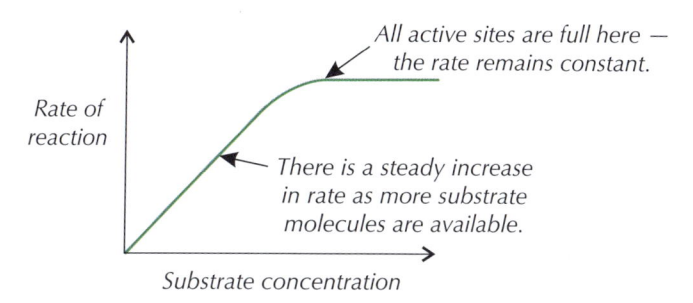

Figure 4: Graph to show how substrate concentration affects enzyme action.

Topic 1b Biological Molecules and Transport in Cells

pH

Tip: A low pH means that an environment is acidic. A high pH means that it is alkaline.

The pH also affects enzymes. If it's too high or too low, the pH interferes with the bonds holding the enzyme together. This changes the shape of the active site and denatures the enzyme.

All enzymes have a pH that they work best at — this is called the optimum pH (see Figure 5).

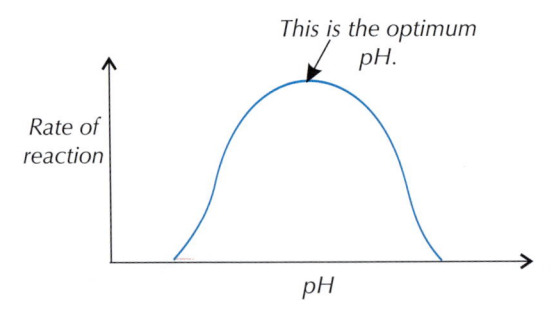

Figure 5: Graph to show how pH affects enzyme action.

The optimum pH is different for different enzymes, depending on where they work. For many enzymes it's neutral pH 7, but not always.

Example

Pepsin is an enzyme used to break down proteins in the stomach. It works best at pH 2, which means it's well-suited to the acidic conditions in the stomach.

Practice Questions — Fact Recall

Q1 Why can enzymes be described as catalysts?

Q2 What is the name of the part of an enzyme that binds to the substrate?

Q3 True or false? All enzymes work best at pH 7.

Practice Question — Application

Tip: Respiration is the process of breaking down glucose, which transfers energy. There's loads more about it on pages 199-201.

Q1 Hexokinase is an enzyme found in the human body that's involved in respiration. It catalyses this reaction:

$$\text{glucose} \xrightarrow{\text{hexokinase}} \text{substance A}$$

Enzymes in the human body work best at 37 °C.

A scientist heats up hexokinase to 50 °C and adds it to some glucose. Suggest the effect this will have on the rate of the reaction compared to if the reaction was at 37 °C. Explain your answer.

2. Investigating Enzymatic Reactions

You need to know how to investigate the effect of pH on the rate of the reaction catalysed by an enzyme. Read on for more.

Investigating the effect of pH on amylase

CORE PRACTICAL

The enzyme **amylase** catalyses the breakdown of starch to maltose. It's easy to detect starch using iodine solution — if starch is present, the iodine solution will change from browny-orange to blue-black. This is how you can investigate how pH affects amylase activity:

1. Put a drop of iodine solution into every well of a spotting tile.

2. Place a Bunsen burner on a heat-proof mat, and a tripod and gauze over the Bunsen burner. Put a beaker of water on top of the tripod and heat the water until it reaches the optimum temperature of the amylase you are using. (Use a thermometer to measure the temperature.) Try to keep the temperature of the water constant throughout the experiment.

3. Use a syringe to add 3 cm^3 of amylase solution and 1 cm^3 of a buffer solution with a pH of 5 to a boiling tube. Using test tube holders, put the boiling tube into the beaker of water and wait for five minutes.

4. Next, use a different syringe to add 3 cm^3 of a starch solution to the boiling tube.

5. Immediately mix the contents of the boiling tube and start a stop clock.

6. Use continuous sampling to record how long it takes for the amylase to break down all of the starch. To do this, use a dropping pipette to take a fresh sample from the boiling tube every thirty seconds and put a drop into a well on the spotting tile. When the iodine solution remains browny-orange, starch is no longer present.

7. Repeat the whole experiment with buffer solutions of different pH values to see how pH affects the time taken for the starch to be broken down.

8. Remember to control any variables each time you repeat the experiment to make it a fair test. Variables that need controlling include the concentration and volume of the amylase and starch solutions and the temperature of the reaction mixture. See p.10 for more on fair tests.

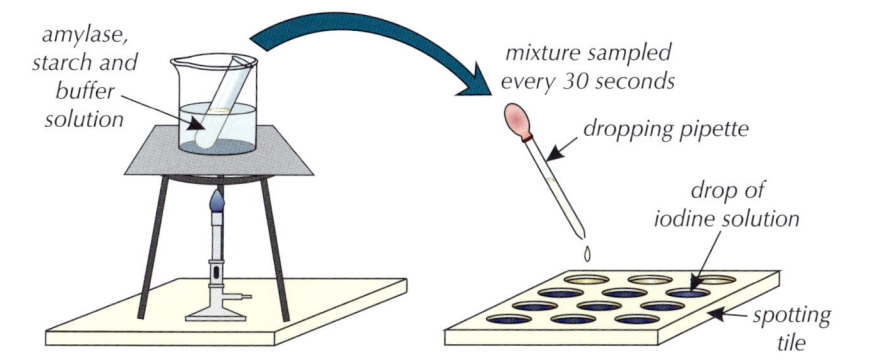

Figure 1: *Apparatus for investigating the breakdown of starch.*

Learning Objectives:

- Be able to investigate the effect of pH on enzyme activity. (Core Practical).
- Be able to understand rate calculations for enzyme activity.

Specification References 1.10, 1.11

Tip: Don't forget to do a risk assessment before you do this experiment. You should always take basic safety precautions like wearing goggles and a lab coat.

Tip: Instead of using the Bunsen burner and beaker of water, you could set an electric water bath to control the temperature. See page 236 for more on water baths.

Tip: You should repeat the experiment at least three times at each pH and work out the mean time taken for the starch to break down.

Tip: You could use a pH meter to accurately measure the pH of your solutions.

Topic 1b **Biological Molecules and Transport in Cells**

Calculating the rate of a reaction

It's often useful to calculate the rate of reaction after an experiment. Rate is a measure of how much something changes over time.

Tip: You could also use the formula '1/time' but '1000/time' will give you a bigger number that is easier to plot on a graph.

For the experiment on the previous page, you can calculate the rate of reaction using this formula:

$$\text{Rate} = \frac{1000}{\text{time}}$$

The units are s^{-1} since rate is given per unit of time.

> **Example**
>
> At pH 6, the time taken for amylase to break down all of the starch in a solution was 90 seconds. So the rate of the reaction
> = 1000 ÷ 90 = **11 s^{-1}**

If an experiment measures how much something changes over time, you calculate the rate of reaction by dividing the amount that it has changed by the time taken.

> **Example**
>
> **The enzyme catalase catalyses the breakdown of hydrogen peroxide into water and oxygen. During an investigation into the activity of catalase, 24 cm^3 of oxygen was released in 50 seconds (s). Calculate the rate of the reaction. Write your answer in cm^3 s^{-1}**
>
> Amount of product formed = change = 24 cm^3
>
> Rate of reaction = change ÷ time
> = 24 cm^3 ÷ 50 s
> = **0.48 cm^3 s^{-1}**

Tip: cm^3 s^{-1} means centimetres cubed per second. It means the same as cm^3/s.

Practice Question — Application

Q1 A group of students were investigating the effect of pH on the rate of starch breakdown by the enzyme amylase. They mixed the enzyme and starch in a boiling tube, then every 10 seconds added a drop of the mixture to a well on a spotting tile containing iodine solution. They timed how long it took for all of the starch to be broken down.

   a) What could the students have used to control the pH level of the starch and enzyme mixture?

   b) How would the students know when all of the starch had been broken down?

   c) It took 120 seconds for all of the starch to be broken down. Calculate the rate of the reaction. Give your answer in s^{-1}.

Topic 1b Biological Molecules and Transport in Cells

3. Enzymes in Breakdown and Synthesis

Learning Objective:
- Be able to explain the importance of enzymes as biological catalysts in the synthesis of carbohydrates, proteins and lipids and their breakdown into sugars, amino acids and fatty acids and glycerol.

Specification Reference 1.12

Organisms need to be able to break down large molecules and build them back up again. Lots of enzymes are needed to catalyse these reactions.

Enzymes in breakdown reactions

Carbohydrates, proteins and lipids are big molecules, which are essential for life. Organisms need to be able to break them down into their smaller components, so they can be used for growth and other life processes. These breakdown reactions are catalysed by enzymes.

Examples
- Many of the molecules in the food we eat are too big to pass through the walls of our digestive system, so digestive enzymes break them down into smaller, soluble molecules. These can pass easily through the walls of the digestive system, allowing them to be absorbed into the bloodstream. They can then pass into cells to be used by the body.
- Plants store energy in the form of starch (a carbohydrate). When plants need energy, enzymes break down the starch into smaller molecules (sugars). These can then be respired to transfer energy to be used by the cells (see p.199).

Tip: Lipids are fats and oils.

Tip: Carbohydrates, lipids and proteins are all biological molecules — this means they're molecules found in living organisms.

Different types of enzymes catalyse the breakdown of carbohydrates, proteins and lipids.

Carbohydrases

Carbohydrases convert carbohydrates into simple sugars. Amylase is an example of a carbohydrase. It breaks down starch — see Figure 1.

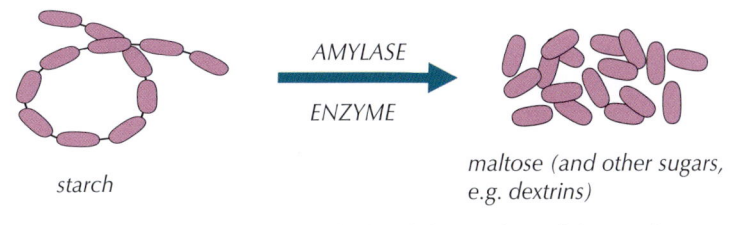

starch → AMYLASE ENZYME → maltose (and other sugars, e.g. dextrins)

Figure 1: Diagram to show the breakdown of starch by amylase.

Proteases

Protease enzymes catalyse the conversion of proteins into amino acids — see Figure 2.

proteins → PROTEASE ENZYMES → amino acids

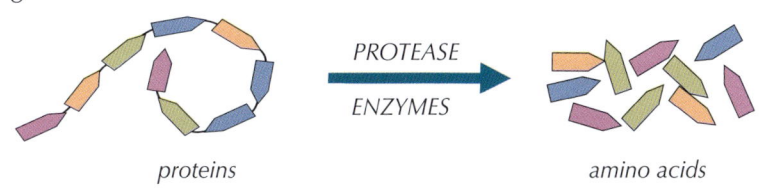

Figure 2: Diagram to show the breakdown of proteins by proteases.

Exam Tip
You need to learn the types of molecules that carbohydrates, proteins and lipids are broken down into.

Topic 1b **Biological Molecules and Transport in Cells**

Lipases

Lipase enzymes catalyse the conversion of lipids into glycerol and fatty acids — see Figure 3.

Tip: When lipids are broken down, the fatty acids will lower the pH of the solution they are in — this is because they're acidic. When proteins are broken down into amino acids, the same thing happens.

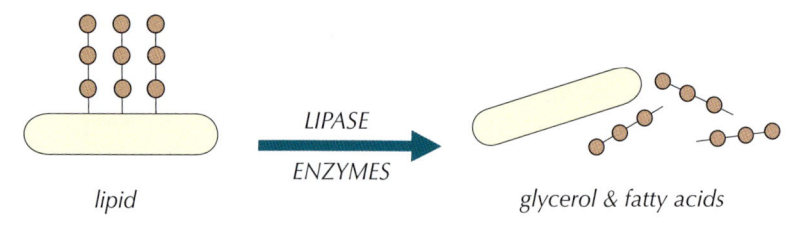

Figure 3: Diagram to show the breakdown of lipids by lipases.

Tip: <u>Carbohydr</u>ase enzymes break down <u>carbohydr</u>ates. <u>Prote</u>ase enzymes break down <u>prote</u>ins. <u>Lip</u>ase enzymes break down <u>lip</u>ids.

Enzymes in synthesis reactions

Organisms also need to be able to synthesise carbohydrates, proteins and lipids from their smaller components. Again, enzymes are used to catalyse the reactions involved. These enzymes are different to the ones used in breakdown reactions.

Carbohydrates can be synthesised by joining together simple sugars.

> **Example**
>
> Glycogen synthase is an enzyme that joins together lots of chains of glucose molecules to make glycogen (a molecule used to store energy in animals).

Proteins are made by joining amino acids together. Enzymes catalyse the reactions needed to do this. Lots of enzymes are also involved in the synthesis of lipids from fatty acids and glycerol.

Practice Questions — Fact Recall

Q1 True or false? Digestive enzymes build small molecules up into larger molecules.

Q2 a) Name the type of enzyme that catalyses the breakdown of lipids.

b) What types of molecules are lipids broken down to produce?

Practice Question — Application

Q1 A protease solution is mixed with a protein solution. Every ten minutes, a sample of the solution is taken and mixed with ninhydrin. Ninhydrin is a yellowish compound which turns a deep-purple colour when reacted with amino acids.

Describe how you would expect the colour of the samples to change over the course of the experiment. Explain your answer.

4. Transport in Cells

Substances can pass into and out of cells by diffusion, osmosis or active transport. The way substances move across cell membranes depends on the type of substance and its concentration across the membrane.

Learning Objective:
- Be able to explain how substances are transported into and out of cells, including by diffusion, osmosis and active transport.

Specification Reference 1.15

Diffusion

"Diffusion" is simple. It's just the gradual movement of particles from places where there are lots of them to places where there are fewer of them. That's all it is — just the natural tendency for stuff to spread out.

Here's fancy way of saying the same thing:

> Diffusion is the spreading out of particles from an area of higher concentration to an area of lower concentration.

Diffusion happens in both solutions and gases — that's because the particles in these substances are free to move about randomly. The simplest type is when different gases diffuse through each other.

Tip: If something moves from an area of higher concentration to an area of lower concentration, it is said to have moved down a concentration gradient.

Example

When you spray perfume, the smell of perfume diffuses through the air in a room:

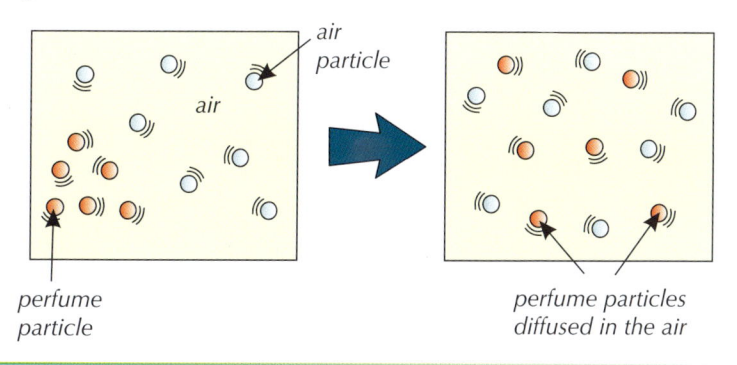

Figure 1: The ink particles in this flask are diffusing into the water — they're moving from an area of high concentration (at the bottom of the flask) to an area of low concentration (higher up).

Diffusion is a passive process — this means that it doesn't need energy to make it work.

Diffusion across cell membranes

Cell membranes are clever because they hold the cell together but they let stuff in and out as well. Dissolved substances can move in and out of cells by diffusion.

Cell membranes are **partially permeable**. This means they let some molecules through but not others. Only very small molecules can diffuse through cell membranes — things like oxygen (needed for respiration — see page 199), glucose, amino acids and water. Big molecules like starch and proteins can't fit through the membrane (see Figure 2 on the next page).

Tip: Partially permeable membranes have very small holes in them. Big molecules can't fit through the holes.

Topic 1b Biological Molecules and Transport in Cells

Exam Tip
If you're struggling to remember which way the particles move in diffusion, think of it like this: if you were in a really crowded place, you'd probably want to get out of there to somewhere with a bit more room. It's the same with particles — they always diffuse from an area of higher concentration to an area of lower concentration.

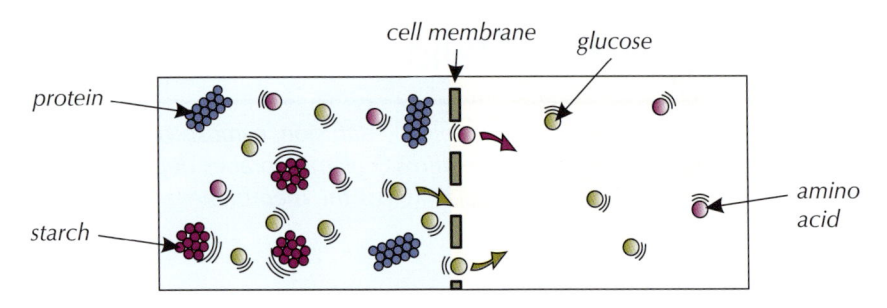

Figure 2: *Diagram to show diffusion across a cell membrane.*

Just like with diffusion in air, particles flow through the cell membrane from where there's a higher concentration (more of them) to where there's a lower concentration (fewer of them).

They're only moving about randomly of course, so they go both ways — but if there are a lot more particles on one side of the membrane, there's a **net** (overall) movement from that side.

> **Example**
>
> Particles are diffusing both in and out of this cell. However, the concentration of particles is higher inside the cell than outside, so the net movement of particles is out of the cell.

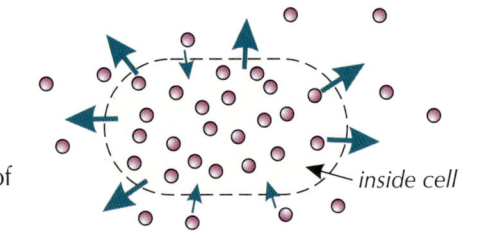

Osmosis

Water molecules can move into and out of cells via a process called osmosis.

> Osmosis is the net movement of water molecules across a partially permeable membrane from a region of higher water concentration to a region of lower water concentration.

Tip: A solute is a molecule that's dissolved in water, e.g. sucrose.

You could also describe osmosis as the net movement of water molecules across a partially permeable membrane from a region of lower solute concentration to a region of higher solute concentration.

The water molecules pass both ways through the membrane during osmosis. This happens because water molecules move about randomly all the time. But because there are more water molecules on one side than on the other, there's a steady net flow of water into the region with fewer water molecules, i.e. into the solution with the higher solute concentration. This means the more concentrated solution gets more dilute. The water acts like it's trying to "even up" the concentration either side of the membrane. This is shown in Figure 3 on the next page.

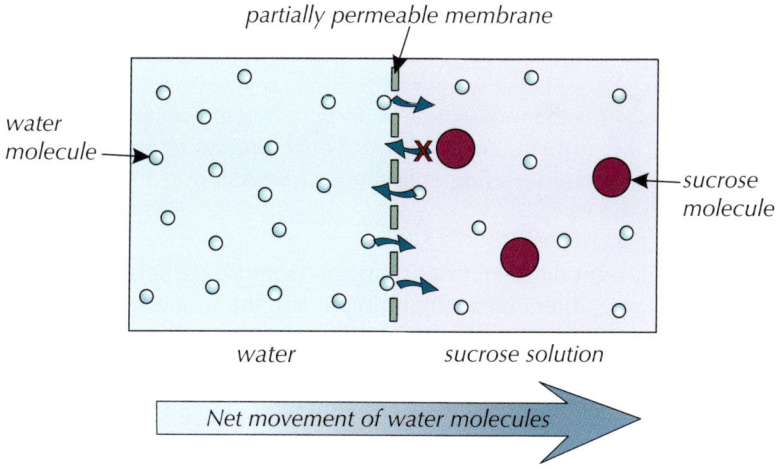

Figure 3: Diagram to show how osmosis works.

Tip: The sucrose solution has a higher concentration of solute (sucrose) than the pure water. So you can see that the net movement of water molecules is from the region of lower solute concentration to the region of higher solute concentration, as well as from the region of higher water concentration to the region of lower water concentration.

Osmosis is a type of **diffusion** — passive movement of water particles from an area of higher water concentration to an area of lower water concentration.

The movement of water in and out of cells

The solution surrounding a cell will usually have a different concentration to the fluid inside the cell. This means that water will either move into the cell from the surrounding solution, or out of the cell, by osmosis.

Tip: Both plant and animal cells gain and lose water by osmosis.

If a cell is short of water, the solution inside it will become quite concentrated (i.e. there'll be a low concentration of water molecules). This usually means the solution outside the cell is more dilute (there's a higher concentration of water molecules), and so water will move into the cell by osmosis. If a cell has lots of water, the solution inside it will be more dilute, and water will be drawn out of the cell and into the fluid outside by osmosis.

This is summarised in Figure 4.

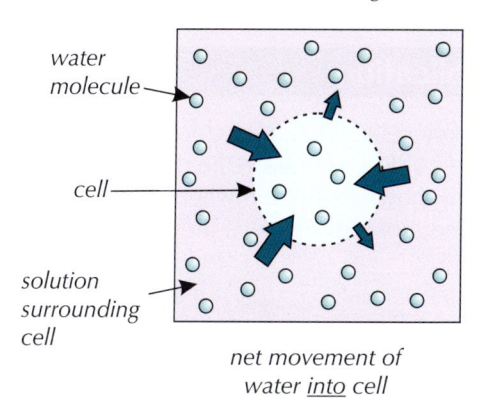

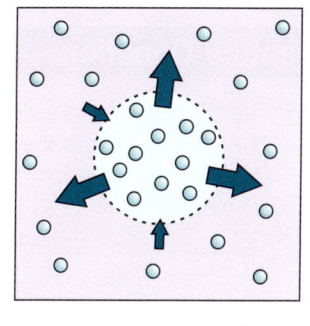

Tip: Cells that gain water by osmosis get a bit bigger (animal cells that gain too much water will eventually burst). Cells that lose water get a bit smaller.

Figure 4: Diagram to show the movement of water molecules into and out of a cell.

Active transport

Exam Tip
You could be asked in the exam to compare diffusion, osmosis and active transport. Make sure you know the similarities and differences between them all.

> Active transport is the movement of particles against a concentration gradient (i.e. from an area of lower concentration to an area of higher concentration) using energy transferred during respiration.

Active transport is a bit different from diffusion because particles are moved up a concentration gradient rather than down, and the process requires energy (unlike diffusion, see page 43). It allows cells to absorb substances from very dilute solutions. Here's an example of active transport at work in the digestive system:

Tip: Active transport is also useful in plants, e.g. to absorb mineral ions from the soil. See page 157 for more.

Example

When there's a higher concentration of nutrients in the gut than in the blood, the nutrients diffuse naturally into the blood. BUT — sometimes there's a lower concentration of nutrients in the gut than in the blood.

Active transport allows nutrients to be taken into the blood, despite the fact that the concentration gradient is the wrong way. This is essential to stop us starving. It means that glucose can be taken into the bloodstream when its concentration in the blood is already higher than in the gut. The glucose can then be transported to cells, where it's used for respiration (see pages 199-201).

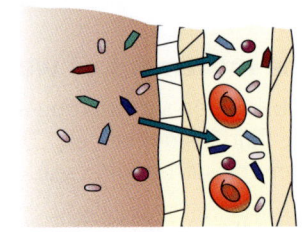

Inside the gut   Inside the blood

Practice Questions — Fact Recall

Q1 What is osmosis?

Q2 Explain how cells can absorb ions from very dilute solutions.

Practice Question — Application

Q1 The diagrams below show three cells in different glucose solutions. The concentration of glucose inside and outside the cell is shown in each case. Which diagram shows a situation where the net movement of glucose will be out of the cell — A, B or C?

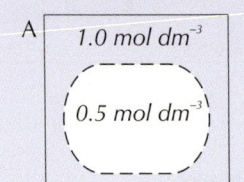

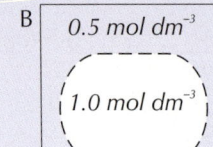

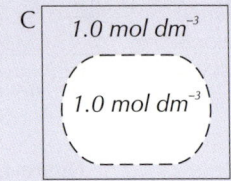

A: outside 1.0 mol dm^{-3}, inside 0.5 mol dm^{-3}

B: outside 0.5 mol dm^{-3}, inside 1.0 mol dm^{-3}

C: outside 1.0 mol dm^{-3}, inside 1.0 mol dm^{-3}

Topic 1b Biological Molecules and Transport in Cells

5. Investigating Osmosis in Plant Cells

Plant cells gain and lose water by osmosis. You can investigate how changing the concentration of the solution surrounding the cell affects osmosis.

Investigating the effect of sugar solutions on plant cells

Here's an experiment you can do to show osmosis at work:
1. Prepare sucrose solutions of different concentrations ranging from pure water to a very concentrated sucrose solution.
2. Use a cork borer to cut a potato into the same sized pieces (the pieces need to be about 1 cm in diameter and preferably from the same potato).
3. Divide the cylinders into groups of three and use a mass balance to measure the mass of each group.
4. Place one group in each solution.
5. Leave the cylinders in the solution, as shown in Figure 1, for at least 40 minutes (making sure that they all get the same amount of time).

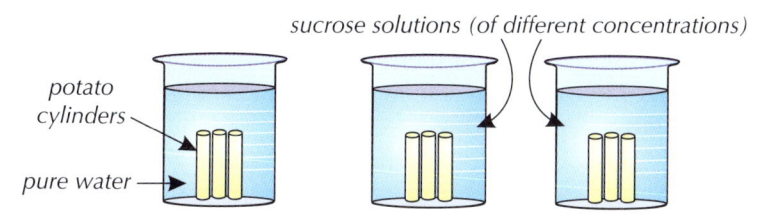

Figure 1: A diagram to show the set-up of the experiment.

5. Remove the cylinders and pat dry gently with a paper towel. This removes excess water from the surface of the cylinders, so you get a more accurate measurement of their final masses.
6. Weigh each group again and record your results.

Variables and errors

The **dependent variable** in this experiment is the cylinder mass and the **independent variable** is the concentration of the sucrose solution. All other variables (volume of solution, the size of potato cylinders, the age and type of potatoes used, the amount of drying, etc.) must be kept the same in each case. Otherwise, the experiment won't be a fair test and your results won't be valid.

Like any experiment, you need to be aware of how errors (see p.13) may arise. Sometimes they may occur when carrying out the method, e.g. if some potato cylinders were not fully dried, the excess water would give a higher mass, or if water evaporated from the beakers, the concentrations of the sugar solutions would change. You can reduce the effect of these errors by repeating the experiment and calculating a mean percentage change at each concentration.

Learning Objectives:
- Be able to investigate osmosis in potatoes. (Core Practical)
- Be able to calculate percentage gain and loss of mass in osmosis.

Specification References 1.16, 1.17

Tip: As with all experiments, make sure you carry out a risk assessment before you start this practical.

Tip: Make sure there's no skin left on your potato cylinders, as this could affect your results.

Tip: You could also carry out this experiment using different salt solutions or by investigating the effect on cylinder length instead of mass.

Tip: There's more on variables on page 10.

Tip: You can read all about how to calculate a mean on page 14.

Tip: By calculating the percentage change, you can compare the effect of sucrose concentration on cylinders that didn't have the same initial mass. An increase in mass will give a positive percentage change and a decrease will give a negative percentage change.

Interpreting the results

Once you have got all your results, you need to calculate the percentage change in mass for each group of cylinders before and after their time in the sucrose.

$$\text{percentage change in mass} = \frac{\text{final mass} - \text{initial mass}}{\text{initial mass}} \times 100$$

Example

A group of cylinders weighed 13.2 g at the start of the experiment. At the end they weighed 15.1 g.
Calculate the percentage change in mass.

The percentage change in mass is:
$$\frac{\text{final mass} - \text{initial mass}}{\text{initial mass}} \times 100$$
$$= \frac{15.1 - 13.2}{13.2} \times 100 = \mathbf{14.4\%}$$

Tip: Make sure your initial mass and final mass have the same units.

Producing a graph of your results

You can create a graph of your results by plotting the percentage change in mass against the concentration of sucrose solution. You can then draw a line of best fit, which you can use to determine the concentration of the solution in the potato cells:

Tip: There's more about plotting graphs on pages 16-18.

Example

An experiment to investigate the effect of sucrose concentration on potato cells gave the results in the table below.

Concentration of sucrose solution (M)	0.1	0.25	0.5	1.0	2.0
Percentage change in mass (%)	16.5	2.5	−8.0	−15.5	−20.0

The results are plotted as a graph, with concentration of sucrose solution on the x-axis and percentage change in mass on the y-axis (see Figure 2).

Tip: 'M' is a unit of concentration. You might also see it written as mol dm^{-3}. A solution with a concentration of 0.00 M would be pure water, so the 0.1 M sucrose solution has a much higher concentration of water molecules than the 2.0 M solution.

- At the points above the x-axis, the concentration of water molecules in the sucrose solutions is higher than in the cylinders. The cylinders gain mass as water is drawn in by osmosis.

- At the points below the x-axis, the concentration of water molecules in the sucrose solutions is lower than in the cylinders. This causes the cylinders to lose water, so their mass decreases.

This point is where the concentration of the sucrose solution is the same as the concentration of the solution inside the potato cells.

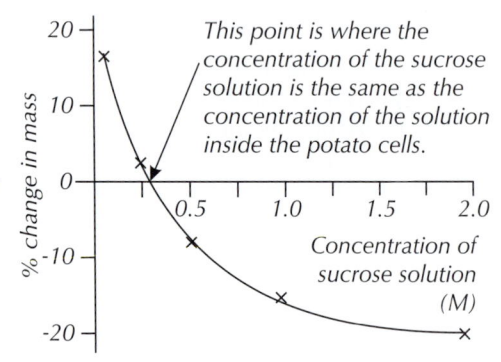

Figure 2: A graph to find the concentration of the solution inside the potato cells.

- The point at which the line of best fit crosses the *x*-axis (where the percentage change in mass is 0) is the point at which the concentration of the sucrose solution is the same as the concentration of the solution in the potato cells. You can estimate the concentration of the solution inside the potato cells by reading the value off the *x*-axis at this point.

Tip: When the fluid inside the cylinders is the same concentration as the sucrose solution, the two fluids are said to be isotonic.

Practice Question — Application

Q1 An experiment is carried out to investigate osmosis.

A potato is cut up into cylinders of the same known length and width. Two different concentrations of sucrose solution are prepared in two separate beakers. Three potato cylinders are then placed into each beaker.

The potato cylinders are left for several hours and then the length of each cylinder is measured again. The final mean cylinder length is recorded for each beaker.

a) What is:

   i) the dependent variable in this experiment?

   ii) the independent variable in this experiment?

b) Give two variables that need to be controlled in this experiment so that the experiment is a fair test.

c) The potato cylinders in one beaker were 9.6 cm long at the start of the experiment. At the end of the experiment, they had a mean length of 8.5 cm. Calculate the percentage change in mean length.

Exam Tip
You could get asked questions about any of the Core Practicals in the exam — so make sure you understand what's happening in each one.

Topic 1b Checklist — Make sure you know...

Enzymes

☐ That enzymes are biological catalysts, speeding up the rate of chemical reactions in living things.

☐ That every enzyme has its own unique active site, and it's the shape of this active site that allows the enzyme to bind to its substrate.

☐ That enzymes will usually only bind to one specific substrate, so if the substrate doesn't fit the active site, the reaction won't be catalysed. This is the 'lock and key' model of enzyme action.

☐ That increasing the temperature increases the rate of an enzyme-controlled reaction until it gets so hot that some of the bonds holding the enzyme together break. The active site then changes shape and no longer fits the substrate — the enzyme is denatured.

☐ That increasing the substrate concentration increases the rate of an enzyme-controlled reaction until there are enough substrate molecules to occupy all available enzyme active sites (after which it has no effect).

☐ That extreme pH levels decrease the rate of an enzyme-controlled reaction by interfering with bonds in the active site, changing the shape of the active site and denaturing the enzyme.

cont...

Investigating Enzymatic Reactions

- [ ] How to investigate the effects of pH on enzyme activity, for example, on the rate of the breakdown of starch by the enzyme amylase (Core Practical).
- [ ] How to calculate the rate of an enzyme controlled reaction.

Enzymes in Breakdown and Synthesis

- [ ] That enzymes catalyse the breakdown of large biological molecules into smaller biological molecules so that they can be used for growth and other life processes.
- [ ] That carbohydrases convert carbohydrates into simple sugars.
- [ ] That proteases catalyse the conversion of proteins into amino acids.
- [ ] That lipases catalyse the conversion of lipids (fats and oils) into glycerol and fatty acids.
- [ ] That enzymes catalyse the synthesis of carbohydrates, proteins and lipids from smaller molecules.

Transport in Cells

- [ ] That diffusion is the spreading out of particles from an area of higher concentration to an area of lower concentration.
- [ ] That dissolved substances such as glucose, oxygen and amino acids move in and out of a cell by diffusion, and that the net (overall) movement will be to an area of lower concentration.
- [ ] That osmosis is the movement of water molecules across a partially permeable membrane from a region of higher water concentration (a dilute solution) to a region of lower water concentration (a more concentrated solution).
- [ ] How differences in the concentration of water molecules inside and outside of a cell will cause water molecules to move into or out of the cell by osmosis.
- [ ] That active transport is the movement of particles against a concentration gradient (i.e. from an area of lower concentration to an area of higher concentration) using energy transferred by respiration.

Investigating Osmosis in Plant Cells

- [ ] How to investigate the effect of different concentrations of a sugar or salt solution on osmosis in potato cells (Core Practical).
- [ ] How to calculate percentage change in mass for plant tissue (e.g. a piece of potato).

Exam-style Questions

1 Respiration is a process used by cells to release energy.

(a) When cells respire, they produce carbon dioxide as a waste product. The carbon dioxide diffuses from the cells into the bloodstream, so it can be removed from the body.

Is the carbon dioxide concentration greater in the bloodstream or inside the respiring cells? Explain your answer.

(1 mark)

(b) The energy released by respiration can be used to absorb glucose into the bloodstream from the small intestine.

Explain why energy may be needed to absorb glucose into the bloodstream.

(2 marks)

2 A student was measuring the rate that carbon dioxide (CO_2) was produced in a reaction controlled by enzyme X. He performed the experiment at three different temperatures — 10 °C, 25 °C and 50 °C. The experiment at 50 °C produced no carbon dioxide at all.

His results are shown in **Figure 1**.

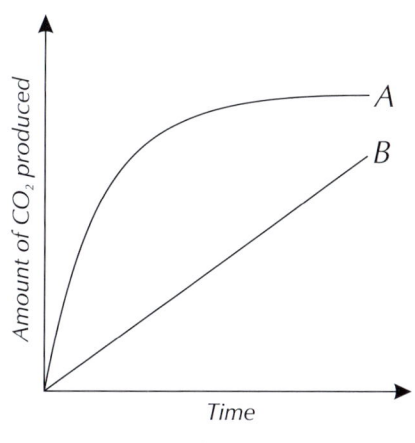

Figure 1 — graph showing Amount of CO_2 produced against Time, with curve A levelling off higher and line B rising more gradually.

(a) Enzyme X is only able to catalyse this reaction.
Explain why most enzymes can only catalyse a single reaction.

(2 marks)

(b) Suggest which line on **Figure 1** (**A** or **B**) represents the experiment carried out at 25 °C. Explain your answer.

(2 marks)

(c) Suggest why the experiment at 50 °C failed to produce any CO_2.

(2 marks)

3 The conditions inside the stomach are acidic due to the presence of hydrochloric acid (HCl acid). An experiment was done to show how digestion in the stomach works. The enzyme pepsin is a protease found in the stomach. In the experiment, three equally sized pieces of meat were added to each of three test tubes.
Then the test tubes were filled with equal volumes of the following substances:

Test tube 1: hydrochloric acid
Test tube 2: pepsin
Test tube 3: pepsin and hydrochloric acid

The results are shown in **Figure 2**.

Figure 2

Describe the results and explain what they suggest about pepsin.

(3 marks)

4 Eleanor is investigating osmosis using potatoes.

She cuts small wells into two pieces of potato, and sets up two experiments (A and B). She then leaves the potatoes for five hours.

Figure 3 shows how the appearance of each experiment changes after five hours.

Experiment A

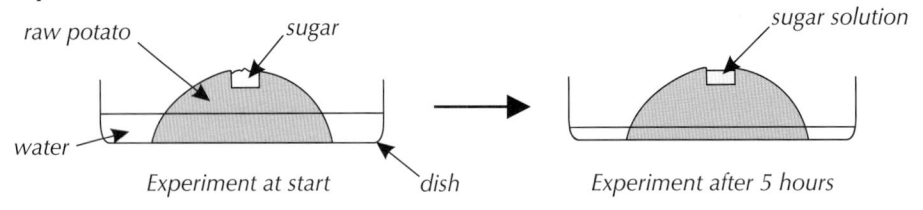

Experiment B

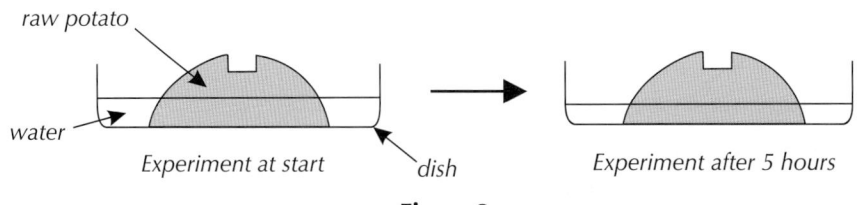

Figure 3

(a) Explain the changes that Eleanor saw in experiment A.

(3 marks)

(b) Suggest an explanation for why the water level in the dish in experiment B didn't decrease as much as much as that in experiment A.

(3 marks)

Topic 2a — Cell Division and Stem Cells

1. Mitosis

Our body cells are able to make copies of themselves so that we can grow or repair any damaged tissue. It's pretty clever stuff...

Body cells and chromosomes

Most cells in your body have a structure called a **nucleus** (see page 23). The nucleus contains your genetic material (the instructions you need to grow and develop). This material is stored in the form of **chromosomes** — see Figure 1.

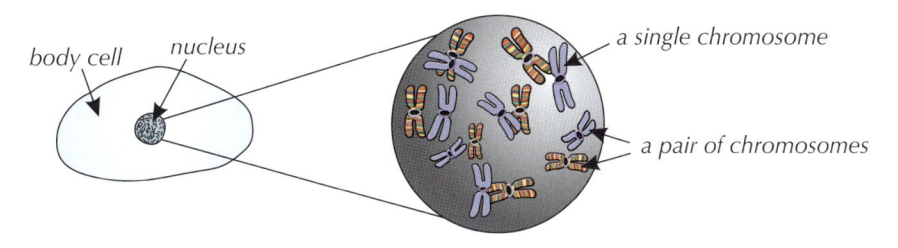

Figure 1: Diagram to show that a cell nucleus contains chromosomes.

Body cells normally have two copies of each chromosome — this makes them '**diploid**' cells. One chromosome comes from the organism's 'mother', and one from its 'father'.

Chromosomes and DNA

Chromosomes are long lengths of a molecule called **DNA**. The DNA is coiled up to form the arms of the chromosome (see Figure 2).

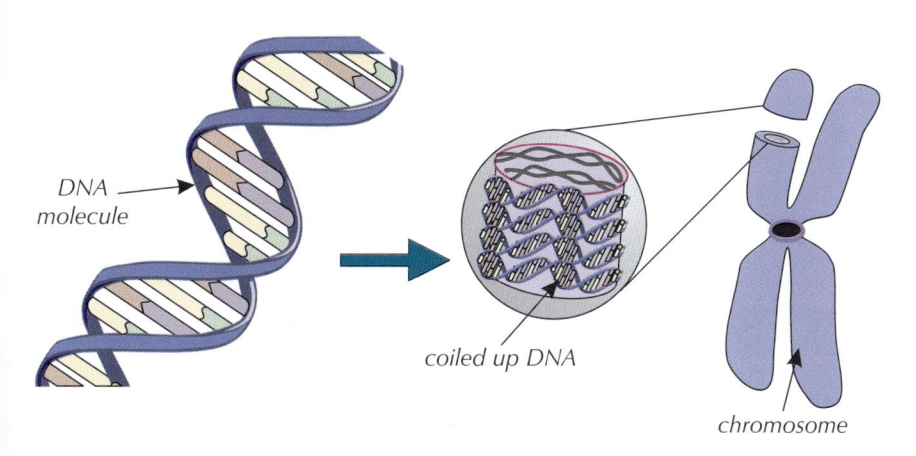

Figure 2: Diagram to show how DNA coils up to form a chromosome.

Figure 3: A pair of human chromosomes seen under a microscope.

Learning Objectives:
- Be able to describe mitosis as part of the cell cycle, including the stages interphase, prophase, metaphase, anaphase and telophase and cytokinesis.
- Be able to describe the division of a cell by mitosis as the production of two daughter cells, each with identical sets of chromosomes in the nucleus to the parent cell, and that this results in the formation of two genetically identical diploid body cells.
- Be able to describe the importance of mitosis in growth, repair and asexual reproduction.

Specification References 2.1 – 2.3

Tip: See pages 75-77 for more on DNA.

Mitosis and the cell cycle

Body cells in multicellular organisms divide to produce new cells during a process called the cell cycle. The cell cycle starts when a cell has been produced by cell division and ends with the cell dividing to produce two identical cells. It can be summarised as a stage of cell growth and DNA replication (called **interphase**, see below), followed by a stage of cell division (see Figure 4).

The stage of the cell cycle when the cell divides is called **mitosis**:

> Mitosis is when a cell reproduces itself by splitting in two to form two genetically identical offspring.

Mitosis can also specifically refer to the division of the nucleus rather than the whole cell. **Cytokinesis** (the division of the cytoplasm) takes place at the same time. The end of the cell cycle results in two new genetically identical diploid cells.

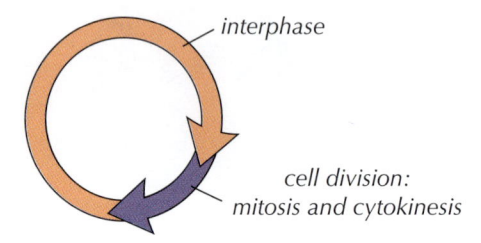

Figure 4: Diagram outlining the cell cycle.

As a cell goes through the cell cycle, it has to undergo some key changes.

What happens during the cell cycle?

Here are the steps involved in the cell cycle:

Interphase

1. In a cell that's not dividing, the DNA is all spread out in long strings (see Figure 5).

2. Before it divides, the cell has to grow and increase the amount of subcellular structures such as mitochondria and ribosomes.

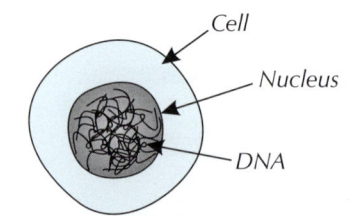

Figure 5: Diagram of a cell in interphase.

3. It then duplicates its DNA — so there's one copy of each chromosome for each new cell. The DNA is copied and forms X-shaped chromosomes. Each 'arm' of the chromosome is an exact duplicate of the other.

Tip: When a cell has copied its DNA, the left arm of an X-shaped chromosome has the same DNA as the right arm.

Now the cell is ready for mitosis...

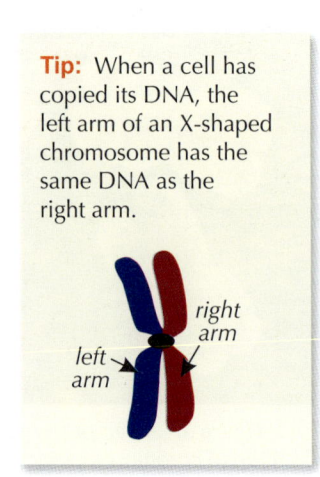

Mitosis

Mitosis is really one continuous process, but it can be divided into four stages:

1. **Prophase**
   The chromosomes condense, getting shorter and fatter. The membrane around the nucleus breaks down and the chromosomes lie free in the cytoplasm.

2. **Metaphase**
   The chromosomes line up at the centre of the cell.

3. **Anaphase**
   Cell fibres pull the chromosomes apart. The two arms of each chromosome go to opposite ends of the cell.

4. **Telophase**
   Membranes form around each of the sets of chromosomes. These become the nuclei of the two new cells — the nucleus has divided.

Cytokinesis

Before telophase ends, the cytoplasm and cell membrane divide to form two separate cells — this process is called **cytokinesis**.

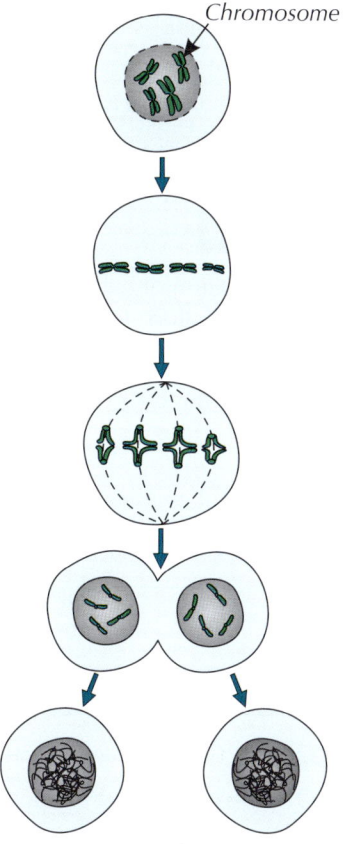

Figure 6: Diagram showing mitosis and cytokinesis in the cell cycle.

At the end of mitosis, the cell has produced two new daughter cells. Each daughter cell contains exactly the same set of chromosomes in its nucleus — the two cells are genetically identical. They're also genetically identical to the diploid parent cell. This makes the daughter cells diploid too.

Uses of mitosis

Mitosis is used:

- By multicellular organisms to grow.
- By multicellular organisms to replace cells that have been damaged.
- By some organisms to reproduce by **asexual reproduction**:

> **Example**
>
> Strawberry plants form runners by mitosis (see Figure 8). These runners take root and new plants grow from them (also by mitosis). These new plants (the offspring) have exactly the same DNA as the parent.
>
> *Figure 8: Strawberry plant with runner (red stem).*

Exam Tip
You need to remember all these stages, and in the correct order too. A memory aid like this one might help you:
In Plymouth My Aunt Teaches Chemistry (interphase, prophase, metaphase, anaphase, telophase, cytokinesis).

Tip: Chromosomes only look like this:

just before the cell divides (see previous page). After the nucleus has divided, the chromosomes in each set look like this:

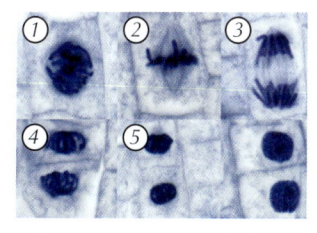

Figure 7: A series of photos showing an onion cell in mitosis. 1 = prophase, 2 = metaphase, 3 = anaphase, 4&5 = telophase.

Exam Tip
In the exam, you might have to identify or describe what's going on in photos of real cells undergoing mitosis, so make sure you learn what the different stages look like.

Topic 2a Cell Division and Stem Cells

Calculating the number of cells

You can calculate the number of cells there will be after multiple divisions of a cell by mitosis. The formula you need is:

$$\text{number of cells} = 2^n$$

'n' is the number of divisions by mitosis.

Tip: Each cell divides to produce 2 cells, so the number of cells increases by a power of 2 for each division.

Tip: 2^5 is the same as $2 \times 2 \times 2 \times 2 \times 2$.

Example

A population of cells is dividing continually by mitosis. The population started with one cell. How many cells were in the population after five divisions of mitosis?

- Stick the value for 'n' into the equation, number of cells = 2^n:

$$\text{number of cells} = 2^5$$

- Calculate the answer:

$$\text{number of cells} = \mathbf{32}$$

Practice Questions — Fact Recall

Q1 Describe what happens to the DNA in a cell during interphase.

Q2 Describe what happens during anaphase of mitosis.

Q3 Name the process by which a cell's cytoplasm and cell membrane divide to form two new cells.

Q4 Give two uses of mitosis in multicellular organisms.

Practice Questions — Application

Q1 This photograph shows the last stage in mitosis — two new daughter cells are formed.

   a) Will these new cells be genetically identical or genetically different to the parent cell?

   b) How many sets of chromosomes will these cells have?

   c) Describe what is happening in the photograph.

Q2 A scientist is studying mitosis in yeast cells. A sample contains one yeast cell, which begins dividing. How many cells will there be in the sample after ten divisions?

Exam Tip
You don't have to know anything to do with the specific cells to answer a mitosis question like this in the exam.

2. Cell Division and Growth

All organisms grow. You need to know the processes involved in both animal and plant growth, as well as how percentile charts are used to monitor growth.

Growth and development

Growth is an increase in size or mass. Plants and animals grow and develop due to these processes:

- **Cell division**
  This happens by mitosis (see pages 54-55).

- **Cell differentiation**
  Cell differentiation is the process by which a cell changes to become specialised for its job. Having specialised cells (see page 26) allows multicellular organisms to work more efficiently because different cell types can carry out different functions.

Plants also grow by **cell elongation**. This is where a plant cell expands, making the cell bigger and so making the plant grow.

Figure 1: A plant cell elongating.

Growth in animals

All growth in animals happens by cell division. Animals tend to grow while they're young, and then they reach full growth and stop growing. So when you're young, cells divide at a fast rate but once you're an adult, most cell division is for repair — the cells divide to replace old or damaged cells. This also means that, in most animals, cell differentiation is lost at an early stage.

Growth in plants

In plants, growth in height is mainly due to cell elongation. Cell division usually just happens in the tips of the roots and shoots (in areas called **meristems** — see pages 60-61). But plants often grow continuously — even really old trees will keep putting out new branches. So, plants continue to differentiate to develop new parts, e.g. leaves, roots.

Cancer

The body controls the amount of cell division that happens for growth, so cells will normally stop dividing when enough new cells have been produced. The rate at which cells divide by mitosis is controlled by the chemical instructions (genes) in an organism's DNA.

If there's a change in one of the genes that controls cell division, the cell may start dividing uncontrollably — growth doesn't stop. This can result in a mass of abnormal cells called a **tumour**. If the tumour invades and destroys surrounding tissue it is called cancer.

Learning Objectives:

- Be able to explain the importance of cell differentiation in the development of specialised cells.
- Be able to describe growth in organisms, including cell division and differentiation in animals.
- Be able to describe growth in organisms, including cell division, elongation and differentiation in plants.
- Be able to describe cancer as the result of changes in cells that lead to uncontrolled cell division.
- Be able to demonstrate an understanding of the use of percentiles charts to monitor growth.

Specification References 2.4 – 2.7

Tip: A random change in a gene is called a mutation — see p. 90.

Percentile charts

Percentile charts can be used to assess a child's growth over time, so that an overall pattern in development can be seen and any problems highlighted (e.g. obesity, malnutrition, dwarfism).

For example, a baby's growth is regularly monitored after birth to make sure it's growing normally. Three measurements are taken — length, mass and head circumference. These results are plotted on percentile growth charts like the one in the example below.

These charts show a number of 'percentiles'. Each percentile represents one percent of the data, so if you were looking at a percentile chart for mass, the 50th percentile would show the mass that 50% of babies will have reached at a certain age.

Tip: Head circumference is the measurement of the distance around the largest area of the head. It's measured to check for things like problems with the development of the brain.

Tip: Percentiles tell you where in the data set a data point lies. The value of a percentile tells you what percentage of data has a value equal to or lower than the data points in that percentile.

Tip: The median is the middle value in a data set (see page 14) so the 50th percentile is the median.

Example

The growth chart in Figure 2 shows that a three-month-old boy who weighs 7 kg is just above 75th percentile for weight — roughly 75% of three-month-old boys are lighter and 25% are heavier.

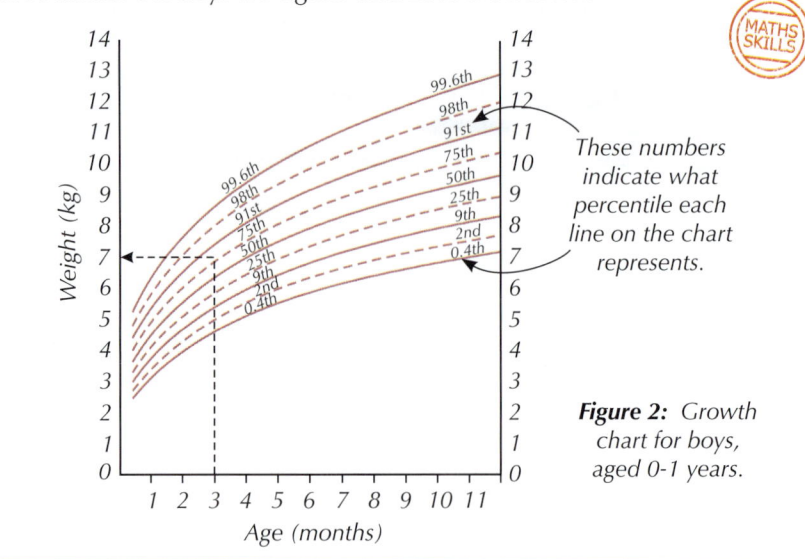

These numbers indicate what percentile each line on the chart represents.

Figure 2: Growth chart for boys, aged 0-1 years.

Babies vary in size, but doctors are likely to investigate if a baby's size is above the top percentile line or below the bottom percentile line, their size increases or decreases by two or more percentile lines over time, or if there's an inconsistent pattern (e.g. a small baby with a very large head).

Practice Questions — Fact Recall

Q1 What is cell differentiation?

Q2 Describe how changes in a cell can result in cancer.

Practice Question — Application

Q1 A baby is in the 60th percentile for weight. What percentage of babies of the same age weigh either the same or less than this baby?

Topic 2a Cell Division and Stem Cells

3. Stem Cells

All the cells in an organism originate from stem cells. Scientists are attempting to use these cells to do some pretty amazing things...

What are stem cells?

Some cells are undifferentiated (i.e. they have not yet changed to become specialised for a particular job). These undifferentiated cells are called **stem cells**. They can divide to produce lots more undifferentiated cells. These new cells can then develop into different types of cell, depending on what instructions they're given.

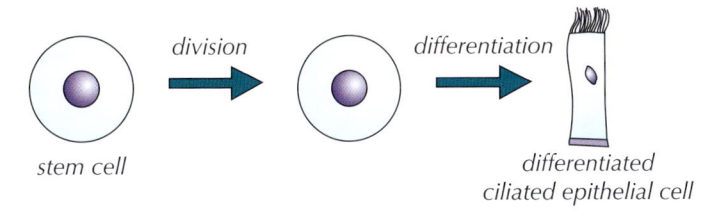

Figure 1: *Diagram showing a differentiated cell resulting from a stem cell.*

Stem cells are found in early human embryos. These embryonic stem cells have the potential to divide and produce any kind of cell at all. This makes sense if you think about it — all the different types of cell found in a human being have to come from those few cells in the early embryo. This means embryonic stem cells are really important for the growth and development of organisms.

Adults also have stem cells, but they're only found in certain places, like bone marrow (the spongy tissue inside bones). These aren't as versatile as embryonic stem cells — they can't produce any cell type at all, only certain ones. In animals, adult stem cells are used to replace damaged cells, e.g. to make new skin or blood cells.

Adult stem cells in medicine

Adult stem cells are already used to cure disease.

> **Example**
>
> People with some blood diseases (e.g. sickle cell anaemia, a disease which affects the red blood cells) can be treated by bone marrow transplants. Bone marrow contains adult stem cells that can turn into new blood cells to replace the faulty old ones.

Embryonic stem cells in medicine

Scientists have experimented with extracting stem cells from very early human embryos and growing them. Under certain conditions, the stem cells can be stimulated to differentiate into specialised cells. In the future, it might be possible to use embryonic stem cells to replace faulty cells in sick people (see Figure 3 on the next page).

Learning Objectives:
- Be able to describe the function of embryonic stem cells and stem cells in animals.
- Be able to discuss the potential benefits and risks associated with the use of stem cells in medicine.
- Be able to describe the function of meristems in plants.

Specification References 2.8, 2.9

Tip: Ciliated epithelial cells are specialised cells. There's more about them on page 27.

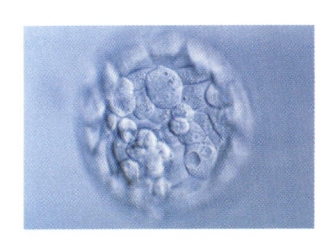

Figure 2: *Microscope image of a human embryo that's about 4 days old. Stem cells can be taken from the embryo at this stage.*

Topic 2a Cell Division and Stem Cells

Tip: The advantage of using embryonic stem cells for therapies over adult stem cells is that they have the potential to differentiate into many different types of cell (unlike adult stem cells, which are limited to differentiating into certain types of cell). They are also easier to grow in culture than adult stem cells.

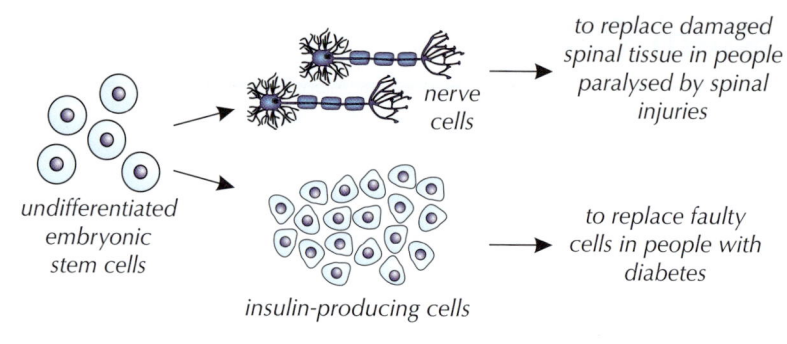

Figure 3: Diagram showing some potential uses of embryonic stem cells in medicine.

Issues involved in using stem cells

Before specialised cells created from stem cells can be used for medical treatments, a lot of research needs to be done. There are many potential risks which scientists need to learn more about.

Examples

- Tumour development — stem cells divide very quickly. If scientists are unable to control the rate at which the transplanted cells divide inside a patient, a tumour may develop (see page 57).

- Disease transmission — viruses live inside cells. If donor stem cells are infected with a virus and this isn't picked up, the virus could be passed on to the recipient and so make them sicker.

- Rejection — if the transplanted cells aren't grown using the patient's own stem cells, the patient's body may recognise the cells as foreign and trigger an immune response to try to get rid of them. The patient can take drugs to suppress this response, but this makes them susceptible to diseases.

Exam Tip
Questions on the issues associated with using stem cells in medicine might crop up in the exam, so make sure you know the potential benefits and the risks associated with using them.

Ethical issues

Research using embryonic stem cells also raises ethical issues.

Some people are against it, because they feel that human embryos shouldn't be used for experiments since each one is a potential human life.

However, others think that curing patients who already exist and who are suffering is more important than the rights of embryos. One fairly convincing argument in favour of this point of view is that the embryos used in the research are usually unwanted ones from fertility clinics which, if they weren't used for research, would probably just be destroyed. However, many campaigners for the rights of embryos think this should be banned too.

Tip: Obtaining stem cells from an embryo destroys the embryo.

Tip: In some countries stem cell research is banned, but it's allowed in the UK as long as it follows strict guidelines.

Stem cells in plants

In plants, the only cells that divide by mitosis are found in plant tissues called **meristems**. Meristem tissue is found in the areas of a plant that are growing, e.g. the tips of the roots and shoots.

Meristems produce unspecialised cells that are able to divide and form any cell type in the plant — they act like embryonic stem cells. But unlike human stem cells, these cells can divide and differentiate to generate any type of cell for as long as the plant lives.

The unspecialised cells go on to form specialised tissues like xylem and phloem (see page 155).

Figure 4: *Plants grown from meristem tissue.*

Practice Questions — Fact Recall

Q1 What is a stem cell?

Q2 In terms of their ability to produce different cell types, what is the difference between early embryonic stem cells and adult stem cells?

Q3 Give two potential risks of using stem cells in medical treatments.

Q4 Name the tissue in plants where stem cells can be found.

Practice Questions — Application

Q1 Adult stem cells can only be found in certain places in the body. One place is the skin. Suggest why adult stem cells are needed in the skin.

Q2 Alzheimer's disease is a condition which damages the neurones (nerve cells) in the brain. These neurones die, but are not replaced, leading to a decrease in the amount of neurones in the brain. Symptoms of Alzheimer's disease include memory loss, confusion and changes in personality.

   a) Suggest a way in which embryonic stem cells could potentially be used to treat people with Alzheimer's disease.

   b) Suggest another possible use of embryonic stem cells in medicine.

Q3 Embryonic stem cells used for medical research are mostly taken from embryos left over from fertility clinics, which would otherwise be destroyed. Suggest a reason why some people are happier with using these embryos for stem cell research, rather than creating embryos purely with the purpose of being used for research.

Topic 2a Checklist — Make sure you know...

Mitosis

- [ ] That body cells divide by mitosis, as part of the cell cycle.
- [ ] That the cell cycle also includes interphase, during which a cell grows, increases the amount of its subcellular structures and makes a copy of its DNA.
- [ ] That the stages of mitosis are prophase, metaphase, anaphase and telophase. During prophase, the chromosomes condense and the membrane around the nucleus breaks down. In metaphase, the chromosomes line up at the centre of the cell. In anaphase, cell fibres pull the chromosomes apart. Then in telophase, membranes form around each of the sets of chromosomes to create the nuclei of the two new cells.
- [ ] That cytokinesis (the division of the cytoplasm and cell membrane to create two separate cells) takes place before telophase ends.
- [ ] That mitosis produces two new genetically identical diploid cells (with two sets of chromosomes each).
- [ ] That mitosis allows organisms to grow and replace damaged cells.
- [ ] That mitosis is used by some organisms to reproduce asexually.

Cell Division and Growth

- [ ] That growth in animals and plants can involve cell division and differentiation.
- [ ] That cell differentiation (where a cell changes to become specialised for its job) is important for allowing multicellular organisms to work efficiently.
- [ ] That growth in plants can also involve cell elongation (where the plant cells expand).
- [ ] That a change in a gene that controls cell division can cause a cell to divide uncontrollably, which can result in cancer.
- [ ] How percentile charts are used to monitor the growth of a child.

Stem Cells

- [ ] That stem cells are undifferentiated cells that can divide to produce new undifferentiated cells, which can then differentiate.
- [ ] That embryonic stem cells can produce any type of cell, and that this makes them important for the growth and development of organisms.
- [ ] That stem cells in adult animals can only produce certain types of cell and are used to replace damaged cells.
- [ ] That stem cells could be used to create specialised cells to replace faulty cells in medical treatments.
- [ ] That the use of stem cells in medical treatments carries risks (e.g. tumour development, disease transmission and rejection of transplanted cells), and that some people object to using stem cells for medical treatments and research on ethical grounds.
- [ ] That plant stem cells are found in tissues called meristems, and that they can differentiate into any type of plant cell throughout the plant's life.

Exam-style Questions

1   **Figure 1** shows four stages of mitosis in a cell. The stages are in the wrong order.

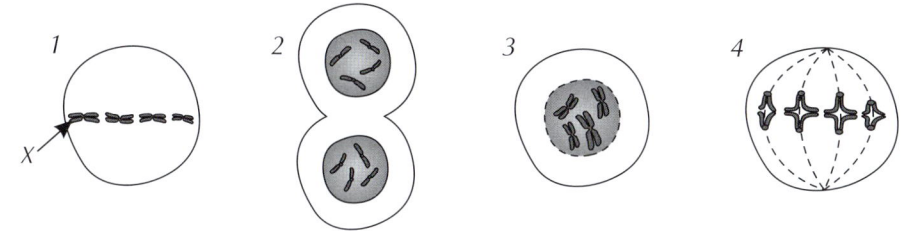

Figure 1

(a)   Name the structure labelled **X**.

(1 mark)

(b)   Which of the following options lists the stages of mitosis from **Figure 1** in the correct order?

     A   1, 2, 4, 3
     B   2, 3, 1, 4
     C   3, 4, 1, 2
     D   3, 1, 4, 2

(1 mark)

(c)   Which of the stages shown in **Figure 1** represents prophase? Explain your answer.

(2 marks)

(d)   Describe the products of mitosis.

(3 marks)

2   The graph in **Figure 2** is a percentile growth chart for boys aged from 0 to 1 years.

(a)   A baby boy who is 9 months old weighs 7.2 kg. What percentile is the baby in?

(1 mark)

(b)   A 6-month-old baby boy is in the 50th percentile for weight. Estimate the weight of the baby.

(1 mark)

(c)   Describe how a growth chart like the one in **Figure 2** is used to monitor growth.

(2 marks)

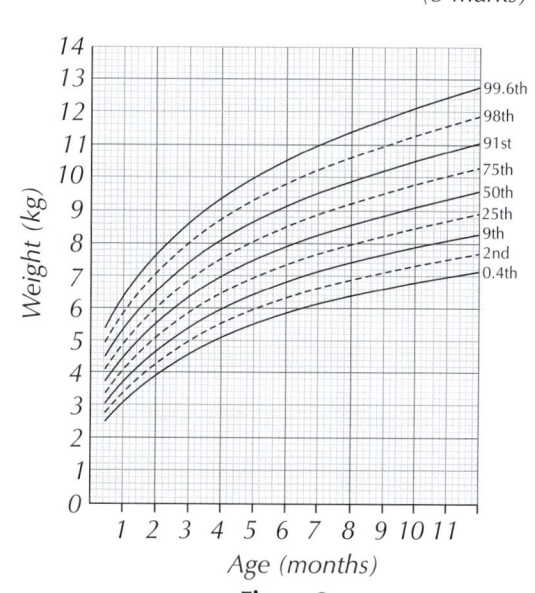

Figure 2

Topic 2b — Nervous Control

Learning Objective:
- Be able to explain the structure and function of sensory receptors, sensory neurones, relay neurones in the CNS and motor neurones in the transmission of electrical impulses, including the roles of the axon, dendron and myelin sheath.

Specification Reference 2.13

1. The Nervous System

First up, an overview of the nervous system...

What is the nervous system?

Organisms need to respond to **stimuli** (changes in the environment) in order to survive. A single-celled organism can just respond to its environment, but the cells of multicellular organisms need to communicate with each other first. So as multicellular organisms evolved, they developed nervous and hormonal communication systems.

Your nervous system is what allows you to react to your surroundings. It also allows you to coordinate your behaviour. It's made up of all the **neurones** (nerve cells) in your body — there's more on these on the next two pages.

Tip: There's more about hormonal communication on pages 165-167.

Sensory receptors

Sensory receptors are groups of cells that detect stimuli and initiate responses to them. Different receptors detect different stimuli.

Tip: Receptors can form part of larger, complex organs, e.g. the retina of the eye is covered in light receptor cells.

> **Examples**
> - Receptors in the eyes detect light.
> - Some receptors in the skin detect touch (pressure). Some detect tissue damage (which causes you to feel pain). Others detect temperature change.

The central nervous system (CNS)

The central nervous system (CNS) is where all the information from sensory receptors is sent, and where reflexes (see p.67) and actions are coordinated.

Tip: The CNS coordinates a response — in other words, it receives information about a stimulus and decides what to do about it.

In vertebrates (animals with backbones) the CNS consists of the brain and spinal cord only. The spinal cord is a long column of neurones that runs from the base of the brain down the spine. The spinal cord relays information between the brain and the rest of the body.

In mammals, the CNS is connected to the body by sensory neurones and motor neurones. Neurones transmit information as electrical impulses to and from the CNS. This happens very quickly.

Effectors

Tip: Nervous impulses are electrical impulses.

'Instructions' from the CNS are sent along neurones to effectors. Effectors are muscles or glands which respond to nervous impulses and bring about a response to a stimulus. Muscles and glands respond to nervous impulses in different ways. Muscles contract and glands secrete chemical substances called hormones (see page 165).

Different types of neurone

Different types of neurone are involved in the transfer of information to and from the CNS:

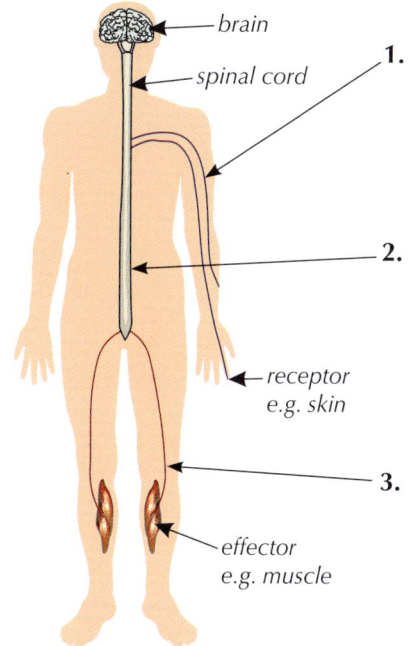

1. **Sensory neurones**
   The neurones that carry information as electrical impulses from sensory receptors to the central nervous system.

2. **Relay neurones**
   The neurones that carry electrical impulses from sensory neurones to motor neurones. They are found in the central nervous system.

3. **Motor neurones**
   The neurones that carry electrical impulses from the central nervous system to the effectors.

(Diagram labels: brain, spinal cord, receptor e.g. skin, effector e.g. muscle)

Exam Tip
The exam isn't just a test of what you know — it's also a test of how well you can apply what you know. For instance, you might have to take what you know about a human and apply it to a horse (e.g. sound receptors in its ears send information to the brain via sensory neurones). The key is not to panic — just think carefully about the information that you are given.

The transmission of information to and from the CNS is summarised in Figure 1:

stimulus → Receptors → (sensory neurone) → CNS (coordinator) → (motor neurone) → Effector → response
(relay neurone within CNS)

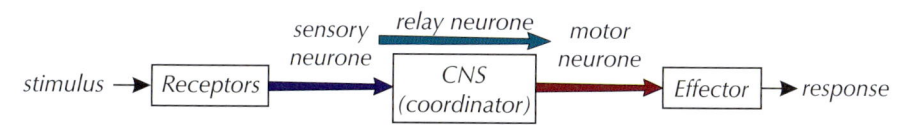

Figure 1: Flow diagram showing the transmission of information to and from the CNS.

The time it takes you to respond to a stimulus is called your **reaction time**.

Exam Tip
Make sure you know which type of neurone transfers information to which place in the nervous system — it's easy to get the different types of neurones confused and they often come up in exams.

Neurone structure

All neurones have a cell body with a nucleus (plus cytoplasm and other subcellular structures found in animal cells). The cell body has extensions that connect to other neurones — dendrites and **dendrons** carry nerve impulses towards the cell body, and **axons** carry nerve impulses away from the cell body. Some axons are surrounded by a **myelin sheath**. This is a fatty layer that acts as an electrical insulator, speeding up the electrical impulse.

Neurones can be very long, which also speeds up the impulse (connecting with another neurone slows the impulse down, so one long neurone is much quicker than lots of short ones joined together).

Tip: Remember, axons carry nerve impulses away from the cell body.

Structure of a sensory neurone

Sensory neurones have one long dendron that carries nerve impulses from receptor cells to the cell body, which is located in the middle of the neurone. One short axon carries nerve impulses from the cell body to the CNS. See Figure 2 on the next page.

Topic 2b Nervous Control

Figure 2: Diagram showing the structure of a sensory neurone.

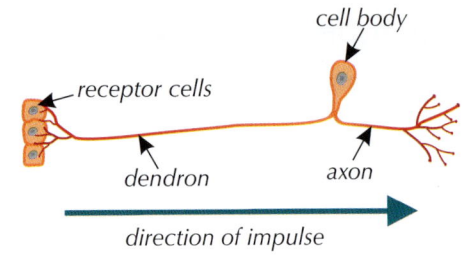

Structure of a motor neurone

Motor neurones have many short dendrites, which carry nerve impulses from the CNS to the cell body. One long axon carries nerve impulses from the cell body to effector cells.

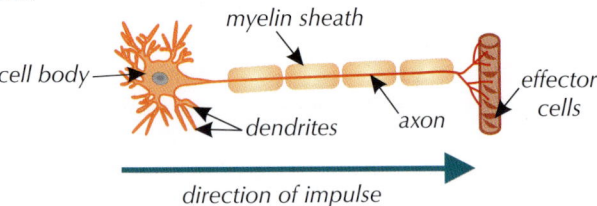

Tip: Figure 3 shows a myelinated motor neurone but you can get unmyelinated ones too. Sensory and relay neurones can also be myelinated.

Figure 3: Diagram showing the structure of a motor neurone.

Figure 5: Motor neurones (black) in muscle tissue, as seen under a light microscope.

Structure of a relay neurone

Relay neurones also have many short dendrites. These carry nerve impulses from sensory neurones to the cell body. An axon carries nerve impulses from the cell body to motor neurones.

Figure 4: Diagram showing the structure of a relay neurone.

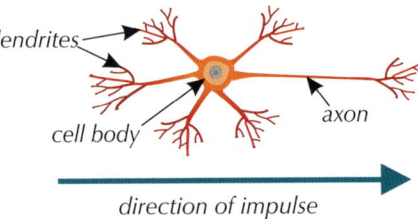

Practice Questions — Fact Recall

Q1 What is the function of an axon?

Q2 Why do some axons have a myelin sheath?

Practice Question — Application

Q1 A dog hears a cat moving in the garden, so runs towards it.

  a) i) Suggest what the stimulus is in this situation and what detects it.

  ii) What name is given to the type of neurone that transmits information about the stimulus to the central nervous system?

  The dog's brain sends an impulse to the dog's muscles which act as effectors.

  b) i) What type of neurone transmits information from the central nervous system to an effector?

  ii) How do the dog's muscles respond to the nerve impulse?

2. Synapses and Reflexes

Reflexes are rapid responses to stimuli that happen without you having to think about them — they're automatic. The neurones involved in a reflex aren't all joined together though — they have gaps between them called synapses.

Synapses

The connection between two neurones is called a synapse. The nerve signal is transferred by chemicals called **neurotransmitters** which diffuse (move) across the gap. The neurotransmitters then set off a new electrical signal in the next neurone. This is shown in Figure 1.

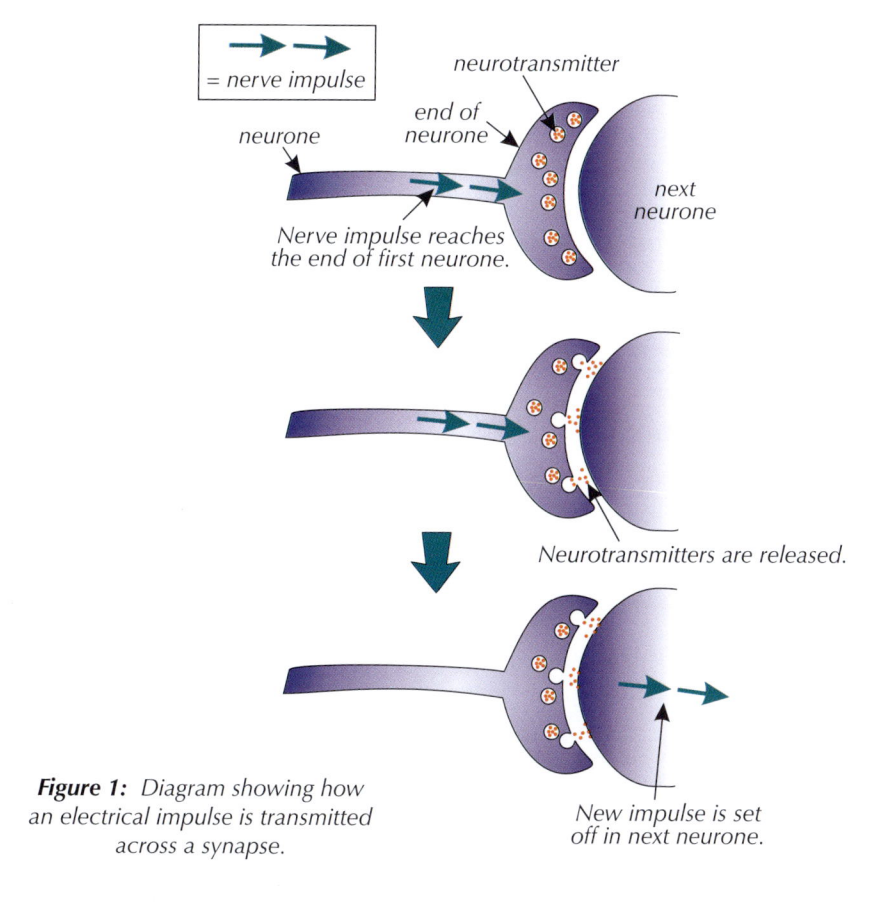

Figure 1: Diagram showing how an electrical impulse is transmitted across a synapse.

Neurones deliver information really quickly because the signal is transmitted by electrical impulses. Synapses slow down the transmission of a nervous impulse because the diffusion of neurotransmitters across the gap takes time (it's still pretty fast though).

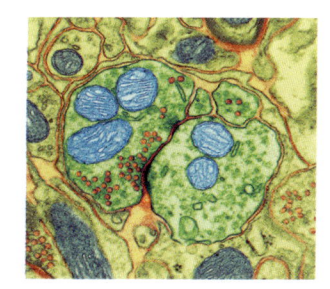

Reflexes

Reflexes are fast, automatic responses to certain stimuli. They bypass your conscious brain completely when a quick response is essential — your body just gets on with things. Reflexes can reduce your chance of being injured, although they have other roles as well.

Learning Objectives:
- Be able to explain the structure and function of synapses in the transmission of electrical impulses, including the role of neurotransmitters.
- Be able to explain the structure and function of a reflex arc including sensory, relay and motor neurones.

Specification References 2.13, 2.14

Figure 2: A synapse viewed under a microscope. The neurones are shown in green. The red dots contain neurotransmitters.

Tip: 'Automatic' means done without thinking.

Topic 2b Nervous Control

Reflex arcs

The passage of information in a reflex (from receptor to effector) is called a reflex arc. The neurones in reflex arcs go through the spinal cord or through an unconscious part of the brain. Here are the main stages in a reflex arc:

1. When a stimulus is detected by receptors, impulses are sent along a sensory neurone to a relay neurone in the CNS.
2. When the impulses reach a synapse between the sensory neurone and the relay neurone, they trigger neurotransmitters to be released (see previous page). These cause impulses to be sent along the relay neurone.
3. When the impulses reach a synapse between the relay neurone and a motor neurone, the same thing happens. Neurotransmitters are released and cause impulses to be sent along the motor neurone.
4. The impulses then travel along the motor neurone to the effector (which is usually a muscle).
5. If the effector is a muscle, it will respond to the impulse by contracting. If it's a gland, it will secrete a hormone.

Because you don't have to think about the response (which takes time) a reflex is quicker than normal responses. Figure 3 summarises a reflex arc:

Tip: Flick back to pages 65-66 for more on sensory, relay and motor neurones.

Tip: Remember, electrical impulses pass between the different neurones via diffusion of chemicals at the synapse. They don't just jump between the neurones.

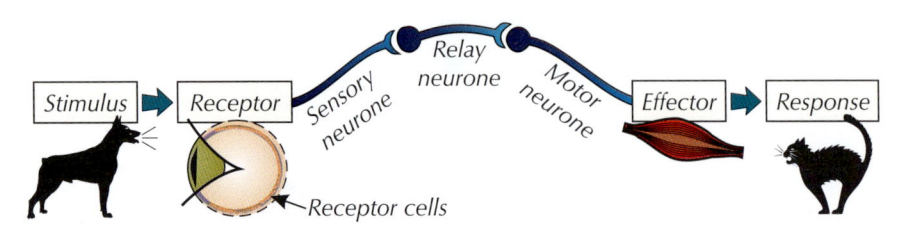

Figure 3: Block diagram of a reflex arc.

Example

If a bee stings a person's finger, the reflex response is that the hand moves away from the source of pain. Here's the pathway taken by this reflex arc:

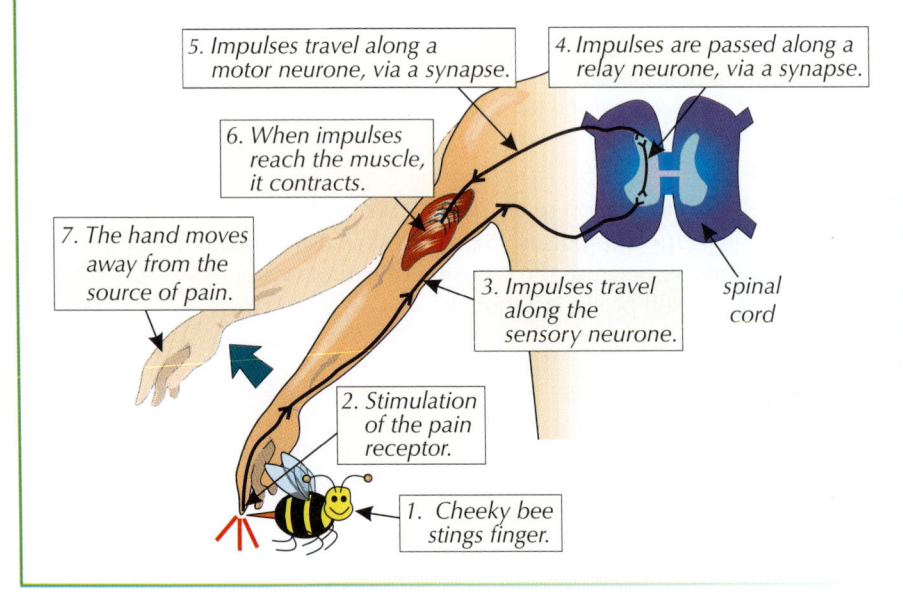

1. Cheeky bee stings finger.
2. Stimulation of the pain receptor.
3. Impulses travel along the sensory neurone.
4. Impulses are passed along a relay neurone, via a synapse.
5. Impulses travel along a motor neurone, via a synapse.
6. When impulses reach the muscle, it contracts.
7. The hand moves away from the source of pain.

Tip: The important things to remember about reflexes are that they're <u>automatic</u> (you don't have to think about them) and <u>rapid</u> (so they're often able to prevent or reduce the chance of injury).

Topic 2b Nervous Control

Example

Very bright light can damage the eye — so you have a reflex to protect it, called the iris reflex.

When light receptors in the eye detect very bright light, a message is sent along a sensory neurone to the brain. The message then travels along a relay neurone to a motor neurone, which tells circular muscles in the iris (the coloured part of the eye) to contract, making the pupil smaller. This reduces the amount of light that can enter the eye.

The opposite process happens in dim light. This time, the radial muscles contract and the circular muscles relax, which makes the pupil wider.

This reflex reaction is shown in Figure 4.

Tip: The pupil doesn't actually <u>do</u> anything during the iris reflex — it's just a hole, so although it looks like the pupil is changing size, it's really the iris that's actively doing the changing.

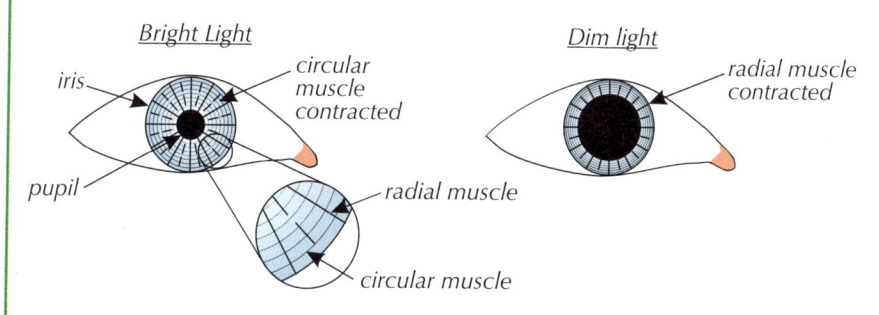

Figure 4: Diagram showing the iris reflex in bright and dim light.

Practice Questions — Fact Recall

Q1 How do nerve impulses travel from one neurone to another?

Q2 What is a reflex?

Q3 Do reflex arcs travel through conscious parts of the brain?

Q4 What neurone comes after the sensory neurone in a reflex arc?

Q5 If the effector in a reflex arc is a gland, what will the response of that reflex arc be?

Practice Question — Application

Q1 David steps on a drawing pin and immediately pulls his foot up off the pin.

   a) What is the stimulus in this response?

   b) What is the effector in this response? How does it respond?

   c) Complete the pathway taken by this reflex arc.

   Stimulus → Receptor → Sensory neurone...

Exam Tip
Questions on reflex arcs are quite common in the exam. Make sure you know the general pathway they take really well, and you'll be able to apply it to any reflex response you're given.

Topic 2b Nervous Control

Topic 2b Checklist — Make sure you know...

The Nervous System
- [ ] That sensory receptors are cells that detect stimuli (changes in the environment) and initiate responses.
- [ ] That the CNS (which is made up of the brain and spinal cord) coordinates responses to stimuli.
- [ ] That sensory neurones carry nervous (electrical) impulses from sensory receptors to the CNS, relay neurones carry nervous impulses through the CNS and motor neurones carry nervous impulses from the CNS to effectors (muscles and glands).
- [ ] The structure of sensory, motor and relay neurones, including: the role of the dendron, dendrites and axon in carrying impulses to and away from the cell body, and the role of the myelin sheath in insulating the axon to speed up nervous impulses.

Synapses and Reflexes
- [ ] The structure of a synapse (the connection between neurones) and how a nerve signal is transferred across a synapse by neurotransmitters.
- [ ] That in a simple reflex arc, stimuli are detected by receptors and transmitted to the CNS as nervous impulses via sensory neurones. The impulses are then transferred via a relay neurone in the CNS to a motor neurone, which sends impulses to an effector. The effector then produces a response.

Exam-style Questions

1 A scientist conducted an experiment on reaction time.

Subjects had an electrode placed on their upper arm to detect when their muscle contracted. The subjects were asked to place their finger on a metal disc, which gave out a small electric shock at random. This shock caused the muscle in the upper arm to contract.

The scientist measured reaction time as the time it took between the initiation of the shock and the contraction of the muscle in the upper arm.

Figure 1 shows the pathway taken in this reflex response.

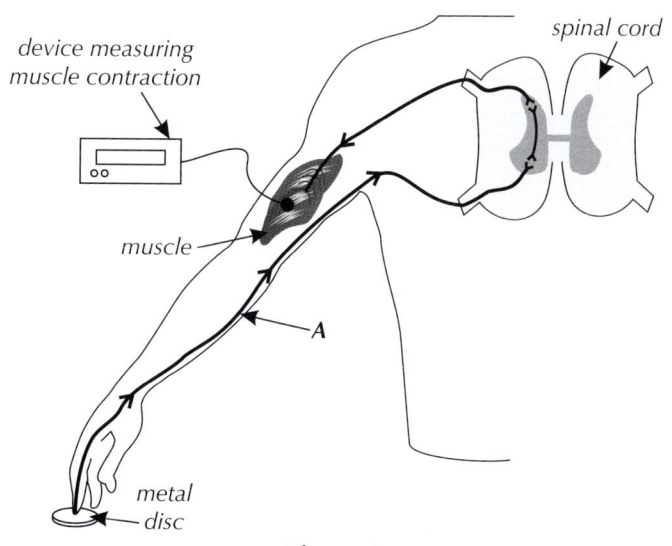

Figure 1

(a) Where are the sensory receptors located in this response?

(1 mark)

(b) Name the type of neurone labelled **A** in the diagram.

(1 mark)

(c) The average reaction time measured during the experiment was 0.024 s.

After he had recorded their reaction times, the scientist gave the subjects a drug which is known to increase the amount of neurotransmitter released at the synapses. He then repeated the experiment.

What do you think would happen to the average reaction time after administration of the drug? Explain your answer.

(2 marks)

(d) Reflexes often help to protect us from injury.
Suggest and explain **two** features of reflexes that help them do this.

(4 marks)

Topic 3a — Reproduction, DNA and Protein Synthesis

Learning Objectives:
- Be able to explain the terms gamete and zygote.
- Be able to explain the role of meiotic cell division, including the production of four daughter cells, each with half the number of chromosomes, and that this results in the formation of genetically different haploid gametes.

Specification References 3.3, 3.13

1. Sexual Reproduction and Meiosis

These next two pages are all about how you were made. Read on — it's fascinating stuff...

What is sexual reproduction?

Sexual reproduction is where genetic information from two organisms (a father and a mother) is combined to produce offspring which are genetically different to either parent. Sexual reproduction involves gametes (sex cells).

Gametes

In sexual reproduction the mother and father produce gametes by meiosis (see next page). Egg and sperm cells in animals are examples of gametes (see Figure 1).

Normal body cells are **diploid** (see page 53). This means they have two copies of each chromosome. Gametes are **haploid** — they contain half the number of chromosomes in a normal cell (see page 27). So instead of having two copies of each chromosome, a gamete has just one of each.

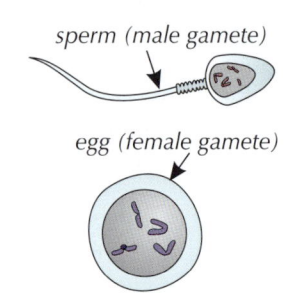

Figure 1: The sperm and egg cells.

Tip: In flowering plants, the male gametes are called pollen and the female gametes are called ovules.

Tip: The genetic information is stored as DNA in chromosomes — see page 53.

Fertilisation

At fertilisation, a male gamete (from the father) fuses with a female gamete (from the mother) to produce a fertilised egg, also known as a **zygote**. The zygote ends up with the full number of chromosomes (half from the father and half from the mother). This is shown in Figure 2.

Tip: The zygote is diploid.

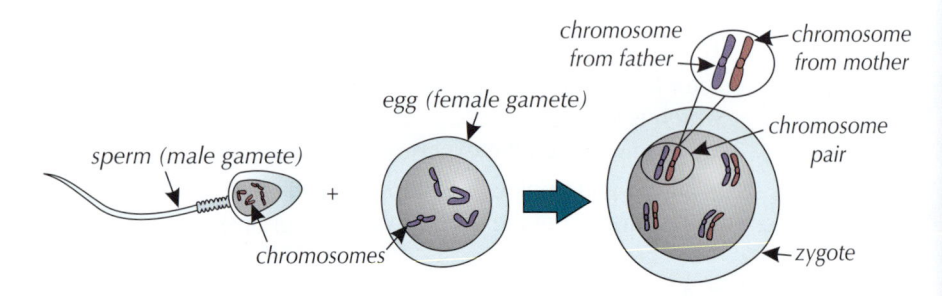

Figure 2: Diagram showing fertilisation.

The zygote then undergoes cell division (by mitosis, see pages 54-55) and develops into an embryo.

Sexual reproduction means that the offspring inherits features from both parents — it receives a mixture of chromosomes from its mum and its dad (and it's the chromosomes that decide how you turn out). This mixture of genetic information produces variation in the offspring. Pretty cool, eh.

Tip: For more on variation, see pages 89-91.

What is meiosis?

Meiosis is a type of cell division. It's different to mitosis because:

- It doesn't produce identical cells.
- It produces cells which have half the normal number of chromosomes.

Gametes are produced by meiosis. In humans, meiosis only takes place in the reproductive organs (ovaries and testes).

Exam Tip
The words 'mitosis' and 'meiosis' look and sound very similar. Make sure that you know how to spell each one. You won't gain marks in the exam if the examiner can't tell which type of cell division you are talking about.

Cell division by meiosis

1. Before the cell starts to divide, it duplicates its genetic information, forming two armed chromosomes — one arm of each chromosome is an exact copy of the other arm. After replication, the chromosomes arrange themselves into pairs.

2. In the first division in meiosis the chromosome pairs line up in the centre of the cell.

3. The pairs are then pulled apart so each new cell only has one copy of each chromosome. Some of the father's chromosomes (shown in blue in Figure 4) and some of the mother's chromosomes (shown in red) go into each new cell. This mixing up of the parents' chromosomes is really important — it mixes up their genes, creating genetic variation in the offspring.

4. In the second division, the chromosomes line up again in the centre of the cell. The arms of the chromosomes are pulled apart.

5. You get four haploid daughter cells — these are the gametes. Each gamete only has a single set of chromosomes in it. Each of the gametes (sperm or egg cells) is genetically different from the others.

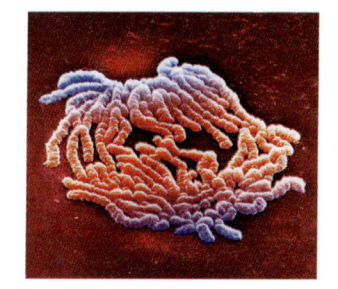

Figure 3: Microscope image showing pairs of chromosomes being pulled apart during the first division in meiosis.

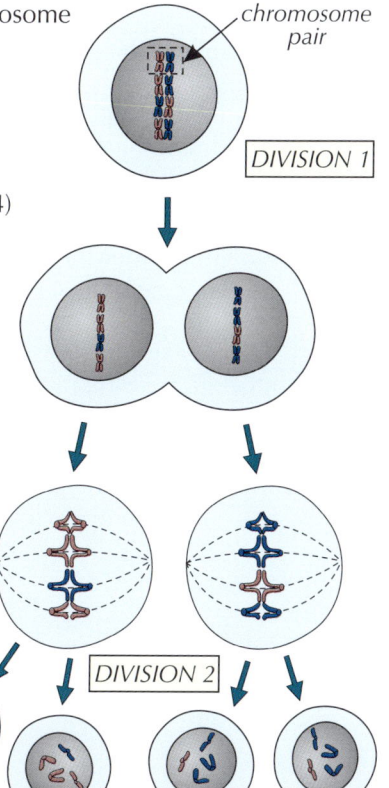

Figure 4: Diagram showing the stages in meiosis.

Topic 3a Reproduction, DNA and Protein Synthesis

Practice Questions — Fact Recall

Q1 How many sets of chromosomes do gametes contain?

Q2 Where are gametes produced?

Q3 How many cell divisions occur in meiosis?

Q4 How many new cells are produced when a cell divides by meiosis?

Q5 True or False? Gametes are all genetically identical.

Practice Questions — Application

Q1 Different animals have different numbers of chromosomes in their body cells and in their gametes, as shown in the table:

Type of animal cell	Number of chromosomes
Dog body cell	78
Cat egg cell	19
Horse sperm cell	32

Using your knowledge and the information provided in the table, suggest:

a) how many chromosomes there are in a dog sperm cell.

b) how many chromosomes there are in the body cell of a cat.

c) how many chromosomes there are in a horse egg cell.

Q2 Mary thinks that after the first division in meiosis, cells will have half a set of chromosomes. Why does this not happen after the first division when a cell divides by meiosis?

2. DNA

DNA is a pretty important molecule because it's what makes us unique. Therefore it's really important that you learn all about it...

Chromosomes and DNA

DNA stands for deoxyribonucleic acid. It's the chemical that all of the genetic material in a cell is made up from. It contains coded information — basically all the instructions to put an organism together and make it work. So it's what's in your DNA that determines what inherited characteristics you have.

DNA is found in the nucleus of eukaryotic cells (e.g. animal and plant cells), in really long structures called chromosomes. The DNA is coiled up to form the 'arms' of the chromosome. In diploid cells, chromosomes come in pairs.

DNA is a polymer — a large molecule built from a chain of smaller molecules. As you can see from Figure 1, DNA is made up of two strands twisted together in the shape of a double helix.

Learning Objectives:
- Be able to explain the term chromosome.
- Be able to describe DNA as a polymer made up of two strands coiled to form a double helix.
- Be able to describe a gene as a section of a DNA molecule that codes for a specific protein and the genome as the entire DNA of an organism.
- Be able to describe DNA as a polymer made up of strands linked by a series of complementary base pairs, which are joined together by weak hydrogen bonds.
- Be able to explain how DNA can be extracted from fruit.

Specification References 3.4 – 3.6, 3.13

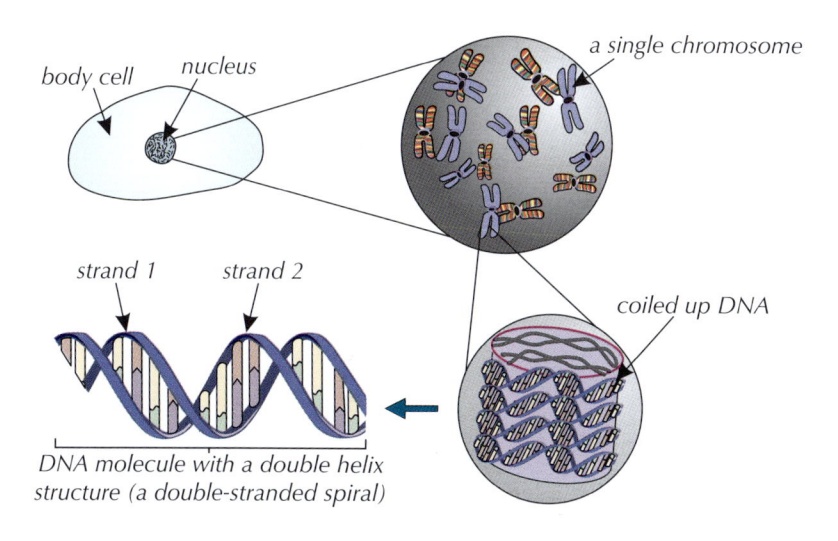

Figure 1: Diagram showing the structure of DNA and where it is found in a eukaryotic cell.

Tip: Chromosomes in bacteria are different to chromosomes in eukaryotic cells. Bacteria have one big loop of chromosomal DNA in their cytoplasm — see p.24 for more.

Genes and the genome

A **gene** is a small section of DNA. Each gene codes for (tells the cells to make) a particular sequence of amino acids which are put together to make a specific protein.

All of an organism's DNA makes up its **genome**.

Topic 3a Reproduction, DNA and Protein Synthesis

The structure of DNA

DNA strands are polymers made up of lots of repeating units. Each unit contains of one of four different 'bases'. The four bases are A (adenine), T (thymine), C (cytosine) and G (guanine).

Complementary base pairing

Each base in a DNA strand links to a base on the opposite strand in the helix — see Figure 2.

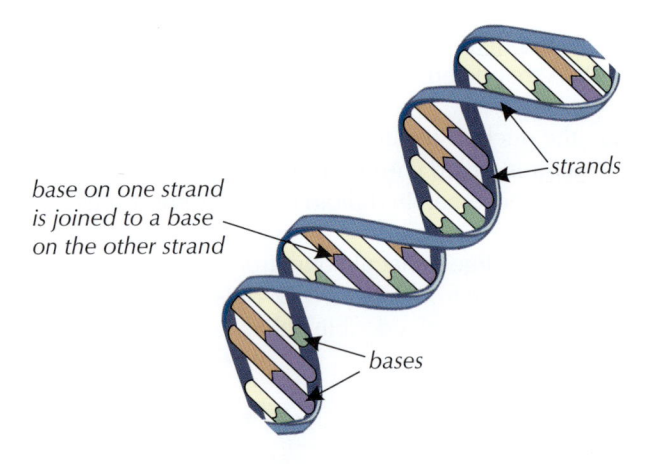

Figure 2: Diagram showing part of a DNA molecule.

A always pairs up with T, and C always pairs up with G (see Figure 3). This is called complementary base pairing. The complementary base pairs are held together by weak hydrogen bonds.

Exam Tip
Make sure you memorise which bases link with which — it could be easy marks in the exam.

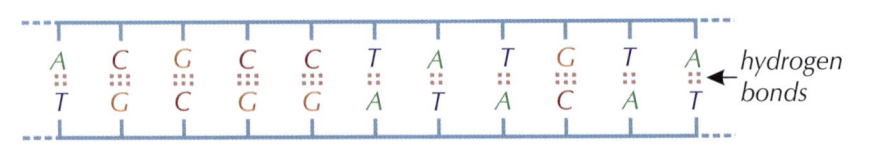

Figure 3: Diagram showing complementary pairing of bases in DNA.

Tip: Always do a risk assessment before carrying out any practical work.

Extracting DNA from fruit

You need to be able to describe how to extract DNA from fruit. Here's what you do:

1. Mash some strawberries and then put them in a beaker containing a solution of detergent and salt. Mix well.

    - The detergent will break down the cell membranes to release the DNA.

Tip: Other soft fruits will work well here, such as kiwi or banana. You can use washing up liquid as the detergent.

   - The salt will make the DNA stick together.

2. Filter the mixture to get the froth and big, insoluble bits of cell out.

3. Gently add some ice-cold alcohol (e.g. ethanol) to the filtered mixture.

4. The DNA will start to come out of solution as it's not soluble in cold alcohol. It will appear as a stringy white precipitate (a solid) that can be carefully fished out with a glass rod (see Figure 4).

Tip: DNA isn't soluble in alcohol — so adding the alcohol causes the DNA to precipitate out of the solution.

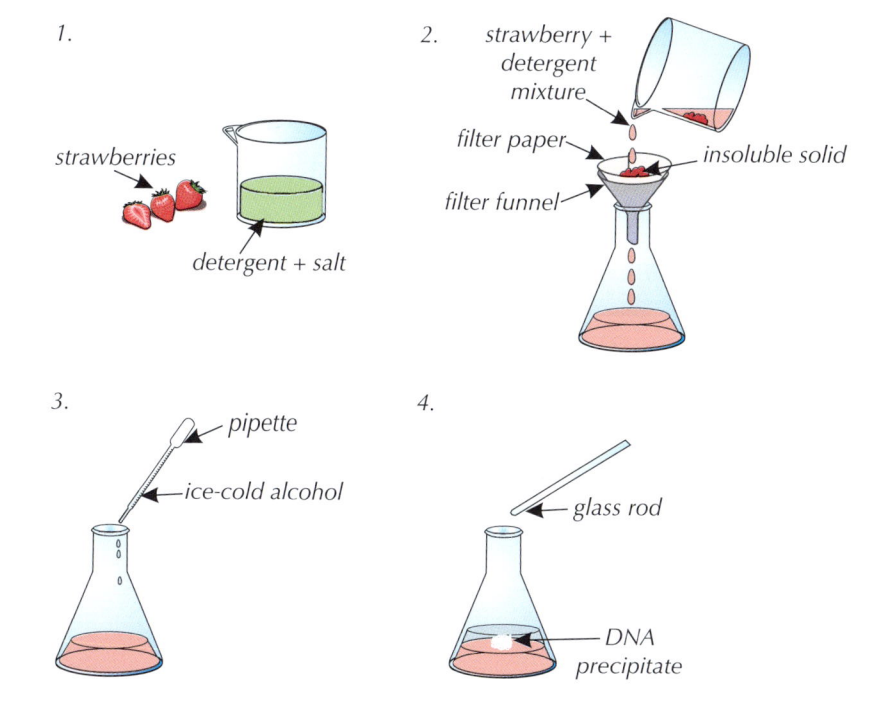

Figure 5: If you're careful, the DNA precipitate you extract from your fruit should look something like this.

Figure 4: Diagram showing method for extracting DNA from strawberries.

Practice Questions — Fact Recall

Q1 What is a DNA double helix?

Q2 What term is used to describe a section of DNA that codes for a particular protein?

Q2 What term is used to describe all of an organism's DNA?

Practice Questions — Application

Q1 A DNA sequence is shown below.
Write the base sequence for the complementary strand.

T C T A C G A A T G A A

Q2 A student is extracting DNA from a kiwi fruit. She mashes up the fruit to form a pulp and adds a solution of washing-up liquid.

a) Why does the student add the washing-up liquid solution to the fruit pulp?

b) What should the student add to make the DNA clump together?

c) After filtering her mixture, the student adds ice-cold alcohol. Describe what the student should expect to see after carrying out this step.

Topic 3a Checklist — Make sure you know...

Sexual Reproduction and Meiosis

☐ That gametes (sex cells) are haploid (they have half the number of chromosomes in normal body cells).

☐ That a zygote (fertilised egg) is formed when two gametes fuse together at fertilisation.

☐ That gametes are produced by meiosis — a type of cell division that results in four genetically different haploid daughter cells.

DNA

☐ That DNA is stored in the cell nucleus as chromosomes (long molecules of coiled-up DNA).

☐ That DNA is a polymer made up of two strands twisted into a double-helix shape.

☐ That a gene is a section of DNA that codes for a particular protein and that the genome is all the DNA in an organism.

☐ That the two strands in a DNA double helix are linked by complementary base pairs (A–T and C–G) held together by weak hydrogen bonds.

☐ How to extract DNA from fruit, using detergent, salt, filter paper and ice-cold alcohol to precipitate out the DNA.

Exam-style Questions

1 A farmer selects a male pig and a female pig and breeds them together. **Figure 1** shows the process.

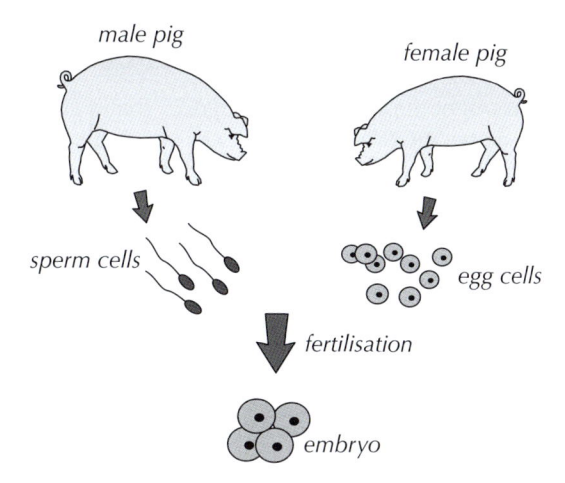

Figure 1

(a) Is the reproduction shown in **Figure 1** an example of sexual or asexual reproduction? Give a reason for your answer.

(1 mark)

(b) The pigs that are born as a result of this process will share characteristics with both the male pig and the female pig. Explain why.

(2 marks)

(c) The sperm cells are gametes.
  (i) Explain why it is important that the sperm cells only have one set of chromosomes.

(1 mark)

  (ii) Name the type of cell division that occurs in the reproductive organs of the male pig to produce the sperm cells.

(1 mark)

2 A scientist analyses a sample of DNA.

(a) There are 2.16×10^6 base pairs in the sample. 46% of the base pairs contain adenine (A). Calculate the number of base pairs that contain cytosine (C).

(2 marks)

(b) Name the bonds that hold base pairs together in DNA.

(1 mark)

(c) The scientist obtained the DNA sample from some cells. Suggest how the scientist could have precipitated the DNA out of a solution containing cell debris.

(1 mark)

Topic 3b — Genetic Diagrams and Inheritance

Learning Objectives:
- Know that most phenotypic features are the result of multiple genes rather than single gene inheritance.
- Be able to explain why there are differences in inherited characteristics as a result of alleles.
- Be able to explain the terms: gene, allele, dominant, recessive, homozygous, heterozygous, genotype and phenotype.

Specification References 3.12, 3.13, 3.19

1. Genes and Alleles

This page is all about how our genes determine our characteristics...

Genes and characteristics

You might remember from page 75 that a gene is a section of DNA that codes for a specific protein. The genes you inherit control what characteristics you develop. Different genes control different characteristics and most characteristics are controlled by multiple genes interacting. However, some characteristics are controlled by a single gene — for example, red-green colour blindness in humans and round vs wrinkly peas (see next page).

What are alleles?

All genes exist in different versions called alleles. Gametes (see p.72) only have one allele, but all the other cells in an organism have two — one on each chromosome in a pair (see Figure 1). This is because we inherit half of our alleles from our mother and half from our father. In genetic diagrams (see pages 81-84), letters are usually used to represent alleles.

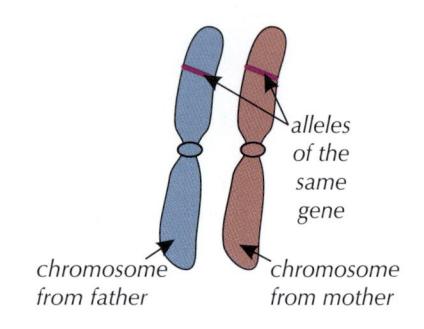

Figure 1: Diagram showing two alleles for the same gene.

For characteristics controlled by a single gene, if an organism has two alleles for that particular gene that are the same, then it's **homozygous** for that trait. If its two alleles for a particular gene are different, then it's **heterozygous**. If the two alleles are different, only one can determine what characteristic is present. The allele for the characteristic that's shown is called the **dominant** allele (use a capital letter for dominant alleles — e.g. 'C'). The other one is called **recessive** (and you show these with small letters — e.g. 'c').

For an organism to display a recessive characteristic, both its alleles must be recessive (e.g. cc). But to display a dominant characteristic the organism can be either CC or Cc, because the dominant allele overrules the recessive one if the plant/animal/other organism is heterozygous.

Your **genotype** is the combination of alleles you have, e.g. CC, cc or Cc. Your alleles work at a molecular level (by coding for slightly different proteins) to determine what characteristics you have — your **phenotype**, e.g. brown eyes, blonde hair, etc.

Practice Question — Fact Recall

Q1 Explain what is meant by each of these terms:

   a) alleles   b) homozygous   c) dominant allele   d) phenotype

2. Genetic Diagrams and Family Pedigrees

The diagrams on the next few pages show how we inherit our characteristics...

Monohybrid inheritance

Characteristics that are determined by a single gene can be studied using **monohybrid crosses**. This is where you cross two parents to look at just one characteristic. In the exam they could ask you about the inheritance of any characteristic controlled by a single gene, as the principle's always the same.

Genetic diagrams of monohybrid inheritance

Genetic diagrams allow you to see how certain characteristics are inherited. The inheritance of round or wrinkly peas from pea plants is an example of monohybrid inheritance and can be shown using genetic diagrams.

Example 1

The gene which causes wrinkly peas is recessive, so you can use a small 'r' to represent it. Round peas are due to a dominant gene, which you can represent with a capital 'R'. If you cross one pea plant which produces wrinkly peas (rr) and one that produces round peas (in this case RR), all of the offspring will produce round peas — but they'll have the alleles Rr.

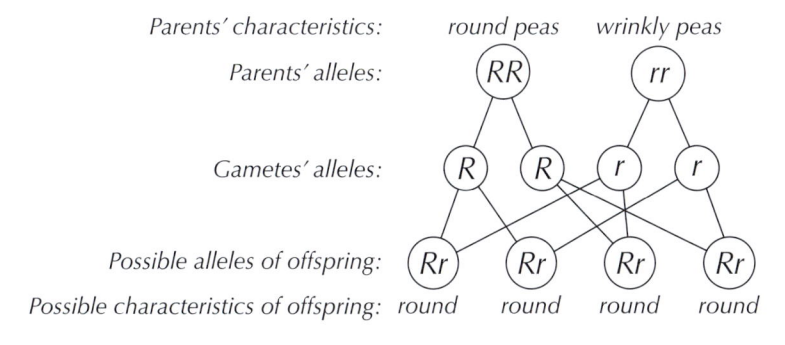

Parents' characteristics: round peas   wrinkly peas
Parents' alleles: (RR)   (rr)

Gametes' alleles: (R) (R)   (r) (r)

Possible alleles of offspring: (Rr) (Rr) (Rr) (Rr)
Possible characteristics of offspring: round round round round

You can also show this genetic cross in a Punnett square:

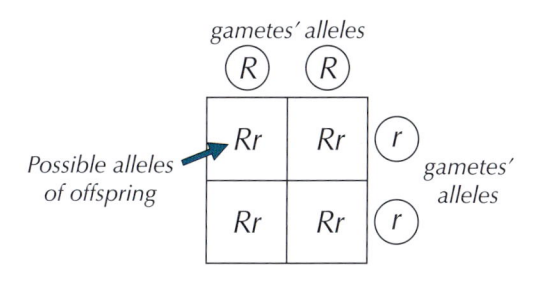

	R	R
r	Rr	Rr
r	Rr	Rr

(gametes' alleles across top and down side; possible alleles of offspring in the squares)

You need to be able to use genetic diagrams to predict and explain the outcomes of monohybrid crosses between individuals for lots of different combinations of alleles. The outcomes are given as ratios and can be used to work out the probability of having offspring with a certain characteristic.

Learning Objectives:
- Be able to explain monohybrid inheritance using genetic diagrams, Punnett squares and family pedigrees.
- Be able to calculate and analyse outcomes (using probabilities, ratios and percentages) from monohybrid crosses and pedigree analysis for dominant and recessive traits.

Specification References 3.14, 3.16

Tip: Monohybrid inheritance is also known as single gene inheritance.

Tip: 'Cross' just means 'breed together'.

Figure 1: The peas produced by pea plants can either be wrinkly (left) or round (right).

Tip: In this example, a plant producing wrinkly peas must be homozygous recessive (it must have 'rr' alleles). However, a plant producing round peas could be homozygous dominant or heterozygous — it can have two possible combinations of alleles — RR or Rr.

Topic 3b Genetic Diagrams and Inheritance

Probability is a measure of how likely something is to happen. In maths, the probability of a certain event happening is written as a number between 0 (impossible) and 1 (certain). It can also be written as a fraction or a percentage.

A 3:1 ratio in the offspring

A cross could produce a 3:1 ratio for a certain characteristic in the offspring. The following example shows that this would happen if two of the heterozygous offspring from Example 1 were crossed.

Example 2

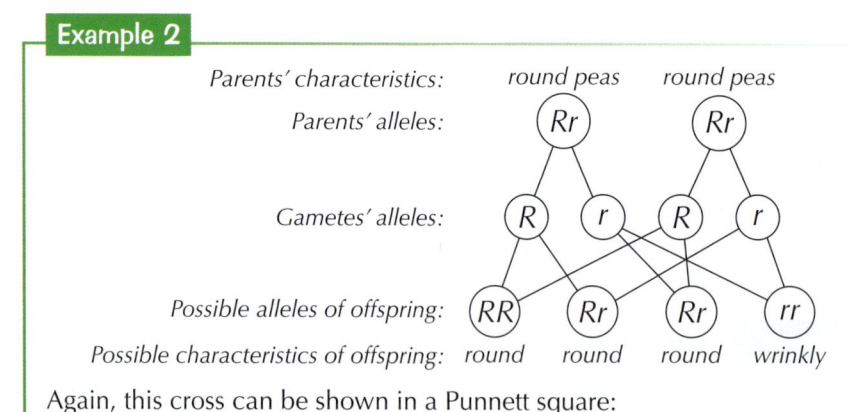

Parents' characteristics: round peas, round peas
Parents' alleles: Rr, Rr

Gametes' alleles: R, r, R, r

Possible alleles of offspring: RR, Rr, Rr, rr
Possible characteristics of offspring: round, round, round, wrinkly

Again, this cross can be shown in a Punnett square:

This cross gives a 3:1 ratio of plants producing round peas to plants producing wrinkly peas. This means there's a 1 in 4, 25%, 0.25 or ¼ chance of any new pea plant having wrinkly peas. Remember that "results" like this are only probabilities — they don't say definitely what'll happen.

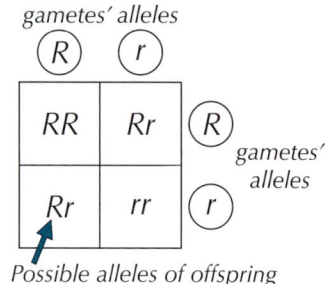

gametes' alleles

	R	r
R	RR	Rr
r	Rr	rr

gametes' alleles

Possible alleles of offspring

Tip: The 3:1 ratio of round to wrinkly peas shows that the round allele is dominant.

Exam Tip
A 3:1 ratio of plants producing round peas to plants producing wrinkly peas means there's a 1 in 4 chance of a new plant having wrinkly peas, not a 1 in 3 chance — it's an easy mistake to make, so be careful when you're talking about proportions and probabilities.

All the offspring are the same

More than one cross could result in all of the offspring showing the same characteristic. Here you have to do some detective work to find out what's gone on:

Example 3

If you cross a homozygous pea plant that produces round peas (so has two dominant alleles — RR), with a homozygous pea plant that produces wrinkly peas (rr), all the offspring will be heterozygous (Rr), so produce round peas:

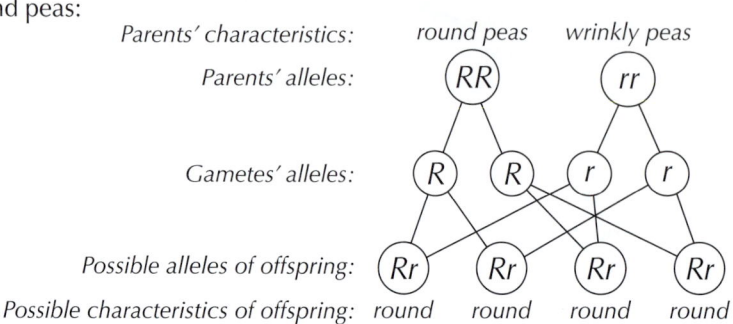

Parents' characteristics: round peas, wrinkly peas
Parents' alleles: RR, rr

Gametes' alleles: R, R, r, r

Possible alleles of offspring: Rr, Rr, Rr, Rr
Possible characteristics of offspring: round, round, round, round

Tip: You can see this cross — and a Punnett square that shows the same thing — in Example 1 on the previous page.

Topic 3b Genetic Diagrams and Inheritance

So, there's a 100% probability of any new pea plant having round peas.

But, if you crossed a homozygous pea plant that produces round peas (RR), with a heterozygous pea plant that produces round peas (so has a dominant and a recessive allele — Rr), you would also only get offspring that produce round peas:

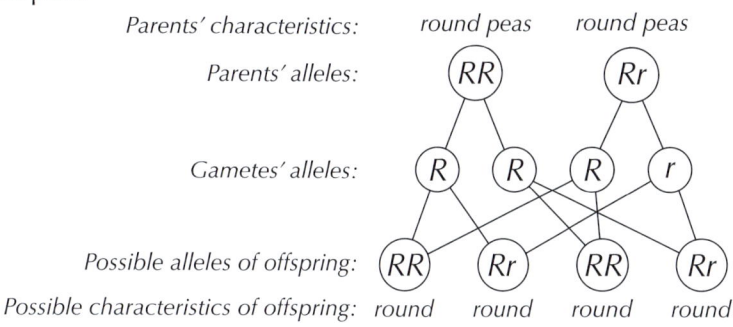

Parents' characteristics: round peas   round peas
Parents' alleles: RR   Rr
Gametes' alleles: R   R   R   r
Possible alleles of offspring: RR   Rr   RR   Rr
Possible characteristics of offspring: round   round   round   round

Tip: You know the drill by now — here's the Punnett square showing this cross:

	R	R
R	RR	RR
r	Rr	Rr

To find out which cross you'd done, you'd have to breed the offspring together and see what kind of ratio you got — then you'd have a good idea. If it was a 3:1 ratio of round to wrinkly in the offspring, it's likely that you originally had RR and rr plants (see Example 2 on the previous page).

A 1:1 ratio in the offspring

Next up is an example of when a cross produces a 1:1 ratio in the offspring — half the offspring are likely to show one characteristic and half are likely to show another characteristic. This time we're using cats with long and short hair. (Peas are a bit dull...)

Example 4

A cat's long hair is caused by a dominant allele 'H'. Short hair is caused by a recessive allele 'h'. A heterozygous cat with long hair (Hh) was bred with a homozygous cat with short hair (hh):

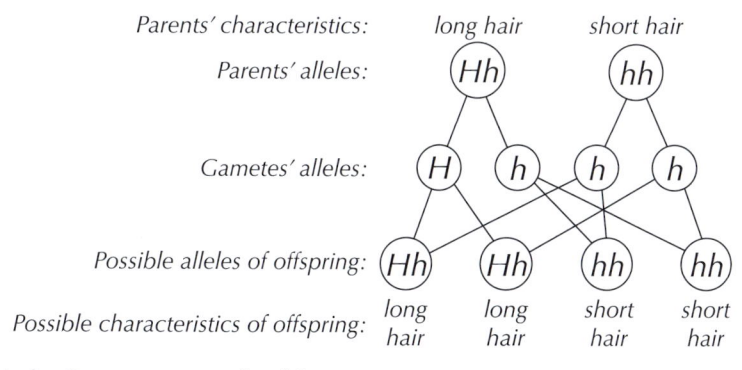

Parents' characteristics: long hair   short hair
Parents' alleles: Hh   hh
Gametes' alleles: H   h   h   h
Possible alleles of offspring: Hh   Hh   hh   hh
Possible characteristics of offspring: long hair   long hair   short hair   short hair

Here's the Punnett square for this cross:

gametes' alleles

	H	h
h	Hh	hh
h	Hh	hh

Possible alleles of offspring / gametes' alleles

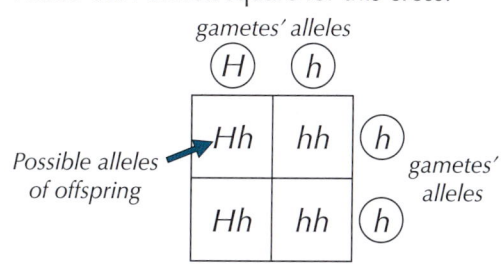

This is a 1:1 ratio, which gives a 50% probability of a new cat being born to these parents having long hair.

Exam Tip
Half the offspring of this cross are homozygous recessive — their genotype is 'hh', which produces a short-haired phenotype. The other half are heterozygous — their genotype is 'Hh', producing a long-haired phenotype. Get used to using terms such as 'homozygous', 'heterozygous', 'dominant', 'recessive' 'genotype' and 'phenotype' now — you need to know them for the exams.

Topic 3b **Genetic Diagrams and Inheritance**

Constructing genetic diagrams

You need to be able to construct genetic diagrams for monohybrid crosses.

Example 1

Drawing a Punnett square to show a cross between a pea plant with round peas (Rr) and a pea plant with wrinkly peas (rr).

1. First, draw a grid with four squares.
2. Put the possible alleles from one parent down the side, and those from the other parent along the top.
3. Then in each middle square you fill in the letters from the top and side that line up with that square — the pairs of letters in the middle show the possible combinations of the alleles.

The steps are shown here:

Exam Tip
If you're asked to produce a genetic diagram in the exam, you should be told what letters to use to represent the alleles.

Example 2

Drawing a genetic diagram to show a cross between a pea plant with wrinkly peas (rr) and a pea plant with round peas (RR).

1. Draw two circles at the top of the diagram to represent the parents. Put the round genotype in one and the wrinkly genotype in the other.
2. Draw two circles below each of the parent circles to represent the possible gametes. Put a single allele from each parent in each circle.
3. One gamete from the female combines with one gamete from the male during fertilisation, so draw criss-cross lines to show all the possible ways the alleles could combine.
4. Then write the possible combinations of alleles in the offspring in the bottom circles.

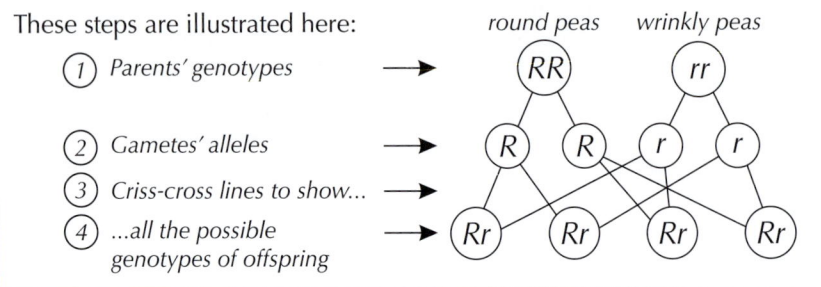

These steps are illustrated here:

① Parents' genotypes
② Gametes' alleles
③ Criss-cross lines to show...
④ ...all the possible genotypes of offspring

Exam Tip
You could be given any gene in a question about monohybrid inheritance. Whether the gene codes for a disease or a physical trait, you always draw and interpret the genetic diagrams in the same way.

Topic 3b Genetic Diagrams and Inheritance

Family pedigrees

In genetics, a family pedigree is a diagram that shows how a characteristic (or disorder) is inherited in a group of related people. You might be asked to interpret one in the exam.

> **Example**
>
> Cystic fibrosis is an inherited disorder of the cell membranes. The allele which causes cystic fibrosis is a recessive allele, carried by about 1 person in 30. Because it's recessive, people with only one copy of the allele won't have the disorder — they're known as **carriers** (they carry the faulty allele, but don't have any symptoms).
>
> For a child to inherit the disorder, both parents must be either carriers or have the disorder themselves. There's a 1 in 4 chance of a child having the disorder if both parents are carriers. This is shown in the diagram below, where 'f' is used for the recessive cystic fibrosis allele. 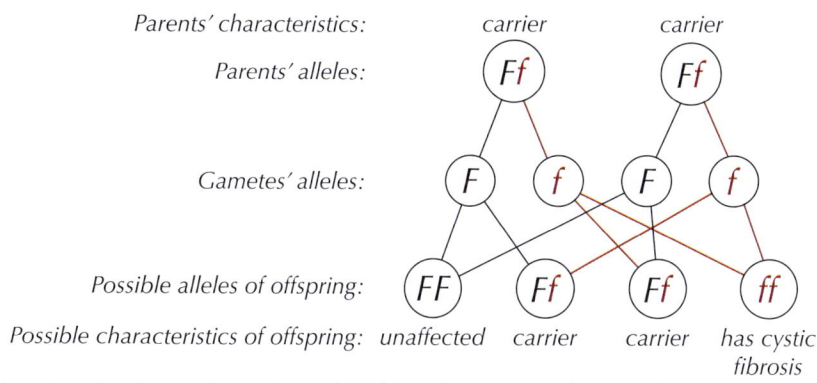
>
> | | | |
> |---|---|---|
> | Parents' characteristics: | carrier | carrier |
> | Parents' alleles: | Ff | Ff |
> | Gametes' alleles: | F   f | F   f |
> | Possible alleles of offspring: | FF   Ff | Ff   ff |
> | Possible characteristics of offspring: | unaffected   carrier | carrier   has cystic fibrosis |
>
> Here is a family pedigree for a family with carriers of cystic fibrosis:

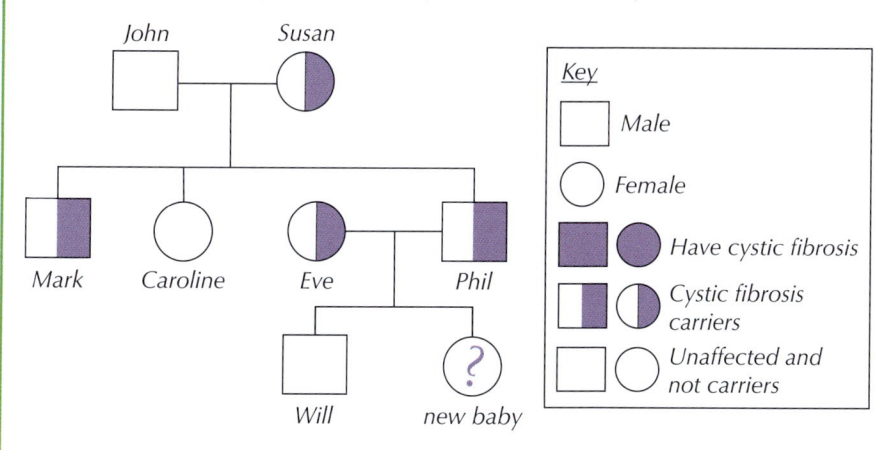

Tip: On this pedigree you can see that John and Susan are parents to Mark, Caroline and Phil. John and Susan are linked to their children by vertical lines. Eve and Phil are parents to Will and the new baby.

From the family pedigree, you can tell that:

1. The allele for cystic fibrosis isn't dominant because plenty of the family carry the allele but don't have the disorder.
2. There is a 25% chance that Eve and Phil's new baby will have the disorder and a 50% chance that it will be a carrier, as Eve and Phil are carriers but are unaffected.

The case of the new baby is just the same as in the genetic diagram above — the baby could be unaffected (FF), a carrier (Ff) or have cystic fibrosis (ff).

Exam Tip
A good way to work out a family pedigree is to write the genotype of each person onto it.

Topic 3b Genetic Diagrams and Inheritance

Exam Tip
Sometimes you can't tell a person's genotype from looking straight at the family pedigree and the key — you might need to do a bit of detective work and figure out the genotypes of other people first.

The probability of each outcome can also be expressed as a ratio — 1 : 2 : 1 for unaffected : carrier : disorder.

Practice Questions — Application

Q1 Charlotte has some guinea pigs with rough coats and some guinea pigs with smooth coats. The allele for a rough coat is represented by 'R'. The allele for a smooth coat is represented by 'r'. The rough coat allele is dominant to the smooth coat allele. She crosses a rough coated guinea pig (RR) with a smooth coated guinea pig (rr). Here is an incomplete genetic diagram of the cross:

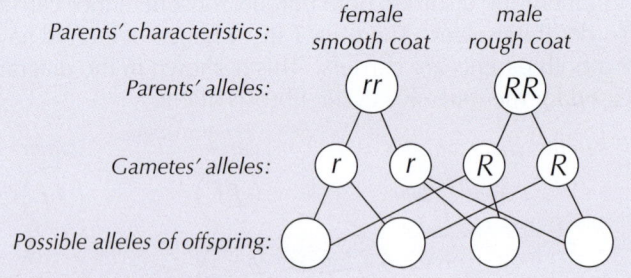

Parents' characteristics: female smooth coat / male rough coat
Parents' alleles: rr / RR
Gametes' alleles: r r R R
Possible alleles of offspring:

a) Complete the diagram to show the possible alleles of the offspring.

b) What type of coat will the offspring have?

Q2 The family pedigree below shows the inheritance of the inherited disorder polydactyly in a family.

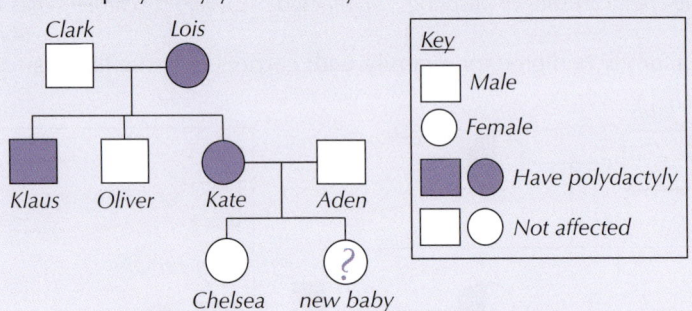

Clark — Lois
Klaus, Oliver, Kate — Aden
Chelsea, new baby (?)

Key:
■ Male
○ Female
■ ● Have polydactyly
□ ○ Not affected

Tip: Polydactyly is an inherited disorder that results in a person being born with extra fingers or toes.

Using the family pedigree, answer the following questions:

a) The allele for polydactyly is dominant. How can you tell this from the family pedigree?

b) If the new baby was a girl with polydactyly, what symbol would she have on the family tree?

For the following questions, use 'D' to represent the allele for polydactyly and 'd' to represent the allele for an unaffected person.

c) Give the genotype of the following individuals:
   i) Clark   ii) Kate

d) Kate and Aden are having a baby. Draw a Punnett square to show the inheritance of polydactyly from Kate and Aden. What is the probability the new baby will have polydactyly?

Topic 3b Genetic Diagrams and Inheritance

3. Sex Determination

Our sex is determined by just two chromosomes, X and Y.

Sex chromosomes

There are 23 pairs of chromosomes in every human body cell. Of these, 22 are matched pairs of chromosomes — these just control your characteristics. The 23rd pair are labelled XY or XX. They're the two chromosomes that decide your sex — whether you turn out male or female.

> **Males** have an **X** and a **Y** chromosome: **XY**
> The Y chromosome causes male characteristics.
>
> **Females** have **two X** chromosomes: **XX**
> The XX combination allows female characteristics to develop.

Gametes are haploid (see p.27) so they only contain one sex chromosome. All eggs have one X chromosome, but a sperm can have either an X chromosome or a Y chromosome.

Sex determination and genetic diagrams

At fertilisation, the sperm fertilises the egg, and the chromosomes from the gametes combine, forming a new individual with the correct number of chromosomes (see page 72). Whether the individual is male or female depends on whether the sperm that fertilises an egg carries an X or a Y chromosome — this is sex determination.

Sex determination can be shown using genetic diagrams like the ones you saw on pages 81-84. These diagrams show the inheritance of chromosomes not alleles, but they work in the same way.

Learning Objectives:
- Be able to describe how the sex of offspring is determined at fertilisation, using genetic diagrams.

Specification Reference 3.15

Figure 1: *The X and Y chromosomes. The Y chromosome is smaller.*

Example

The Punnett square in Figure 2 shows sex determination. The pairs of letters in the middle show the possible combinations of chromosomes in the offspring.

	X	X
X	XX	XX
Y	XY	XY

female gametes (eggs) — top
male gametes (sperm) — side
possible chromosomes in offspring...

...two males (XY) and two females (XX).

Figure 2: *Punnett square showing sex determination.*

Tip: You can construct genetic diagrams to show sex determination in the same way as for monohybrid inheritance (see p.84). Just put the possible chromosomes from each gamete where you would normally put the alleles from each gamete. Then fill in the possible combinations of the offspring — XX or XY.

Figure 3 on the next page is another type of genetic diagram showing sex determination. The possible chromosomes in the offspring are shown in the bottom circles.

Tip: Remember, one gamete from the female combines with one gamete from the male during fertilisation. It's quite easy to get confused, so check you aren't drawing lines that put both the male's gametes or both the female's gametes into the same circle.

Tip: Only one of these possible combinations would actually happen for any one offspring.

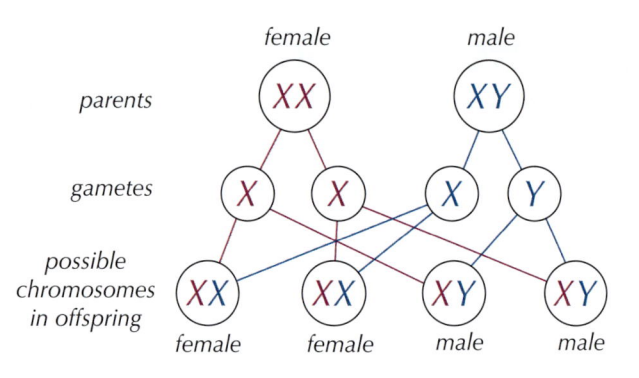

Figure 3: *Genetic diagram showing sex determination.*

Both Figure 2 and Figure 3 show two XX results and two XY results, so there's an equal probability of getting a boy or a girl. This can be written as a 50:50 ratio, which is the same as 1:1. Alternatively, you could say the probability of getting a boy is 1 in 2, 50%, 0.5 or ½.

Don't forget that this 50:50 ratio is only a probability at each pregnancy. If you had four children, they could all be boys.

Practice Questions — Fact Recall

Q1 How many of the 23 pairs of human chromosomes determine sex?

Q2 True or False? All sperm cells carry the Y chromosome.

Practice Questions — Application

Rachael and her husband Luca are expecting their first child. The incomplete genetic diagram below shows sex inheritance.

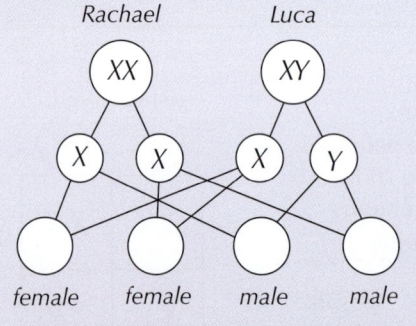

Q1 Copy and complete the genetic diagram above to show the possible combinations of sex chromosomes that the baby could have.

Q2 What is the probability that their child will be a boy?

Q3 Draw a Punnett square to show the possible combinations of sex chromosomes that Rachael and Luca's baby could have.

4. Variation

These pages are all about the differences between you, me, and well... everyone else really. It's fascinating stuff...

What is variation?

Different species look... well... different — my dog definitely doesn't look like a daisy. But even organisms of the same species will usually look at least slightly different — e.g. in a room full of people you'll see different colour hair, individually shaped noses, a variety of heights, etc.

These differences are called the variation within a species — and there are two types of variation: **genetic variation** and **environmental variation**.

Genetic variation

Genetic variation within a species is caused by organisms having different alleles (versions of genes) which can lead to differences in phenotype (the characteristics an organism displays).

Genetic variation can be caused by new alleles arising through mutations (see next page). Sexual reproduction also causes genetic variation since it results in alleles being combined in lots of different ways in offspring (see page 73). Sexual reproduction means no two members of a species are genetically identical (apart from identical twins).

Some characteristics are determined only by genes.

> **Examples**
> - Flower colour in violets.
> - Eye colour.
> - Blood group.
> - Inherited disorders (e.g. haemophilia or cystic fibrosis).

Environmental variation

The environment that organisms live and grow in also causes differences between members of the same species — this is called environmental variation. Environmental variation covers a wide range of differences — from losing your toes in a piranha attack, to getting a suntan, to having yellow leaves and so on. Basically, any difference that has been caused by the conditions something lives in is an environmental variation.

Environmental variations in phenotype are also known as **acquired characteristics**. They're characteristics that organisms acquire (get) during their lifetimes.

Learning Objectives:
- Be able to describe the causes of variation that influence phenotype, including:
    - genetic variation — different characteristics as a result of mutation and sexual reproduction;
    - environmental variation — different characteristics caused by an organism's environment (acquired characteristics).
- Know that there is usually extensive genetic variation within a population of a species and that this arises through mutations.
- Know that most genetic mutations have no effect on the phenotype, some mutations have a small effect on the phenotype and, rarely, a single mutation will significantly affect the phenotype.

Specification References 3.20, 3.22, 3.23

Figure 1: Identical twins have exactly the same genes, which is why they look so alike.

Tip: Plants are strongly influenced by environmental factors, e.g. sunlight, moisture level, temperature and soil mineral content.

> **Example**
>
> A plant grown on a nice sunny windowsill would grow luscious and green.
>
> The same plant grown in darkness would grow tall and spindly and its leaves would turn yellow — these are acquired characteristics (environmental variations).

Genetic and environmental variation

Most characteristics are determined by a mixture of genetic and environmental factors.

> **Examples**
>
> - Height — the maximum height that an animal or plant could grow to is determined by its genes. But whether it actually grows that tall depends on its environment, e.g. how much food it gets.
>
> - Intelligence — one theory is that although your maximum possible IQ might be determined by your genes, whether or not you get to it depends on your environment, e.g. your upbringing and school life.
>
> - Health — some people are more likely to get certain diseases (such as cancer or heart disease) because of their genes. But lifestyle also affects the risk, e.g. whether you smoke or how much junk food you eat.

Tip: Environmental factors aren't just the physical things around you. They can include things like the way you were brought up too.

Mutations

Occasionally a gene may mutate. A mutation is a random change in the base sequence of an organism's DNA.

Mutations mean that the gene is altered, which produces an allele, or a different version of the gene. As the gene codes for the sequence of amino acids that make up a protein, gene mutations sometimes lead to changes in the protein that it codes for.

Most mutations have very little or no effect on the protein that the gene codes for. Some will change it to such a small extent that its function is unaffected. This means that most mutations have no effect on an organism's phenotype — they are neutral.

Tip: Mutations in DNA happen at random — it doesn't matter whether or not they'll result in a beneficial change.

> **Examples**
>
> - A mutation to a gene may produce an allele that codes for the same sequence of amino acids, so the same protein is produced.
> - The mutation may cause a change in one amino acid in a protein, but the change has no effect on the protein's function.

There tends to be a lot of genetic variation within a population of a species. This is mostly due to neutral mutations.

Topic 3b Genetic Diagrams and Inheritance

Some mutations have a small influence on the organism's phenotype — they alter the individual's characteristics but only slightly.

> **Example**
>
> Some characteristics, e.g. eye colour, are controlled by more than one gene. A mutation in one of the genes may change the eye colour a bit, but the difference might not be huge.

Very occasionally, a mutation can have a dramatic effect on phenotype. This could be because it results in the production of a protein that is so different, it can no longer carry out its function.

Tip: Mutations that result in a large change in phenotype are very rare.

> **Example**
>
> The genetic disorder, cystic fibrosis, is caused by a mutation that has a huge effect on phenotype. The gene codes for a protein that controls the movement of salt and water into and out of cells. However, the protein produced by the mutated gene doesn't work properly. This leads to the production of thick, sticky mucus in the lungs and digestive system, which can make it difficult to breathe and to digest food.

Tip: If the environment changes, and the new phenotype makes an individual more suited to the new environment, it can become common throughout the species relatively quickly by natural selection (see p.97).

New combinations of alleles may also interact with each other to produce new phenotypes.

Practice Questions — Fact Recall

Q1 True or False? Only differences in genes can cause variation within a population.

Q2 a) What is a mutation?

b) Explain why most mutations have no effect on an organism's phenotype.

Practice Questions — Application

Q1 For the plant characteristics below, say whether they are determined by genes only, the environment only, or both.

a) stem height

b) spots caused by a fungus

Q2 Identical twins have exactly the same genes. Non-identical twins don't. Studies have shown that:

- identical twins tend to have more similar IQs than non-identical twins (Study 1).
- identical twins who are brought up together tend to have more similar IQs than identical twins who are brought up separately (Study 2).

What do the results of Studies 1 and 2 suggest about the influence of genes and the environment on IQ? Explain your answer.

Topic 3b Genetic Diagrams and Inheritance

Learning Objective:
- Be able to discuss the outcomes of the Human Genome Project and its potential applications within medicine.

Specification Reference 3.21

5. The Human Genome Project

Scientist have worked hard to identify genes within our genome that contribute to disease. This was achieved through the Human Genome Project.

Mapping the human genome

Thousands of scientists from all over the world collaborated (worked together) on the Human Genome Project. The big idea was to find every single human gene. The project officially started in 1990 and a complete map of the human genome, including the locations of around 20 500 genes, was completed in 2003.

Now that the genes have all been found, scientists are trying to figure out what they all do. So far, the project has helped to identify about 1800 genes related to disease, which has huge potential benefits for medicine (see below).

Tip: A genome is the entire set of genetic material in an organism (see p.75).

Medical applications

Understanding the human genome is a really important tool for many branches of medicine.

Prediction and prevention of disease

Many common diseases like cancers and heart disease are caused by the interaction of different genes, as well as lifestyle factors. If doctors knew what alleles predisposed people to what diseases, we could all get individually tailored advice on the best diet and lifestyle to avoid our likely problems. Doctors could also check us regularly to ensure early treatment if we do develop the diseases we're susceptible to. This could increase the chance of a full recovery.

Tip: Just because somebody has genes which make them susceptible to a disease, it does not mean that they will definitely develop it — they are just at a greater risk.

Testing and treatment for inherited disorders

Inherited disorders (e.g. cystic fibrosis) are caused by the presence of one or more faulty alleles in a person's genome. Thanks to the Human Genome Project, scientists are now able to identify the genes and alleles that are suspected of causing an inherited disorder much more quickly than they could do in the past. Once an allele that causes an inherited disorder has been identified, people can be tested for it and it may be possible to develop better treatments or even (eventually) a cure for the disease.

> **Example**
>
> Gene therapy is when a working copy of a gene is introduced into cells to treat a genetic disease. For example, research is being carried out to try to find a way to use gene therapy to treat cystic fibrosis patients.

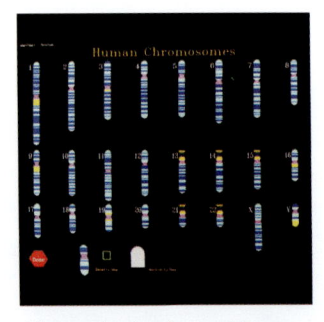

Figure 1: *Analysis of human chromosomes during the Human Genome Project.*

New and better medicines

Some alleles affect how our individual bodies will react to certain diseases and to the possible treatments for them. Scientists can use this knowledge to design new drugs that are specifically tailored to people with a certain allele. They can also determine how well an existing drug will work for an individual.

> **Example**
>
> Some breast cancer drugs are only effective in women who have certain alleles. So patients can be tested to see whether or not they will respond to a particular drug.

Genetic tests can also help determine what dosage is most appropriate for particular drugs in different patients.

> **Example**
>
> Children with leukaemia may get a certain genetic test so that doctors can prescribe the correct dosage of medicine to prevent toxic side-effects.

Tip: More generally, knowing how a disease affects us on a molecular level should make it possible to design more effective treatments with fewer side-effects.

Ethical issues raised by genetic analysis

Despite the many advantages of the Human Genome Project, the genetic analysis it has enabled could have some drawbacks.

> **Examples**
>
> - If a person knows they have alleles which make them susceptible to a particular disease, it could lead to increased stress levels. E.g. someone who knows they are susceptible to a brain disease could panic every time they get a headache (even if they never go on to develop the disease).
> - Someone who knows they carry a faulty allele could come under pressure not to have children (to prevent them potentially passing on that allele).
> - Employers and insurers could also discriminate against those who have a genetic likelihood of a disease. This could result in difficulty finding employment or getting life insurance.

Practice Questions — Application

Sarah's mother has breast cancer caused by a harmful mutation in the *BRCA1* gene. A genetic test determines that Sarah has inherited the gene, putting her at increased risk of developing breast cancer.

Q1 Suggest one advantage of Sarah having this genetic test.

Q2 Suggest two disadvantages of Sarah having this genetic test.

Topic 3b Genetic Diagrams and Inheritance

Topic 3b Checklist — Make sure you know...

Genes and Alleles

☐ That most characteristics are controlled by several genes, but some are controlled by just one gene.

☐ That all genes exist in different forms called alleles, and that if an organism has two alleles for a gene that are the same then it is homozygous. If the two alleles are different then it's heterozygous.

☐ That if an individual is heterozygous for a characteristic, the allele for the characteristic that is displayed is dominant and the other allele is recessive. You need to be homozygous recessive for a recessive characteristic to be displayed.

☐ That your genotype is the combination of alleles you have and that these alleles work at the molecular level to determine your phenotype — the characteristics that you have.

Genetic Diagrams and Family Pedigrees

☐ That monohybrid inheritance is where the alleles of a single gene control a characteristic, and that this can be explained using genetic diagrams, Punnett squares and family pedigrees.

☐ How to express the results of monohybrid crosses and pedigree analysis using probabilities, ratios and percentages.

Sex Determination

☐ That the 23rd pair of chromosomes are called sex chromosomes and how these determine sex.

☐ How to use genetic diagrams to describe sex determination.

Variation

☐ That variation within a species is the differences between individuals, and that these differences are caused by genetic variation, environmental variation (acquired characteristics), or both.

☐ That there is usually a lot of genetic variation within a population of a species and that this arises through mutations in DNA and sexual reproduction.

☐ That most mutations have no effect on phenotype, some have a small effect on phenotype and a few have a big effect on phenotype.

The Human Genome Project

☐ That the work of the Human Genome Project has medical applications and what these might be.

Exam-style Questions

1 Huntington's disease is an example of an inherited disorder.
It is caused by a dominant faulty allele, which is represented by the letter 'H'.
The other allele for the gene is represented by the letter 'h'.

(a) Give the possible genotype(s) of a person with Huntington's disease.

(1 mark)

(b) A person is homozygous for the Huntington's disease allele.
Which of the following shows the person's genotype?
- A   HH
- B   hh
- C   Hh
- D   H

(1 mark)

(c) The person's parents are both heterozygous for the Huntington's disease allele.

Complete the Punnett square below to show the probability of any offspring of these two heterozygous individuals inheriting Huntington's disease.

Give the probability as a percentage.

mother's alleles

father's alleles

(2 marks)

2 Kevin and Roy are identical twins.
They have an older biological brother called Dave.

(a) Explain why Dave and Roy have the same natural hair colour, but different eye colours.

(2 marks)

(b) Roy is a much better runner than Kevin.
Suggest **one** factor that may cause this difference in sporting ability.

(1 mark)

3 Kaye and Mark are expecting a baby. They already have three daughters.

(a) State the probability that Kaye and Mark will have another baby girl.
(1 mark)

(b) Kaye has dimples in her cheeks, but Mark does not. The presence of dimples is thought to be caused by a dominant allele represented by the letter **D**. The recessive allele is represented by the letter **d**. Kaye is heterozygous for the dimples gene.
Predict the ratio of dimpled to undimpled children amongst Kaye and Mark's offspring. Draw a Punnet square to explain your answer.
(2 marks)

(c) Kaye and Mark have a baby boy.
State the chromosome that causes male characteristics.
(1 mark)

4 Family pedigrees can show the inheritance of genetic disorders, such as cystic fibrosis. **Figure 1** is a family pedigree showing the inheritance of cystic fibrosis in a family.

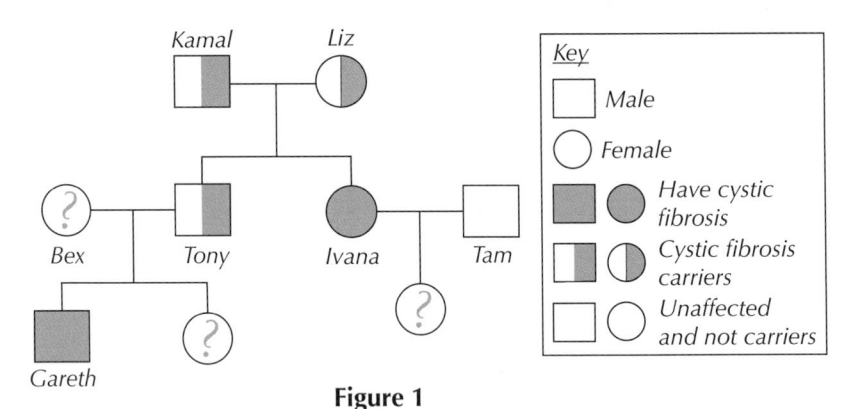

Figure 1

(a) Is Gareth heterozygous or homozygous for the cystic fibrosis allele?
Explain your answer.
(1 mark)

f represents the allele for cystic fibrosis and **F** represents the healthy allele.

(b) Bex and Tony have a child with cystic fibrosis. Bex does not have cystic fibrosis.
State the combination of alleles Bex must have for the cystic fibrosis gene.
Explain your answer.
(2 marks)

(c) Looking at the family pedigree, could Ivana and Tam have a child with cystic fibrosis?
Draw a Punnett square to explain your answer.
(2 marks)

Topic 3b Genetic Diagrams and Inheritance : Exam-style Questions

Topic 4a — Natural Selection and Evolution

1. Natural Selection and Evidence for Evolution

The very first organisms on Earth, were simple and single-celled. Evolution is how those organisms became the many, complex species we know today.

What is evolution?

Evolution is the slow and continuous change of organisms' inherited characteristics from one generation to the next. The scientist Charles Darwin came up with the theory of natural selection to explain how evolution occurs.

The theory of evolution by natural selection

Scientists have developed Darwin's theory over time, using what we now know about genetics. It works like this:

1. Individuals in a population show genetic variation — differences in their characteristics that are caused by different **alleles** (see page 89). New alleles arise through **mutations** (see page 90).

2. Things like predation, competition for resources (e.g. food, water, mates, etc.) and disease act as **selection pressures**. This means they affect an organism's chance of surviving and reproducing.

3. Those individuals with characteristics that make them better adapted to the selection pressures in their environment have a better chance of survival and so are more likely to breed successfully.

4. This means the alleles that are responsible for the useful characteristics are more likely to be passed on to the next generation.

5. However, some individuals will be less well adapted to the selection pressures in their environment and may be less able to compete. These individuals are less likely to survive and reproduce.

6. The beneficial characteristics become more common in the population over time.

Evidence for evolution — antibiotic resistance

Antibiotics are drugs that are designed to kill bacteria or prevent them from reproducing.

Like all organisms, bacteria sometimes develop random mutations in their DNA. These can create new alleles which can change the bacteria's characteristics, e.g. being less affected by a particular antibiotic.

Learning Objectives:
- Be able to explain Darwin's theory of evolution by natural selection.
- Be able to explain how the emergence of resistant organisms supports Darwin's theory of evolution including antibiotic resistance in bacteria.

Specification References 4.2, 4.3

Tip: Darwin published his theory in 1859 — over 150 years ago.

Tip: Alleles are versions of genes (see page 80).

Tip: A species that can't compete is likely to become extinct (die out).

Exam Tip
You need to learn how bacteria evolve to become antibiotic resistant for your exam.

Tip: Antibiotic-resistant strains are a problem for people who become infected with these bacteria because they aren't immune to the new strain and there is no effective treatment. 'Superbugs' (e.g. MRSA) that are resistant to most known antibiotics are getting more common.

For the bacterium, the ability to resist this antibiotic is a big advantage. In a host who's being treated to get rid of the infection, a resistant bacterium is better able to survive than a non-resistant bacterium. This means it lives for longer and reproduces many more times — and so the allele for antibiotic resistance is passed on to lots of offspring (see Figure 1).

This is how antibiotic resistance spreads and becomes more common in a population of bacteria over time.

Variation in the population — bacterium with resistance allele; bacterium without resistance allele.

Survival — Treatment with antibiotic. Resistant bacteria are more likely to survive. Non-resistant bacteria die.

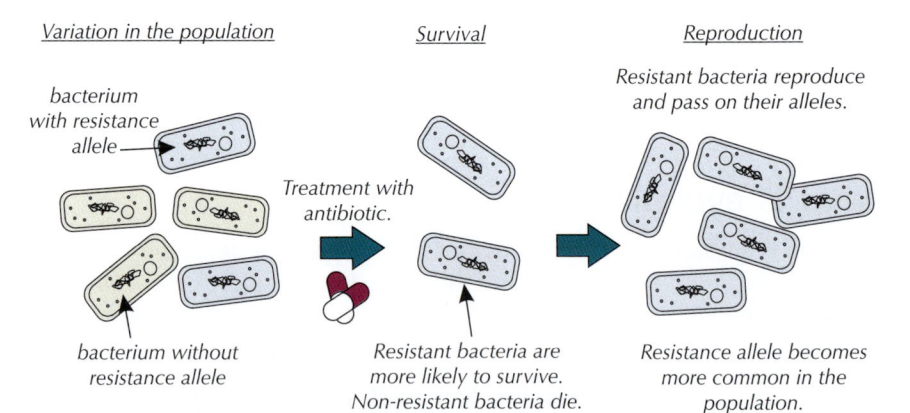

Reproduction — Resistant bacteria reproduce and pass on their alleles. Resistance allele becomes more common in the population.

Figure 1: Diagram to show how antibiotic resistance develops.

Tip: It's easy to see evolution happening in bacteria because they reproduce so rapidly.

The emergence of antibiotic resistance provides evidence for evolution because it's an example of natural selection taking place that we can observe. Antibiotic resistance makes the bacteria better adapted to an environment in which a selection pressure (antibiotics) are present. As a result, antibiotic resistance becomes more common in the population over time.

Tip: Natural selection is a theory — an accepted hypothesis (see p.2). Evidence is really important when it comes to accepting or rejecting scientific hypotheses — if there's no evidence to support a hypothesis, it won't become a theory.

Other organisms have developed resistance to chemicals that are designed to kill them too — e.g. many rats are now resistant to the chemical Warfarin™ (which used to be used to kill rats). The emergence of these organisms also provides evidence for evolution.

Evidence for evolution — fossils

A fossil is any trace of an animal or plant that lived a long time ago (usually many millions of years ago). They are most commonly found in rocks. Generally, the deeper the rock, the older the fossil.

By arranging fossils in chronological (date) order, gradual changes in organisms can be observed. This provides evidence for evolution, because it shows how species have changed and developed over billions of years. Fossils that provide evidence for human evolution are covered on pages 100-101.

Figure 2: A fossil of a dinosaur's skull.

Practice Questions — Fact Recall

Q1 How do new alleles arise in a population?

Q2 What is a selection pressure?

Q3 True or false? Organisms that are less well adapted to the selection pressures in their environment are better able to compete.

Practice Questions — Application

Q1 Glyphosate is a chemical that is commonly used in weedkillers. Some weeds have become resistant to it.

Use the theory of evolution by natural selection to explain how a population of weeds could become glyphosate-resistant.

Q2 In 1810, a herd of reindeer were taken from the Arctic to an area with a warmer climate. The herd were then left to live and reproduce in the area and were revisited in 1960. Some information about the herd is shown in the graph.

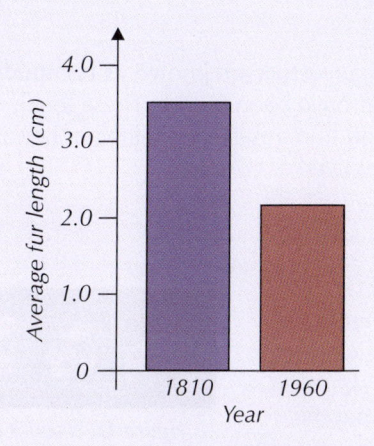

a) By roughly how much did the average fur length of the herd change between 1810 and 1960?

b) Explain this change in terms of natural selection.

Tip: To help you answer Q2 b), think about how the change in fur length might affect the reindeer in their new environment.

Learning Objective:
- Be able to describe the evidence for human evolution, based on fossils, including:
  - Ardi from 4.4 million years ago,
  - Lucy from 3.2 million years ago,
  - Leakey's discovery of fossils from 1.6 million years ago.

Specification Reference 4.4

Tip: An ancestor is a relative that lived a long time before you, e.g. your grandad's grandad. If two species have a common ancestor, it means that they are both descended from the same ancestor.

2. Evidence for Human Evolution — Fossils

Like all organisms alive today, humans have evolved from other, less complex organisms. The evidence for this comes from fossils.

Who did humans evolve from?

Evidence from fossils suggests that humans and chimpanzees evolved from a common ancestor — a species of ape that existed around 6 million years ago.

Human beings and their ancestors are known as **hominids**. Fossils of several different hominid species have been found. These fossils have characteristics that are between apes and humans — by looking at hominid fossils you can see how humans have evolved over time.

> **Example**
>
> Figure 1 shows a selection of hominid skulls. The skulls are arranged in chronological (date) order, with the oldest skulls on the left. You can see that the oldest skulls are smaller and more ape-like. The skulls gradually get more human-like as you go from left to right. The skull on the far right is 92 000 years old. It belonged to a modern human (*Homo sapiens*).

Figure 1: *A series of hominid skulls.*

Hominid fossils

Certain hominid fossils have been found that are key to our understanding of how humans evolved. These include the fossils known as "Ardi" and "Lucy", as well as the fossils discovered by the scientist Richard Leakey and his team in Kenya. You need to learn about them all for your exam.

Figure 2: *An artist's sketch of what Ardi might have looked like. Here, she's shown climbing a tree.*

"Ardi"

Ardi is a hominid fossil of the species *Ardipithecus ramidus*. She was found in Ethiopia and is 4.4 million years old. Ardi's features are a mixture of those found in humans and in apes:

- The structure of her feet suggests she climbed trees — she had an ape-like big toe to grasp branches.

- She also had long arms and short legs (more like an ape than a human).

- Her brain size was about the same as a chimpanzee's.

- But the structure of her legs suggests that she walked upright. Her hand bone structure also suggests she didn't use her hands to help her walk (like apes do).

Tip: Brain size is found by working out 'cranial capacity' — the space taken up by the brain in the skull.

Topic 4a Natural Selection and Evolution

"Lucy"

Lucy is a hominid fossil of the species *Australopithecus afarensis*. She was found in Ethiopia and is 3.2 million years old. Lucy also has a mixture of human and ape features, but she is more human-like than Ardi.

- Lucy had arched feet, more adapted to walking than climbing, and no ape-like big toe.
- The size of her arms and legs was between what you would expect to find in apes and humans.
- Her brain was slightly larger than Ardi's but still similar in size to a chimp's brain.
- The structure of Lucy's leg bones and feet suggest she walked upright, but more efficiently than Ardi.

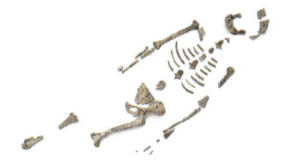

Figure 3: The remains of Lucy's skeleton. Although the remains are incomplete, other fossils of the same species have been found, which tell us more about her.

Leakey's fossils

In 1984 scientist Richard Leakey organised an expedition to Kenya to look for hominid fossils. He and his team discovered many important fossils of different *Australopithecus* and *Homo* species.

- One of their finds was "Turkana Boy" — a 1.6 million year old fossil skeleton of the species *Homo erectus*. He has a mixture of human and ape-like features, but is more human-like than Lucy.
- His short arms and long legs are much more like a human than an ape, and his brain size was much larger than Lucy's — similar to human brain size.
- The structure of his legs and feet suggest he was even better adapted to walking upright than Lucy.

Figure 4: A model made to show what Lucy might have looked like when she was alive.

A timeline of human evolution

So you know that the *Ardipithecus* and *Australopithecus* species were more ape-like, compared to the *Homo* species, which are human-like.

They can all be put on a timeline, showing how humans have evolved — see Figure 6.

Figure 5: A model made to show what Turkana Boy might have looked like.

Tip: Turkana Boy was more closely related to modern humans than either Lucy or Ardi — that's why his model looks more like us than Lucy's model does.

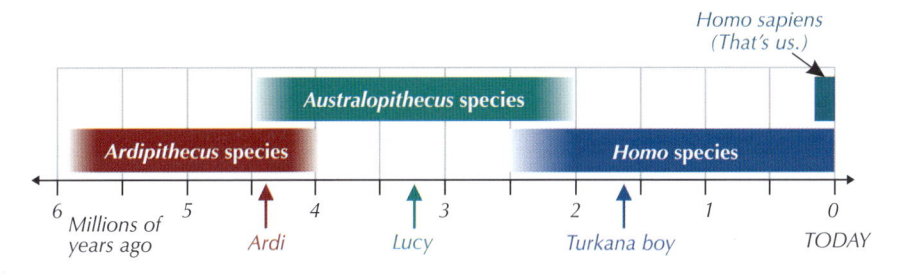

Figure 6: A timeline showing humans and their ancestors (hominids).

Topic 4a Natural Selection and Evolution

Practice Questions — Fact Recall

Q1 Briefly explain how hominid fossils provide evidence for human evolution.

Q2 True or false? The fossil "Ardi" is younger than the fossil "Lucy".

Q3 Briefly describe the fossil "Turkana Boy" discovered by Richard Leakey and his team. Include the age of the fossil.

Practice Questions — Application

Q1 For each of the fossils described below, state whether it is "Ardi", "Lucy" or Richard Leakey's "Turkana Boy".

   A This fossil is 3.2 million years old. The size of the arms and legs are in between what you would expect to find in apes and humans.

   B This fossil has long arms and short legs similar to those of an ape. It also has an ape-like big toe.

   C This fossil has short arms and long legs. The skulls suggests that the brain size was similar to a human brain size.

Q2 Put the fossils described in Q1 in age order, starting with the oldest.

Q3 A scientist finds a hominid fossil that is more recent than Lucy. How would you expect the arm and leg lengths of this fossil to compare to Lucy's?

3. Evidence for Human Evolution — Stone Tools

Learning Objective:
- Be able to describe the evidence for human evolution based on stone tools, including:
  - the development of stone tools over time;
  - how these can be dated from their environment.

Specification Reference 4.5

Fossils of hominid remains aren't the only evidence for human evolution — the tools they used also gives us clues about how we evolved.

Tool development

The different *Homo* species (see page 101) continued to evolve. You can tell this because they started using stone tools and these gradually became more complex — so their brains must have been getting larger.

Homo habilis

Homo habilis lived between 2.5 and 1.5 million years ago. They made simple stone tools called pebble tools by hitting rocks together to make sharp flakes. These could be used to scrape meat from bones or crack bones open.

Homo erectus

Homo erectus lived between 2 and 0.3 million years ago. They sculpted rocks into shapes to produce more complex tools like simple hand-axes. These could be used to hunt, dig, chop and scrape meat from bones.

Homo neanderthalensis

Homo neanderthalensis lived between 300 000 and 25 000 years ago. They made even more complex tools. There is evidence that they used flint tools, with sharp, pointed edges, and wooden spears.

Figure 1: *A selection of flint tools.*

Homo sapiens

Homo sapiens are modern humans. The first *Homo sapiens* appeared about 200 000 years ago. By this point flint tools were widely used. More complex pointed tools, including fish hooks, needles and arrowheads appeared around 50 000 years ago.

Some of these developments are summarised in Figure 2.

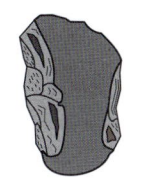

A simple pebble tool made by Homo habilis.

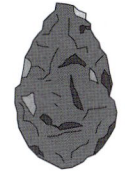

A sculpted hand axe made by Homo erectus.

A pointed flint arrowhead made by Homo sapiens.

Figure 2: *A diagram to show how stone tools have increased in complexity over time.*

Tip: Flint is a type of hard, sedimentary rock. It can be used to make tools because it splits into thin layers, with a sharp edge (called flakes) when struck with a hammer or other similar object. Flint tools are more difficult to make than, e.g. a simple pebble tool.

Exam Tip
You don't need to learn the names of the different hominid species for your exam, but you might see them used in exam questions — don't be thrown by it.

Dating stone tools and fossils

When an ancient stone tool or hominid fossil (see page 100) is found, scientists need to be able to work out how old it is. There are several different ways they can try to do this. These include:

- Looking at the structural features of the tool or fossil. For example, simpler tools are likely to be older than more complex tools.

- Using **stratigraphy** — the study of rock layers. For a tool or fossil to be found in a rock layer, it must have been present at the time the layer was formed. Older rock layers are normally found below younger layers, so tools or fossils in deeper layers are usually older — see Figure 3.

Tip: Dating tools and fossils isn't always very accurate, e.g. rock layers can move over time.

Most recent fossils likely to be found in this layer.

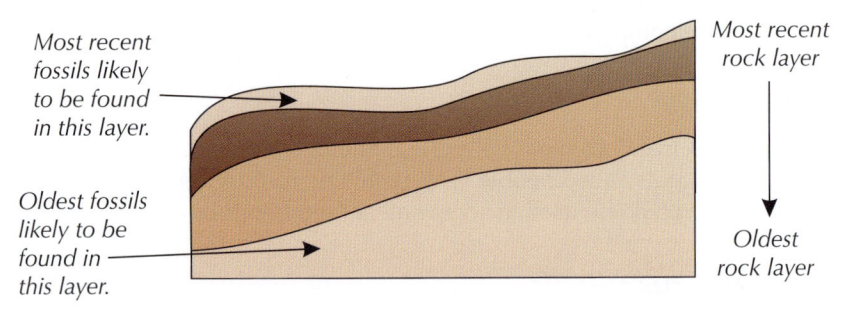

Most recent rock layer

Oldest fossils likely to be found in this layer.

Oldest rock layer

Figure 3: A diagram to show how stratigraphy works.

- Stone tools are often found with carbon-containing material, e.g. a wooden handle. A process called carbon-14 dating can be used to date this material. Carbon-14 dating works on the basis that all carbon-based material contains a small amount of a radioactive form of carbon called ^{14}C and that the amount of ^{14}C decreases over time as it decays. Carbon-14 dating is a form of radiometric dating and other methods of radiometric dating can be used to date the rocks that tools or fossils are found in. These methods include potassium-argon and uranium-lead dating.

Tip: Carbon-14 dating only works to date carbon-containing material that's around 70 000 years old or less. Both potassium-argon and uranium-lead dating can be used to date materials that are billions of years old.

Practice Questions — Application

Q1 Three stone tools are shown below.

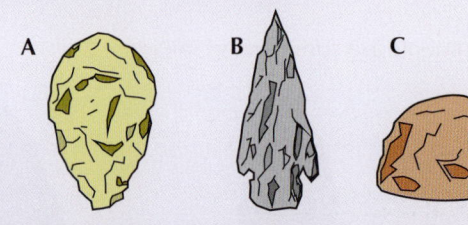

A   B   C

a) Using only the structural features of the tools, put the tools in the most likely order of age, starting with the oldest.

b) Give reasons for your answer to part a).

c) Which tool is most likely to have been made by modern humans?

d) The tool labelled A was found in a layer of rock above the tool labelled C. Does this support or contradict your answer to part a)? Explain your answer.

Topic 4a Natural Selection and Evolution

4. Classification

Classification means sorting things into groups — like organisms, for example. The way in which we classify organisms has changed over time and with advances in scientific knowledge and technology.

Learning Objective:
- Be able to describe how genetic analysis has led to the suggestion of the three domains rather than the five kingdoms classification method.

Specification Reference 4.7

Five kingdom classification

Traditionally, organisms were classified according to similarities and differences in their observable characteristics, i.e. things you can see (like how many legs something has). As technology improved, this included things you can see with a microscope, e.g. cell structure.

These characteristics were used to classify organisms in the five kingdom classification system. In this system, living things are first divided into five groups called kingdoms. These are:

- Animals — fish, mammals, reptiles, etc.
- Plants — grasses, trees, etc.
- Fungi — mushrooms and toadstools, yeasts, mould.
- Prokaryotes — all single-celled organisms without a nucleus (e.g. bacteria).
- Protists — eukaryotic single-celled organisms, e.g. algae.

The kingdoms are then subdivided into smaller and smaller groups that have common features — phylum, class, order, family, genus, species.

The five kingdom classification method is illustrated in Figure 1.

Tip: All eukaryotic organisms have a nucleus in their cells. There's more on eukayotic and prokaryotic organisms on pages 23-24.

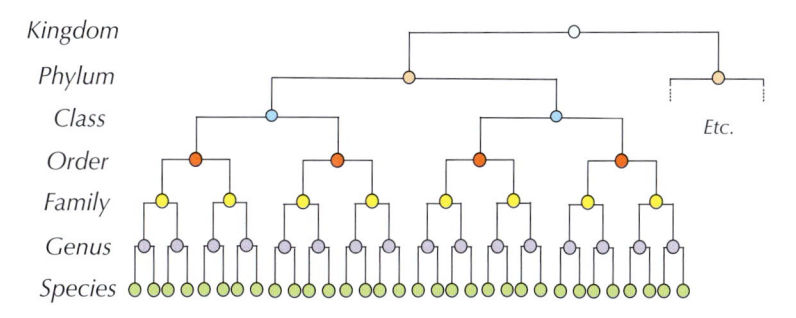

Figure 1: Diagram to show the five kingdom system of classification.

Three domain classification

The five kingdom classification system is still used, but it's now a bit out of date.

Over time, technology has developed further and our understanding of things like biochemical processes and genetics has increased. For example, we are now able to determine the sequence of DNA bases in different organisms' genes and compare them — the more similar the sequence of a gene, the more closely related the organisms. Scientists are also able to compare RNA sequences in a similar way.

Tip: It's the sequence of DNA bases in a gene that codes for a protein. In order to make proteins, the code in DNA is first copied over into another molecule called RNA. The RNA has a complementary base sequence to DNA.

Tip: More closely related species will have more classification groups in common. E.g. humans and apes share all the same classification groups down to family, but humans and mice only share them down to class — they are not part of the same order or family.

> **Example**
>
> The diagram below shows part of the DNA base sequence for a particular protein in found in three different species.
>
> Species A: ATTGTCTGATTGGTGCTAGTCGTCGATGCTAGGATCG
>
> Species B: ATTGTATGATTGGTGCTAGTCGGCGATGCTAGGATCG
>
> Species C: ATTGATTGAAAGGAGCTACTCGTAGATATAAGGAGGT
>
> There are 13 differences between the base sequences in species A and C, but only 2 differences between the base sequences in species A and B. This suggests that species A and B are more closely related than A and C.

Genetic analysis led to a bit of a rethink about the way organisms are classified and to the proposal of the three domain system of classification by a scientist called Carl Woese.

Using RNA sequencing, Woese found that some members of the Prokaryote kingdom were not as closely related as first thought. He proposed that this kingdom should be split into two groups called Archaea and Bacteria. Organisms in the Archaea domain look similar to bacteria but are actually quite different (as their DNA and RNA sequences show). The Bacteria domain contains "true bacteria" — for example *E. coli* and *Chlamydia*.

Tip: Archaea were first found in extreme places such as hot springs and salt lakes.

In fact, Woese suggested that all organisms should first be divided into three large groups called domains. Archaea and Bacteria are two of these domains. The third domain is Eukarya — all eukaryotic organisms are in this domain.

The three domains are then subdivided into smaller groups used in the five kingdom classification system (beginning with kingdom and finishing with species). The three domain system of classification is summarised in Figure 2.

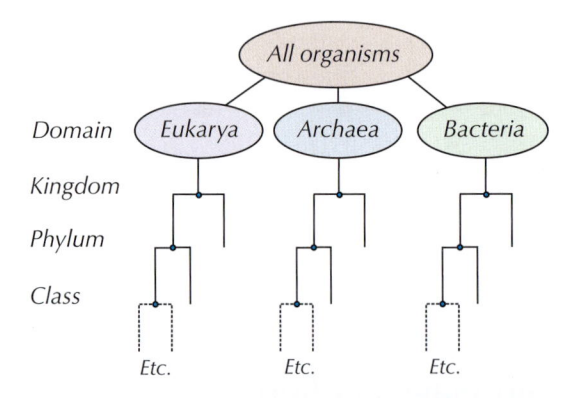

Figure 2: Diagram to show the three domain system of classification.

Practice Questions — Fact Recall

Q1 What is the smallest group in the five kingdom classification system?
  A kingdom   B class   C species   D genus

Q2 Explain how the three domain classification system was developed.

Q3 Name each of the three domains.

Topic 4a Natural Selection and Evolution

Topic 4a Checklist — Make sure you know...

Natural Selection and Evidence for Evolution

☐ How to explain Darwin's theory of evolution by natural selection. Genetic variation in a population gives some organisms a survival advantage over others when faced with certain selection pressures. The better adapted organisms are more likely to survive, reproduce and pass on the alleles that control their advantageous characteristic(s) to their offspring.

☐ How the spread of antibiotic resistance in bacterial populations provides evidence for evolution.

Evidence for Human Evolution — Fossils

☐ That "Ardi" (4.4 million years old) and "Lucy" (3.2 million years old) are fossils of human ancestors, as are the fossils discovered by Richard Leakey (for example, "Turkana Boy", which is 1.6 million years old).

☐ How Ardi, Lucy and Leakey's fossils (e.g. Turkana Boy) provide evidence for the evolution of humans from an ape ancestor.

Evidence for Human Evolution — Stone Tools

☐ That human ancestors used stone tools, which became more complex over time, providing evidence to suggest that these ancestors were evolving (and their brain size was increasing).

☐ How stone tools and fossils can be dated by their structural features and by their environment — for example, by studying the rock layers in which the tools and fossils were found or by carbon-14 dating any carbon-containing material the tools and fossils were found with.

Classification

☐ How advances in DNA and RNA sequencing led to the proposal of the three domain system of classification (in which prokaryotic organisms are split into the two separate domains of Archaea and Bacteria) instead of the five kingdom classification system.

Exam-style Questions

1   **Figure 1** shows a stone hand axe from South Africa that's about 1.5 million years old.

Figure 1

(a)   Describe **one** way in which scientists could have determined the age of the hand axe in **Figure 1** from its surroundings.

(1 mark)

(b)   "Lucy" is a fossil of the species *Australopithecus afarensis*.

    (i)   Approximately how much older is "Lucy" than the hand axe in **Figure 1**?
         A   0.1 million years
         B   1.2 million years
         C   1.7 million years
         D   2.9 million years

(1 mark)

    (ii)   When she was alive, Lucy is not likely to have used tools like the one in **Figure 1**. Explain why.

(2 marks)

2*   **Figure 2** shows a type of snake called a Sinaloan milk snake.

The milk snake is relatively harmless, but it has evolved to have a very similar pattern and colouring to the deadly poisonous coral snake, which lives in the same environment. The coral snake's colouring warns predators that it is dangerous to eat.

Figure 2

Using the idea of natural selection, explain how the milk snake may have evolved to have a similar colouring to the coral snake.

(6 marks)

| Topic 4b | Genetic Modification |

1. Selective Breeding

Selective breeding is all about getting the characteristics you want in animals and plants.

What is selective breeding?

Selective breeding is when humans artificially select the plants or animals that are going to breed so that the genes for particular characteristics remain in the population. Organisms are selectively bred to develop features that are useful or attractive:

Examples
- Animals that produce more meat or milk.
- Crops with disease resistance.
- Dogs with a good, gentle temperament.
- Plants that produce bigger fruit.

The process of selective breeding

This is the basic process involved in selective breeding:

1. From your existing stock, select the ones which have the characteristics you're after.
2. Breed them with each other.
3. Select the best of the offspring, and breed them together.
4. Continue this process over several generations, and the desirable trait gets stronger and stronger. Eventually, all the offspring will have the characteristic.

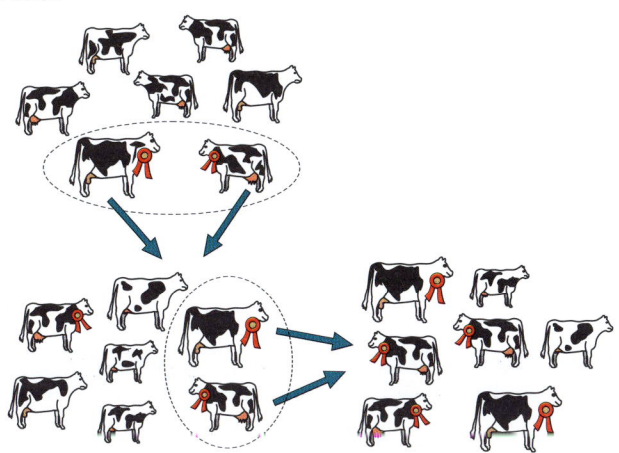

Figure 1: *Diagram showing the best offspring being selectively bred together over many generations — the desirable trait becomes more common.*

Learning Objectives:
- Be able to explain selective breeding and its impact on food plants and domesticated animals.
- Be able to evaluate the benefits and risks of selective breeding in modern agriculture and medicine, including practical and ethical implications.

Specification References 4.8, 4.14

Tip: Selective breeding is also known as 'artificial selection'.

Exam Tip
You could be asked how an organism would be selectively bred for a characteristic you've not come across before. Don't worry — the general process would still be exactly the same.

Selective breeding is nothing new — people have been doing it for thousands of years. It's how we ended up with edible crops from wild plants and how we got domesticated animals like cows and dogs.

Uses of selective breeding

In agriculture (farming), selective breeding can be used to improve yields (the amount of food a crop or some livestock produce).

> **Example**
>
> **Genetic variation** (see page 89) means that some cattle will have better characteristics for producing meat than others (e.g. a larger size).
>
> To improve meat yields, a farmer could select the cows and bulls with these characteristics and breed them together. After doing this, and selecting the best of the offspring for several generations, the farmer would get cows with a very high meat yield.

Figure 2: *The Belgian Blue breed of cow has been produced by selective breeding to produce lots of meat.*

Tip: Selective breeding can be used to improve yields with plants too, e.g. it can be used to increase the amount of grain produced by a cereal crop.

Selective breeding can also be used in medical research.

> **Example**
>
> In several studies investigating the reasons behind alcoholism, rats have been bred with either a strong preference for alcohol or a weak preference for alcohol. This has allowed researchers to compare the differences between the two different types of rats, including differences in their behaviour and in the way that their brains work.

Reducing the gene pool

The main problem with selective breeding is that it reduces the gene pool — the number of different alleles (forms of a gene) in a population. This is because the farmer keeps breeding from the "best" animals or plants — which are all closely related. This is known as **inbreeding**.

Inbreeding can cause health problems because there's more chance of the organisms inheriting harmful genetic defects when the gene pool is limited. Some dog breeds are particularly susceptible to certain defects because of inbreeding (e.g. pugs often have breathing problems). This leads to ethical considerations — particularly if animals are deliberately bred to have negative characteristics for medical research.

There can also be serious problems if a new disease appears. There's not much variation in the population, so there's less chance of resistance alleles being present. All the stock are closely related to each other, so if one of them is going to be killed by a new disease, the others are also likely to succumb to it.

Practice Questions — Fact Recall

Q1 Outline the process of selective breeding.

Q2 Explain one problem associated with selective breeding.

2. Genetic Engineering

Humans are able to change an organism's genes through a process called genetic engineering. It's really quite clever...

What is genetic engineering?

The basic idea of genetic engineering is to transfer a gene from one organism's genome into another organism's genome, in order to introduce a desirable characteristic. The organism into which the gene has been transferred is known as a **genetically modified** (**GM**) **organism** (or GMO).

Uses of genetic engineering

Scientists use genetic engineering to do all sorts of things:

> **Examples**
>
> - Bacteria have been genetically modified to produce human insulin that can be used to treat diabetes (see next page).
> - GM crops have had their genes modified, e.g. to improve the size and quality of their fruit, or make them resistant to disease, insects and herbicides (chemicals used to kill weeds).
> - Sheep and cows have been genetically engineered to produce useful human proteins in their milk, e.g. antibodies used in therapy to treat illnesses like arthritis, some types of cancer and multiple sclerosis.

How genetic engineering works [Higher]

This is the process involved in genetic engineering:

1. The DNA (gene) that is going to be transferred is cut out with a **restriction enzyme**. Restriction enzymes recognise specific sequences of DNA and cut the DNA at these points. The cut leaves one of the DNA strands with unpaired bases — this is called a "**sticky end**".

2. The same restriction enzyme is used to cut open the **vector** DNA. A vector is something used to transfer DNA into a cell. It could be a plasmid (a small, circular molecule of DNA that can be transferred between bacteria) or a virus.

3. The vector DNA and the DNA you're inserting are left with complementary (matching) sticky ends. They are mixed together with **ligase** enzymes. Ligase joins the sticky ends together to produce recombinant DNA (two different bits of DNA stuck together).

4. The recombinant DNA (i.e. the vector containing the new DNA) is inserted into other cells, e.g. bacteria.

5. The cells can now use the inserted gene to make the protein it codes for.

Learning Objectives:
- Be able to describe genetic engineering as a process which involves modifying the genome of an organism to introduce desirable characteristics.
- [H] Be able to describe the main stages of genetic engineering including the use of: restriction enzymes, ligase, sticky ends, vectors.
- Be able to evaluate the benefits and risks of genetic engineering in modern agriculture and medicine, including practical and ethical implications.

Specification References 4.10, 4.11, 4.14

Tip: In the future, it might be possible to do even more with genetic engineering. For example, produce animals with organs suitable for organ transplantation.

Tip: [H] Plasmids occur naturally in many bacterial cells. See page 24 for more. Viruses naturally insert DNA into the organisms they infect.

Topic 4b Genetic Modification

> **Example — Higher**
>
> The human insulin gene can be inserted into bacteria. The bacteria will then produce human insulin. This process is shown in Figure 1.
>
> *human insulin gene*
>
> 1. Restriction enzymes cut the insulin gene out. *sticky ends*
>
> *plasmid*
>
> *sticky ends*
>
> 2. The same restriction enzymes are used to cut open the plasmid.
>
> *recombinant DNA*
>
> 3. Ligase enzymes are used to join the two pieces of DNA together.
>
> 4. The recombinant DNA is inserted into bacterial cells.
>
> 5. The bacteria are grown in large numbers in a fermenter and start to produce human insulin.
>
> **Figure 1:** The steps involved in producing human insulin using genetically engineered bacteria.

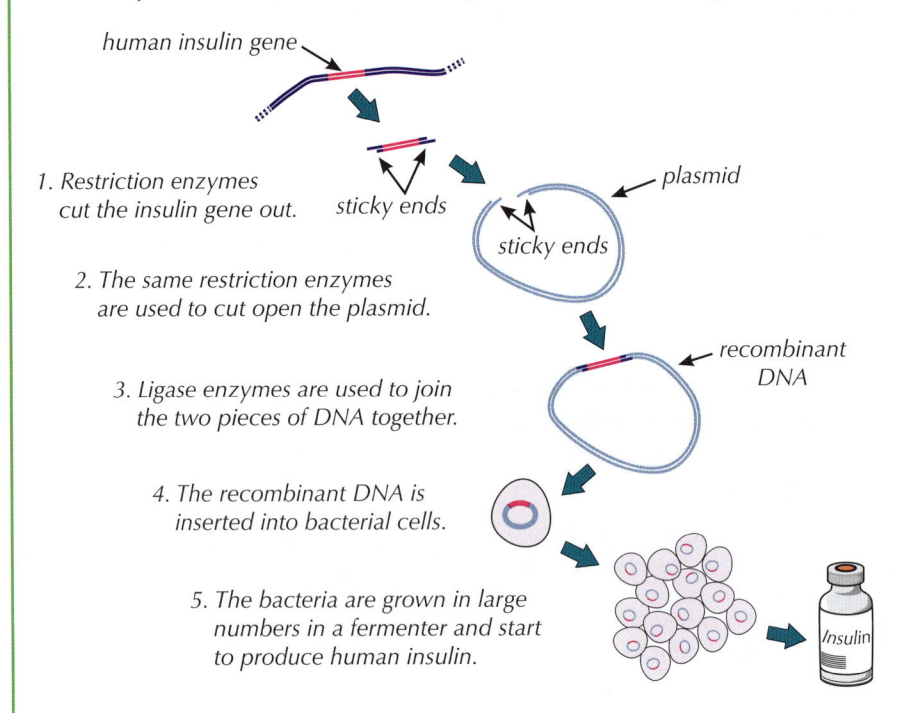

Figure 2: Genetically engineered bacteria being grown in an industrial vat.

Benefits and risks

Genetic engineering has a lot of benefits.

> **Examples**
>
> - In agriculture, genetically modifying crops to be herbicide-resistant means farmers can spray their crops to kill weeds, without affecting the crop itself. This can increase crop yield (the amount of food a crop produces).
> - In medicine, genetically modifying bacteria has allowed human insulin for the treatment of diabetes to be produced relatively easily and cheaply in large quantities.

Tip: Insulin from pigs and cows used to be used to treat diabetes. However, some people have an adverse reaction to these animal insulins. They can also be difficult to obtain in large quantities.

However, there are ethical concerns about the genetic engineering of animals. It can be hard to predict what effect modifying its genome will have on the organism — many genetically modified embryos don't survive and some genetically modified animals suffer from health problems later in life.

There are also practical concerns about growing genetically modified crops. One is that transplanted genes may get out into the environment, e.g. a herbicide resistance gene may be picked up by weeds, creating a new 'superweed' variety. Another concern is that genetically modified crops could adversely affect food chains — or even human health.

Topic 4b Genetic Modification

Practice Questions — Fact Recall

Q1 What is genetic engineering?

Q2 What is the role of each of the following in genetic engineering:
    a) restriction enzymes?   b) ligases?   c) vectors?

Practice Question — Application

Q1 There is a vaccine that protects against the liver disease hepatitis B. Like most vaccines it is injected using a needle (which must be sterilised). The vaccine must also be transported and stored in a refrigerator, which can be expensive.

Scientists are working on genetically modifying corn plants to produce the hepatitis B vaccine in their corn kernels. The kernels could be made into a foodstuff which is eaten, and which would not need to be refrigerated.

a) Suggest and explain two advantages of the corn-based hepatitis B vaccine compared to a normal hepatitis B vaccine, particularly in developing countries where hepatitis B is common.

b) Suggest one concern people may have about growing these genetically engineered corn plants.

Exam Tip
If you're asked to 'suggest' an answer in the exam, you're not expected to already know the correct answer. You're expected to use your scientific knowledge to put forward a sensible idea.

Topic 4b Checklist — Make sure you know...

Selective Breeding

- [ ] That selective breeding involves humans selecting organisms to breed over several generations, so that a desirable characteristic gets stronger.
- [ ] That selective breeding has resulted in the edible crops and domesticated animals we have today.
- [ ] Some of the benefits and risks of selective breeding in agriculture and medicine, including ethical implications (e.g. the health problems caused by inbreeding in selectively bred animals) and practical implications (e.g. the risks associated with reducing the gene pool).

Genetic Engineering

- [ ] That during genetic engineering, a gene is transferred from one organism's genome into another organism's genome, in order to introduce a desirable characteristic.
- [ ] H The process of genetic engineering, including: the use of restriction enzymes to cut out the desired gene and cut open the vector DNA leaving unpaired bases (sticky ends), the use of ligase enzymes to join the gene to the vector DNA and the use of that vector (e.g. a plasmid or virus) to transfer the desired gene into other cells (e.g. bacteria).
- [ ] Some of the benefits and risks of genetic engineering in agriculture and medicine, including ethical implications (e.g. genetically engineered animals may suffer from health problems) and practical implications (e.g. genes from genetically engineered crops may get out into the environment).

Exam-style Questions

1 Tomato plants were among the first crop plants to be genetically engineered. Which of the following is an example of genetic engineering?

    A Tomato plants being bred over several generations to produce large fruit.
    B Tomato plants being grown on an artificial growth medium.
    C A gene for disease resistance being transferred to tomato plants from another plant species.
    D Tomato plants being grown without the use of chemical pesticides.

(1 mark)

2 A farmer is using selective breeding to try to produce a type of wheat that is resistant to a particular disease.

  (a) (i) Suggest **one** benefit to the farmer of growing disease-resistant wheat.

(1 mark)

    (ii) Suggest and explain **one** advantage to the farmer of using selective breeding to produce the wheat, rather than genetic engineering.

(2 marks)

  (b) Describe how the farmer could produce disease-resistant wheat using selective breeding.

(4 marks)

  (c) Suggest and explain **one** problem that could be caused by the selective breeding of wheat that is resistant to a particular disease.

(2 marks)

3 Factor VIII is a human protein which helps blood to clot. People with haemophilia A do not make enough functional factor VIII and their blood does not clot properly.

Non-human animal cells can be genetically engineered to produce human factor VIII. The cells can then be grown and the factor VIII harvested for the treatment of people with haemophilia A.

  (a) Describe how non-human animal cells could be genetically engineered to produce human factor VIII.

(4 marks)

  (b) Suggest **one** advantage of genetically engineering animal cells in isolation, over genetically engineering whole animals to produce the factor VIII protein.

(1 mark)

Topic 5a — Health and Disease

1. Introduction to Health and Disease

Diseases are one cause of poor health. Sometimes, different diseases interact, leading to further health complications that don't appear related at first.

Diseases

A disease is a condition where part of an organism doesn't function properly. Diseases are often responsible for causing ill health, but being healthy is not just about being free from disease. The World Health Organisation (the WHO) has developed a definition for health:

> Health is a state of complete physical, mental and social well-being, and not merely the absence of disease or infirmity.

Diseases can be communicable or non-communicable.

Communicable diseases

Communicable diseases are those that can spread between individuals. They are caused by things like bacteria, viruses, parasites and fungi (see next page). They're sometimes described as contagious or infectious diseases. Tuberculosis and malaria are examples of communicable diseases. There's more about them on pages 117-119.

Non-Communicable diseases

Non-communicable diseases are those that can't spread between individuals. They generally last for a long time and get worse slowly. Asthma, cancer and coronary heart disease are examples of non-communicable diseases. See pages 135-137 for more on non-communicable diseases.

Susceptibility to other diseases

If you are affected by one disease, it could make you more susceptible to others — your body may become weakened by the disease, so it's less able to fight off others.

Example

People who have problems with their immune system, e.g. AIDS patients (see p.119), have an increased chance of suffering from communicable diseases such as influenza (flu), because their body is less able to defend itself against the pathogen that causes flu.

Practice Questions — Fact Recall

Q1 What is meant by the term 'health'?

Q2 What is the main difference between communicable and non-communicable diseases?

Learning Objectives:
- Be able to describe health as a state of complete physical, mental and social well-being and not merely the absence of disease or infirmity, as defined by the World Health Organisation (WHO).
- Be able to describe the difference between communicable and non-communicable diseases.
- Be able to explain why the presence of one disease can lead to a higher susceptibility to other diseases.

Specification References 5.1, 5.2, 5.3

Tip: Infirmity means weakness or frailness.

Tip: The WHO definition of health means that even if someone is physically fit, they still might be unhealthy (e.g. they have mental health issues or are socially isolated).

Tip: Being susceptible to a disease means that you have an increased chance of getting that particular disease.

Learning Objectives:
- Be able to describe a pathogen as a disease-causing organism, including bacteria, viruses, protists and fungi.
- Be able to describe how pathogens are spread and how this spread can be reduced or prevented, including: tuberculosis (airborne), cholera (water), Chalara ash dieback (airborne) and malaria (animal vectors).
- Be able to describe some common bacterial infections, including tuberculosis and cholera.
- Be able to describe some common fungal infections, including Chalara ash dieback.
- Be able to describe some common protist infections, including malaria.
- Be able to describe some common viral infections, including HIV.
- Be able to explain how sexually transmitted infections (STIs) are spread and how this spread can be reduced or prevented, including the *Chlamydia* bacteria and the HIV virus.

Specification References 5.4-5.6, 5.8

2. Communicable Diseases

Disease isn't a particularly pleasant thing, but you've still got to learn about it. First up in the section is meeting the organisms that cause disease.

Pathogens

Pathogens are organisms that cause disease. They can cause **communicable (infectious) diseases** — diseases that can spread (see previous page). Both plants and animals can be infected by pathogens. There are several types of pathogen, including bacteria, viruses, protists and fungi.

Bacteria

Bacteria are very small cells, which can reproduce rapidly inside your body. They can make you feel ill by producing toxins (poisons) that damage your cells and tissues.

> **Example**
> *Vibrio cholerae* — these bacteria cause cholera (p.117-118).

Viruses

Viruses are not cells. Like bacteria, they can reproduce rapidly inside your body. They live inside your cells and replicate themselves using the cells' machinery to produce many copies of themselves. The cell will usually then burst, releasing all the new viruses. This cell damage is what makes you feel ill.

> **Example**
> HIV (see page 119) — this virus infects and destroys cells that normally help to defend the body against disease (like white blood cells, see p.123-124).

Protists

There are lots of different types of protists. But they're all eukaryotes (see page 23) and most of them are single-celled. Some protists are parasites. Parasites live on or inside other organisms and can cause them damage. They are often transferred to the organism by a **vector**, which doesn't get the disease itself — e.g. an insect that carries the protist.

> **Example**
> Malaria is caused by a protist that lives inside a mosquito (p.118).

Fungi

Some fungi are single-celled. Others have a body which is made up of hyphae (thread-like structures). These hyphae can grow and penetrate human skin and the surface of plants, causing diseases. The hyphae can produce spores, which can be spread to other plants and animals.

> **Example**
> The ash dieback fungus infects ash trees — see page 118 for more.

The spread of pathogens

Pathogens can be spread in many ways. Here are a few that you should know about.

- Some pathogens can be picked up by drinking or bathing in dirty water e.g. the bacterium that causes cholera.

- Pathogens can be airborne (carried in the air) and can then be breathed in, e.g. the bacterium that causes tuberculosis.

- Some pathogens can be carried and transmitted by organisms known as animal **vectors**. For example, mosquitos are animal vectors which carry the protist that causes malaria.

Bacterial diseases

There are two examples of bacterial diseases that you need to know about.

Tuberculosis

Being exposed to the bacterium *Mycobacterium tuberculosis* can lead to an infection called tuberculosis (TB). Signs and symptoms of TB include coughing and lung damage.

The bacterium is spread through the air in droplets when infected individuals cough and sneeze. There are a variety of ways in which the spread of TB can be reduced.

> **Examples**
> - Infected individuals should avoid crowded public spaces and sleep alone.
> - They should also practise good hygiene. This includes washing their hands regularly, covering their mouth and nose with tissues or a face mask when coughing or sneezing and disposing of tissues and face masks following use.
> - A well-ventilated home can also reduce the likelihood of transmission.

Figure 1: *An electron microscope image of* Mycobacterium tuberculosis.

Exam Tip
How to prevent the spread of a disease is linked to how it spreads.

Cholera

Cholera is a disease that is spread by the bacterium *Vibrio cholerae*. The main symptom of a cholera infection is diarrhoea that lasts for a few days. This can lead to severe dehydration and further complications, including death.

The pathogen spreads through contaminated water sources. Most cases of cholera occur in developing countries, where clean water is not widely available. The spread of cholera can be reduced by making sure that people have access to clean water supplies.

Fungal and protist diseases

You also need to know about some diseases caused by fungi and protists.

Chalara ash dieback

A fungus is responsible for the disease known as Chalara ash dieback. The fungus infects ash trees, with symptoms including loss of leaves and bark lesions (wounds). In most cases it leads to the death of the entire tree, either directly or by weakening the tree to a point where it cannot defend itself from other diseases.

The fungus is carried through the air by the wind. It can also spread when ash trees already infected with the disease are moved between different areas.

There are two main strategies for slowing down the spread of the disease.

- Removing young, infected ash trees and replanting with a different species of tree (e.g. birch) can slow down the spread of the fungus.

- Efforts have also been made to reduce the spread of the disease by placing restrictions on the import and movement of ash trees.

Figure 2: *A lesion on the trunk of an ash tree caused by the fungal disease Chalara ash dieback.*

Malaria

Malaria is caused by a protist. Part of the malarial protist's life cycle takes place inside the mosquito. The mosquitoes are vectors — they pick up the malarial protist when they feed on an infected animal, but don't get the disease themselves. Every time the mosquito feeds on another animal, it infects it by inserting the protist into the animal's blood vessels.

Malaria causes repeating episodes of fever. It can be fatal. It also causes damage to red blood cells and, in severe cases, to the liver.

The spread of malaria can be reduced by stopping the mosquitoes from breeding.

> **Example**
>
> Mosquitoes can breed in standing water, so mosquitoes can be prevented from breeding by removing these water sources. For example, people who live in areas with a risk of malaria should make sure that they empty or get rid of any containers on their land that fill with rainwater.

People can also be protected from mosquito bites to stop the spread of the disease.

> **Examples**
> - Spraying any exposed skin with an insect repellant can prevent people from being bitten by mosquitoes.
> - Sleeping under a mosquito net can prevent people from being bitten when they're asleep.

Sexually transmitted infections

Sexually transmitted infections (STIs) are spread through sexual contact, including sexual intercourse. They can be caused by a bacteria, virus, fungus or protist. There are two STIs that you need to know about.

Chlamydia

Chlamydia is a kind of bacterium, but it behaves in a similar way to a virus because it can only reproduce inside host cells (see p.116 for more on viruses).

Although it doesn't usually cause symptoms, it can result in infertility in men and women. In some cases, *Chlamydia* can be passed on from an infected woman to her child during childbirth.

The spread of *Chlamydia* can be reduced by wearing a condom when having sex or avoiding sexual contact. Since the disease doesn't often cause any symptoms, screening is available to help with early detection. Once the infection is diagnosed, the individual can be treated. This reduces the time that they could unknowingly pass the infection on to other individuals.

HIV

HIV is the Human Immunodeficiency Virus. It attacks white blood cells, which are a key part of the body's immune response (see pages 123-124). Following infection with HIV, some people experience flu-like symptoms, whereas others may not experience any symptoms at all. Usually, the person doesn't then experience any symptoms for several years. During this time, HIV can be controlled with antiretroviral drugs, which stop the virus replicating in the body.

Over time, HIV will destroy enough white blood cells that the infection leads to **AIDS** (Acquired Immune Deficiency Syndrome). This is when the infected person's immune system deteriorates and eventually fails. Because of this, the person becomes very vulnerable to opportunistic infections by other pathogens that the body would normally be able to fight off.

HIV is spread by exchanging certain infected bodily fluids (e.g. blood, semen, vaginal fluids). This most commonly occurs through sexual intercourse and by sharing needles when taking drugs. This means that the spread of HIV can be greatly reduced by using a condom when having sex and by drug users not sharing needles. Medication can reduce the risk of an infected individual passing the virus on to others during sex (or of a mother passing the virus to her baby during pregnancy) so screening and proper treatment are also important.

Figure 3: A mosquito net hangs over a bed.

Tip: Some STIs, including chlamydia, are spread by genital contact, not just sexual intercourse.

Tip: *Chlamydia* bacteria cause the disease chlamydia.

Tip: Condoms are the only type of contraception that protects against STIs.

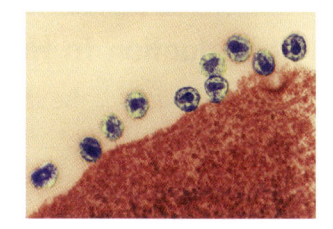

Figure 4: HIV particles (blue) infecting a white blood cell.

Tip: Opportunistic infections are caused by pathogens that take advantage of a weakened or impaired immune system.

Practice Questions — Fact Recall

Q1 a) List two signs or symptoms of tuberculosis.

b) Describe how *Mycobacterium tuberculosis* is spread.

Q2 How can the spread of cholera be reduced?

Q3 a) Name a type of plant that can be infected by the Chalara fungus.

b) Give two symptoms seen in a plant infected with the Chalara fungus.

Q4 Why are mosquito nets used in areas with a high risk of malaria?

Q5 Describe what is meant by the term 'sexually transmitted infection'.

Q6 Give two ways in which the spread of *Chlamydia* can be reduced.

Q7 Describe how HIV affects the body.

Practice Questions — Application

Q1 Gonorrhea is a sexually transmitted infection caused by bacteria. Suggest one way in which the spread of gonorrhea can be reduced.

Q2 A nurse working in a GP surgery washes his hands carefully after seeing patients. Suggest how this will prevent the spread of disease.

Topic 5a Checklist — Make sure you know...

Introduction to Health and Disease

☐ That health is the state of complete physical, mental and social wellbeing and that simply being free from disease does not necessarily make an individual healthy.

☐ That diseases can be communicable or non-communicable, and what is meant by these terms.

☐ That the presence of one disease can increase the likelihood of an individual catching other diseases.

Communicable Diseases

☐ That pathogens are organisms that cause disease, and include bacteria, viruses, protists and fungi.

☐ That tuberculosis is an airborne bacterial disease that causes lung damage, and its spread can be reduced in ways such as practising good hygiene and ensuring patients avoid public spaces.

☐ That cholera is a bacterial disease that causes diarrhoea and spreads via contaminated drinking water, and that transmission of cholera can be prevented by having clean water supplies.

cont...

- ☐ That Chalara ash dieback is an airborne fungal disease that causes leaf loss and bark lesions in ash trees, and that the spread of the fungus can be reduced by replacing infected trees with a different species and placing restrictions on the import and movement of ash trees.
- ☐ That malaria is a disease caused by a protist that causes damage to red blood cells and the liver, and that it's spread via animal vectors (mosquitoes) can be reduced by preventing mosquitoes from breeding and by taking precautions to avoid being bitten (e.g. mosquito nets).
- ☐ That the sexually transmitted infection chlamydia (caused by *Chlamydia* bacteria) is spread through sexual contact, and that transmission can be reduced by wearing a condom when having sex or avoiding sexual contact, and screening individuals so they can be treated for the infection.
- ☐ That the HIV virus destroys the white blood cells of the immune system, leading to the onset of AIDS.
- ☐ That HIV is the spread through the exchange of certain bodily fluids, often during sex, and that its spread can be reduced by wearing a condom when having sex, screening and taking medication.

Exam-style Questions

1 A patient in a UK hospital has been diagnosed with malaria after returning from Kenya. In order to diagnose the patient, a doctor analysed a sample of the patient's blood under a microscope slide. The sample was found to contain the malarial pathogen.

  (a) (i) Define the term 'pathogen'.
(1 mark)

      (ii) Name the type of pathogen that causes malaria.
(1 mark)

  (b) (i) Give **one** effect that malaria has on the body, which might be visible to the doctor analysing the patient's blood sample under the microscope.
(1 mark)

      (ii) Suggest why the doctor is not concerned about other patients in the hospital contracting malaria from the patient.
(2 marks)

  (c) People visiting areas where malaria is present are advised to take anti-malarial medication to reduce the risk of them contracting the disease.
Suggest **two** other pieces of advice people may be given to further reduce the risk of catching malaria.
(2 marks)

  (d) The patient is treated and is declared fit to go home, as the pathogen has been eradicated and he is free from disease.
Suggest why, despite being disease-free, the patient may not necessarily be healthy.
(1 mark)

2 HIV is a virus that kills white blood cells in the body.

  (a) (i) Describe how HIV is spread between humans.
(1 mark)

      (ii) Suggest **two** ways in which the spread of HIV can be reduced.
(2 marks)

  (b) HIV can be described as a communicable disease.
Explain what is meant by this term.
(1 mark)

  (c) Explain how an infection of HIV affects the susceptibility of the body to other diseases.
(3 marks)

Topic 5b — Fighting Disease

1. Defences Against Disease

Part of being healthy means being free from disease. But that's easier said than done...

The body's defences

In order to cause disease, pathogens (disease causing organisms — see p.116) first need to enter the body. Luckily, the human body has got features that stop a lot of nasties getting inside in the first place. These features are known as 'barriers' and are the body's first line of defence against disease. They are non-specific, which means that they work against many different types of pathogen. There are two types of barrier that you need to know about — physical barriers and chemical barriers.

Physical barriers

Physical barriers act to block the entrance of pathogens into the body.

Examples
- The skin acts as a barrier to pathogens. If it gets damaged, blood clots can quickly seal any cuts to help keep microorganisms out of the body.
- Hairs and mucus in your nose trap particles that could contain pathogens.
- Some cells in the trachea and bronchi (airways in the lungs) secrete mucus to trap pathogens.
- Other cells that line the trachea and bronchi have cilia. These are hair-like structures, which waft the mucus up to the back of the throat where it can be swallowed.

Chemical barriers

The body produces a variety of chemicals which can destroy pathogens. These are known as chemical barriers.

Examples
- The stomach produces hydrochloric acid. This kills pathogens that make it that far from the mouth.
- The body produces enzymes called lysozymes that can kill bacteria. Lysozymes are present in several substances secreted by the body, such as in tears where they kill bacteria on the surface of the eye.

The immune system

If pathogens do make it into your body, your immune system kicks in to destroy them. The most important part of your immune system is the **white blood cells**. They travel around in your blood and crawl into every part of you, constantly patrolling for pathogens.

Learning Objectives:
- Be able to describe how the physical barriers of the human body provide protection from pathogens, including skin, mucus and cilia.
- Be able to describe how the chemical defences of the human body provide protection from pathogens, including hydrochloric acid and lysozymes.
- Be able to explain the role of the specific immune system of the human body in defence against disease, including exposure to the pathogen, and the role of antigens in triggering an immune response which causes the production of antibodies.

Specification References 5.12, 5.13

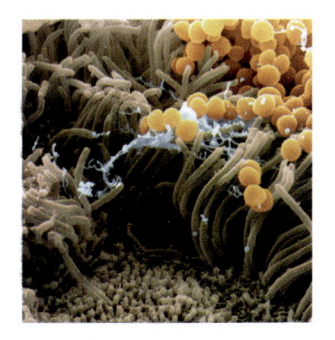

Figure 1: Bacteria (yellow) sticking to mucus (blue) on microscopic hairs in the nose.

When white blood cells come across an invading pathogen, they can respond in different ways, for example:

1. Consuming them

Some white blood cells can engulf foreign cells and digest them. This is called **phagocytosis**. It's a non-specific response.

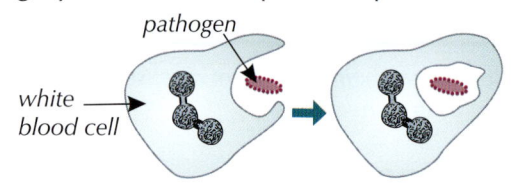

Figure 3: A white blood cell engulfing a pathogen.

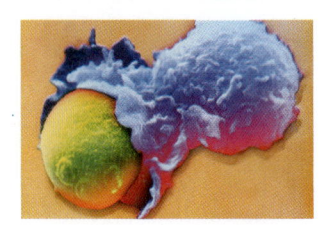

Figure 2: A white blood cell (blue/pink) engulfing a pathogen (yellow/green). Seen under a microscope.

Tip: Antigens found on the surface of pathogens can be described as 'foreign' — they're not recognised by the B-lymphocytes.

2. Producing antibodies

B-lymphocytes are a type of white blood cell that are involved in the specific immune response — this is the immune response to a specific pathogen.

Every invading pathogen has unique molecules (e.g. proteins) called **antigens** on its surface. When your B-lymphocytes come across an antigen on a pathogen, they will start to produce proteins called **antibodies.** These antibodies bind (lock on) to the invading cells so that they can be found and destroyed by other white blood cells.

Tip: Memory lymphocytes are also produced after an immune response to an antigen (see next page for more).

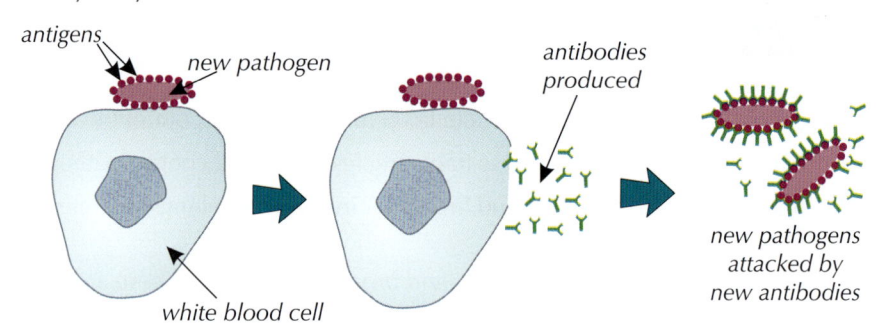

Figure 4: Diagram showing the production of antibodies.

Exam Tip
Don't get antigens and antibodies mixed up in the exam. Remember, the body makes antibodies against the antigens on pathogens.

The antibodies produced are specific to that type of pathogen — they won't lock on to any others. Antibodies are then produced rapidly and carried around the body to find all similar pathogens.

Practice Questions — Fact Recall

Q1 Give three physical barriers to disease.

Q2 Give two ways in which white blood cells help to defend the body against disease.

Exam Tip
In the exam, you might get asked questions about pathogens or diseases you've never heard of before. Don't let that put you off though — you should be able to work out the answers by applying what you already know.

Practice Question — Application

Q1 The SARS coronavirus (SARS-CoV) causes SARS, a respiratory disease. It can enter the body by being inhaled in droplets. Describe one feature of the body that helps to protect the body from infection with SARS-CoV.

Topic 5b Fighting Disease

2. Memory Lymphocytes and Immunisation

Our immune system contains special cells which can remember what pathogens have invaded our bodies in the past. This means our bodies can respond faster if they invade again...

Memory lymphocytes

When a pathogen enters the body for the first time, the response of the immune system is slow. This is because there aren't many B-lymphocytes that can make the antibody needed to bind with the new antigen. Eventually the body will produce enough of the right antibody to overcome the infection. During this time, the infected person will show symptoms of the disease.

As well as antibodies, special white blood cells called **memory lymphocytes** are produced in response to a foreign antigen. Memory lymphocytes remain in the body for a long time, and can 'remember' a specific antigen. The person is now **immune** to the pathogen, as their immune system has the ability to respond quickly to a second infection. If the same pathogen enters the body again, there are more cells that will recognise it and produce antibodies against it.

This secondary immune response is faster and stronger than the primary response which occurred when the body was first exposed to the new pathogen. The secondary response often gets rid of the pathogen before you begin to show any symptoms (see Figure 1).

Learning Objectives:
- Be able to explain the role of the specific immune system of the human body in defence against disease, including how antigens trigger the production of memory lymphocytes, and the role of memory lymphocytes in the secondary response to the antigen.
- Be able to explain the body's response to immunisation using an inactive form of a pathogen.

Specification References 5.13, 5.14

Tip: The secondary response is always faster than the primary response. This is shown by a steeper line in graphs of blood antibody concentration against time.

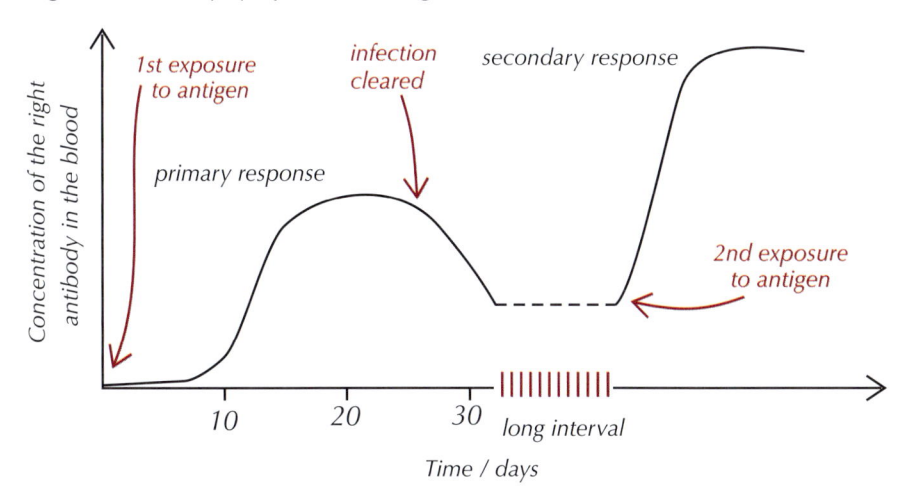

Figure 1: *A graph of antibody concentration against time since antigen exposure.*

Immunisation

When you're infected with a new pathogen, it takes your white blood cells a few days to learn how to deal with it. But by that time, you can be pretty ill. You can be immunised against some diseases (e.g. measles), which can stop you getting ill in the first place.

Immunisation usually involves injecting a vaccine into the body which contains small amounts of dead or inactive pathogens.

Topic 5b Fighting Disease

Tip: A vaccination is when you give someone a vaccine. It's a method of immunisation.

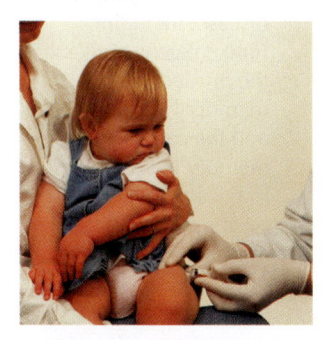

The pathogens are antigenic (they carry antigens). This causes your white blood cells to produce antibodies to target them — even though the pathogens are harmless (because they're dead or inactive).

Example

Children can be immunised against measles, mumps and rubella using the MMR vaccine. It contains weakened versions of the viruses that cause these diseases, all in one vaccine.

The antigens will also trigger the production of memory lymphocytes (see previous page). So, if live pathogens of the same type then get into the body at a later date, the memory lymphocytes can rapidly mass-produce antibodies to help destroy the pathogen in a secondary immune response. The immunised person is immune to that pathogen so won't get ill (see Figure 3).

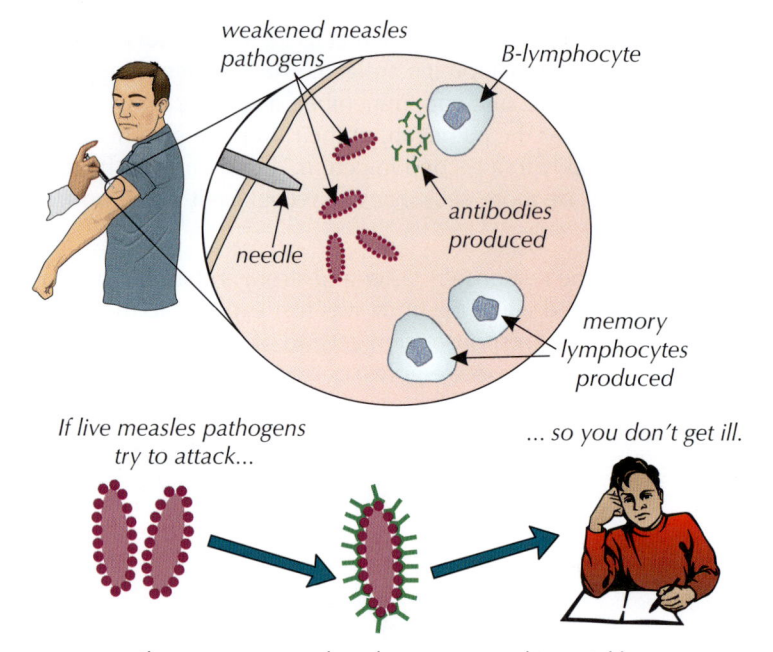

Figure 2: A baby being given the MMR vaccine.

Tip: Remember, antibodies are specific to a particular type of pathogen (see p.124). So a vaccination against the typhoid bacterium will only protect you against typhoid — it won't make you immune to anything else.

If live measles pathogens try to attack...

... so you don't get ill.

... there are memory lymphocytes around to quickly recognise them and produce antibodies against them...

Figure 3: A diagram of how immunisation works.

Tip: Don't get white blood cells confused with red blood cells. Red blood cells transport oxygen around the body, whilst white blood cells are part of the immune system.

Practice Questions — Application

Q1 Whooping cough is a severe cough that can cause serious breathing difficulties in young babies.
Suggest how a whooping cough vaccination might work.

Q2 A child was exposed to the virus that causes chickenpox, and developed symptoms of the disease. Six months later, the child was exposed to the same virus but did not develop any symptoms. Explain why.

Topic 5b Fighting Disease

3. Developing Drugs

Drugs have to go through many stages, including discovery, development and testing before they can be made commercially available.

Drug discovery

The first stage in the development of a drug is discovery. This could happen in many different ways.

> **Example**
>
> Penicillin is an antibiotic (see p.131). It was discovered by Alexander Fleming when he was clearing out Petri dishes containing bacteria. He noticed that one of the dishes had mould on it, and the area around the mould was free of bacteria. The mould was producing penicillin, which was killing the bacteria.

Nowadays, most scientists use their knowledge of how a disease works to try and identify molecules that could be used as drugs to fight the disease. Once a new potential drug has been discovered, it needs to be developed. This involves preclinical and clinical testing.

Drug testing

Before newly discovered drugs can be given to the general public, they have to go through a thorough testing procedure to make sure they are safe and effective.

There are three main stages in drug testing — preclinical testing on human cells and tissues, preclinical testing on live animals, and clinical testing on human volunteers.

Preclinical testing

Cells and tissues

In preclinical testing, drugs are tested on human cells and tissues in the lab. However, you can't use human cells and tissues to test drugs that affect whole or multiple body systems, e.g. testing a drug for blood pressure must be done on a whole animal because it has an intact circulatory system.

Live animals

The next step in preclinical testing is to test the drug on live animals. This is to test efficacy (whether the drug works and produces the effect you're looking for), to find out about its toxicity (how harmful it is) and to find the best dosage (the concentration that should be given, and how often it should be given).

Learning Objective:
- Be able to describe that the process of developing new medicines, including antibiotics, has many stages, including discovery, development, preclinical and clinical testing.

Specification Reference 5.20

Tip: Like all drugs, antibiotics (see p.131) undergo thorough drug testing.

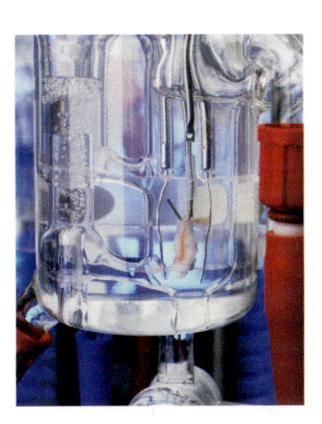

Figure 1: *A piece of tissue from a human intestine being used in drug testing.*

Topic 5b Fighting Disease

Clinical testing

If the drug passes the tests on animals then it's tested on human volunteers in a clinical trial.

First, the drug is tested on healthy volunteers. This is to make sure that it doesn't have any harmful side effects when the body is working normally. At the start of the trial, a very low dose of the drug is given and this is gradually increased.

If the results of the tests on healthy volunteers are good, the drugs can be tested on people suffering from the illness. The optimum dose is found — this is the dose of drug that is the most effective and has few side effects.

Placebos

To test how well the drug works, patients are randomly put into two groups. One is given the new drug, the other is given a **placebo** (a substance that looks like the drug being tested but doesn't do anything, e.g. a sugar pill). This is so the doctor can see the actual difference the drug makes — it allows for the placebo effect (when the patient expects the treatment to work and so feels better, even though the treatment isn't doing anything).

Tip: People in the control group of a clinical trial should be similar to people in the treatment group, e.g. of a similar age, gender, etc. This helps to make sure the study is a fair test — see page 10 for more on making a study a fair test.

Example

A pharmaceutical company has developed a drug, Drug X, to help people with high blood cholesterol to lower their cholesterol level. The drug was tested on 1500 patients with high cholesterol. The patients were divided into two groups and over six months each patient had one tablet per day. One group had a tablet containing Drug X and the other group had a tablet without Drug X — the placebo.

Blind and double-blind trials

Clinical trials are **blind** — the patient in the study doesn't know whether they're getting the drug or the placebo. In fact, they're often **double-blind** — neither the patient nor the doctor knows until all the results have been gathered (see Figure 2). This is so the doctors monitoring the patients and analysing the results aren't subconsciously influenced by their knowledge.

	Blind trial	Double-blind trial
Does the **patient** know whether they're getting the drug or the placebo?	no	no
Does the **doctor** know whether the patient is getting the drug or the placebo?	yes	no

Figure 2: Table summarising blind and double-blind trials.

Tip: Peer review is when other scientists check that the work is valid and has been carried out rigorously — see page 2.

The results of drug testing and drug trials aren't published until they've been through peer review. This helps to prevent false claims.

When a drug has finally passed all of these tests, it still needs to be approved by a medical agency before it can be used to treat patients. All of this means that drugs are as effective and safe as possible.

The importance of drug testing

It's really important that drugs are tested thoroughly before being used to make sure they're safe. An example of what can happen when drugs are not thoroughly tested is the case of thalidomide...

> **Example**
>
> Thalidomide is a drug that was developed in the 1950s. It was intended as a sleeping pill, and was tested for that use. But later it was also found to be effective in relieving morning sickness in pregnant women.
>
> Unfortunately, thalidomide hadn't been tested as a drug for morning sickness, and so it wasn't known that it could pass through the placenta and affect the fetus, causing abnormal limb development. In some cases, babies were born with no arms or legs at all. About 10 000 babies were affected by thalidomide, and only about half of them survived.
>
> The drug was banned, and more rigorous testing procedures were introduced. More recently thalidomide has been used in the treatment of leprosy and other diseases, e.g. some cancers.

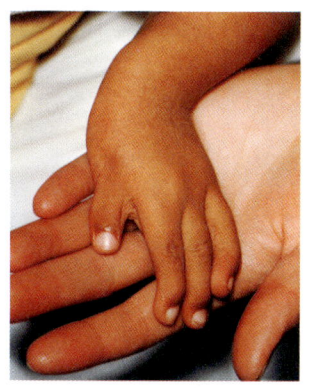

Figure 3: This baby was born with a deformed hand due to thalidomide.

Practice Questions — Fact Recall

Q1 What are drugs tested on in preclinical testing?

Q2 Give two things that drug testing aims to find out.

Q3 a) In a clinical trial, what type of volunteer is the drug tested on first — healthy volunteers or people suffering from the illness?

b) Describe the dosage of drug that is first used in a clinical trial.

Q4 What is a placebo?

Q5 Explain the difference between a blind and a double-blind trial.

Exam Tip
If you're asked what a placebo is in the exam, remember that it's not a drug — this is because it doesn't actually do anything.

Practice Questions — Application

Q1 For each of the drugs below, suggest what would have been given as a placebo when that drug went through clinical trials.

a) a paracetamol capsule

b) a steroid inhaler

c) a cortisone injection

Q2 A new weight-loss pill has been developed called Drug Y.

The pill was tested in a double-blind clinical trial. It involved three groups of obese volunteers (50 per group), all of whom wanted to lose weight. Each group member took a pill three times a day for a year, alongside diet and exercise:

- Group 1 took Drug Y.
- Group 2 took a similar weight-loss pill already available (Drug Z).
- Group 3 took a placebo.

The average weight loss per person after one year is shown on the graph.

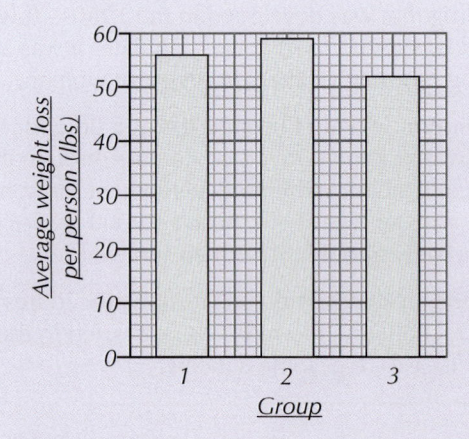

a) i) Would the doctors involved in this trial have known which patients were being given the placebo? Explain your answer.

   ii) Suggest what could have been used as a placebo in this trial.

b) Suggest why Group 2 was included in the trial.

c) From these results, what can you conclude about Drug Y? Use data from the graph to support your answer.

Exam Tip
When answering a question about a clinical trial in the exam, make sure you read all the information you're given. Here you need to have spotted that it's a double-blind trial — this will help you answer Q2 a) i).

Topic 5b Fighting Disease

4. Antibiotics

Sometimes, your immune system isn't enough when it comes to fighting off infections. That's where medicines such as antibiotics come in...

What are antibiotics?

Antibiotics are drugs that are used to treat bacterial infections. Antibiotics work by inhibiting processes in bacterial cells, but not in the host organism.

> **Example**
>
> Some antibiotics (e.g. penicillin) inhibit the building of bacterial cell walls — this prevents the bacteria from dividing, and eventually kills them, but has no effect on cells in the human host (which don't have cell walls).

Different antibiotics target different types of bacteria, so it's important to be treated with the right one.

> **Example**
>
> Doxycycline is one of several antibiotics that can be given to patients suffering from an infection of chlamydia (caused by the bacterium *Chlamydia* — see p.119). Doxycycline works by interrupting the synthesis of important proteins inside the bacteria that are needed for the bacteria to survive. As with all bacterial infections, many antibiotics are ineffective (e.g. daptomycin) or less effective (e.g. penicillin) at treating chlamydia, so doctor's need to make sure that they prescribe the correct antibiotic.

Learning Objective:
- Be able to explain that antibiotics can only be used to treat bacterial infections because they inhibit cell processes in the bacterium but not in the host organism.

Specification Reference 5.16

Tip: Protein synthesis in bacteria is different to protein synthesis in host organisms so antibiotics won't affect protein synthesis in the host.

Antibiotics and viruses

Antibiotics don't destroy viruses (e.g. flu or cold viruses). This is because viruses are not cells (unlike bacteria) so they don't contain a cell wall or any of the machinery needed for growth and reproduction — this means antibiotics have no effect on them. Viruses can only reproduce inside a host organism's cells using the host cell's machinery. Since antibiotics don't affect the host cell either, the virus inside survives. It is very difficult to develop drugs that destroy just the virus without killing the body's cells.

Tip: A drug that targets a virus is known as an 'antiviral'.

Practice Questions — Fact Recall

Q1 What are antibiotics?

Q2 What can't all bacterial infections be treated with the same antibiotic?

Q3 Explain why antibiotics can't be used to kill viruses.

Topic 5b Checklist — Make sure you know...

Defences Against Disease

☐ That the body has physical barriers to disease, which include the skin, mucus in the nose and airways, and cilia which line the trachea and bronchi.

cont...

- [ ] That the body has chemical barriers to disease, which include hydrochloric acid produced in the stomach and lysozymes.
- [ ] That if pathogens do manage to enter the body, the immune system can attack them — some white blood cells non-specifically engulf pathogens by phagocytosis, and other white blood cells called B-lymphocytes produce antibodies in response to antigens in the specific immune response.
- [ ] That antibodies bind to antigens on pathogens so that the pathogens can be found and destroyed by other white blood cells.

Memory Lymphocytes and Immunisation

- [ ] That when a foreign antigen on the surface of a pathogen enters the body for the first time, it triggers the production of specialised white blood cells called memory lymphocytes.
- [ ] That memory lymphocytes remain in the body for a long period of time and can 'remember' the antigen that triggered their production in the primary immune response to that antigen.
- [ ] That the secondary immune response is faster and stronger than the primary immune response, as memory lymphocytes recognise the antigens on the pathogen and mass produce antibodies specific to that antigen.
- [ ] That immunisation usually involves injecting dead or inactive pathogens to trigger the production of antibodies and memory lymphocytes. If a live version of the same pathogen then enters the body, memory lymphocytes will rapidly mass-produce the right antibodies to kill it so that the person doesn't get ill.

Developing Drugs

- [ ] That modern drug discovery involves scientists using knowledge of how a disease works to try and find molecules that could be used to treat the disease.
- [ ] That drugs have to be tested to make sure that they are safe and effective.
- [ ] That new drugs are first tested in preclinical trials on human cells and tissues as well as on live animals.
- [ ] That during preclinical drug trials on live animals, new drugs are tested for efficacy and toxicity, and also to find the best dose.
- [ ] That after preclinical testing, drugs are tested in clinical trials on healthy volunteers at low doses. They're then tested on ill volunteers to find the optimum dose of a drug.
- [ ] That a placebo is a substance that looks similar to the drug being tested but that doesn't do anything, and is used in clinical trials to find out if any improvement in the patients' conditions was from the drug, or if it was caused by the placebo effect.
- [ ] That in a blind trial, the volunteers don't know which volunteers have been given the drug and which volunteers have been given the placebo and in a double-blind trial, neither the doctors nor the volunteers know.

Antibiotics

- [ ] That antibiotics are used only to treat bacterial infections as they specifically target processes in bacterial cells, leaving the cells of the host organism unharmed.

Exam-style Questions

1 Pathogens can enter the body in several ways.
  (a) Outline how the stomach helps to defend the body against the entry of pathogens.
   (1 mark)
  (b) The human airways include the trachea and bronchi.
    Outline how the trachea and bronchi help to defend the body against pathogens.
   (3 marks)
  (c) Describe how lysozyme acts as a chemical barrier to infection.
   (1 mark)

  Sometimes pathogens get past the body's defences.
  This leads to the production antibodies by B-lymphocytes.
  (d) Describe the role that antibodies play in the specific immune response.
   (2 marks)

2 **Figure 1** shows the number of measles cases reported each year worldwide, along with the estimated immunisation coverage, from 1980 to 2014.

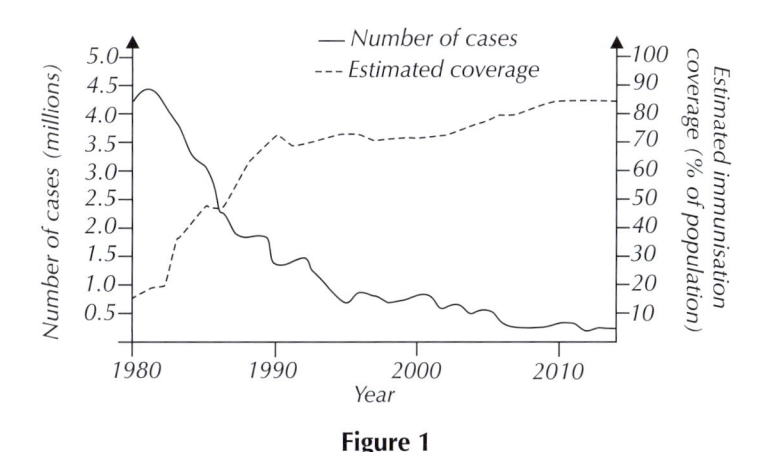

Figure 1

  (a) Describe the trends shown in the graph.
    Use data from the graph to support your answer.
   (4 marks)
  (b) Evaluate how far this data supports the case for immunising people against measles.
   (2 marks)
  (c) A vaccine can contain small amounts of the disease-causing pathogen.
    Suggest why the pathogens in the vaccine do not cause the disease themselves.
   (1 mark)

3 A new drug is being developed.

(a) Describe how modern scientists discover drugs with the potential to cure disease.

(1 mark)

(b) The new drug enters preclinical testing. Preclinical testing happens on cells and tissues, and it is sometimes done using live animals too.
Suggest why a drug designed to affect the absorption of nutrients from the small intestine into the bloodstream might be tested on live animals rather than just on cells and tissues.

(2 marks)

The drug then enters clinical trials.

(c)* Describe what happens at this stage.
Refer to placebos and double-blind testing in your answer.

(6 marks)

4 The role of the immune system is to remove or destroy pathogens that enter the body. This is partly achieved through the production of antibodies.

Figure 2 shows how the level of an antibody in the blood changes during the primary and secondary immune responses.

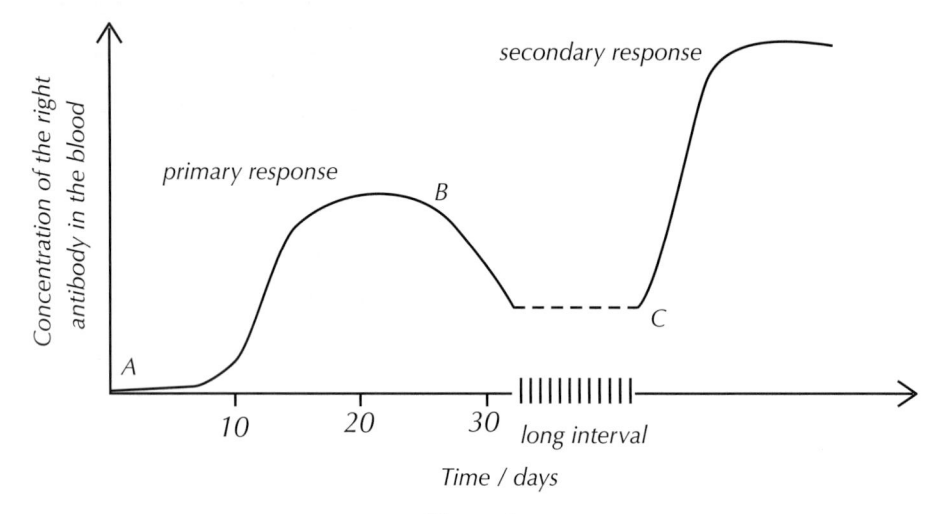

Figure 2

(a) What is occurring at point **B** in **Figure 2**?

 A The concentration of antibody is decreasing as the infection begins.
 B The concentration of antibody is decreasing as the infection ends.
 C The concentration of antibody is decreasing as white blood cells die.
 D The concentration of antibody is decreasing as it is destroyed by the pathogen.

(1 mark)

(b) Point **A** in **Figure 2** represents the first exposure to the pathogen.
Point **C** represents the second exposure to the pathogen.
Describe why the concentration of antibody in the blood increases more quickly following point **C** than at point **A**.

(3 marks)

Topic 5b Fighting Disease : Exam-style Questions

Topic 5c | Non-Communicable Diseases

1. Risk Factors for Non-Communicable Diseases

Non-communicable diseases can't be transmitted between individuals — see page 115. However, there are certain things that make developing a non-communicable disease more likely...

What are risk factors?

Risk factors are things that are linked to an increase in the likelihood that a person will develop a certain disease during their lifetime. They don't guarantee that someone will get the disease.

Risk factors can be unavoidable, e.g. a person's age or gender may make them more likely to get a disease. They can also be environmental (e.g. exposure to air pollution). But some risk factors are lifestyle factors that people can change, e.g. how much exercise they do or whether or not they smoke.

Many non-communicable diseases (including cardiovascular disease, cancer, liver and lung diseases, and obesity) are caused by several different risk factors interacting with each other rather than one factor alone. This means that the more risk factors you have for a disease, the more likely you are to get it.

Lifestyle-related risk factors for disease

You need to be able to explain the effect of the following lifestyle-related risk factors on disease.

Smoking

Smoking is a major risk factor associated with **cardiovascular disease** — that's any disease associated with the heart or blood vessels, e.g. a heart attack or stroke (see p.140). Heart attacks and strokes occur when the blood supply to the heart or brain is cut off. This stops oxygen reaching the heart or brain cells, causing them to die.

Smoking is a risk factor for these diseases for several reasons. One is that nicotine in cigarette smoke increases heart rate, which increases blood pressure. High blood pressure damages artery walls, which contributes to the build up of fatty deposits in the arteries. These deposits restrict blood flow and increase the risk of a heart attack or stroke. Smoking also increases the risk of blood clots forming in arteries, which can further restrict or block blood flow and lead to a heart attack or stroke.

Smoking is also a risk factor for **cancer** — in particular lung cancer. This is because cigarette smoke contains chemicals called carcinogens. These cause mutations in the genes that control cell division, which can lead to cancer (uncontrolled cell growth, see p.57).

Learning Objectives:
- Be able to describe that many non-communicable human diseases are caused by the interaction of a number of factors, including cardiovascular diseases, many forms of cancer, some lung and liver diseases and diseases influenced by nutrition.
- Be able to explain the effect of lifestyle factors on non-communicable diseases at local, national and global levels, including:
  - smoking on cardiovascular diseases;
  - alcohol on liver diseases;
  - exercise and diet on obesity and malnutrition.

Specification References 5.23, 5.24

Tip: The alleles you inherit may also make you more susceptible to developing a certain disease (see p.92).

Tip: Smoking is a risk factor for several lung diseases besides cancer, including emphysema and bronchitis.

Figure 1: A liver with cirrhosis (top) and a normal liver (bottom).

Exam Tip
In the exam, you might need to identify a correlation between risk factors and diseases from a graph. To recap what correlation is, look at page 18.

Exam Tip
In the exam, you might need to read off data related to disease risk factors from a table, graph or chart, or explain what the data is showing. Remember to always check any units or graph scales carefully before answering any questions.

Drinking alcohol

Drinking too much alcohol is a major risk factor for liver diseases, e.g. cirrhosis (scarring of the liver) and liver cancer.

Enzymes in the liver break down alcohol, but the breakdown products can damage liver cells. Liver cells may also be damaged when toxic chemicals leak from the gut due to damage to the intestines caused by alcohol. Drinking too much over a long period of time can cause permanent liver damage. It's also a risk factor for cardiovascular disease.

Diet

A diet with too few nutrients can lead to **malnutrition** (a condition where you don't have the right balance of nutrients to stay healthy). There are many different diseases associated with malnutrition.

> **Example**
>
> Scurvy is a disease caused by a deficiency (lack) of vitamin C in the diet. This affects the body's ability to produce collagen — an important protein found in tissues such as bone and tendons. Symptoms of scurvy include painful joints and muscles, as well as bleeding gums.

Malnutrition can also be caused by a diet with too many nutrients.

> **Example**
>
> A diet that's high in fat and sugar can lead to problems such as **obesity** (see page 138) and being overweight. Obesity itself is a risk factor for other non-communicable diseases, e.g. type 2 diabetes (see p.181) and cardiovascular disease.

Low levels of exercise (physical activity)

Exercise is an important factor in maintaining a healthy weight. Those who don't get enough exercise are more likely to become overweight and obese, which can lead to further health problems. Inactive people are also more likely to develop high blood pressure and cardiovascular disease, as well as increasing their risk of certain cancers.

Local, national and global impacts

Lifestyle factors can have different impacts locally, nationally and globally.

Local impacts

Non-communicable diseases can have knock-on effects for local areas. For example, in areas where there are high levels of obesity, smoking or excess alcohol consumption, there's likely to be a high occurrence of certain non-communicable diseases, e.g. cardiovascular or liver disease. This can put pressure on the resources (money, beds, staff, etc.) of local hospitals.

National impacts

Non-communicable diseases are also costly at a national level because the National Health Service provides the resources for the treatment of patients all over the UK. And sometimes, people suffering from a non-communicable disease may not be able to work. A reduction in the number of people able to work can affect a country's economy.

Global impacts

As well as being costly, non-communicable diseases are very common, e.g. cardiovascular disease is the number one cause of death worldwide. In developing countries, malnutrition is also a big problem because people are not able to access enough food. The high cost and occurrence of these diseases can hold back the development of a country — so they have an effect at a global level.

Practice Questions — Fact Recall

Q1 What is meant by the term 'risk factor'?

Q2 Give two risk factors for disease that can be changed.

Q3 Give two diseases that smoking is a risk factor for.

Q4 Give a risk factor that is thought to cause type 2 diabetes.

Q5 Give an example of the effect of non-communicable diseases caused by lifestyle factors at a national level in the UK.

Learning Objective:

- Be able to explain the effect of lifestyle factors on obesity and malnutrition, including BMI, using the BMI equation:

$$BMI = \frac{\text{weight (kg)}}{(\text{height (m)})^2}$$

and waist : hip calculations.

Specification Reference 5.24

2. Measures of Obesity

You might remember from p.136 that obesity is a risk factor for several different non-communicable diseases. This means that it's important for doctors to be able to determine whether or not somebody is obese.

What is obesity and how is it measured?

Obesity means being very overweight and having too much body fat. However, you can't just say that anybody over a certain weight is obese. That's because people come in all sorts of shapes and sizes — your weight is affected by things like your height and your muscle mass, as well as the amount of fat your body stores. So doctors use measures such as the Body Mass Index (BMI) and waist-to-hip ratio to help them decide whether somebody is overweight or obese.

Body Mass Index (BMI)

The Body Mass Index (BMI) is can be used a guide to help decide whether someone is underweight, normal weight, overweight or obese. It's calculated from a person's height and weight, using this formula:

$$BMI = \frac{\text{weight (kg)}}{(\text{height (m)})^2}$$

Tip: (height (m))² means you multiply the height in metres by itself.

Once you have calculated a value for a person's BMI, you can refer to a table that shows how the different values are classified — see Figure 1.

Tip: As you can see from Figure 1, BMI can be used to tell if someone is underweight (and therefore that they might not be getting enough nutrients) as well as if they are overweight.

Body Mass Index	Weight Description
below 18.5	underweight
18.5 - 24.9	normal
25 - 29.9	overweight
30 - 39.9	moderately obese
above 40	severely obese

Figure 1: Table showing weight classification by BMI.

Example

Calculate the BMI of a person who weighs 63.0 kg and is 1.70 m tall. Is this person overweight?

1. Put the numbers you've been given into the formula above. Give your answer to an appropriate number of significant figures (see p.15).

$$BMI = \frac{\text{weight (kg)}}{(\text{height (m)})^2} = \frac{63.0 \text{ kg}}{1.70 \text{ m}^2} = 21.799... = \mathbf{21.8 \text{ kg m}^{-2} \text{ (3 s.f.)}}$$

2. Look at the table in Figure 1. Find the category in which the BMI value you have calculated lies. Read across to find the weight description.

   This person is not overweight — their BMI lies between 18.5 and 24.9 (the normal weight range).

Exam Tip
Make sure you're using the correct units for height and weight in any BMI calculations. E.g. if you're given the height in cm, you'll need to convert it to m before you start your calculation. There's more on converting units on pages 19-20.

If you eat a high fat, high sugar diet and you don't do enough exercise, you're likely to take in more energy than you use. The excess energy is stored as fat, so you're more likely to have a high BMI and be obese.

BMI isn't always a reliable measure of obesity. For example, athletes have lots of muscle, which weighs more than fat, so they can come out with a high BMI even though they're not overweight.

Waist-to-hip ratio

A waist-to-hip ratio helps to measure fat distribution. To calculate it, you need to measure a person's hip circumference at its widest part, as well as the circumference of their waist. You can then use the following formula to figure out their waist-to-hip ratio:

Tip: The circumference of a person's waist or hips is the distance the whole way around their body at that point.

$$\text{waist-to-hip ratio} = \frac{\text{waist circumference}}{\text{hip circumference}}$$

Example

Calculate the waist-to-hip ratio of a person who has a waist circumference of 69 cm and a hip circumference of 98 cm.

$$\text{waist-to-hip ratio} = \frac{\text{waist circumference}}{\text{hip circumference}} = \frac{69 \text{ cm}}{98 \text{ cm}} = 0.7040... = \mathbf{0.70} \text{ (2 s.f.)}$$

Exam Tip
When calculating the waist-to-hip ratio, make sure that the waist circumference and the hip circumference are in the same units.

The higher your waist-to-hip ratio, the more weight you're likely to be carrying around your middle. A ratio above 1.0 for males and above 0.85 for females indicates that too much weight is being carried around the middle — this is known as abdominal obesity. A person with abdominal obesity has a greater risk of developing obesity-related health problems, such as cardiovascular disease (see next page) and type 2 diabetes (see p.181), than someone who carries more weight around their hips.

It can be helpful to look at both a person's BMI and waist-to-hip ratio to measure their health. It's possible that a person could have a normal BMI but carry more weight around their stomach than their hips, therefore putting them at greater risk of certain non-communicable diseases.

Figure 2: A woman measuring the circumference of her waist.

Practice Question — Application

Q1 Robyn weighs 77.0 kg and is 178 cm tall.
Lauren weighs 75.0 kg and is 155 cm tall.

a) Calculate the BMI of each of the women.

b) Use Figure 1 on the previous page to find the weight description of each of the women. Which woman may be recommended to lose weight by a doctor?

Topic 5c Non-Communicable Diseases

Learning Objective:
- Be able to evaluate some of the treatments for cardiovascular disease, including lifestyle changes, life-long medication and surgical procedures.

Specification Reference 5.25

3. Treating Cardiovascular Disease

Cardiovascular disease is one of the main causes of death in the UK. We have many ways to effectively treat it. Read on for more...

What is cardiovascular disease?

Cardiovascular disease (CVD) is a term used to describe diseases of the heart or blood vessels. It is generally associated with the narrowing and blockage of **arteries** (blood vessels that carry blood away from the heart).

Arteries narrow when fatty deposits build up inside them (see Figure 1). The deposits occur in areas where the artery wall has been damaged, e.g. by high blood pressure. The deposits can also trigger blood clots to form, which can block blood flow completely.

Tip: See pages 193-197 for more on blood vessels and the heart.

Tip: Lifestyle-related risk factors for CVD include smoking, drinking too much alcohol, obesity, a diet high in saturated fats and a lack of exercise. There's more on risk factors on p.135-137.

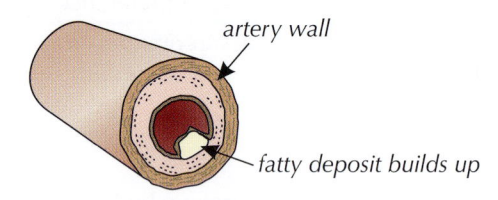

Figure 1: Fatty deposits building up in an artery.

Several different diseases can be classed as cardiovascular diseases.

Examples

- Coronary heart disease is when fatty deposits build up in the arteries that supply blood to the heart muscle (the coronary arteries). This causes the arteries to become narrow, so blood flow to the heart is restricted. If blood clots also form and completely block the blood flow in the coronary arteries, the heart muscle will be deprived of oxygen. This causes a heart attack.
- A stroke occurs when an already narrowed artery supplying the brain with blood is blocked by a blood clot. This cuts off the blood supply to the brain and deprives the brain of oxygen.

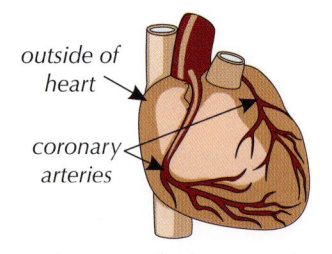

Figure 2: The location of the coronary arteries.

Depending on the extent of the severity of the disease, CVD can be treated in a few different ways.

Tip: There are other factors which can also increase the risk of developing CVD, such as age, gender and family history. While these risk factors can't be changed, it is possible to control and modify lifestyle-related risk factors.

Lifestyle changes

Making changes to your lifestyle can reduce your risk of developing CVD. If you already have CVD, these changes can form part of the treatment, helping to reduce the risk of a further heart attack or stroke. Lifestyle changes are often recommended first because they don't really have any downsides.

People with (or at risk of) CVD may be encouraged to eat a healthy, balanced diet, which is low in saturated fat (as saturated fat can increase the level of 'bad' cholesterol in the blood — see next page). They may also be encouraged to exercise regularly, lose weight if necessary and stop smoking.

Life-long medication

Lifestyle changes aren't always enough to treat CVD. Sometimes medicines are needed too. Some people may need to take these medicines for the rest of their lives.

Statins

Statins are drugs that can reduce the amount of 'bad' cholesterol (also known as LDL cholesterol) present in the bloodstream. Having too much 'bad' cholesterol in the bloodstream can cause fatty deposits to form inside arteries, which can lead to coronary heart disease. Taking statins slows down the rate of fatty deposits forming, which can reduce the risk of strokes and heart attacks.

Unfortunately, statins also have their disadvantages. Statins are a long-term drug that must be taken regularly. There's the risk that someone could forget to take them. Also, statins can sometimes cause negative side effects, e.g. headaches and aching muscles. Some of these side effects can be serious, e.g. kidney failure, liver damage and memory loss. Another disadvantage is that the effect of statins isn't instant. It takes time for their effect to kick in.

Tip: Cholesterol is an essential lipid that your body produces and needs to function properly. However, high levels of 'bad' (LDL) cholesterol in your bloodstream can cause health problems.

Antihypertensives

Antihypertensives reduce blood pressure. This helps to prevent damage to blood vessels and so reduces the risk of fatty deposits forming. This reduces the risk of cardiovascular disease. There are different types of antihypertensive medications, which reduce blood pressure in different ways.

> **Examples**
> - Diuretics — help flush out excess water.
> - ACE inhibitors — relax blood vessels.
> - Beta blockers — cause the heart to beat slower and less forcefully.

Each type of medication has it's own set of side effects, such as headaches and dizziness.

Exam Tip
In the exam, you could be asked to evaluate different treatments for CVD — if so, make sure you write about both the advantages and disadvantages of the treatments you're asked about.

Anticoagulants

Blood clots are more likely to form in patients with cardiovascular disease. This, coupled with the narrowing of arteries in CVD, increases the likelihood of blood clots blocking blood flow to vital organs. Anticoagulants (e.g. Warfarin™) are drugs which make blood clots less likely to form. This reduces the risk of blood clots causing problems such as heart attacks and strokes.

However, blood clotting is needed to prevent excessive bleeding. Patients taking anticoagulants are more likely to suffer from heavy bleeding if they're injured. This can result in significant blood loss if the injury is severe. Anticoagulants can also sometimes increase the risk of internal bleeding.

Exam Tip
When prescribing medicine, doctors have to weigh up the possible side effects against the risk of disease.

Surgical procedures

Sometimes the damage caused by cardiovascular disease needs to be treated with surgery. Any heart surgery is a major procedure and so there is always risk of bleeding, clots and infection. The longer and more complex the surgery, the greater the risk of such complications.

Stents

Stents are wire mesh tubes that can be inserted inside arteries to widen them and keep them open. They are particularly useful in people with coronary heart disease.

Stents keep the coronary arteries open, making sure blood can pass through to the heart muscles (see Figure 3). This keeps the person's heart beating (and the person alive).

> **Exam Tip**
> Make sure that you're clear about what you're being asked to do when answering data questions. If you're asked to describe what some data shows, you'll just need to give any patterns or trends. If the question wants you to explain the data, you'll need to apply your scientific knowledge to give reasons for the trends.

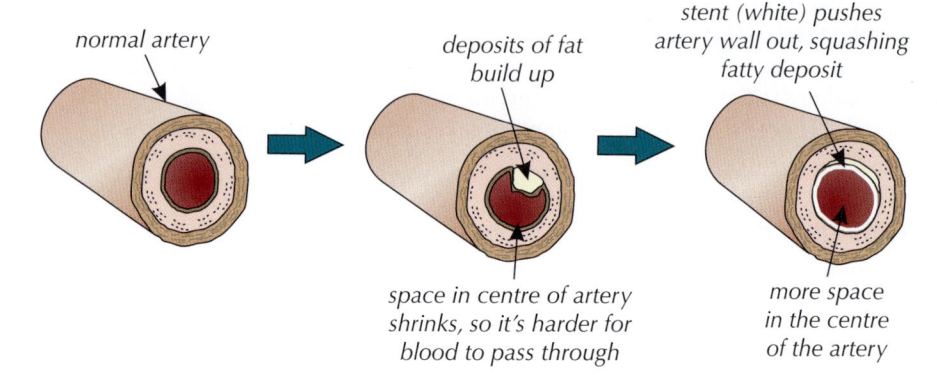

Figure 3: A diagram showing how a stent can help to widen an artery.

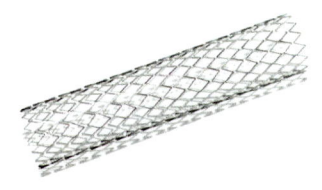

Figure 4: A stent that can be used to widen an artery.

Stents are a way of lowering the risk of a heart attack in people with coronary heart disease. They are effective for a long time and the recovery time from the surgery is relatively quick.

However, there is a risk of complications during the operation (e.g. a heart attack) and a risk of infection from surgery. Over time, the artery can narrow again as the stents can irritate the artery and make scar tissue grow. There's also the risk of a patient developing a blood clot near the stent — the patient needs to take anticoagulants to reduce this risk.

> **Tip:** Sampling is often used when collecting data related to health and disease. This is because it would take too long and cost too much to collect data from the entire population. Large samples are better than small samples. See p.238-239 for more on sampling.

Coronary bypass surgery

It's not always appropriate to insert a stent (for example, in cases when a patient has several blocked blood vessels). In such cases, blood flow to the heart can be improved by carrying out coronary bypass surgery. This is where a piece of healthy vessel is taken from elsewhere in the body and used to bypass a blocked section of the coronary arteries.

Coronary bypass surgery is longer and more invasive than surgery to insert a stent and so carries greater risk of complications. It also requires a longer stay in hospital following the operation and has a longer recovery time. However, there's a lower chance that the surgery will need to be repeated. (Repeat surgery can be necessary with stents if the artery narrows again.)

Donor hearts

Heart transplants are necessary in cases where heart disease is severe. The whole heart can be replaced with a donor heart. Although heart transplants can be life saving operations, they do have disadvantages.

> **Examples**
> - The new heart does not always start pumping properly, so further treatment is needed to help blood circulation until it improves.
> - Sometimes the immune system recognises the donor heart as foreign and attacks it. This is called rejection. To reduce the risk of rejection, patients must take immunosuppressant drugs for the rest of their life. These drugs suppress the immune system, but by doing so, make the patient more vulnerable to infection.

Tip: Patients must be compatible with the donor heart so that their body doesn't reject it. This means that there can be a long waiting list for donor hearts.

Practice Questions — Fact Recall

Q1 What is cardiovascular disease?

Q2 How do drugs that help to reduce blood pressure (antihypertensives) treat cardiovascular disease?

Q3 Give one risk of having any kind of surgery to treat cardiovascular disease.

Practice Question — Application

Q1 Clifford is diagnosed with cardiovascular disease. The doctor advises Clifford to stop smoking. Explain why.

Q2 A patient has been told he has cardiovascular disease. The doctors tell the patient he needs a surgical procedure to treat his condition. He is given information about having a stent inserted and about coronary bypass surgery. Some of the information is shown in the table below.

	Stent	Coronary bypass surgery
Time surgery takes	30 minutes - 2 hours	3-6 hours
Length of hospital stay	0-1 days	7 days or more
Approximate recovery time	1 week	6-12 weeks
Other information	Repeat surgery may be needed if artery narrows again	Less likely to need repeat surgery

After discussing his options with his doctor, the patient chooses to have a stent inserted rather than have coronary bypass surgery. Using information from the table, evaluate why the patient may have made this choice.

Topic 5c Checklist — Make sure you know...

Risk Factors for Non-Communicable Diseases
- [ ] That risk factors are things linked to an increased likelihood that a person will develop a disease.
- [ ] That many non-communicable diseases, including cardiovascular disease, cancer, liver and lung diseases and obesity are caused by several different risk factors interacting with each other.
- [ ] Why smoking is a risk factor for cardiovascular disease and alcohol is a risk factor for liver disease.
- [ ] Why a diet with too few or too many nutrients is a risk factor for malnutrition, and that a diet high in fat and sugar and a lack of exercise are risk factors for obesity.
- [ ] How non-communicable diseases have effects at local, national and global levels.

Measures of Obesity
- [ ] That Body Mass Index (BMI) and waist-to-hip ratio can be used as measures of obesity.
- [ ] That BMI can be used as a guide to determine whether a person is underweight, normal weight, overweight or obese.
- [ ] That BMI is calculated using the formula: BMI = weight (kg) ÷ (height (m))^2.
- [ ] Why diets high in fat and sugar, coupled with physical inactivity, can increase the likelihood of a high BMI and obesity.
- [ ] That the waist-to-hip ratio is a measure of fat distribution, which is calculated using the formula: waist-to-hip ratio = waist circumference ÷ hip circumference.
- [ ] That a high waist-to-hip ratio indicates that a person is carrying too much weight around their middle, increasing the risk of obesity-related problems.

Treating Cardiovascular Disease
- [ ] That cardiovascular disease can be treated by making lifestyle changes to reduce risk and that such changes are recommended for treatment first as they don't really have any downsides.
- [ ] That cardiovascular disease can be treated using life-long medications, such as statins to reduce 'bad' cholesterol in the blood, antihypertensives to reduce blood pressure and anticoagulants to reduce blood clotting, and that these medications have both advantages and disadvantages.
- [ ] That surgical procedures can be used to treat cardiovascular disease, including stents, coronary bypass surgery and heart transplants, and that all types of heart surgery carry major risks.
- [ ] How to evaluate relevant information and data describing treatments for cardiovascular disease.

Exam-style Questions

1

(a) Moira has a hip circumference of 89 cm and a waist circumference of 0.72 m.
Calculate Moira's waist-to-hip ratio. Give your answer to 2 significant figures.

(2 marks)

(b) Nadira has a waist-to-hip ratio of 0.92. Using your answer to part a), suggest whether Moira or Nadira is at more risk of developing type 2 diabetes. Explain your answer.

(2 marks)

(c) It is recommended that adults should not regularly drink more than 14 units of alcohol a week. Moira drinks 22 units of alcohol a week. Suggest **one** non-communicable disease that Moira is at risk of developing. Explain why.

(2 marks)

2 After a heart attack, many patients have a stent fitted into the affected coronary artery. A stent is a tube inserted into an artery to keep it open. It could be a bare-metal stent or a drug-eluting stent, which gradually releases a drug to prevent new cells from growing over the stent.

In a trial, patients needing a stent were randomly given either a bare-metal stent or a drug-eluting stent. Following their surgery, the patients were monitored and any problems recorded.

154 patients received the drug-eluting stent and 153 patients received the bare-metal stent. **Figure 1** shows how many patients experienced certain problems following stent surgery:

Figure 1

	Number of patients who died following treatment	Number of patients who had another heart attack	% of patients whose artery renarrowed
Drug-eluting stent	3	3	9
Bare-metal stent	7	3	21

(a) Calculate the percentage of patients that died after receiving the drug-eluting stent.

(1 mark)

(b) Suggest why stents are often used in people who have had a heart attack.

(2 marks)

(c) Based on the information given, some doctors may conclude that drug-eluting stents are more beneficial than bare-metal stents. Do you think this is a valid conclusion? Explain your answer.

(3 marks)

Topic 6   Plant Structures and Their Functions

Learning Objectives:
- Be able to describe photosynthesis in plants and algae as an endothermic reaction that uses light energy to react carbon dioxide and water to produce glucose and oxygen.
- Be able to describe photosynthetic organisms as the main producers of food and therefore biomass.

Specification References 6.1, 6.2

Tip: Plants can use glucose to make a variety of things, such as cell walls and proteins.

Tip: Exothermic reactions transfer energy to the surroundings and endothermic reactions transfer energy from the surroundings.

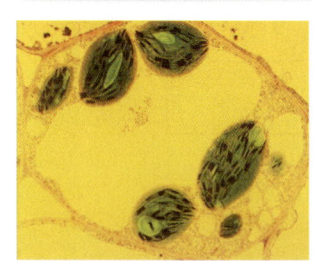

Figure 1: *Microscope image of a plant cell. The green structures are chloroplasts.*

Tip: Xylem is the tissue that transports water around a plant (see page 155).

1. Photosynthesis

Plants make their own food using energy from the Sun, a substance called chlorophyll, carbon dioxide from the air and water from the soil.

What is photosynthesis?

Photosynthesis is the process that produces 'food' in organisms such as green plants and algae. The 'food' it produces is **glucose** (a sugar). Photosynthesis uses energy from the Sun to convert carbon dioxide and water into glucose and oxygen.

Some of the glucose is used to make larger, complex molecules that the organisms need to grow. These make up the organisms' **biomass** — the mass of living material in the organisms. The energy stored in the plants' and algae's biomass works its way through the food chain as animals eat them and each other. So photosynthetic organisms are the main producers of food for nearly all life on Earth.

Where does photosynthesis happen?

Photosynthesis takes place in **chloroplasts** in green plant cells — they contain pigments like **chlorophyll** that absorb light. Energy is transferred to the chloroplasts by light. Photosynthesis is **endothermic** — this means energy is transferred from the environment in the process.

Photosynthesis happens in the leaves of all green plants — this is largely what the leaves are for. Figure 2 shows a cross-section of a leaf showing the four raw materials (carbon dioxide, water, light and chlorophyll) needed for photosynthesis.

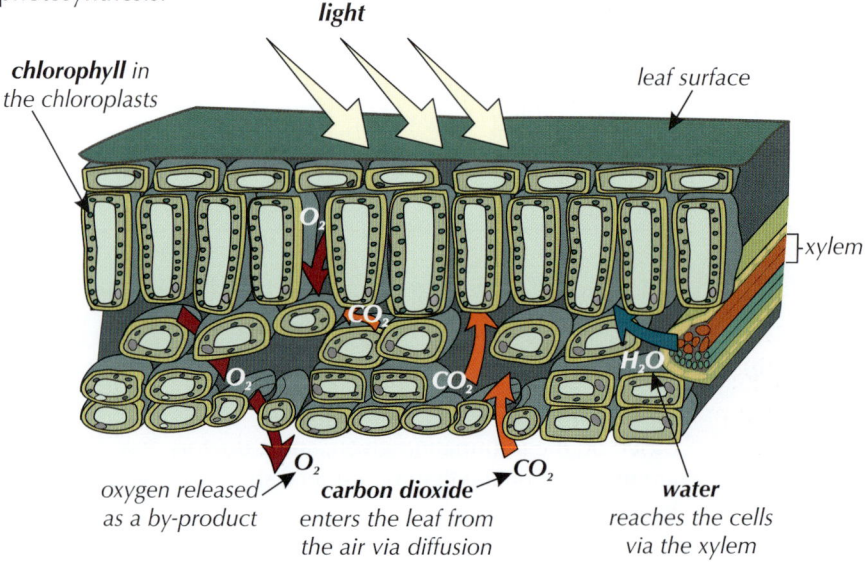

Figure 2: *Diagram of a cross-section through a leaf, showing the four raw materials required for photosynthesis.*

- **chlorophyll** in the chloroplasts
- light
- leaf surface
- xylem
- oxygen released as a by-product
- **carbon dioxide** enters the leaf from the air via diffusion
- **water** reaches the cells via the xylem

Word equation

The word equation for photosynthesis is:

$$\text{carbon dioxide} + \text{water} \xrightarrow{\text{light}} \text{glucose} + \text{oxygen}$$

Exam Tip
You should learn these photosynthesis equations — they could get you easy marks in the exam.

Symbol equation

There's a symbol equation for photosynthesis too:

$$6CO_2 + 6H_2O \xrightarrow{\text{light}} C_6H_{12}O_6 + 6O_2$$

Practice Questions — Fact Recall

Q1 Which product produced by photosynthesis is 'food' for the plant?

Q2 Which gas is used in photosynthesis?

Q3 Which gas is produced by photosynthesis?

Q4 a) Name the parts of a plant cell that contain chlorophyll.

b) What role does chlorophyll play in photosynthesis?

Q5 Photosynthesis is a reaction that takes in energy from the surroundings. Give the name for this type of reaction.

Q6 Write out the word equation for photosynthesis.

Q7 Name the chemical substance with the symbol $C_6H_{12}O_6$.

Practice Question — Application

Q1 Three identical plants were grown for a week. They were treated in exactly the same way, except they each received different amounts of sunlight per day, as shown in this table:

Plant	Hours of sunlight received per day
A	3
B	7
C	10

The plants didn't have any source of light other than sunlight.

Which plant do you think will have produced the most glucose after one week? Explain your answer.

Topic 6 Plant Structures and Their Functions

Learning Objectives:
- Be able to explain the effect of light intensity, carbon dioxide concentration and temperature as limiting factors on the rate of photosynthesis.
- **H** Be able to explain the interactions of light intensity, carbon dioxide concentration and temperature in limiting the rate of photosynthesis.

Specification References 6.3, 6.4

2. Limiting Factors in Photosynthesis

Photosynthesis doesn't always happen at the same rate — factors such as light intensity, carbon dioxide level and temperature can all affect the rate.

What is a limiting factor?

The rate of photosynthesis is affected by the intensity of light, the concentration of carbon dioxide (CO_2), and the temperature. All three of these things need to be at the right level to allow a plant to photosynthesise as quickly as possible. If any one of these factors is too high or too low, it will become the **limiting factor**. This just means it's the factor which is stopping photosynthesis from happening any faster.

Which factor is limiting at any particular time depends on the environmental conditions:

> **Examples**
> - At night there's much less light than there is during the day, so light intensity is usually the limiting factor at night.
> - In winter it's usually cold, so a low temperature is often the limiting factor.
> - If it's warm enough and bright enough, the amount of CO_2 is usually limiting.

Tip: Plants also need water for photosynthesis, but when a plant is so short of water that it becomes the limiting factor in photosynthesis, it's already in such trouble that this is the least of its worries.

Limiting factors in photosynthesis

You need to be able to explain how light intensity, carbon dioxide concentration and temperature affect the rate of photosynthesis.

1. Effect of light intensity

Light provides the energy needed for photosynthesis. As the light intensity (strength of light) increases, photosynthesis gets faster.

H After a certain point, if you increase the light intensity, it won't make any difference — as light intensity increases, the rate will no longer increase. This is because it will be either the temperature or the carbon dioxide level which is now the limiting factor, not light. This is shown in Figure 1.

Tip: **H** In Figure 1, photosynthesis hasn't stopped happening when the graph levels off — it's just that the <u>rate</u> of photosynthesis is not increasing anymore.

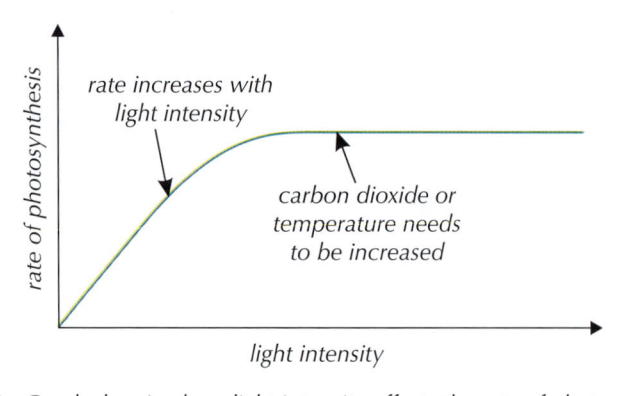

Figure 1: Graph showing how light intensity affects the rate of photosynthesis.

H In the lab you can change the light intensity by moving a lamp closer to or further away from your plant (see page 152 for this experiment). But if you just plot the rate of photosynthesis against "distance of lamp from the plant", you get a weird-shaped graph. To get a graph like the one in Figure 1, you either need to measure the light intensity at the plant using a light meter or calculate the relative light intensity using a nifty bit of maths called the inverse square law — see page 154.

Figure 2: The number of bubbles produced in a set time can be counted to estimate the rate of photosynthesis, but a more accurate set-up can be seen on pages 152-153.

2. Effect of carbon dioxide concentration

CO_2 is one of the raw materials needed for photosynthesis, so the rate of photosynthesis increases as the carbon dioxide concentration increases.

H As with light intensity, the amount of CO_2 will only increase the rate of photosynthesis up to a point. After this the graph flattens out — as the amount of CO_2 increases, the rate no longer increases (see Figure 3). This shows that CO_2 is no longer the limiting factor — at this point, either temperature or light intensity will be limiting the rate of photosynthesis.

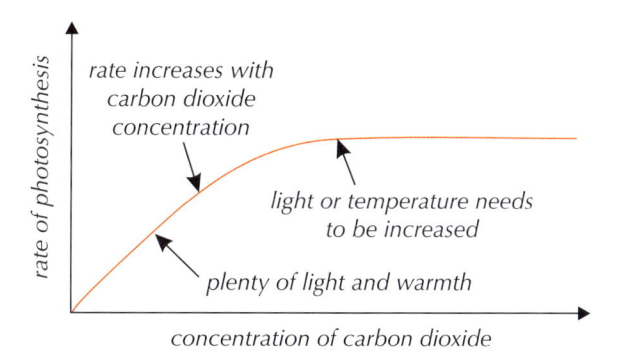

Figure 3: Graph showing how carbon dioxide concentration affects the rate of photosynthesis.

Tip: If you're investigating the rate of photosynthesis using a plant in water, you can increase the CO_2 level by dissolving sodium hydrogencarbonate in the water. This gives off carbon dioxide.

3. Effect of temperature

Photosynthesis gets faster as the temperature increases, but only up to a certain temperature. If it gets too hot, the rate of photosynthesis slows down and it can even stop altogether.

Enzymes are proteins which increase the speed of chemical reactions in living things — so enzymes increase the rate of photosynthesis in plant cells. The speed at which enzymes work is affected by temperature.

Tip: You can read more about enzymes on pages 36-38.

Usually, if the temperature is the limiting factor in photosynthesis it's because it's too low — the enzymes needed for photosynthesis work more slowly at low temperatures. But if the plant gets too hot, the enzymes it needs for photosynthesis and its other reactions will be damaged. This happens at about 45 °C (which is pretty hot for outdoors, although greenhouses can get that hot if you're not careful).

Figure 4, on the next page, shows the effect that temperature has on the rate of photosynthesis.

Topic 6 Plant Structures and Their Functions

Tip: The highest point (the peak) of the graph in Figure 4 is the optimum temperature of the reaction. See page 37 for more.

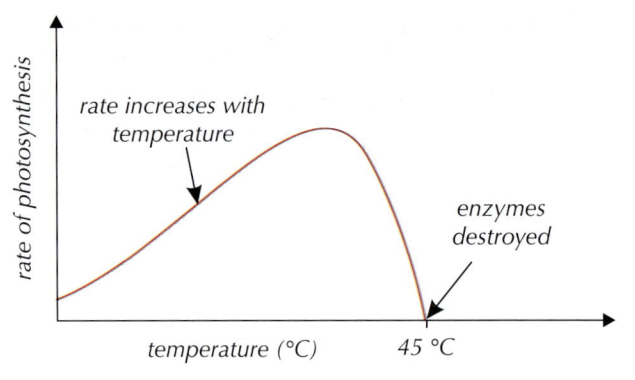

Figure 4: Graph showing how temperature affects the rate of photosynthesis.

4. Graphs showing more than one limiting factor `Higher`

You can show the effect of more than one limiting factor on the same graph:

> **Example** — **Higher**
>
> Figure 5 shows how the rate of photosynthesis is affected by changing light intensity for two reactions carried out at different temperatures.
>
> At the start of the graph, the rate of photosynthesis increases steadily as the light intensity increases for both reactions. At this point, light intensity is the limiting factor for both.
>
> The lines level off when light intensity is no longer the limiting factor. The 15 °C line levels off at a lower point than the 25 °C line — at this point temperature must have become the limiting factor for the reaction at 15 °C. 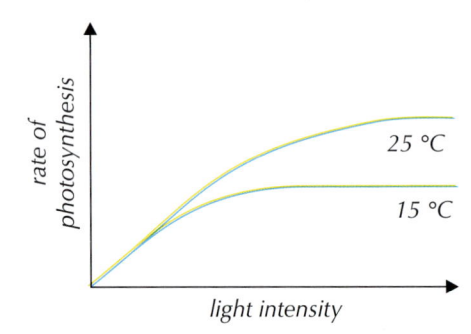
>
> *Figure 5: Graph showing how rate of photosynthesis is affected by both light intensity and temperature.*

Practice Question — Fact Recall

Q1 The rate of photosynthesis is affected by limiting factors.

　a) What is meant by a 'limiting factor' of photosynthesis?

　b) Apart from light intensity, name two other factors that affect the rate of photosynthesis.

　c) Describe the effect of increasing light intensity on the rate of photosynthesis.

Practice Questions — Application

Q1 Complete the table to show what is most likely to be the limiting factor of photosynthesis in the environmental conditions listed.

Environmental conditions	Most likely limiting factor
Outside on a cold winter's day.	
In an unlit garden at 1:30 am, in the UK, in summer.	
On a windowsill on a warm, bright day.	

Q2 Peter was investigating the rate of photosynthesis in pondweed. He put equally sized samples of pondweed in two separate flasks, A and B. Flask A had a lower carbon dioxide concentration than flask B. Peter put the flasks an equal distance away from a light source. He gradually increased the intensity of the light during the experiment. He kept both flasks at a constant temperature of 25 °C. Peter's results are shown on the graph below:

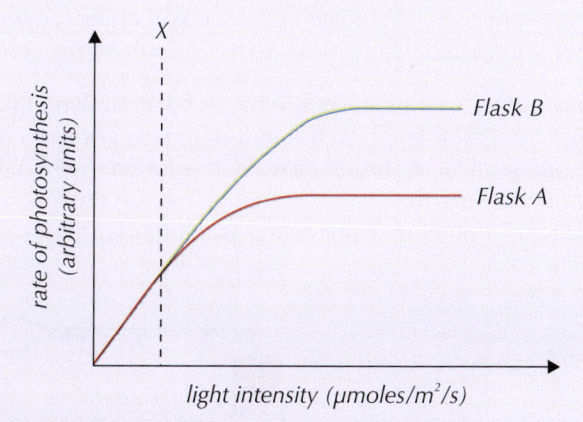

a) Peter thinks that the limiting factor before point X in his experiment is light. Explain why he is right.

b) Suggest why the line for Flask A levels off at a lower point than the line for Flask B. Explain your answer.

Exam Tip H
µmoles/m^2/s is a unit used to measure light intensity. Don't panic if you see unfamiliar units in the exam — just focus on what the axis is showing you, e.g. here it's light intensity.

Learning Objective:
- Be able to carry out an experiment to investigate the effect of light intensity on the rate of photosynthesis (Core Practical).

Specification Reference 6.5

3. Investigating the Rate of Photosynthesis

You need to know how to collect data about how light intensity affects the rate of photosynthesis. Handily, that's what these pages are all about.

Investigating the rate of photosynthesis

To investigate the effect of different light intensities on the rate of photosynthesis, you need to be able to measure the rate. One way to do this involves an aquatic plant, such as Canadian pondweed. The rate at which the pondweed produces oxygen corresponds to the rate at which it's photosynthesising — the faster the rate of oxygen production, the faster the rate of photosynthesis. Here's how the experiment works:

- A source of white light is placed at a specific distance from a conical flask containing the pondweed. Leave the pondweed for a couple of minutes to adjust to the new light intensity before starting the experiment.

Tip: Make sure you do a risk assessment before you start this investigation, so that you carry it out safely.

- When you're ready to start, connect a gas syringe to the conical flask and leave the pondweed to photosynthesise for a set amount of time.

Tip: Canadian pondweed is not native to the UK, so it must be disposed of carefully after the experiment — it shouldn't be released into the environment.

- As it photosynthesises, the oxygen released will collect in the gas syringe. This allows you to accurately measure the volume of oxygen produced.

The apparatus for the experiment should be set up as shown in Figure 2. The gas syringe should be empty at the start of the experiment. Sodium hydrogencarbonate releases carbon dioxide in solution — it is usually added to the water to make sure the plant has enough carbon dioxide (so that carbon dioxide concentration is not acting as a limiting factor.)

Figure 1: Pondweed giving off oxygen bubbles as a by-product of photosynthesis.

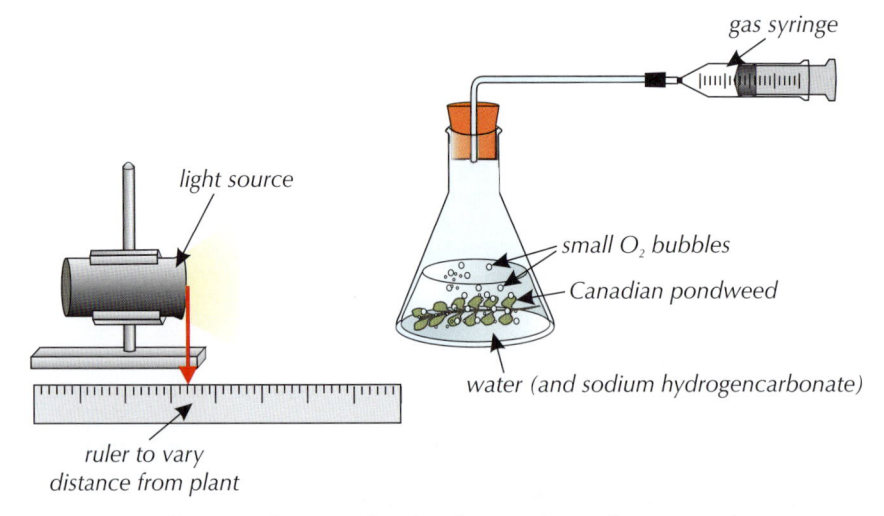

Figure 2: Diagram showing the experimental set up used to measure the rate of photosynthesis in water plants.

You should repeat the experiment a few times with the light source at the same distance and calculate the mean volume of O_2 produced. Then you can repeat the whole procedure with the light source placed at different distances from the pondweed.

Tip: You can also investigate the rate of photosynthesis with algal balls, instead of pondweed. These are little balls of jelly which contain algae.

Controlling variables

In this experiment, you're investigating the effect of different light intensities on the rate of photosynthesis — the light intensity is the **independent variable**. The **dependent variable** (the variable you're measuring) is the amount of oxygen produced. You have to try to keep all the other variables constant, so that it's a fair test.

> **Examples**
>
> - If your plant's in a flask, keep the flask in a water bath to help keep the temperature constant.
> - It's harder to control the carbon dioxide concentration. But if you add the same amount of sodium hydrogencarbonate to the same volume of water each time, it should mean that roughly the same amount of carbon dioxide is available to the plant in each experiment.

Tip: The independent variable is the variable that you change in an experiment — see page 10.

Tip: For more on designing investigations and controlling variables see pages 9-11.

Tip: The experiment can be modified to test the effect of temperature of carbon dioxide concentration too. Just remember to only change one variable at a time.

Calculating the rate of photosynthesis

You can compare the results at different light intensities by giving the rate of oxygen production as the volume of gas produced per unit time, e.g. $cm^3\ min^{-1}$.

To calculate the rate, just divide the total volume of gas that the plant produced by the time taken to produce it.

> **Example**
>
> A student measured the amount of oxygen produced by a piece of pondweed by collecting it in a gas syringe. After 5 minutes, 2.5 cm^3 of oxygen had been collected. Calculate the rate of oxygen production. Give your answer in $cm^3\ min^{-1}$.
>
> Divide the volume of oxygen produced by the time taken:
>
> Rate = 2.5 cm^3 ÷ 5 min = **0.5 $cm^3\ min^{-1}$**

Tip: When you're working out a rate, you should always be dividing by time.

Practice Question — Application

Q1 A student set up an experiment to investigate the rate of photosynthesis using a piece of Canadian pondweed.

She placed the pondweed in a flask of water, and measured the amount of oxygen produced using a gas syringe, as shown in the diagram.

In 3 minutes, the pondweed produced 0.5 cm^3 of oxygen. Calculate the rate of photosynthesis for the pondweed. Give your answer in $cm^3\ min^{-1}$, to 1 significant figure.

Tip: There are other ways that you could carry out this experiment too. For example, instead of measuring the volume of oxygen produced, you could count the number of bubbles released by the plant in a set time.

Topic 6 Plant Structures and Their Functions

Learning Objective:

- **H** Be able to explain how the rate of photosynthesis is directly proportional to light intensity and inversely proportional to the distance from a light source, including the use of the inverse square law calculation.

Specification Reference 6.6

4. The Inverse Square Law *Higher*

This can be a bit tricky to get your head around, but stick with it...

What is the inverse square law?

The rate of photosynthesis is **directly proportional** to light intensity. So when you increase the light intensity, the rate of photosynthesis increases at the same rate, and when you decrease the light intensity, the rate of photosynthesis decreases at the same rate.

When a plant is moved away from a light source (e.g. a lamp), the amount of light reaching the plant decreases — in other words, as the distance increases, the light intensity decreases. So both the light intensity and the rate of photosynthesis are **inversely proportional** to the distance from a light source.

However, it's not quite as simple as that. It turns out that light intensity decreases in proportion to the square of the distance. This is called the **inverse square law** and is written out like this:

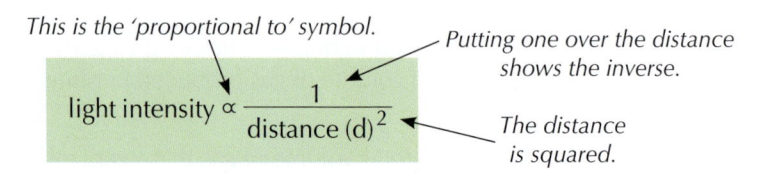

$$\text{light intensity} \propto \frac{1}{\text{distance (d)}^2}$$

This is the 'proportional to' symbol.
Putting one over the distance shows the inverse.
The distance is squared.

Tip: **H** If two variables are proportional to each other, when one variable changes, the other will change at the same rate. Inverse proportion just means that as one variable increases, the other decreases at the same rate.

The inverse square law means that if you halve the distance, the light intensity will be four times greater and if you third the distance, the light intensity will be nine times greater. Likewise, if you double the distance, the light intensity will be four times smaller and if you treble the distance, the light intensity will be nine times smaller.

You can use $1/d^2$ as a measure of light intensity.

Example — *Higher*

Use the inverse square law to calculate the light intensity when the lamp is 10 cm from the pondweed. *(MATHS SKILLS)*

- Use the formula $\frac{1}{d^2}$: $\quad$ light intensity $= \frac{1}{d^2}$
- Fill in the values you know — you're given the distance, so put that in. $\quad$ light intensity $= \frac{1}{10^2}$
- Calculate the answer. $\quad \frac{1}{10^2} = 0.01$ a.u.

Tip: **H** a.u. stands for arbitrary units.

Practice Question — Application

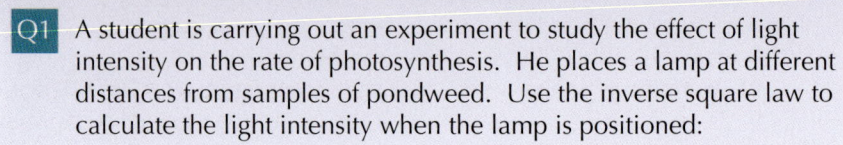

Q1 A student is carrying out an experiment to study the effect of light intensity on the rate of photosynthesis. He places a lamp at different distances from samples of pondweed. Use the inverse square law to calculate the light intensity when the lamp is positioned:

a) 15 cm from the pondweed,   b) 30 cm from the pondweed.

5. Transport in Plants

Like all living things, plants need transport systems to move substances around...

Transport tissues in plants

Flowering plants have two separate types of tissue — phloem and xylem — for transporting substances around. Both types of tissue form 'tubes', which go to every part of the plant, but they are totally separate.

Phloem

Phloem tubes are made of columns of elongated living cells with small pores in the end walls to allow cell sap to flow through (see Figures 1 and 2). Cell sap is a liquid that's made up of the substances being transported and water.

Phloem tubes transport food substances (mainly dissolved sucrose) made in the leaves to the rest of the plant for immediate use (e.g. in growing regions) or for storage. The transport goes in both directions — from the leaves down to the roots, and from the roots up to the leaves. This process is called **translocation** and requires energy from respiration.

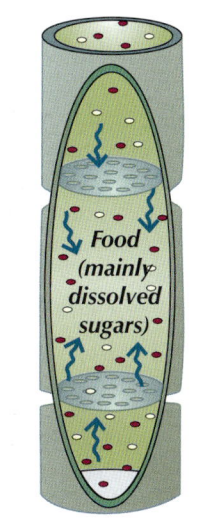

Figure 1: Diagram showing the inside of a phloem tube.

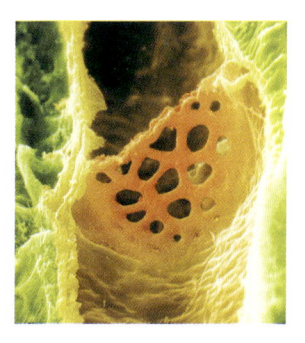

Figure 2: Microscope image of the inside of a cut phloem tube — the small holes between the cells can be seen clearly.

Xylem

Xylem tubes are made of dead cells joined end to end with no end walls between them and a hole down the middle (see Figures 3 and 4). They're strengthened with a material called lignin.

Xylem tubes carry water and mineral ions up the plant — from the roots to the stem and leaves. The movement of water from the roots, through the xylem and out of the leaves is called the **transpiration stream** (see next page).

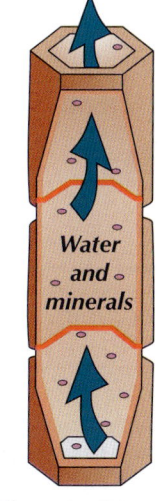

Figure 3: Diagram showing the inside of a xylem tube.

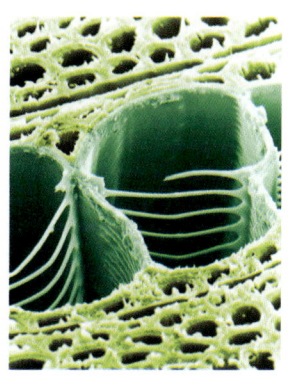

Figure 4: Microscope image showing a cut xylem tube (dark green).

Learning Objectives:
- Be able to explain how the structures of the xylem and the phloem are adapted to their function in the plant, including:
  - living cells in the phloem using energy to transport sucrose around the plant.
  - lignified dead cells in the xylem transporting water and minerals through the plant.
- Be able to describe how sucrose is transported around the plant by translocation.
- Be able to describe how water and mineral ions are transported through the plant by transpiration.
- Be able to explain how the structure of the root hair cells is adapted to absorb water and mineral ions.

Specification References 6.7 – 6.10

Tip: Cells in the root (called root hair cells) take up water from the soil by osmosis, and take up mineral ions by active transport. There's more information about how they're adapted for this on page 157.

Topic 6 Plant Structures and Their Functions

surface of leaf

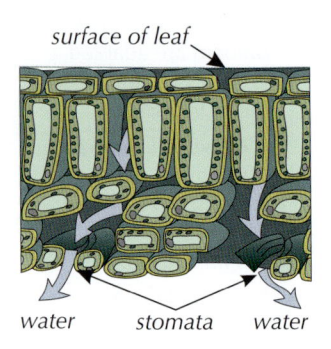

water   stomata   water

Figure 5: *Cross-section of a leaf showing how water moves out during transpiration.*

The transpiration stream

Transpiration is the loss of water from a plant's surface. It is caused by the evaporation and diffusion (see p.43) of water from surface of the plant (usually the leaves). The transpiration stream is the movement of water and mineral ions through a plant from the roots to the leaves.
It happens like this:

1. Water from inside a leaf evaporates and diffuses out of the leaf, mainly through the stomata (tiny holes found mainly on the lower surface of the leaf) — see Figure 5.

2. This creates a slight shortage of water in the leaf, and so more water is drawn up from the rest of the plant through the xylem vessels to replace it.

3. This in turn means more water is drawn up from the roots, and so there's a constant transpiration stream of water through the plant.

The transpiration stream carries mineral ions that are dissolved in the water along with it.

The transpiration stream is shown in Figure 6.

Tip: The rate of transpiration depends on the conditions in the plant's environment. Transpiration happens fastest in bright, hot and dry conditions where the air flow around the leaves is good, because this is when evaporation happens fastest — see page 158 for more.

① *water evaporates and diffuses from the leaves*

② *water is drawn up through the plant*

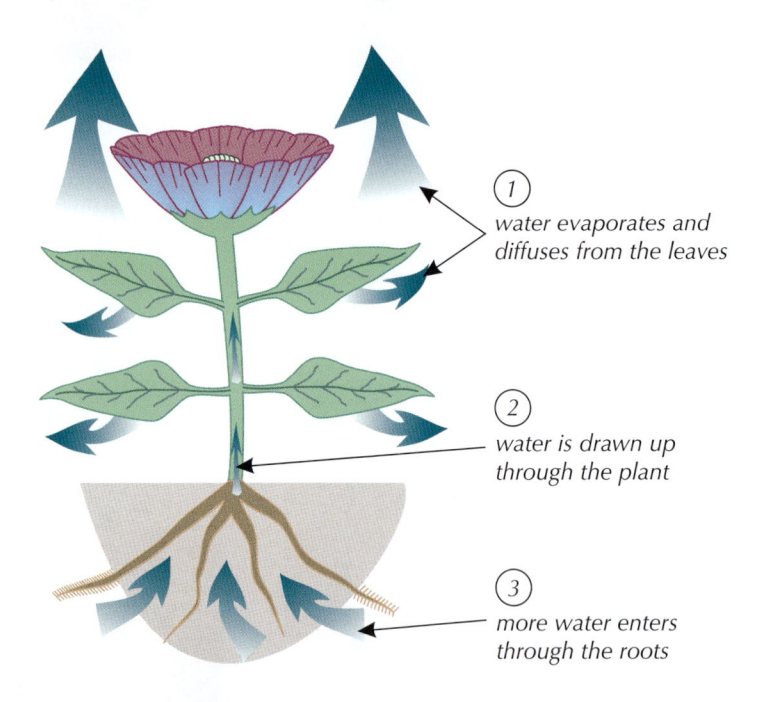

③ *more water enters through the roots*

Figure 6: *Diagram showing how water moves through a plant in the transpiration stream.*

Transpiration is just a side-effect of the way leaves are adapted for photosynthesis. They have to have stomata in them so that gases can be exchanged easily (see page 159). Because there's more water inside the plant than in the air outside, the water escapes from the leaves through the stomata by diffusion.

Root hair cells

The cells on the surface of plant roots grow into "hairs", which stick out into the soil (see Figure 7). Each branch of a root will be covered in millions of these microscopic hairs.

The hairs give the plant a large surface area for absorbing water and mineral ions from the soil. The concentration of mineral ions is usually higher in the root hair cells than in the soil around them, so mineral ions are absorbed by active transport (see page 46). There is normally more water in the soil than in the roots, so water is absorbed by osmosis (see pages 44-45).

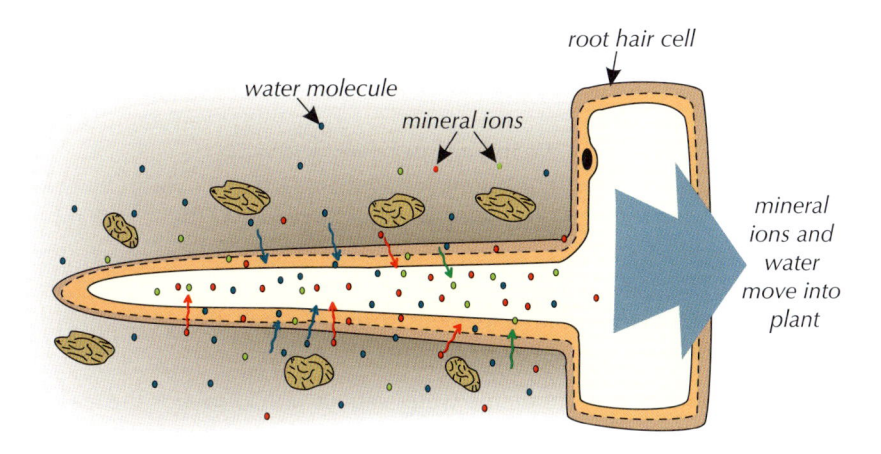

Figure 7: Diagram to show the absorption of water and mineral ions by a root hair cell.

Practice Questions — Fact Recall

Q1 What is transported in phloem tubes?

Q2 Describe the structure of the phloem tubes.

Q3 Give two substances that are transported in xylem tubes.

Q4 Explain how the transpiration steam works to move water through a plant.

Q5 Explain how the shape of root hair cells help a plant to absorb water and mineral ions through its roots.

Learning Objectives:
- Be able to explain the effect of environmental factors on the rate of water uptake by a plant, including light intensity, air movement and temperature.
- Be able to demonstrate an understanding of rate calculations for transpiration.
- Be able to describe the structure and function of the stomata.

Specification References 6.9, 6.12, 6.13

6. Transpiration and Stomata

How quickly transpiration takes place is affected by several factors...

Factors affecting transpiration rate

Transpiration rate is affected by three main environmental factors:

Light intensity
The brighter the light, the greater the transpiration rate. Stomata begin to close as it gets darker. Photosynthesis can't happen in the dark, so they don't need to be open to let CO_2 in. When the stomata are closed, very little water can escape.

Temperature
The warmer it is, the faster transpiration happens. When it's warm, the water particles have more energy to evaporate and diffuse out of the stomata.

Air flow
The better the air flow around a leaf (e.g. stronger wind), the greater the transpiration rate.

If air flow around a leaf is poor, the water vapour just surrounds the leaf and doesn't move away. This means there's a high concentration of water particles outside the leaf as well as inside it, so diffusion doesn't happen as quickly.

If there's good air flow, the water vapour is swept away, maintaining a low concentration of water in the air outside the leaf. Diffusion then happens quickly, from an area of higher concentration to an area of lower concentration.

Tip: Wet clothes dry as water evaporates from the fabric. You wouldn't expect clothes hung out in the garden to dry very quickly on a cold, wet day — so don't expect evaporation from a plant to be quick under those conditions either.

Investigating transpiration rate

You can estimate the rate of transpiration by measuring the uptake of water by a plant using a **potometer**. This is because you can assume that water uptake by the plant is directly related to water loss by the leaves (transpiration). Figure 1 shows the apparatus you'll need.

Tip: You can use a potometer to estimate how light intensity, temperature or air flow around the plant affect the transpiration rate. Just remember to only change one variable at a time and control the rest to make it a fair test.

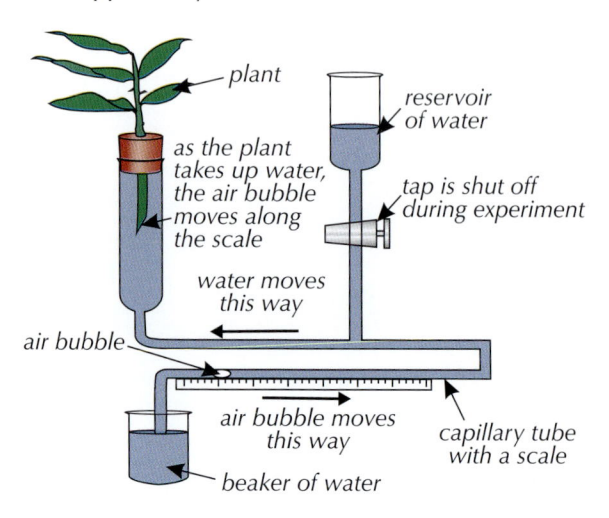

Figure 1: *A potometer — apparatus for measuring the uptake of water by a plant.*

To investigate the rate of transpiration, set up the apparatus as in Figure 1, and then record the starting position of the air bubble. Start a stopwatch and record the distance moved by the bubble per unit of time, e.g. per hour. Keep the conditions constant throughout the experiment, e.g. the temperature and air humidity. Calculating the speed of the air bubble movement gives an estimate of the transpiration rate.

Tip: It's quite tough to set up a potometer. See page 236 for some tips.

Estimating the rate of transpiration

You can use the data you collect in your experiment to estimate the rate of transpiration. Take a look at this example:

Tip: The faster the transpiration rate, the faster the water uptake by the plant.

> **Example**
>
> **A potometer was set up to estimate the rate of transpiration of a plant. In 60 minutes, the bubble in the potometer moved 6.6 cm. Calculate the rate of transpiration. Give your answer in mm min^{-1}.**
>
> 1. First, convert 6.6 cm into mm:
>
>   6.6 × 10 = 66 mm
>
> 2. Then divide the distance moved by the time taken:
>
>   66 ÷ 60 = **1.1 mm min^{-1}**

Tip: Rates of transpiration can also be given in mm^3 min^{-1}, but this requires a bit more maths to find the actual volume of water that the plant has taken up.

Stomata and guard cells

Stomata are tiny pores on the surface of a plant. They're mostly found on the lower surface of leaves. Stomata allow CO_2 and oxygen to diffuse directly in and out of a leaf. They also allow water vapour to escape during transpiration.

Two guard cells surround each stoma. Guard cells have a kidney shape — having this shape helps to open and close the stomata.

- When the plant has lots of water, the guard cells fill with water and go turgid (swollen with water). This opens the stomata so gases can be exchanged for photosynthesis (see Figure 2).

- When the plant is short of water, the guard cells lose water and become flaccid (limp), closing the stomata (see Figure 2). This helps stop too much water vapour escaping.

Tip: Stoma is the singular word, stomata is the plural.

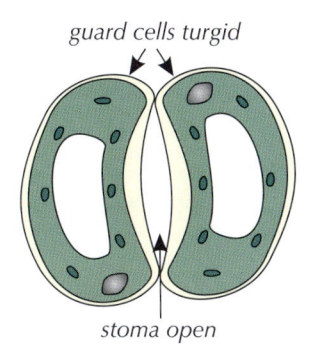

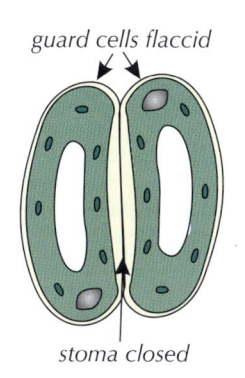

Figure 2: Diagram showing how guard cells open and close a stoma.

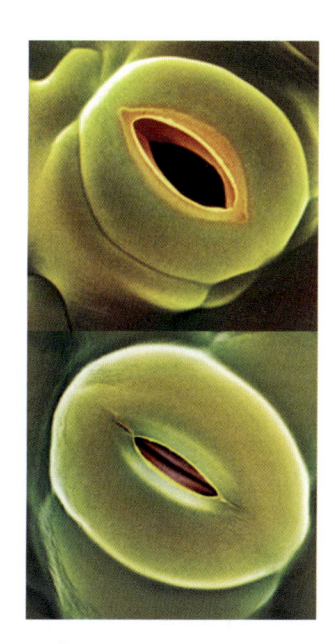

Figure 3: An open stoma (top) and a closed stoma (bottom).

Topic 6 **Plant Structures and Their Functions**

159

Guard cells have other adaptations besides their shape which help with their roles in gas exchange and controlling water loss within a leaf:

- They have thin outer walls and thickened inner walls, which helps to make the opening and closing mechanism work.

- They're sensitive to light, so they can close the stomata at night to save water without losing out on photosynthesis.

You usually find more stomata on the undersides of leaves than on the top. The lower surface is shaded and cooler — so less water is lost through the stomata than if they were on the upper surface.

Practice Questions — Fact Recall

Q1 What is the effect of increasing light intensity on the rate of transpiration?

Q2 Potometers can be used to estimate the rate of transpiration. What does a potometer actually measure?

Q3 a) Name the cells that control the size of the stomata.
b) Explain how these cells close the stomata.

Practice Question — Application

Q1 A student used a potometer to measure the effect that changing the temperature had on the rate of transpiration of a plant cutting.

For each temperature she tested, she kept the equipment at that temperature and measured the distance that the air bubble in the potometer moved in 30 minutes. She repeated the experiment at three different temperatures. Her results are shown below.

Temperature / °C	Distance moved by bubble / mm
10	26
15	31
20	37

a) Calculate the rate of transpiration of the plant in mm min^{-1} at:

i) 10 °C

ii) 15 °C

b) Explain why the bubble moved a greater distance when the plant was kept at 20 °C than when it was kept at 10 °C.

Tip: Rate is measured as a given quantity per unit time. In Q1a, it's a measure of distance divided by time.

Topic 6 Checklist — Make sure you know...

Photosynthesis
- [ ] That photosynthesis is a process used by green plants and algae that converts carbon dioxide and water into glucose and oxygen.
- [ ] That plants use some of the glucose produced during photosynthesis to build up their biomass.
- [ ] That plants are responsible for producing most of the food and biomass in the food chain.
- [ ] That photosynthesis is an endothermic reaction that requires light energy.
- [ ] That photosynthesis takes place in chloroplasts.
- [ ] The word equation and symbol equation for photosynthesis.

Limiting Factors in Photosynthesis
- [ ] That photosynthesis requires light, a suitable temperature and carbon dioxide to occur.
- [ ] How light intensity, carbon dioxide concentration and temperature act as limiting factors on the rate of photosynthesis.
- [ ] **H** How light intensity, carbon dioxide concentration and temperature all act together to control the rate of photosynthesis in a plant.

Investigating the Rate of Photosynthesis
- [ ] How to carry out an experiment to investigate the effect of light intensity on the rate of photosynthesis (Core Practical).

The Inverse Square Law
- [ ] **H** That the rate of photosynthesis is directly proportional to light intensity.
- [ ] **H** That the rate of photosynthesis is inversely proportional to the distance from a light source.
- [ ] **H** How to use the inverse square law in calculations involving light intensity and distance from an object (such as a plant).

Transport in Plants
- [ ] That phloem tubes are made of elongated living cells, which have pores (holes) between them to allow cell sap to pass through.
- [ ] That the phloem carries sucrose and other substances between the leaves and the rest of the plant (including the roots) in a process called translocation.
- [ ] That translocation requires energy from respiration.
- [ ] That xylem tubes are made of dead cells with no end walls between them.

cont...

- [ ] That xylem tubes are strengthened with lignin.
- [ ] How the xylem carries water and mineral ions from the roots to the leaves in the transpiration stream.
- [ ] How the root hair cells of plants are adapted to efficiently absorb mineral ions and water from the soil.

Transpiration and Stomata

- [ ] How light intensity, temperature and air flow affect the rate of transpiration.
- [ ] How to estimate the rate of transpiration from the results of an experiment to investigate the water uptake of a plant.
- [ ] How the stomata (pores) on a leaf are opened and closed by the guard cells.
- [ ] How the stomata and guard cells are adapted for their role in gas exchange in a plant.

Exam-style Questions

1 Tim read the following information in a science magazine:

> You can measure the rate of photosynthesis in plants by doing the following:
>
> Cut discs from a plant leaf. Put them into dilute sodium hydrogencarbonate solution (which serves as a source of carbon dioxide). Put the solution and leaf discs in a syringe and then remove all the air from the syringe — this removes any gases from the air spaces in the leaf, which will cause the leaf discs to sink.
>
> Then put the syringe containing the leaf discs under a light source. As the leaf discs photosynthesise, their cells produce oxygen. The oxygen will fill the air spaces in the leaf — with enough oxygen in the air spaces they'll begin to float. You can use the time this takes as a measure of the rate of photosynthesis.

(a) Where in a plant cell does photosynthesis take place?

(1 mark)

(b) Complete the word equation for photosynthesis:

carbon dioxide + ... ⟶ .... + oxygen

(1 mark)

Tim decided to use this experiment to investigate the effect of light intensity on the rate of photosynthesis. He conducted the experiment at three different light intensities. For each light intensity he cut 10 equally sized discs from a leaf, and set up the experiment as described in the magazine. He then timed how long it took for all of the leaf discs to float to the surface in the syringe. His results are shown in **Figure 1**.

Light intensity	Time it took for all discs to float (minutes)
A	18
B	9
C	11

Figure 1

(c) Which light intensity do you think was the highest, **A**, **B** or **C**? Explain your answer.

(3 marks)

(d) Tim thinks that if he keeps increasing the light intensity, he will keep increasing the rate of photosynthesis. Is he right? Explain your answer.

(3 marks)

(e) Tim conducts the experiment again at light intensity **C**. This time, instead of using sodium hydrogencarbonate solution, he uses the same volume of distilled water. Would you expect it to take more or less than 11 minutes for all of the discs to float? Explain your answer.

(2 marks)

2 Plants have tissues that are adapted for different functions.

(a) Translocation is a process where food substances are moved around the plant.
Name the tissue responsible for translocation in plants.

(1 mark)

(b) Xylem tubes transport minerals and water around a plant.
Describe the structure of the xylem tubes.

(3 marks)

(c) **Figure 2** shows a type of plant cell.

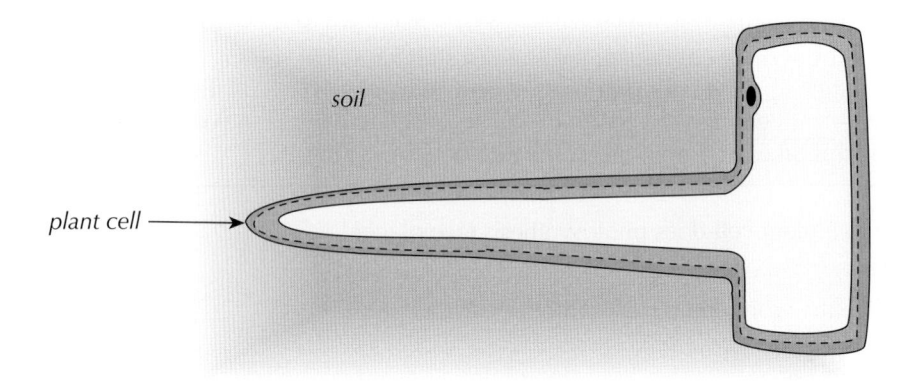

Figure 2

Name the type of plant cell shown.
Describe the role of this cell within the plant.

(2 marks)

3 Transpiration is the loss of water from a plant's surface.

(a) A scientist investigating transpiration finds that a plant she is studying has lost 0.84 cm³ of water over the course of 10 minutes.
Calculate the rate of transpiration of the plant during this 10 minute period.
Give your answer in $cm^3\ s^{-1}$.

(2 marks)

(b) Water is lost from the surface of a leaf through the stomata.
Stomata are tiny pores that are surrounded by guard cells.

(i) What is the role of the guard cells?

(1 mark)

(ii) Describe what would happen to the guard cells around the stomata if a plant was moved from a light room to a completely dark room.
Explain your answer.

(4 marks)

Topic 7a — Hormones and Fertility

1. Hormones

Along with the nervous system (see pages 64-66) hormones allow us to react to changes in the environment and in our bodies. Hormones are secreted by the glands of the endocrine system.

Learning Objective:
- Be able to describe where hormones are produced and how they are transported from endocrine glands to their target organs, including the pituitary gland, thyroid gland, pancreas, adrenal glands, ovaries and testes.

Specification Reference 7.1

What are hormones?

Hormones are chemical molecules released directly into the blood to regulate bodily processes. They are carried in the blood plasma (the liquid part of the blood) to other parts of the body, but only affect particular cells in particular organs (called **target organs**). Hormones control things in organs and cells that need constant adjustment.

Here's a definition of hormones:

> Hormones are chemical messengers which travel in the blood to activate cells in target organs.

The endocrine system

Hormones are produced in (and secreted by) various glands, called **endocrine glands**. These glands make up the endocrine system.

The endocrine system uses hormones to react to changes in the environment or changes inside the body.

Endocrine glands

There are many glands in the endocrine system, including:

- The **pituitary gland** — this produces many hormones that regulate body conditions. It is sometimes called the 'master gland' because these hormones act on other glands, directing them to release hormones that bring about change.

- The **thyroid gland** — this produces thyroxine, which is involved in regulating things like the rate of metabolism, heart rate and temperature (see p.168).

- The **pancreas** — this produces insulin, which is used to regulate the blood glucose level (see page 179).

- The **adrenal glands** — these produce adrenaline, which is used to prepare the body for a 'fight or flight' response (see page 168).

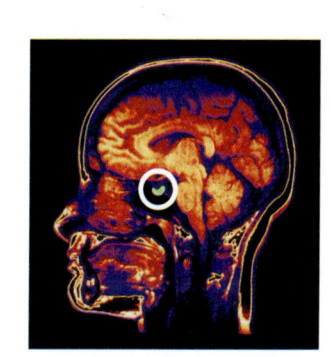

Figure 1: Scan of the brain. The pituitary gland (green structure) is circled in white.

> **Exam Tip**
> Make sure you know which gland produces which hormone. Some of their names give you clues — the <u>thyro</u>id gland produces <u>thyro</u>xine, the <u>adrenal</u> glands produce <u>adrenal</u>ine, the <u>o</u>varies produce <u>o</u>estrogen and the <u>tes</u>tes produce <u>tes</u>tosterone.

- The **ovaries** (females only) — these produce oestrogen, which is involved in the menstrual cycle (see pages 170-172).

- The **testes** (males only) — these produce testosterone, which controls puberty and sperm production in males.

> **Exam Tip**
> These are the glands you need to learn for the exam. There are loads more glands in the body though, each doing its own thing.

> **Tip:** Testis is the singular of testes.

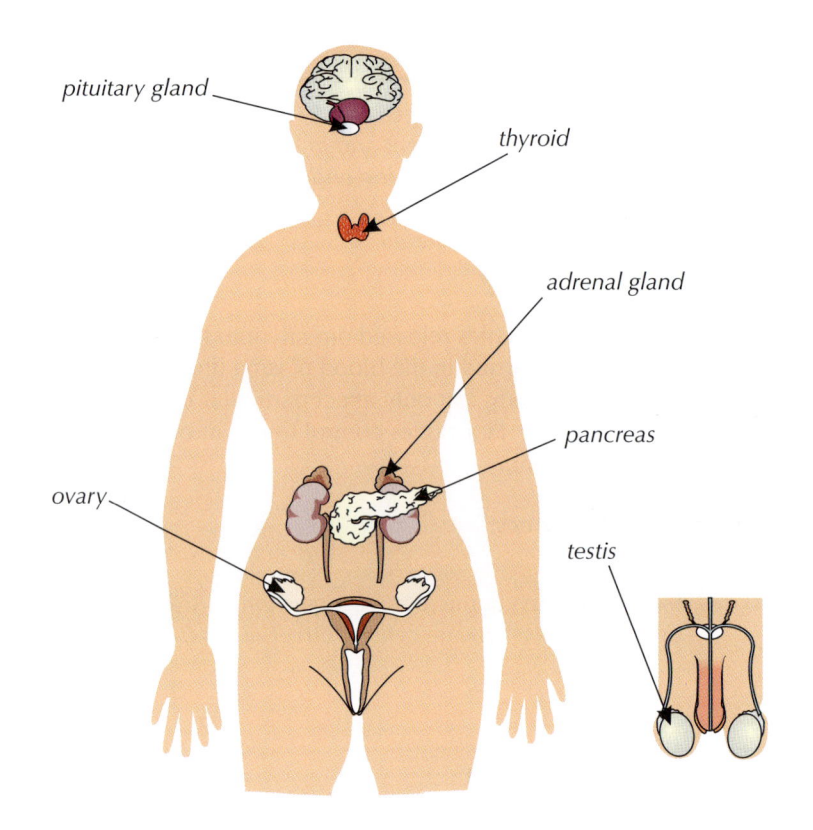

Figure 2: *Diagram showing the location of some of the endocrine glands.*

Comparing nerves and hormones

As hormones are carried in the blood, they tend to travel around the body relatively slowly (compared to nervous impulses anyway). They also tend to have relatively long-lasting effects. Hormones and nerves do similar jobs in the body, but with a few differences. These are summarised in Figure 3.

> **Tip:** There's more about the nervous system on pages 64-66.

Nerves	Hormones
Fast action	Slower action
Act for a short time	Act for a long time
Acts on a very precise area	Acts in a more general way

Figure 3: *Table summarising the differences between nerves and hormones.*

Topic 7a **Hormones and Fertility**

If you're not sure whether a response is nervous or hormonal, have a think...

- If the response is really quick, it's probably nervous.
  Some information needs to be passed to effectors (muscles or glands) really quickly (e.g. pain signals, or information from your eyes telling you about a car heading your way), so it's no good using hormones to carry the message — they're too slow.

- If a response lasts for a long time, it's probably hormonal.
  For example, when you get a shock, a hormone called adrenaline is released into the body (causing the 'fight or flight' response, where your body is hyped up ready for action). You can tell it's a hormonal response (even though it kicks in pretty quickly) because you feel a bit wobbly for a while afterwards.

Practice Questions — Fact Recall

Q1 How are hormones carried around the body?
Q2 True or false? A particular hormone will have an effect on all organs.
Q3 What are hormones secreted from?
Q4 Name a hormone secreted from the testes.
Q5 Which produces a faster response — nerves or hormones?

Exam Tip
Try to learn to spell difficult words like 'pituitary'. It'll help to make sure the examiner knows what you're talking about.

Learning Objectives:

- **H** Be able to explain that adrenaline is produced by the adrenal glands to prepare the body for 'fight or flight', including: increased heart rate, increased blood pressure, increased blood flow to the muscles, and raised blood sugar levels by stimulating the liver to change glycogen into glucose.
- **H** Be able to explain how thyroxine controls metabolic rate as an example of negative feedback, including that:
  - **H** low levels of thyroxine stimulates production of TRH in the hypothalamus, which causes the release of TSH from the pituitary gland;
  - **H** TSH acts on the thyroid to produce thyroxine;
  - **H** when thyroxine levels are normal, thyroxine inhibits the release of TRH and the production of TSH.

Specification References 7.2, 7.3

Tip: H You can think about negative feedback working like a thermostat — if the temperature gets too low, the thermostat will turn the heating on, then if the temperature gets too high, it'll turn the heating off again.

2. Adrenaline and Thyroxine **Higher**

Adrenaline and thyroxine are both pretty useful hormones for us humans.

Adrenaline

Adrenaline is a hormone released by the **adrenal glands** (found just above the kidneys — see Figure 2 on page 166).

It is released in response to stressful or scary situations. Your brain detects fear or stress and sends nervous impulses to the adrenal glands, which respond by secreting adrenaline. Adrenaline gets the body ready for 'fight or flight' — in other words, standing your ground in the face of a threat (e.g. a predator) or bravely running away. It does this by triggering mechanisms that increase the supply of oxygen and glucose to cells.

Examples **Higher**

- Adrenaline binds to specific receptors in the heart. This causes the heart muscle to contract more frequently and with more force, so heart rate and blood pressure increase. This increases blood flow to the muscles, so the cells receive more oxygen and glucose for increased respiration. This gives the muscles the extra energy they need for muscle contraction — allowing you to 'fight' or to run away.

- Adrenaline also binds to receptors in the liver. This causes the liver to break down its glycogen stores (see. p.179) to release glucose. This increases the blood glucose level, so there's more glucose in the blood to be transported to the cells. This increased glucose can be used to fuel muscle contraction in the 'fight or flight' response.

Thyroxine

Thyroxine is a hormone released by the **thyroid gland**, which is found in the neck. It plays an important role in regulating the basal metabolic rate — the speed at which chemical reactions in the body occur while the body is at rest.

Negative feedback

Your body can control the levels of hormones (and other substances) in the blood. When the levels of certain substances in the body go above or below a normal level, the body triggers responses that help to bring these levels back into a normal range. This is called negative feedback (see Figure 1).

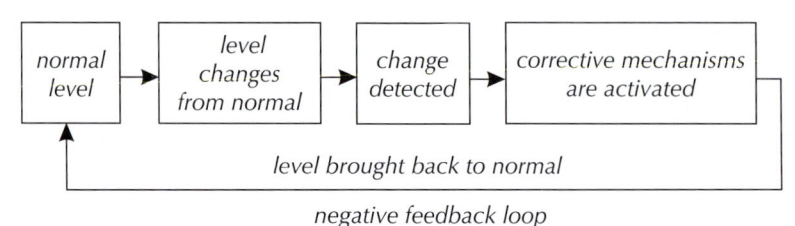

normal level → level changes from normal → change detected → corrective mechanisms are activated → level brought back to normal

negative feedback loop

Figure 1: *A negative feedback mechanism.*

A negative feedback system keeps the amount of thyroxine in the blood at the right level (see Figure 2).

Decrease from normal detected

- When the level of thyroxine in the blood is lower than normal, the hypothalamus (a structure in the brain) is stimulated to release thyrotropin releasing hormone (TRH).
- TRH stimulates the pituitary gland to release thyroid stimulating hormone (TSH).
- TSH stimulates the thyroid gland to release thyroxine, so the blood thyroxine level rises back towards normal.

Increase from normal detected

- When the level of thyroxine in the blood is higher than normal, the release of TRH from the hypothalamus is inhibited (stopped).
- This reduces the production of TSH, which reduces the amount of thyroxine released from the thyroid gland. The level of thyroxine in the blood falls back towards normal.

Exam Tip H
In the exam you could be asked to interpret graphs like Figure 2. Even if they look different, just apply your understanding of negative feedback to help you work out what the graph is showing you.

Tip: H A higher than normal thyroxine level also directly inhibits the secretion of TSH from the pituitary gland.

Tip: H An underactive thyroid can cause weight gain. Less thyroxine is produced, so your metabolic rate drops. This means that less of the glucose you take in gets broken down in respiration (see page 199), so more is stored as fat.

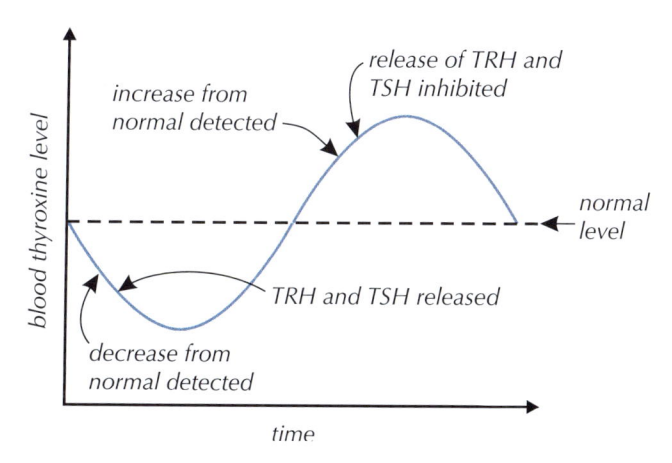

Figure 2: *Graph showing how the level of thyroxine in the blood is controlled by negative feedback.*

Practice Questions — Fact Recall

Q1 Name the glands that release adrenaline.
Q2 Give a role of thyroxine in the body.

Practice Question — Application

Q1 Pierre is surprised when a dog jumps up at him. His heart starts to beat faster.
   a) Name the hormone that has caused this response.
   b) Explain the purpose of this response.

Learning Objectives:
- Be able to describe the stages of the menstrual cycle, including the roles of the hormones oestrogen and progesterone, in the control of the menstrual cycle.
- **H** Be able to explain the interactions of oestrogen, progesterone, FSH and LH in the repair and maintenance of the uterus wall, ovulation and menstruation.

Specification References 7.4, 7.5

3. The Menstrual Cycle

Hormones secreted by the ovaries and the pituitary gland are responsible for controlling the changes that occur during a woman's menstrual cycle.

The menstrual cycle

The menstrual cycle is the monthly sequence of events in which the female body releases an egg and prepares the uterus (womb) in case the egg is fertilised. The menstrual cycle has four stages:

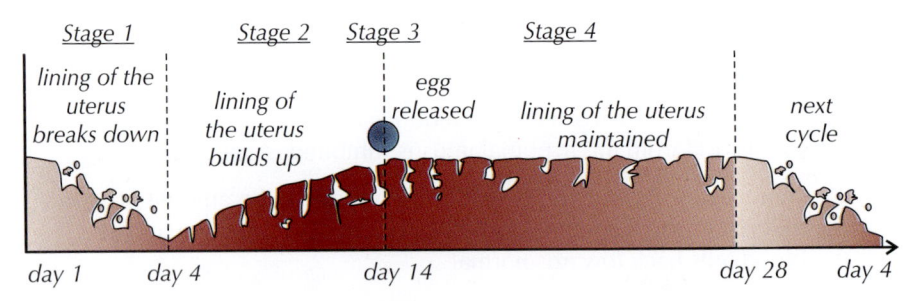

Figure 1: Diagram showing the four stages of the menstrual cycle.

- **Stage 1**
  Day 1 is when **menstruation** (bleeding) starts. The uterus lining breaks down and is released. This lasts for about four days.

- **Stage 2**
  The lining of the uterus is repaired, from day 4 to day 14, into a thick spongy layer full of blood vessels, ready for a fertilised egg to implant there.

- **Stage 3**
  An egg is released from the ovary at day 14. This is called **ovulation**.

- **Stage 4**
  The lining is then maintained for about 14 days, until day 28. If no fertilised egg has landed on the uterus wall by day 28, the spongy lining starts to break down again and the whole cycle starts again.

Oestrogen and **progesterone** are hormones with important roles in the menstrual cycle. Oestrogen stimulates the growth of the uterus lining during stage 2 of the menstrual cycle, whereas progesterone is needed to maintain the uterus lining during stage 4.

Tip: The lining of the uterus is also called the endometrium.

Exam Tip **H**
Make sure you don't talk about egg 'production' or 'development' if you're asked about the menstrual cycle in the exam. Eggs already exist in a woman's ovaries at birth. FSH causes these eggs to <u>mature</u> and LH causes them to be <u>released</u>.

Hormonal interaction in the menstrual cycle `Higher`

As well as oestrogen and progesterone, you also need to know about two more important hormones with roles in the menstrual cycle:

- **Follicle-stimulating hormone (FSH)** — causes a **follicle** (an egg and its surrounding cells) to mature in one of the ovaries.

- **Luteinising hormone (LH)** — stimulates the release of an egg at day 14 (ovulation).

Topic 7a   Hormones and Fertility

The levels of oestrogen, progesterone, FSH and LH fluctuate throughout the menstrual cycle (see Figure 2). They also interact with each other to promote or inhibit the release of other hormones.

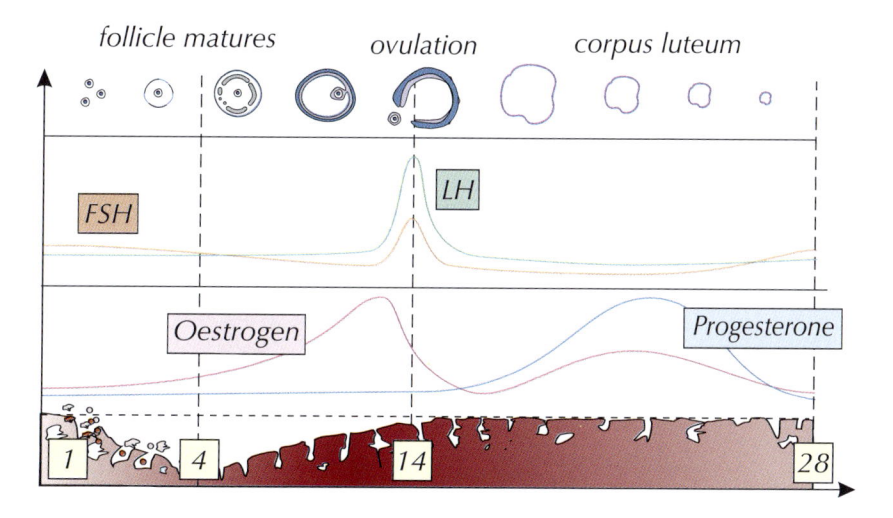

Figure 2: Diagram showing hormonal changes during the menstrual cycle.

Exam Tip H
In the exam you might be asked to interpret a graph like the one in Figure 2. It might look confusing at first, but if you get your head around what each of the four hormones does, it should start to make more sense. A graph is a really useful way to visualise how the hormones interact when controlling the cycle.

1. **FSH** is produced in the pituitary gland. It causes a follicle to mature in one of the ovaries. It also stimulates the ovaries to produce oestrogen.

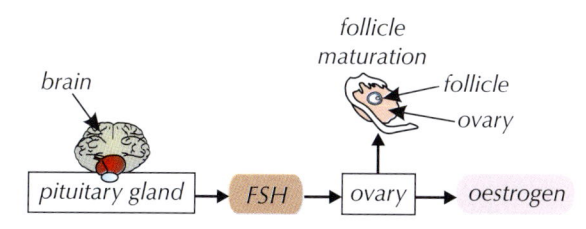

    Figure 3: Diagram showing the role of FSH in the menstrual cycle.

2. **Oestrogen** is produced in the ovaries and causes the lining of the uterus to thicken and grow. A high level of oestrogen stimulates an LH surge (a rapid increase in LH).

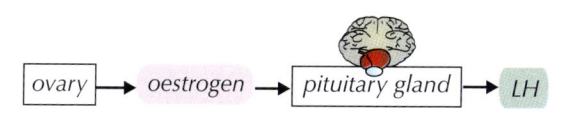

    Figure 4: Diagram showing the role of oestrogen in the menstrual cycle.

3. **LH** is produced by the pituitary gland. The LH surge causes the follicle to rupture and the egg to be released (ovulation). LH also stimulates the remains of the follicle to develop into a structure called a **corpus luteum**.

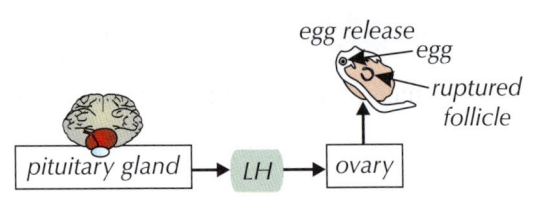

Figure 5: Diagram showing the role of LH in the menstrual cycle.

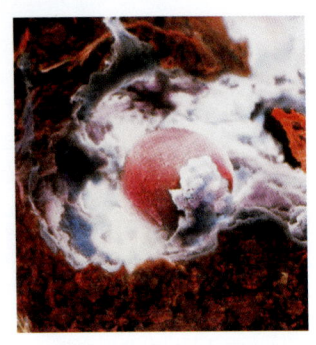

Figure 6: A microscope image showing an egg (pink oval) being released from an ovary (brown).

4. **Progesterone** is released by the corpus luteum after ovulation. It maintains the lining of the uterus during the second half of the cycle and inhibits the release of FSH and LH.

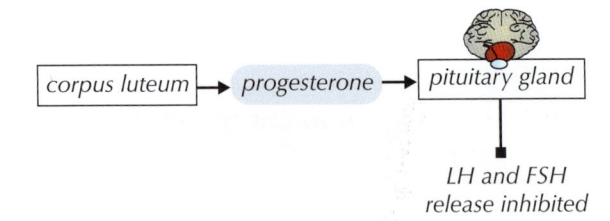

Figure 7: Diagram showing the role of progesterone in the menstrual cycle.

When the level of progesterone falls, and there's a low oestrogen level, the uterus lining breaks down. A low progesterone level allows FSH to increase. This allows the whole cycle to start again.

> **Exam Tip** H
> A change in the level of one hormone can be used to predict a change in the level of another hormone. E.g. an increase in oestrogen while progesterone levels are low should be followed by an increase in LH.

Pregnancy

If a fertilised egg implants in the uterus (i.e. the woman becomes pregnant) then the level of progesterone will stay high to maintain the lining of the uterus during pregnancy.

Practice Questions — Fact Recall

Q1 Describe what happens during menstruation.
Q2 Name the two hormones involved in the growth and maintenance of the uterus lining.
Q3 What effect does FSH have on follicles in the ovaries?
Q4 Give one function of LH.
Q5 Name a hormone that inhibits the release of FSH.
Q6 Which two glands secrete the hormones that control the menstrual cycle?

Practice Question — Application

Q1 The graph below shows the level of a hormone measured in the bloodstream of one woman during her 28 day menstrual cycle.

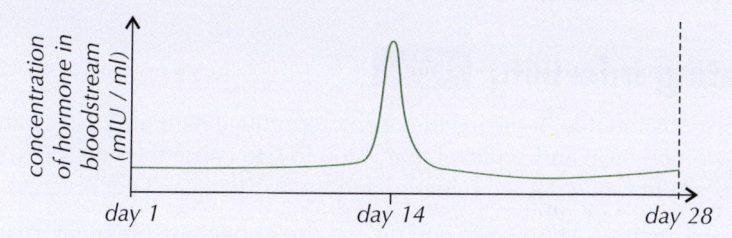

a) Which hormone do you think is shown on the graph? Give a reason for your answer.

b) Where is the hormone you gave in part a) produced?

c) The graph below shows the level of the same hormone measured in another woman during her 28 day menstrual cycle. This woman is struggling to have children. Suggest why this might be.

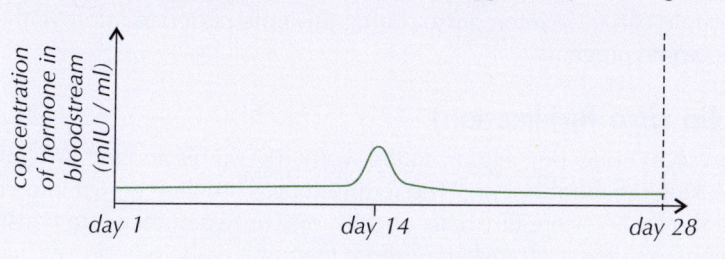

Tip: [H] Think about what happens around the middle of the menstrual cycle.

Tip: [H] Both graphs are drawn to the same scale.

Learning Objectives:

- **H** Be able to explain the use of hormones in Assisted Reproductive Technology (ART) including IVF and clomifene therapy.
- Be able to explain how hormonal contraception influences the menstrual cycle and prevents pregnancy.
- Be able to evaluate hormonal and barrier methods of contraception.

Specification References 7.6 – 7.8

Tip: **H** Have a look back at pages 170-171 for a reminder of what the hormones FSH and LH do.

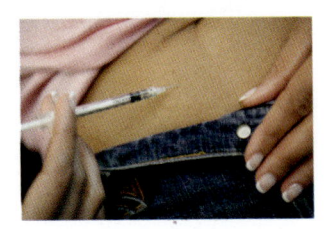

Figure 1: A woman having a hormone injection to prepare for IVF treatment.

4. Controlling Fertility

Hormones are a key factor in fertility, so they can be used to increase or decrease the chance of becoming pregnant.

Treating infertility Higher

If a person is infertile, it means they can't reproduce naturally. For example, some women have an FSH level that is too low to cause their eggs to mature. This means that no eggs are released and the women can't get pregnant.

There are methods an infertile couple can use to become pregnant, many of which involve hormones. You need to learn these two examples:

Clomifene therapy

Some women are infertile because they don't ovulate or they don't ovulate regularly. These women can take a drug called clomifene. This works by causing more FSH and LH to be released by the body, which stimulate egg maturation and ovulation. By knowing when the woman will be ovulating, the couple can have intercourse during this time period to improve the chance of becoming pregnant.

IVF (*in vitro* fertilisation)

IVF involves collecting eggs from the woman's ovaries and fertilising them in a lab using the man's sperm. The fertilised eggs are then grown into embryos. Once the embryos are tiny balls of cells, one or two of them are transferred to the woman's uterus. (Transferring more than one embryo improves the chance of pregnancy.) FSH and LH are given before egg collection to stimulate egg production (so more than one egg can be collected).

IVF is an example of **Assisted Reproductive Technology** (ART) — fertility treatments that involve eggs being handled (and usually fertilised) outside of the body in a lab.

Hormonal methods of contraception

Contraceptives are used to prevent pregnancy. The hormones oestrogen and progesterone can be taken by women to reduce their **fertility** (their ability to get pregnant) and so are often used as contraceptives.

Oestrogen

Oestrogen can be used to prevent egg release. This may seem kind of strange (since naturally oestrogen helps stimulate the release of eggs — see page 171). But if oestrogen is taken every day to keep the level of it permanently high, it inhibits FSH production, and after a while egg maturation and therefore egg release stop and stay stopped.

Progesterone

Progesterone also reduces fertility. It works in several different ways. For example, it stimulates the production of thick cervical mucus which prevents any sperm getting through the entrance to the uterus (the cervix) and reaching an egg. Some progesterone-only contraceptives can also inhibit egg maturation and therefore the release of an egg too.

Types of hormonal contraceptive

Hormonal contraceptives can come in different forms:

> **Examples**
>
> - The combined pill is an oral contraceptive. In a 28 day cycle, it is taken once a day for 21 days, followed by a 7 day break. It contains both oestrogen and progesterone.
> - The mini-pill is a progesterone-only pill. It is useful for women who can't take contraceptives containing oestrogen (e.g. because of a medical condition). It has to be taken every day.
> - The contraceptive patch is a thin, plastic patch that sticks to the skin. Oestrogen and progesterone are released through the skin into the bloodstream. Each patch lasts for 1 week.
> - The contraception injection contains progesterone only. Each dose lasts 2 to 3 months.

Tip: An oral contraceptive is taken by mouth.

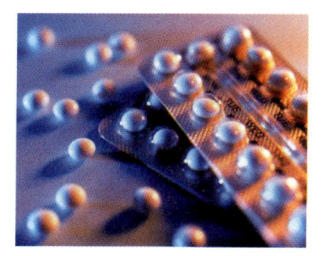

Figure 2: The combined contraceptive pill.

Barrier methods of contraception

Barrier forms of contraception are designed to put a barrier between the sperm and egg so they don't meet. Barrier methods are non-hormonal.

- Condoms are worn over the penis during intercourse to prevent the sperm entering the vagina. There are also female condoms that are worn inside the vagina. Condoms are the only form of contraception that will protect against sexually transmitted diseases.
- A diaphragm is a flexible, dome-shaped device that fits over the cervix (the entrance to the uterus) to form a barrier. It is inserted before sex.

Tip: Diaphragms must be used with spermicide — a chemical that disables or kills sperm. Spermicide can be used alone as a contraceptive, but it's not as effective as when used with a diaphragm.

Evaluating methods of contraception

Generally, when used correctly, hormonal methods are more effective at preventing pregnancy than barrier methods. Also, hormonal methods mean that the couple don't have to stop and think about contraception each time they have intercourse (as they would if they relied on barrier methods).

However, hormonal methods can have unpleasant side-effects, such as headaches, acne and mood changes. Barrier methods are generally free from side effects, although some people can experience allergic reactions to them. Also, hormonal methods don't protect against sexually transmitted infections — condoms are the only form of contraception to do this.

Tip: The method of contraception that is most suitable will differ based on the individual(s) using it.

Exam Tip
In the exam, you could be given data and asked to compare and contrast the effectiveness of different types of contraception. If so, you need to give both the similarities and differences between each type. You won't get all the marks available if you just describe each type individually.

> **Practice Questions — Fact Recall**
>
> Q1 Why is a woman undergoing IVF treatment given FSH and LH before egg collection?
>
> Q2 Explain the function of oestrogen in hormonal contraceptives.
>
> Q3 How do barrier methods of contraception prevent pregnancy?

Topic 7a Checklist — Make sure you know...

Hormones
- [ ] That hormones are produced in endocrine glands and secreted into the bloodstream where they are carried to target organs.
- [ ] That the pituitary gland produces many hormones that regulate body conditions, that the pancreas produces insulin, that the adrenal glands produce adrenaline, that the ovaries found in females produce oestrogen and that the testes in males produce testosterone.

Adrenaline and Thyroxine
- [ ] [H] That adrenaline produced in the adrenal glands is released to prepare the body for fight or flight.
- [ ] [H] That adrenaline increases heart rate and blood pressure so that blood flow to the muscles is increased and the muscle cells receive more oxygen and glucose, allowing for more respiration to occur.
- [ ] [H] That adrenaline acts on the liver to stimulate the breakdown of glycogen into glucose to be transported to cells for increased respiration.
- [ ] [H] That thyroxine regulates metabolic rate, and that its levels in the blood are controlled by negative feedback.
- [ ] [H] That the hypothalamus is stimulated to produce thyrotropin releasing hormone (TRH) when levels of thyroxine are low, and that TRH causes the pituitary gland to release thyroid stimulating hormone (TSH) which stimulates the production of thyroxine in the thyroid.
- [ ] [H] That the release of TRH and the production of TSH are inhibited when the levels of thyroxine in the blood are higher than normal.

The Menstrual Cycle
- [ ] That the menstrual cycle involves the breakdown of the uterus lining during menstruation (bleeding), followed by the repair of the uterus lining, ovulation and maintenance of the uterus lining.
- [ ] That oestrogen stimulates the growth of the uterus lining and progesterone maintains it.
- [ ] [H] That follicle-stimulating hormone (FSH) causes a follicle and its egg to mature in the ovaries and that luteinising hormone (LH) stimulates the release of an egg (ovulation).
- [ ] [H] How oestrogen, progesterone, FSH and LH interact during the stages of the menstrual cycle.

Controlling Fertility
- [ ] [H] How FSH and LH are used in fertility treatments including clomifene therapy and IVF (an example of Assisted Reproductive Technology).
- [ ] How different types of hormonal contraception (containing oestrogen and/or progesterone) can be used to prevent pregnancy by influencing the menstrual cycle.
- [ ] How to evaluate hormonal and barrier methods of contraception, using their advantages and disadvantages.

Exam-style Questions

1 A woman is considering taking a hormonal contraceptive to prevent pregnancy.

  (a) (i) Give **one** advantage of using hormonal contraceptives over barrier contraceptives.

(1 mark)

    (ii) Suggest **one** reason why the woman may decide to continue to use barrier contraceptives alongside a hormonal contraceptive.

(1 mark)

The woman decides to have the contraceptive injection, where she is injected with progesterone every three months.

  (b) Suggest **one** way that the injection will help to prevent her from getting pregnant.

(1 mark)

Another woman and her partner decide to try for a baby.
After unsuccessful attempts at getting pregnant, the woman's doctor explains that she isn't ovulating regularly.

  (c) (i) Suggest a drug-based treatment that could increase the chance of pregnancy for this woman.

(1 mark)

    (ii) Explain how the treatment you suggested in part **(c)(i)** increases the chance of a woman becoming pregnant.

(3 marks)

  (d) Following treatment, the woman becomes pregnant.
During pregnancy the lining of the uterus needs to be maintained.
Name the hormone responsible for maintaining the uterus lining during pregnancy.

(1 mark)

2 Thyroxine is an important hormone of the endocrine system.

  (a) In which of the following glands of the endocrine system is thyroxine produced?

    A pituitary
    B ovary
    C thyroid
    D pancreas

(1 mark)

  (b) Describe how the body responds to low levels of thyroxine in the blood.

(3 marks)

One role of thyroxine is the regulation of the basal metabolic rate.
Basal metabolic rate can be given as the number of calories burned at rest in a certain time.

  (c) A man's basal metabolic rate is 1860 kcal/day.
Calculate how many calories the man burns at rest during six hours.

(2 marks)

Topic 7b — Homeostasis

Learning Objective:
- Be able to explain the importance of maintaining a constant internal environment in response to internal and external change.

Specification Reference 7.9

1. Homeostasis

The internal conditions in the body must be kept constant — this stops cell damage that could happen if we didn't keep on top of things. Luckily there are some clever systems in place to keep everything plodding along steadily.

What is homeostasis?

The conditions inside your body need to be kept steady, even when the external environment changes. This is really important because your cells need the right conditions in order to function properly, including the right conditions for enzyme action (see pages 37-38). Homeostasis is the way in which everything is kept at the right level.

> Homeostasis is the regulation of the conditions inside your body (and cells) to maintain a constant internal environment, in response to changes in both internal and external conditions.

Tip: It can be dangerous for your health if conditions in the body vary too much from normal levels.

Examples of homeostasis in action include:

Examples

- Osmoregulation (regulating water content) — you need to keep a balance between the water you gain (in drink, food, and from respiration) and water you urinate, sweat and breathe out.

- Thermoregulation (regulating body temperature) — you need to reduce your body temperature when you're hot, but increase it when the environment is cold.

- Blood glucose regulation — you need to make sure the amount of glucose in your blood doesn't get too high or too low (see p.179-180).

Negative feedback

Negative feedback systems (see p.168) help to keep conditions in your body steady. This means that if a condition changes away from the normal level, a response is triggered that counteracts the change. E.g. a rise in blood glucose level causes a response that lowers blood glucose level (and vice versa).

Tip: A negative feedback system responds when a level changes from normal, in order to bring the level back to normal. It's a continuous, looping process.

Practice Questions — Fact Recall

Q1   Define homeostasis.

Q2   Give two examples of conditions in your internal environment that need regulating and maintaining.

2. Controlling Blood Glucose

Your blood glucose level needs to be carefully regulated. This is done with the help of hormones produced by the pancreas. However, if things don't work quite as they should, it can result in a condition called diabetes...

Glucose concentration of the blood

Glucose is a type of sugar. Throughout the day the blood glucose level varies:

> **Examples**
>
> - Eating foods containing carbohydrate puts glucose into the blood from the small intestine.
> - The normal metabolism of cells removes glucose from the blood.
> - Vigorous exercise removes much more glucose from the blood.

Excess glucose is stored as **glycogen** in the liver and in the muscles. When these stores are full, the excess glucose is stored as lipid (fat) in the tissues.

Hormonal control of blood glucose

The level of glucose in the blood must be kept steady. Changes in the blood glucose level are monitored by the **pancreas**. The pancreas produces hormones which help to control the blood glucose level.

Insulin

Insulin is a hormone produced by the pancreas. It decreases the blood glucose level when it gets too high. Here's what happens:

1. After a meal containing carbohydrate, a person's blood glucose level rises. This rise is detected by the pancreas.

2. The pancreas responds by producing insulin, which is secreted into the blood.

3. Insulin causes body cells to take up more glucose from the blood. Cells in the liver and muscles can take up glucose and convert it into the storage molecule glycogen.

4. This causes the blood glucose level to fall.

This process is shown in Figure 1.

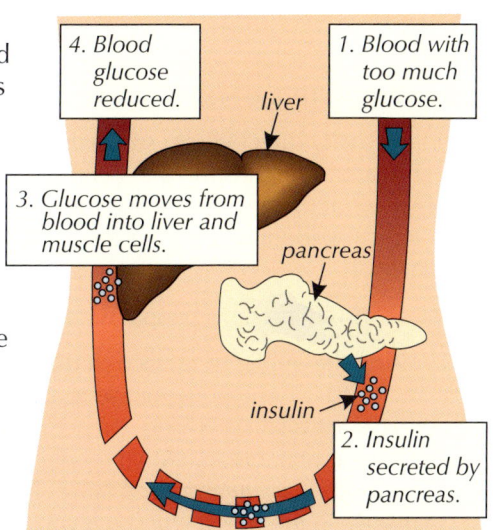

Figure 1: Diagram showing the role of insulin in the control of blood glucose.

Learning Objectives:
- Be able to explain how the hormone insulin controls blood glucose concentration.
- **H** Be able to explain how blood glucose concentration is regulated by glucagon.
- Be able to explain the cause of type 1 diabetes and how it is controlled.
- Be able to explain the cause of type 2 diabetes and how it is controlled.
- Be able to evaluate the correlation between body mass and type 2 diabetes including waist:hip calculations and BMI, using the BMI equation:

$$\text{BMI} = \frac{\text{weight (kg)}}{(\text{height (m)})^2}$$

Specification References 7.13 – 7.17

Topic 7b **Homeostasis**

Exam Tip H
The words 'glucagon' and 'glycogen' look and sound very similar. You need to make sure you get the spelling of these words spot on in the exam. E.g. if you write 'glycogon' the examiner won't know whether you mean glucagon or glycogen so you won't get the marks.

Tip: H Glucagon works with insulin to control blood glucose level in a negative feedback cycle — together they keep blood glucose around its optimum. (See page 168 for more on negative feedback.)

Glucagon Higher

Glucagon is another hormone produced by the pancreas. It increases the blood glucose level when it gets too low. Here's what happens:

1. Blood with too little glucose.
2. Glucagon secreted by pancreas.
3. Glucagon makes liver turn glycogen into glucose.
4. Blood glucose increased.

1. If a person's blood glucose level decreases, the fall is detected by the pancreas.

2. The pancreas responds by producing glucagon, which is secreted into the blood.

3. Glucagon causes the glycogen stored in the liver and muscles to be converted back into glucose, which enters the blood.

4. This causes the blood glucose level to rise.

This process is shown in Figure 2.

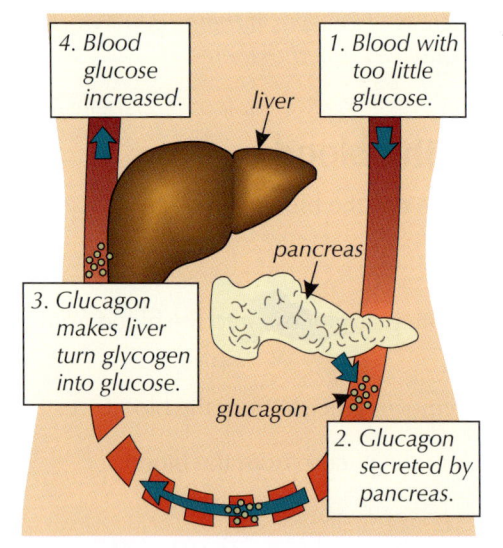

Figure 2: Diagram showing the role of glucagon in the control of blood glucose.

Tip: Remember, insulin <u>reduces</u> blood glucose level.

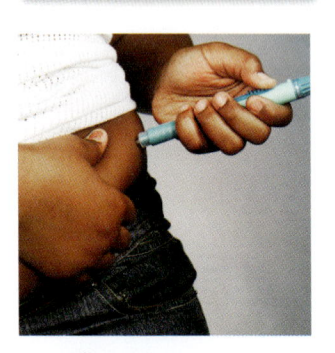

Figure 3: A person injecting insulin.

Tip: Insulin can't be taken in a pill or tablet — the enzymes in the stomach completely destroy it before it reaches the bloodstream. That's why it's normally injected.

Type 1 diabetes

Type 1 diabetes is a condition where the pancreas produces little or no insulin. The result is that a person's blood glucose can rise to a level that can kill them.

Controlling type 1 diabetes

Type 1 diabetes needs to be controlled with **insulin therapy** — this usually involves injecting insulin into the blood. People with type 1 diabetes usually have several injections of insulin throughout the day, which are likely to be at mealtimes. Insulin injections make sure glucose is removed from the blood quickly once the food has been digested. This stops the level of glucose in the blood from getting too high and is a very effective treatment.

Insulin is usually injected into subcutaneous tissue (fatty tissue just under the skin). The amount of insulin that needs to be injected depends on the person's diet and how active they are, since these things will affect their blood glucose level. Injecting too much insulin could lead to a dangerously low blood glucose level.

As well as insulin therapy, people with type 1 diabetes need to think about:

- **Limiting the intake of foods rich in simple carbohydrates** — i.e. sugars (which cause the blood glucose level to rise rapidly). People with type 1 diabetes are also advised to spread their intake of starchy carbohydrates (e.g. pasta, rice, bread, etc.) throughout the day and to pick varieties of these foods that are absorbed more slowly (so they don't cause such a sharp rise in the blood glucose level).

- **Taking regular exercise** — this helps to lower the blood glucose level as the increased metabolism of cells during exercise removes more glucose from the blood.

Type 2 diabetes

Type 2 diabetes is a condition where the pancreas doesn't produce enough insulin, or when a person becomes resistant to their own insulin (their body's cells don't respond properly to the hormone). This can also cause a person's blood glucose level to rise to a dangerous level.

Being overweight can increase your chance of developing type 2 diabetes, as obesity is a major risk factor in the development of the disease (see below).

Tip: Prolonged periods of high blood glucose levels can cause damage to organs such as the eyes, heart and kidneys, resulting in long-term health problems.

Controlling type 2 diabetes

Type 2 diabetes can be controlled by eating a healthy diet, getting regular exercise and losing weight if needed. These things can all help to lower the blood glucose level. Some people with type 2 diabetes also need to have medication or insulin injections to control their blood glucose level.

Tip: There are different medications available for type 2 diabetes. Some can make body cells more sensitive to insulin.

Correlation between type 2 diabetes and obesity

There is a correlation (see p.18) between type 2 diabetes and obesity — this means that obese people have an increased risk of developing type 2 diabetes. People are classified as obese if they have a body mass index (BMI) of over 30. BMI is calculated using this formula:

$$\text{BMI} = \frac{\text{weight (kg)}}{\left(\text{height (m)}\right)^2}$$

Exam Tip
In the exam you might be asked to compare type 1 and type 2 diabetes. It might help to draw a table comparing the two. You could include what they are and how they can be controlled.

Where the body stores excess fat is also important — storing a lot of fat around the abdomen (tummy area) is associated with an increased risk of developing type 2 diabetes. Calculating a person's waist-to-hip ratio gives an indication of how fat is stored. This is the formula you need:

$$\text{waist-to-hip ratio} = \frac{\text{waist circumference (cm)}}{\text{hip circumference (cm)}}$$

Tip: See pages 138-139 for more on calculating BMI and waist-to-hip ratios.

A ratio above 1.0 for men and above 0.85 for women is associated with an increased risk of type 2 diabetes because it indicates that a lot of fat is being stored around the abdomen.

Interpreting blood glucose level graphs

The changes in a person's blood glucose level over time can be shown by a graph. The shape of the graph can vary, depending on whether the person has diabetes — see Figure 4 on the next page. You might need to explain what graphs like this are showing in the exam.

Topic 7b **Homeostasis**

Tip: If the blood glucose concentration rises high then decreases slowly, the person may be resistant to insulin — this is type 2 diabetes. E.g.

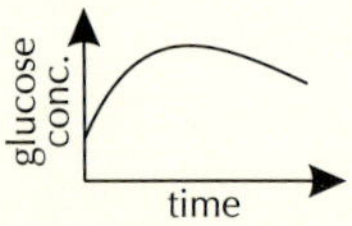

Their pancreas is producing insulin but it's not having the proper effect on the body cells.

Tip: There is a time delay between the release of insulin and the reduction of blood glucose concentration. This is because the insulin first needs to travel in the blood to its target cells.

Tip: H As the glucose level falls below normal, the pancreas responds by releasing glucagon into the blood. Glucagon works to bring the blood glucose back up to its normal level.

Example

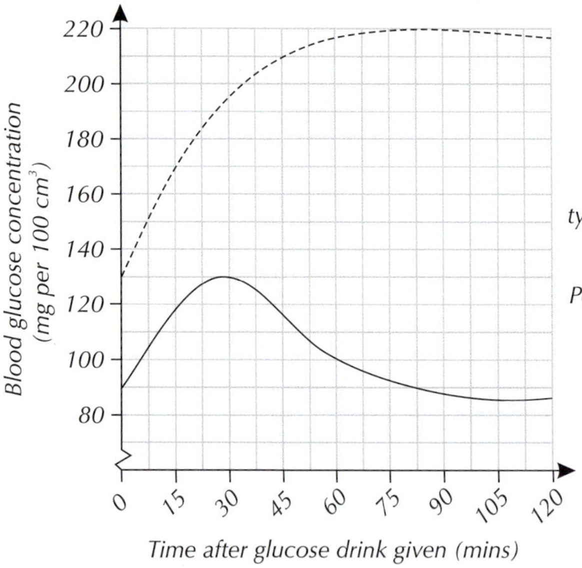

Figure 4: *Graph showing the change in blood glucose concentration over time after consuming a glucose drink for a person with type 1 diabetes and a person without diabetes.*

Here's what Figure 4 is showing:

Person without diabetes

In the initial 30 minutes after consuming the glucose drink, their blood glucose concentration rises from 90 mg/100 cm^3 to 130 mg/100 cm^3. After 30 minutes, their blood glucose concentration begins to fall. This is because as the glucose level rises above normal, the pancreas responds by releasing insulin into the blood. The insulin causes body cells to take up the glucose.

After about 80 minutes, the blood glucose concentration is back to its normal level of 90 mg/100 cm^3, so the pancreas stops releasing insulin. However, the blood glucose concentration then falls slightly below normal — this is due to some insulin still remaining in the blood.

Person with type 1 diabetes

After the person with type 1 diabetes consumes the glucose drink, their blood glucose concentration rises higher than that of the person without diabetes, from 130 mg/100 cm^3 to 220 mg/100 cm^3. Their glucose level then remains high.

This is because their pancreas produces little or no insulin in response to the rising amount of glucose in the blood, so they are not able to control their blood glucose level.

Practice Questions — Fact Recall

Q1 Where in the body is the hormone insulin produced?

Q2 What effect does insulin have on the body's cells?

Q3 Where in the body is the hormone glucagon produced?

Q4 How does glucagon increase blood glucose levels?

Q5 What is type 1 diabetes?

Q6 Give two ways type 2 diabetes can be controlled.

Practice Question — Application

Q1 In a study, a hormone was injected into a subject while their blood glucose level was monitored. The results are shown in the graph.

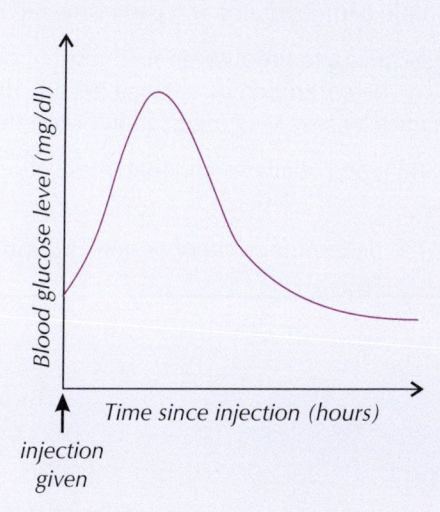

Blood glucose level (mg/dl) vs *Time since injection (hours)*
↑ injection given

a) What hormone do you think was injected? Explain your answer.

b) i) Name the other main hormone that affects the blood glucose level.

   ii) What do you think would happen to the blood glucose level if this hormone had been injected instead? Explain your answer.

Exam Tip
If you are given a graph on blood glucose level in the exam, it's a good idea to look at it carefully and try to work out what it is showing before you start answering the questions. It sounds obvious, but if you just jump straight in you might miss something important.

Topic 7b Checklist — Make sure you know...

Homeostasis

☐ That homeostasis is the regulation of the conditions inside your body (and cells) to maintain a constant internal environment in response to changes in both internal and external conditions.

☐ That the conditions in the body need to be kept steady in order for body cells to function properly.

Controlling Blood Glucose

☐ That insulin is a hormone secreted by the pancreas to reduce the blood glucose level and that it works by causing cells in the liver and muscles to take up more glucose from the blood and convert it into glycogen for storage.

☐ **H** That glucagon is a hormone secreted by the pancreas to increase the blood glucose level and that it works by causing glycogen in the liver and muscles to be converted back into glucose.

☐ That type 1 diabetes is caused by the pancreas producing little or no insulin, and can be controlled through insulin therapy, limiting intake of simple carbohydrates and exercising regularly.

☐ That type 2 diabetes is caused by the pancreas failing to produce enough insulin, or when a person becomes resistant to their own insulin, and can be controlled by eating a healthy diet, exercising regularly, losing weight if needed and sometimes by receiving medication or insulin injections.

☐ That there is a correlation between obesity and type 2 diabetes and that obese people have an increased risk of developing type 2 diabetes.

☐ How to calculate BMI and waist-to-hip ratios to determine whether or not a person is obese.

Exam-style Questions

1 Kaye has recently been diagnosed with type 1 diabetes.

(a) Which of the following statements about type 1 diabetes is true?

    A People with type 1 diabetes are advised to eat a high sugar diet.
    B Type 1 diabetes allows the blood glucose concentration to get too high.
    C Type 1 diabetes is caused by the liver and stomach failing to produce vital hormones.
    D Type 1 diabetes is directly caused by the overproduction of testosterone.

(1 mark)

Kaye's doctor prescribed her hormone injections to control her condition.

(b) Name the hormone that the injections will contain.

(1 mark)

(c) Explain why injecting this hormone can be an effective treatment for type 1 diabetes.

(3 marks)

(d) Diabetes is sometimes described as a "failure of homeostasis". Suggest an explanation as to why diabetes can be described in this way.

(2 marks)

2 **Figure 1** shows the percentage of adults in different age groups with type 2 diabetes that are underweight or of a healthy weight, overweight or obese.

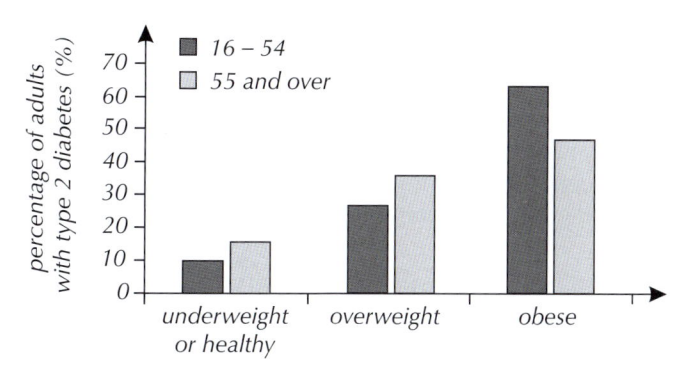

Figure 1

(a) Give **two** conclusions that you can draw from the data in **Figure 1**.

(2 marks)

(b) If a person's body mass index (BMI) is over 30, they are classified as obese.
A 24 year old man weighs 80.0 kg and is 1.89 m tall.
Calculate the man's BMI.

(2 marks)

Topic 8 — Exchange and Transport in Animals

1. Exchange of Materials

Learning Objectives:
- Be able to describe the need to transport substances into and out of a range of organisms, including oxygen, carbon dioxide, water, dissolved food molecules, mineral ions and urea.
- Be able to explain the need for exchange surfaces and a transport system in multicellular organisms including the calculation of surface area : volume ratio.

Specification References 8.1, 8.2

Living organisms need to be able to exchange substances with their environment in order to survive. An organism's size and surface area affect how quickly this is done.

Movement of substances

All organisms must take in substances they need for life processes from the environment. They must also get rid of any waste products from these processes. For example:

- Cells need oxygen for aerobic respiration (see page 199), which produces carbon dioxide as a waste product. These two gases move between cells and the environment by diffusion (see pages 43-44).

- Water is taken up by cells by osmosis (see pages 44-45). In animals, dissolved food molecules (the products of digestion, e.g. glucose, amino acids) and mineral ions diffuse along with it.

- Urea (a waste product produced by animals from the breakdown of proteins) diffuses from cells into the blood plasma for removal from the body by the kidneys.

How easy it is for an organism to exchange substances with its environment depends on the organism's surface area to volume ratio (SA : V).

Tip: Dissolved substances can also move to where they need to be by active transport (see p.46).

Surface area to volume ratios

A **ratio** shows how big one value is compared to another. The larger an organism is, the smaller its surface area is compared to its volume. You can show this by calculating surface area to volume ratios. To do that, you first need to know an organism's volume and surface area. The easiest way to find them is to estimate the size of the organism in the form of a block.

Calculating volume and surface area

The volume of a block (e.g. a cube or cuboid) is found by the equation:

$$\text{volume} = \text{length} \times \text{width} \times \text{height}$$

Example

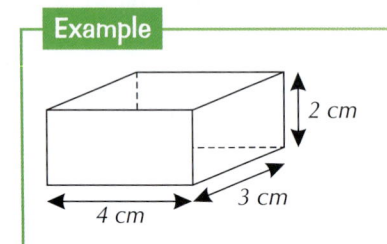

A block that measures 4 cm by 3 cm by 2 cm has the volume:

4 cm × 3 cm × 2 cm = **24 cm³**

Tip: The units of volume are given in units cubed (e.g. µm³).

The area of a square or rectangular surface is found by the equation:

$$\text{area} = \text{length} \times \text{width}$$

To calculate the surface area of an object, just calculate the area of each side and add them all together.

Tip: The area of a triangle is found by the equation: ½ × height × base.
E.g.
height = 4 cm
base = 6 cm
Area = ½ × 4 cm × 6 cm = 12 cm²

Example

A block that measures 4 cm by 3 cm by 2 cm has six surfaces:

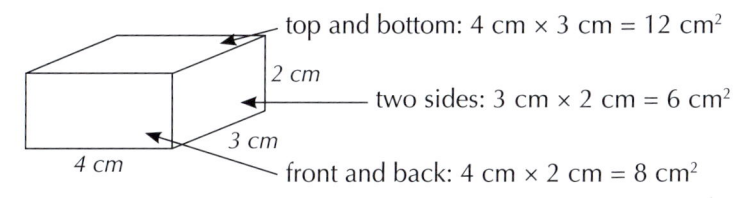

- top and bottom: 4 cm × 3 cm = 12 cm²
- two sides: 3 cm × 2 cm = 6 cm²
- front and back: 4 cm × 2 cm = 8 cm²

So the total surface area of the block is:
12 + 12 + 6 + 6 + 8 + 8 = **52 cm²**

Tip: The units of area are given in units squared (e.g. µm²).

Comparing surface area to volume ratios

Here's how to calculate surface area to volume ratios:

Example

A mouse can be represented by a cube measuring 1 cm × 1 cm × 1 cm.

Its volume is: 1 × 1 × 1 = 1 cm³

Its surface area is: 6 × (1 × 1) = 6 cm²

So the mouse has a surface area : volume ratio of **6 : 1**.

"cube mouse"

Tip: To write a ratio, you just need to write the number of one thing compared to the number of another thing, separated by a colon.

Compare this to a cube hippo measuring 2 cm × 4 cm × 4 cm.

Its volume is: 2 × 4 × 4 = 32 cm³

Its surface area is:

2 × (4 × 4) = 32 cm²
(top and bottom surfaces)

+ (4 × 2) × 4 = 32 cm² (four sides)

Total surface area = 64 cm²

"cube hippo"

The surface area to volume ratio of the hippo can be written as 64 : 32.

To get the ratio in the form n : 1, divide both sides of the ratio by the volume.

So the hippo has a surface area : volume ratio of **2 : 1**.

Tip: To compare two ratios, it's easier if you write both of them in the form n : 1. There's more about writing and simplifying ratios on page 242.

Topic 8 Exchange and Transport in Animals

Figure 1: A hippo (top) has a small surface area:volume ratio. A mouse (bottom) has a large surface area:volume ratio.

Now you can compare the ratios:

The cube mouse's surface area is six times its volume, but the cube hippo's surface area is only twice its volume. So the mouse has a larger surface area compared to its volume.

Why are exchange surfaces needed?

In single-celled organisms, gases and dissolved substances can diffuse directly into (or out of) the cell across the cell membrane. It's because they have a large surface area compared to their volume, so enough substances can be exchanged across the membrane to supply the volume of the cell.

Multicellular organisms (such as animals) have a smaller surface area compared to their volume. This makes it difficult to exchange enough substances to supply their entire volume across their outside surface alone. This means they need some sort of **exchange surface** for efficient diffusion and a transport system to move substances between the exchange surface and the rest of the body.

> **Example**
>
> Oxygen is able to diffuse from the air into a bacterial cell across the cell surface. A bacterium can get all the oxygen it needs for respiration this way.
>
> But in the human body, there are trillions of cells and they all need to get enough oxygen to respire. Oxygen can't just diffuse in through your skin — it would never reach the cells deep inside you.
>
> So humans need a specialised gas exchange surface (the alveoli, see next page) for the oxygen to diffuse across and a specialised breathing system to get it there. They also need a circulatory system (see pages 191-198) to transport the oxygen to every cell.

Tip: One trillion is 10^{12} or 1 000 000 000 000. I wonder who counted all those cells...

Tip: These cells are not drawn to scale.

Practice Question — Application

Q1 Two different cells can be represented by the shapes below:

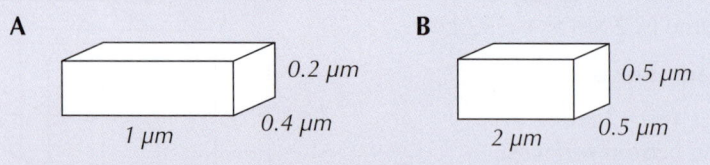

A: 1 μm × 0.4 μm × 0.2 μm

B: 2 μm × 0.5 μm × 0.5 μm

a) Calculate the surface area to volume ratio for each cell. Write each ratio in the form n : 1.

b) Predict which cell is most efficient at absorbing substances by diffusion. Explain your answer.

2. The Alveoli

In humans (and other mammals), gases are exchanged by diffusion in little air sacs in the lungs called alveoli.

Gas exchange in mammals

The job of the lungs is to transfer oxygen (O_2) to the blood and to remove waste carbon dioxide (CO_2) from it. To do this the lungs contain millions of little air sacs called **alveoli** (see Figure 1) where gas exchange takes place.

Learning Objective:
- Be able to explain how alveoli are adapted for gas exchange by diffusion between air in the lungs and blood in the capillaries.

Specification Reference 8.3

Tip: Gas exchange in animals means taking in oxygen from the environment and releasing carbon dioxide.

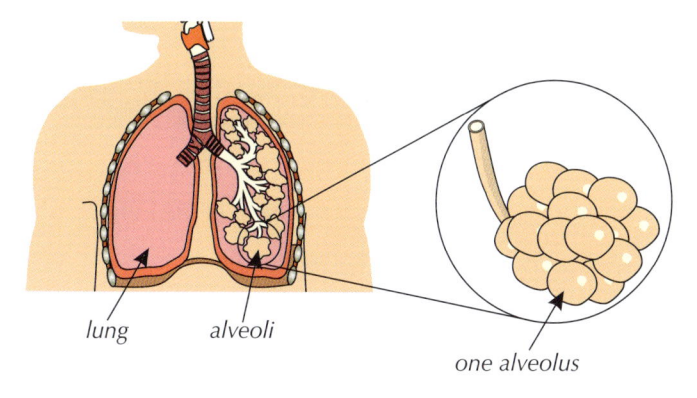

Figure 1: Diagram to show the location and structure of the alveoli.

Tip: It's one alveo<u>us</u> and two or more alveo<u>li</u>.

The alveoli are surrounded by a network of tiny blood vessels known as capillaries (see Figure 2). Blood arriving at the alveoli has just returned to the lungs from the rest of the body, so it contains lots of carbon dioxide and not much oxygen. This maximises the **concentration gradient** for the diffusion of both gases:

- There is a higher concentration of oxygen in the air than in the blood, so oxygen diffuses out of the air in the alveoli and into the blood in the capillaries.

- Carbon dioxide diffuses in the opposite direction, from a high concentration in the blood to a low concentration in the alveoli (see Figure 3), to be breathed out.

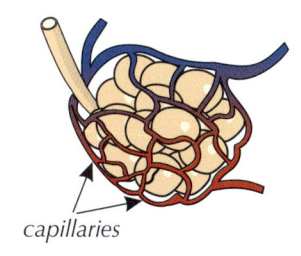

Figure 2: The alveoli are surrounded by a network of capillaries.

Tip: Substances diffuse from an area of higher concentration to an area of lower concentration (see p.43) i.e. down a concentration gradient.

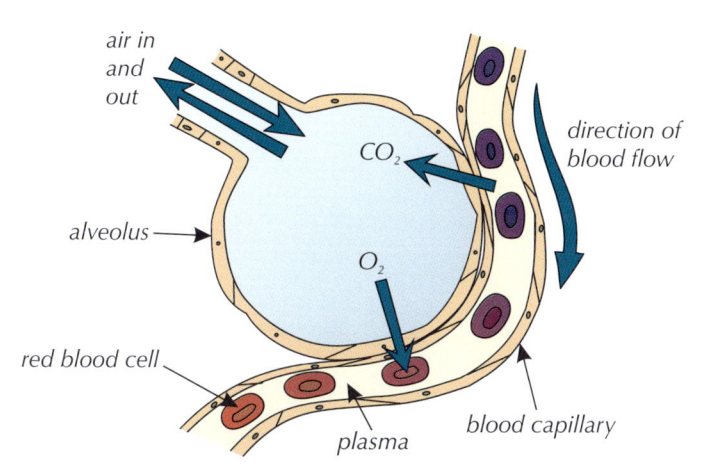

Figure 3: Diagram to show gas exchange across an alveolus.

Topic 8 Exchange and Transport in Animals

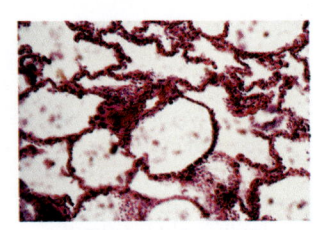

Figure 4: Alveoli and surrounding capillaries as seen under a light microscope.

Tip: Oxygen and carbon dioxide diffuse across the membranes of the cells that make up the walls of the capillary and alveolus. These membranes are partially permeable — see p.43.

Adaptations of the alveoli

The alveoli are specialised to maximise the diffusion of oxygen and CO_2. They have:

- An enormous surface area (about 75 m^2 in humans).
- A moist lining for dissolving gases — the gases need to be dissolved before they can diffuse through the alveolar walls.
- Very thin walls.
- A good blood supply to maintain the concentration gradients of oxygen and carbon dioxide.

Practice Questions — Fact Recall

Q1 Name the structures in the lungs where gas exchange takes place.

Q2 In which direction does oxygen diffuse in the lungs?

  A   From the capillaries into the alveoli.

  B   From the alveoli into the capillaries.

  Explain your answer.

Q3 Give three ways in which the alveoli are adapted to maximise the diffusion of oxygen and carbon dioxide.

Practice Question — Application

Q1 Chronic obstructive pulmonary disease (COPD) can be caused by long-term exposure to irritants which results in destruction of the alveolar walls.

  Suggest how COPD will affect gas exchange in the lungs. Explain your answer.

3. Circulatory System — The Blood

Blood is a major component of the circulatory system. It is used by multicellular organisms to transport materials between their cells.

Function of the circulatory system

The circulatory system's main function is to get food and oxygen to every cell in the body. As well as being a delivery service, it's also a waste collection service — it carries waste products like carbon dioxide and urea to where they can be removed from the body. The circulatory system includes the blood, blood vessels and the heart.

Learning Objective:
- Be able to explain how the structure of the blood is related to its function, including: red blood cells (erythrocytes), white blood cells (phagocytes and lymphocytes), platelets and plasma.

Specification Reference 8.6

What is blood?

Blood is a tissue — it's a group of similar cells which work together to perform a specific function. The function of the blood is to transport substances around the body. It's made up of **red blood cells**, **white blood cells** and **platelets**, which are all suspended in a liquid called **plasma**.

Red blood cells

The job of red blood cells (also called **erythrocytes**) is to transport oxygen around the body. They have a biconcave disc shape (see Figure 1) to give them a large surface area for absorbing oxygen. They also contain a red pigment called **haemoglobin**, which contains iron. The haemoglobin carries the oxygen.

Red blood cells are different from most types of animal cell because they don't have a nucleus — this allows more room for haemoglobin, which means they can carry more oxygen.

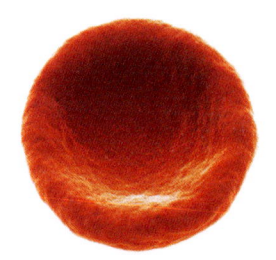

Figure 1: *A red blood cell has a biconcave shape — it looks like it's been squashed in the middle on both sides.*

Transporting oxygen

All body cells need oxygen for respiration — a process which releases energy (see pages 199-201). Oxygen enters the lungs when you breathe in, then red blood cells transport the oxygen from the lungs to all the cells in the body:

- In the lungs, oxygen diffuses into the blood. The oxygen combines with haemoglobin in red blood cells to become oxyhaemoglobin (see Figure 2).

- In body tissues, the reverse happens — oxyhaemoglobin splits up into haemoglobin and oxygen, to release oxygen to the cells.

In the lungs...   *In tissues...*

oxygen + haemoglobin → oxyhaemoglobin   oxyhaemoglobin → haemoglobin + oxygen

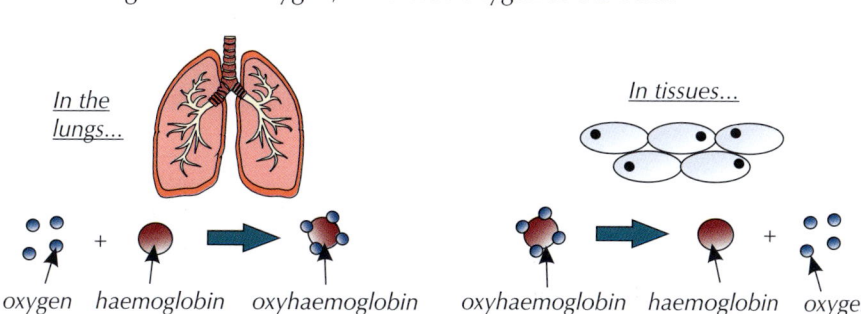

Figure 2: *Diagram illustrating the formation and breakdown of oxyhaemoglobin.*

Tip: The more red blood cells you've got, the more oxygen can get to your cells. At high altitudes there's less oxygen in the air — so people who live there produce more red blood cells to compensate.

Topic 8 Exchange and Transport in Animals

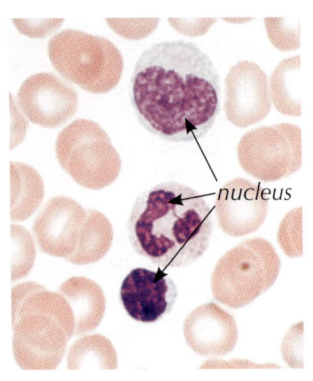

Figure 3: A picture taken down a light microscope showing three different types of white blood cell (stained purple) surrounded by red blood cells (pale red).

White blood cells

Unlike red blood cells, white blood cells have a nucleus. White blood cells help to defend against microorganisms that cause disease (see pages 123-125). There are different types of white blood cell. For example:

- **Phagocytes** are white blood cells that change shape to engulf unwelcome microorganisms — this is called phagocytosis.

- **Lymphocytes** are a group of white blood cells that have different functions depending on their type. For example, B lymphocytes produce antibodies against microorganisms (see p.124). Some also produce antitoxins to neutralise any toxins produced by the microorganisms.

Figure 4: A white blood cell.

When you have an infection, your white blood cells multiply to fight it off — so a blood test will show a high white blood cell count.

Platelets

Platelets are small fragments (pieces) of cells. They have no nucleus. They help the blood to **clot** (clump together) at a wound — this seals the wound and stops you from losing too much blood (see Figure 5). It also stops microorganisms from getting in at the wound. A lack of platelets can cause excessive bleeding and bruising.

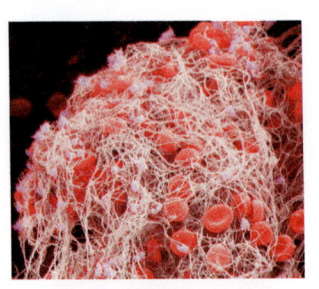

Figure 5: A blood clot formed by the action of platelets.

Plasma

Plasma is a pale straw-coloured liquid which carries just about everything in blood. It carries:

- Red and white blood cells and platelets.
- Nutrients like glucose and amino acids. These are the soluble products of digestion, which are absorbed from the small intestine and taken to the cells of the body.
- Carbon dioxide from the organs to the lungs.
- Urea from the liver to the kidneys.
- Hormones.
- Proteins.
- Antibodies and antitoxins produced by the white blood cells.

Figure 6: A pouch of plasma, which has been extracted from donated blood.

Tip: Urea is a waste product produced from the breakdown of amino acids in the liver.

Practice Questions — Fact Recall

Q1 a) Name the red pigment found in red blood cells.
   b) Describe the role of this red pigment.

Q2 What is the function of white blood cells?

Q3 What is the role of platelets?

Q4 Name the part of blood that's used to transport cells and platelets.

4. Circulatory System — The Blood Vessels

Learning Objective:
- Be able to explain how the structure of the blood vessels is related to their function.

Specification Reference 8.7

Our blood makes its way around our body in blood vessels. There are three different types of blood vessels you need to know about...

Arteries

Arteries are blood vessels which carry blood away from the heart, towards the organs. The heart pumps the blood out at high pressure, so the artery walls are strong and elastic. They contain thick layers of muscle to make them strong, and elastic fibres to allow them to stretch and spring back. The walls are thick compared to the size of the hole down the middle (the lumen) — see Figure 1.

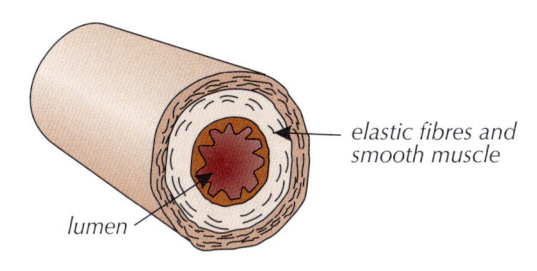

Figure 1: *Diagram to show the structure of an artery.*

Capillaries

Arteries branch into capillaries. Capillaries are involved in the exchange of materials at the tissues — they carry the blood really close to every cell in the body to exchange substances with them. They supply food and oxygen to the cells, and take away waste products like carbon dioxide.

Capillaries are really tiny — too small to see. They have permeable walls, so the substances being exchanged with the cells can diffuse in and out. Their walls are usually only one cell thick (see Figure 2). This increases the rate of diffusion by decreasing the distance over which it occurs. Capillaries are also very narrow, so they can squeeze into the gaps between cells. It also gives them a large surface area compared to their volume, which increases the rate of diffusion.

Tip: Remember, diffusion is the process by which substances move from an area of higher concentration to an area of lower concentration.

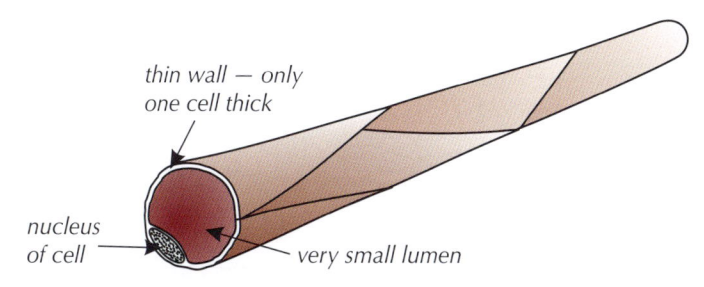

Figure 2: *Diagram to show the structure of a capillary.*

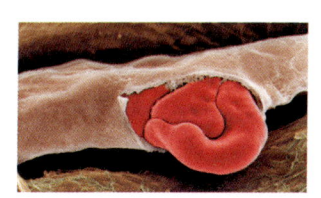

Figure 3: *A torn capillary with blood cells leaking out — you can see how thin the walls of the capillary are.*

Topic 8 Exchange and Transport in Animals

Exam Tip
If you're struggling to remember which way arteries and veins carry blood in the exam, think: <u>arteries</u> are the '<u>way art</u>' (way out) of the heart, and <u>veins</u> are the '<u>vey in</u>' (way in).

Veins

Capillaries eventually join up to form veins. Veins carry blood to the heart.

The blood is at lower pressure in the veins, so the walls don't need to be as thick as artery walls. Veins have a bigger lumen than arteries to help the blood flow despite the lower pressure (see Figure 4).

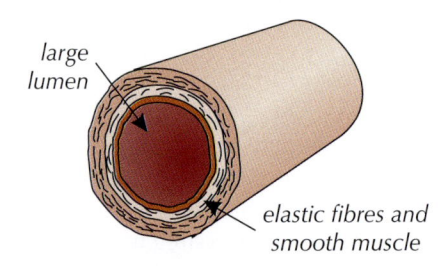

Figure 4: Diagram to show the structure of a vein.

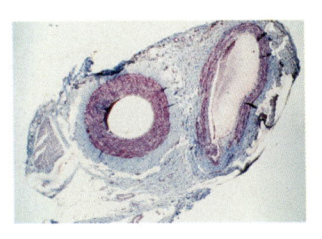

Figure 5: A cross-section through an artery and a vein — the walls of the blood vessels are pink. The walls of the artery (left) are much thicker than the walls of the vein (right).

They also have **valves** to help keep the blood flowing in the right direction to prevent backflow (see Figure 6).

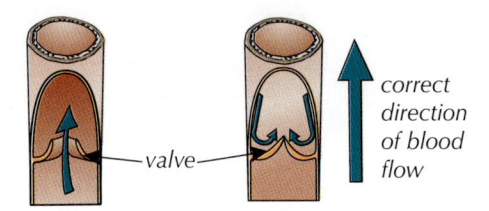

Figure 6: Diagram to show how valves prevent the backflow of blood.

Practice Question — Fact Recall

Q1 What type of blood vessel has walls that are only one cell thick?

Practice Question — Application

Q1 The graph below shows the relative pressure inside two different blood vessels — one is a vein and one is an artery.

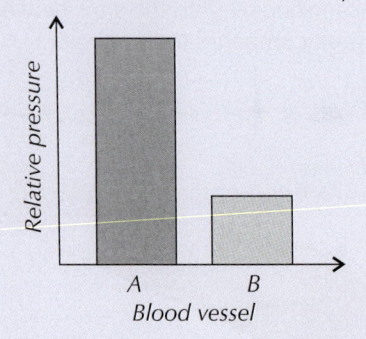

Which blood vessel (A or B) would you expect to contain a higher proportion of muscle tissue in its walls? Explain your answer.

Topic 8 Exchange and Transport in Animals

5. Circulatory System — The Heart

The heart plays a major role in the circulatory system. It is needed to pump the blood through the blood vessels so that material can be transported to and from the cells.

Types of circulatory system

There are different types of circulatory system. In all types of circulatory system, a heart is needed to pump blood around the body.

A double circulatory system

Mammals (including humans) have a double circulatory system. This means that the heart pumps blood around the body in two circuits.

- In the first circuit, the heart pumps deoxygenated blood (blood low in oxygen) to the lungs to take in oxygen. The oxygenated blood then returns to the heart (see Figure 1a).

- In the second circuit, the heart pumps oxygenated blood around all the other organs of the body. The blood gives up its oxygen at the body cells and the deoxygenated blood returns to the heart to be pumped out to the lungs again (see Figure 1b).

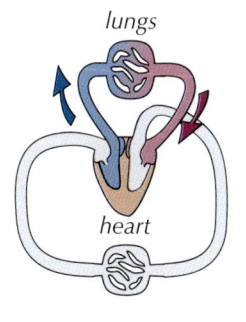

Figure 1a: Blood circulation between the heart and the lungs in mammals.

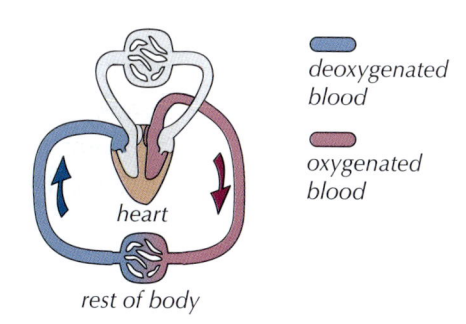

Figure 1b: Blood circulation between the heart and the rest of the body in mammals.

A single circulatory system

Fish have a single circulatory system. Deoxygenated blood from the fish's body travels to the heart, which then pumps it right round the body again in a single circuit. The blood goes via the gills where it picks up oxygen. In single circulatory systems, only deoxygenated blood goes through the heart (see Figure 2).

Figure 2: Blood circulation in a fish.

> **Learning Objectives:**
> - Be able to explain how the structure of the heart and circulatory system is related to its function, including the role of the major blood vessels, the valves and the relative thickness of chamber walls.
> - Be able to calculate heart rate, stroke volume and cardiac output, using the equation:
>   cardiac output = stroke volume × heart rate
>
> **Specification References 8.8, 8.12**

Topic 8 Exchange and Transport in Animals

The blood pressure in single circulatory systems is limited to prevent damage to the capillaries in the gills. In a double circulatory system, blood can be pumped at a low safe pressure in the circuit to the lungs, and at a higher pressure in the circuit to the rest of the body (so material in the blood can reach the cells faster).

Structure of the mammalian heart

The mammalian heart has four chambers (the **right atrium**, **right ventricle**, **left atrium** and **left ventricle**) which it uses to pump blood around (see Figure 3). The major blood vessels leading into and out of these chambers are the **vena cava**, **pulmonary artery**, **aorta** and **pulmonary vein**. The walls of the heart are mostly made of muscle tissue, which contracts to pump the blood.

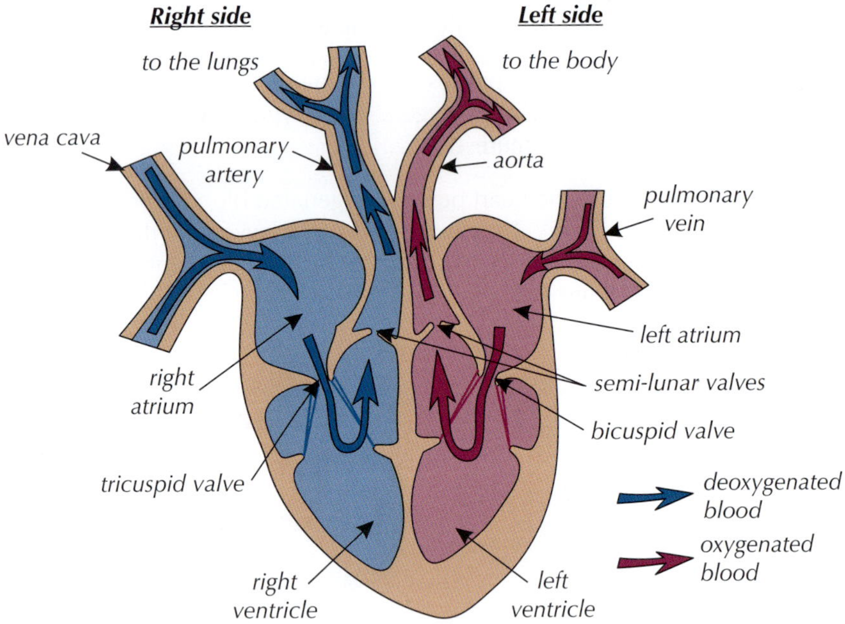

Exam Tip
You need to learn the names of these chambers and the main blood vessels leading into and out of the heart for your exam.

Tip: A fish's heart only has two chambers — a ventricle and an atrium.

Tip: Don't be confused about the way the right and left side of the heart are labelled in this diagram — this is the right and left side of the person whose heart it is.

Tip: The heart also needs its own supply of oxygenated blood. Arteries called coronary arteries branch off the aorta and surround the heart, making sure that it gets all the oxygenated blood it needs. If they become blocked, the heart can become starved of oxygen, potentially leading to a heart attack (see p.140).

Figure 3: Diagram showing the structure of the heart and the direction of blood flow through the heart.

The heart has **valves** to make sure that blood goes in the right direction — they prevent it flowing backwards.

Blood flow through the heart

Deoxygenated blood flows through the right side of the heart to the lungs. Oxygenated blood flows through the left side of the heart to the rest of the body.

1. The right atrium of the heart receives deoxygenated blood from the body through the vena cava (see Figure 4 on the next page). The left atrium receives oxygenated blood from the lungs through the pulmonary vein.

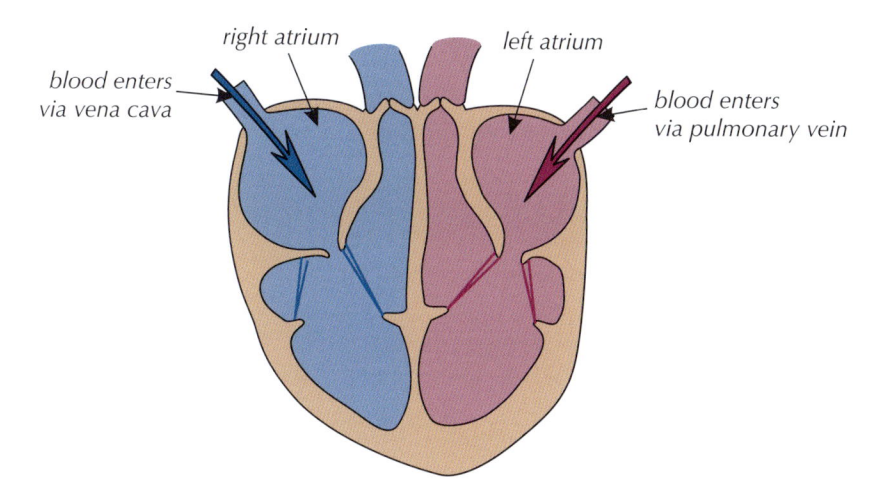

Figure 4: Diagram showing blood flowing into the heart.

2. The atria contract, pushing the blood into the ventricles.

3. The ventricles contract. Deoxygenated blood moves from the right ventricle to the lungs via the pulmonary artery. The oxygenated blood moves from the left ventricle to the whole body via the aorta (see Figure 5).

Tip: 'Atria' is the plural of 'atrium'. So you get one atrium, but two atria.

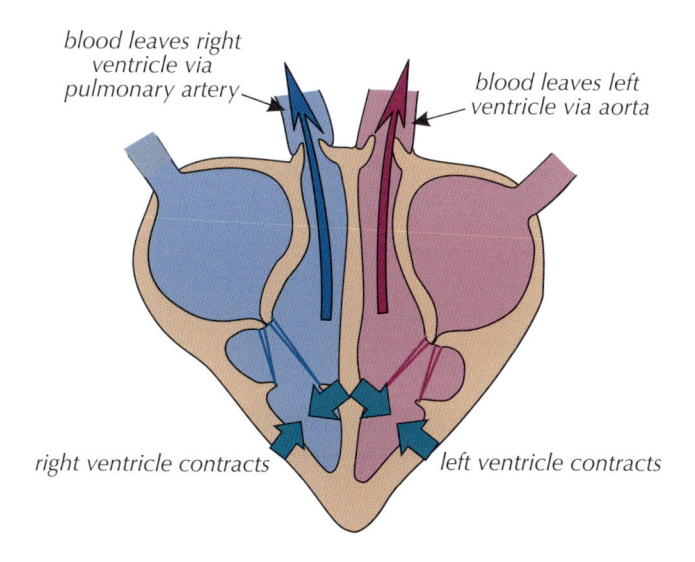

Figure 5: Diagram showing blood being forced out of the heart.

Thickness of the chamber walls

The thickness of each chamber wall in the heart is related to its function.

Both atria walls are relatively thin. They only need to pump blood a short distance to the ventricles, so they don't require much muscle.

The ventricles have to pump blood further, so their chamber walls are thicker than those of the atria. The wall of the left ventricle is much thicker than the wall of the right ventricle. This is because the left ventricle needs more muscle to pump blood around the whole body at high pressure, whereas the right ventricle only has to pump blood to the lungs.

Calculating cardiac output

Cardiac output is the total volume of blood pumped by a ventricle every minute. You can calculate it using this equation:

$$\text{cardiac output} = \text{heart rate} \times \text{stroke volume}$$

in $cm^3\ min^{-1}$; in beats per minute (bpm) ; in cm^3

The **heart rate** is the number of beats per minute (bpm). The **stroke volume** is the volume of blood pumped by one ventricle each time it contracts.

Tip: A cardiac output of 4760 $cm^3\ min^{-1}$ means that 4760 cm^3 of blood are pumped by a ventricle in 1 minute.

Example

Calculate the cardiac output of a person with a heart rate of 68 bpm and an average stroke volume of 70 cm^3.

cardiac output ($cm^3\ min^{-1}$) = heart rate (bpm) × stroke volume (cm^3)
= 68 × 70
= **4760 $cm^3\ min^{-1}$**

Exam Tip
If you find rearranging formulas hard, you can use a formula triangle to help:

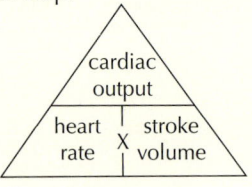

```
     cardiac
     output
   ─────────
   heart  │ stroke
   rate  x│ volume
```

All you do is put your finger over the one you want and read off the formula. E.g. if you want the heart rate, you put your finger over that and it leaves behind cardiac output ÷ stroke volume.

You might be asked to find the stroke volume or the heart rate in the exam instead of the cardiac output — if so, you can just rearrange the equation above.

Example

What is the heart rate of a person with an average stroke volume of 72 cm^3 and a cardiac output of 5420 $cm^3\ min^{-1}$?

heart rate (bpm) = cardiac output ($cm^3\ min^{-1}$) ÷ stroke volume (cm^3)
= 5420 ÷ 72
= **75 bpm**

Practice Questions — Fact Recall

Q1 The circulatory system in mammals is made up of two separate circuits. What is the function of each circuit?

Q2 Name the four chambers of the mammalian heart.

Q3 Name the two blood vessels which:
   a) carry blood into the heart,   b) carry blood out of the heart.

Exam Tip
Make sure you check the units of measurements you're given in the exams. You may need to convert them before you carry out a calculation with them. See p.19-20 for more on converting units.

Practice Questions — Application

Q1 Alan has a condition known as SVCS. This condition is very serious as it obstructs blood flow in the vessel going into the heart from the rest of the body. Name the blood vessel which is affected in SVCS.

Q2 A man has a heart rate of 85 bpm and a cardiac output of 6.46 $dm^3\ min^{-1}$. Calculate the man's stroke volume in cm^3.

6. Respiration

We, and other organisms, need energy to do... well... everything really. This energy comes from the reactions of respiration.

What is respiration?

Respiration is not breathing in and breathing out, as you might think. It's a process that goes on continuously in every cell of all living organisms. For this reason, it's also known as cellular respiration.

Cellular respiration is the process of transferring (releasing) energy from the breakdown of organic compounds (usually glucose). This energy is used to fuel metabolic processes — the necessary chemical reactions that take place inside living organisms. Because energy is transferred to the environment, respiration is an **exothermic reaction**. Some of this energy is transferred by heat. In summary:

> Cellular respiration is an exothermic reaction, which releases energy for metabolic processes, and occurs continuously in every cell of living organisms.

There are two types of respiration — aerobic and anaerobic.

Energy from respiration

Organisms use the energy transferred by respiration to fuel all sorts of metabolic processes.

Examples

- Organisms use energy for reactions that involve building up larger molecules from smaller ones (like proteins from amino acids).

- Animals use energy in the chemical reactions that allow their muscles to contract (which in turn allows them to move about).

- Mammals and birds use energy to keep their body temperature steady (unlike other animals, mammals and birds keep their bodies constantly warm).

Aerobic respiration

Aerobic respiration is respiration using oxygen. It's the most efficient way to transfer energy from glucose. Aerobic respiration goes on all the time in plants and animals.

Most of the reactions in aerobic respiration happen inside cell structures called **mitochondria** (see page 23).

Learning Objectives:
- Be able to describe cellular respiration as an exothermic reaction which occurs continuously in living cells to release energy for metabolic processes, including aerobic and anaerobic respiration.
- Be able to compare the process of aerobic respiration with the process of anaerobic respiration.

Specification References 8.9, 8.10

Tip: Organic compounds are compounds containing carbon. They include carbohydrates, lipids and proteins.

Tip: Respiration itself is a metabolic process.

Figure 1: *Animals, including humans, need energy from respiration to contract their muscles and move.*

Word equation

You need to learn the overall word equation for aerobic respiration:

$$\text{glucose} + \text{oxygen} \rightarrow \text{carbon dioxide} + \text{water}$$

Tip: The equations for aerobic respiration are the reverse of the photosynthesis equations (see p.147).

Symbol equation

There's a symbol equation for aerobic respiration too:

$$C_6H_{12}O_6 + 6O_2 \rightarrow 6CO_2 + 6H_2O$$

Anaerobic respiration

When you do vigorous exercise, your body can't supply enough oxygen to your muscles for aerobic respiration, even though your heart rate and breathing rate increase as much as they can. So your muscles have to start respiring anaerobically as well.

"Anaerobic" just means "without oxygen". It's the incomplete breakdown of glucose, making **lactic acid**. Here's the word equation for anaerobic respiration in animals:

$$\text{glucose} \rightarrow \text{lactic acid}$$

Tip: An increased breathing rate gets more oxygen into your lungs. An increased heart rate means that blood is pumped round the body faster, so the cells receive oxygen more quickly.

Since glucose is only partially broken down, anaerobic respiration does not transfer nearly as much energy as aerobic respiration, making it much less efficient. So, anaerobic respiration is only useful in emergencies, e.g. during exercise when it allows you to keep on using your muscles for a while longer.

During vigorous exercise, lactic acid builds up in the muscles which gets painful and leads to cramp.

Anaerobic respiration in plants

Anaerobic respiration in plants is slightly different. Plants cells can respire without oxygen too, but they produce ethanol (alcohol) and carbon dioxide instead of lactic acid.

This is the word equation for anaerobic respiration in plants:

$$\text{glucose} \rightarrow \text{ethanol} + \text{carbon dioxide}$$

Tip: Fungi, such as yeast, also respire anaerobically to produce ethanol and carbon dioxide. Anaerobic respiration in yeast is used to make beer.

Comparing aerobic and anaerobic respiration

You need to be able to compare aerobic and anaerobic respiration.

	Aerobic respiration	Anaerobic respiration
Is oxygen needed?	yes	no
What products are made?	CO_2 and water	lactic acid (animals) / CO_2 and ethanol (plants)
How much energy is transferred?	A large amount.	A small amount.

Figure 2: Table comparing aerobic and anaerobic respiration.

Practice Questions — Fact Recall

Q1 Give three ways in which mammals use energy from respiration.

Q2 What is aerobic respiration?

Q3 Aerobic respiration is an exothermic reaction. What does this mean?

Q4 Explain when the body uses anaerobic respiration.

Q5 Give the word equation for anaerobic respiration in animals.

Practice Questions — Application

Q1 This diagram shows the equation for aerobic respiration.

glucose + A → carbon dioxide + B

a) What is A in the equation?

b) What is B in the equation?

Q2 Rice is grown in flooded fields called paddy fields. There is very little oxygen available in flooded soils. Suggest why the roots of rice plants need a high tolerance for ethanol (a poison).

Exam Tip
Make sure you know the word equations for both aerobic an anaerobic respiration off by heart. They could get you easy marks in the exam.

Learning Objective:
- Be able to investigate the rate of respiration in living organisms. (Core Practical)

Specification Reference 8.11

7. Investigating Respiration

CORE PRACTICAL

The rate at which an organism respires will change depending on different factors. You can do an experiment to see how temperature affects the rate of respiration.

Measuring the rate of respiration

In aerobic respiration, organisms use up oxygen from the air. By measuring the amount of oxygen consumed by organisms in a given time, you can calculate their rate of respiration.

Here's an experiment which uses woodlice, a water bath and a piece of equipment called a **respirometer**. It allows you to measure the effect of temperature on the rate of respiration of the woodlice. (You could use germinating peas or beans instead of woodlice. Germinating seeds respire to provide energy for growth.)

Tip: Make sure that you carry out a risk assessment before you begin. Soda lime is corrosive, so your teacher or a lab technician should add it to the test tubes for you. Safety goggles and gloves should be worn during the experiment to protect the eyes and skin.

1. Take two test tubes, each containing soda lime granules covered by a ball of cotton wool. Soda lime absorbs the carbon dioxide produced by the respiring woodlice in the experiment. The cotton wool stops both you and the woodlice coming into contact with the soda lime.

2. Place woodlice on top of the cotton wool in one tube. Add glass beads with the same mass as the woodlice to the control tube.

3. Set up the respirometer as shown in Figure 1, with the water bath set to 15 °C.

Tip: The control tube helps you check that the movement of the fluid in the respirometer (see next page) is caused by the woodlice respiring and not as a result of something else. There's more on controls on page 10.

Tip: There's more on using water baths on page 236.

Tip: You could also use cotton wool soaked in a few drops of potassium hydroxide solution to absorb the CO_2. You would need to prevent the woodlice from coming into contact with this though, e.g. by using a layer of gauze.

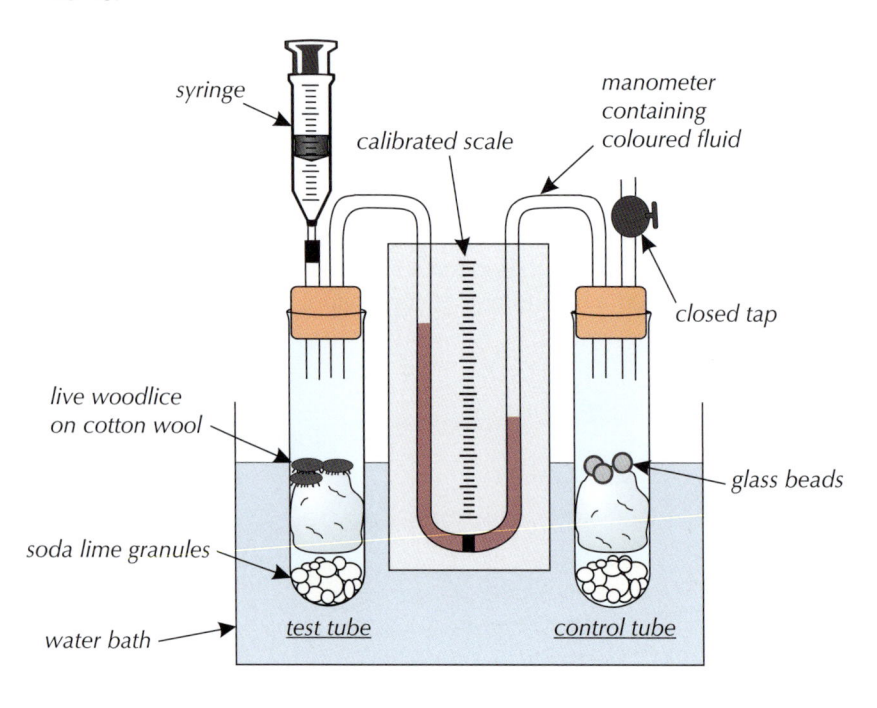

Figure 1: Apparatus for investigating the effect of temperature on respiration.

Topic 8 Exchange and Transport in Animals

4. Leave the apparatus for 5 minutes to allow the temperature inside the test tubes to reach the temperature of the water bath.

5. Use the syringe to set the fluid in the manometer to a known level.

6. Leave the apparatus for a set period of time.

7. During this time, there'll be a decrease in the volume of the air in the test tube containing the woodlice. This is because the woodlice use up oxygen in the tube as they respire. (The carbon dioxide they produce is absorbed by the soda lime so it doesn't affect the experiment.)

8. The decrease in volume reduces the pressure in the tube, causing the coloured liquid in the manometer to move towards the test tube containing the woodlice. The higher the rate of respiration, the more the coloured liquid will move.

9. The distance moved by the liquid in a given time is measured. This value can then be used to calculate the volume of oxygen taken in by the woodlice per unit of time. This gives you the rate of respiration in, e.g. $cm^3\ min^{-1}$.

Tip: You can work out the volume of oxygen taken in by the woodlice by multiplying the distance moved by the liquid in the manometer by πr^2, where 'r' is the radius of the manometer.

Example

In an experiment measuring the respiration in woodlice, 2.7 cm³ of oxygen were taken up in a 30 minute time period.

Calculate the rate of respiration in $cm^3\ min^{-1}$.

Divide the volume of oxygen taken up by the woodlice by the number of minutes that it was consumed in.

rate of respiration = 2.7 ÷ 30 = **0.09 $cm^3\ min^{-1}$**.

Exam Tip
Pay close attention to the units given in the question. Volume of oxygen uptake could be given in ml, mm³ or cm³. You could also be asked to calculate the rate of respiration per second — just divide the time in minutes by 60 and then follow the steps for working out the rate.

10. Repeat steps 1-9 with the water bath set at different temperatures, e.g. 20 °C and 25 °C. This will allow you to see how changing the temperature affects the rate of respiration.

You should think carefully about what temperatures to use in your experiment before you start. The process of respiration uses enzymes. If the temperature is too high, enzymes will denature (see p.37) and so respiration will not occur. If you are using live animals, you also need to make sure you pick temperatures that are safe and do not cause discomfort (see below).

Ethical issues from using live organisms

Any live animals you use in this experiment should be treated ethically. For example, it's important not to leave the woodlice in the respirometer for too long, or they may run out of oxygen and die. They should also be kept away from the soda lime (or potassium hydroxide) as it is corrosive. There's more on the ethical treatment of organisms in experiments on page 240.

Practice Question — Application

Q1 A student carries out an investigation using a respirometer. Her experimental set-up is shown in the diagram below.

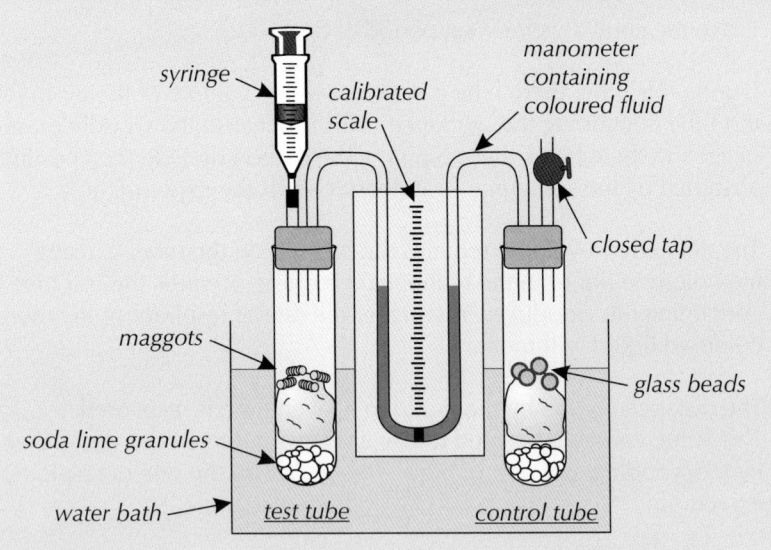

The student measures the rate of respiration in maggots over a 30 minute time period at 10 °C and then again at 20 °C. All other variables are kept the same.

a) What is the role of the cotton wool in the test tubes?

b) Explain why there is soda lime in the test tubes.

c) In which direction would you expect the coloured fluid in the manometer to move during the experiments?

    A Towards the test tube containing maggots.

    B Towards the control tube containing glass beads.

Explain your answer.

d) During the experiment at 20 °C, the fluid in the manometer moves further than the experiment at 10 °C. What does this suggest about the effect of temperature on the rate of respiration? Explain your answer.

Topic 8 Checklist — Make sure you know...

Exchange of Materials

☐ That organisms need to take in substances (e.g. oxygen, water, dissolved food molecules and mineral ions) from the environment for life processes, and that they need to remove the waste products (e.g. carbon dioxide and urea) from such processes.

☐ How to calculate and compare surface area to volume ratios.

☐ That exchanging materials with the environment is more difficult in multicellular organisms than in single-celled organisms due to their smaller surface area to volume ratios, so multicellular organisms need specialised exchange surfaces and transport systems for exchanging and carrying materials.

The Alveoli

☐ How alveoli (tiny air sacs) in the lungs are adapted to maximise the diffusion of oxygen into the blood and carbon dioxide out of the blood by having a large surface area, a moist lining, very thin walls and an efficient blood supply.

Circulatory System — The Blood

☐ That red blood cells (erythrocytes) have no nucleus, have a biconcave shape and contain haemoglobin that binds to oxygen, allowing them to carry oxygen from the lungs to the rest of the body.

☐ That white blood cells (e.g. phagocytes and lymphocytes) have a nucleus and help to defend against disease caused by microorganisms.

☐ That platelets are fragments of cells which don't have a nucleus and help blood to clot at a wound.

☐ That plasma carries just about everything in the blood including blood cells and platelets, nutrients released from digestion, carbon dioxide, urea, hormones, proteins, antibodies and antitoxins.

Circulatory System — The Blood Vessels

☐ That there are three types of blood vessel found in the body — arteries, which carry blood away from the heart, capillaries, which carry blood close to the cells to allow substances to be exchanged, and veins, which carry blood back to the heart.

☐ How the structures of the different blood vessels are adapted to allow them to carry out their roles in the circulatory system.

Circulatory System — The Heart

☐ That mammals (including humans have a double circulatory system to transport substances around the body via the blood, which is pumped around the body by the heart. One circuit, powered by the right ventricle, pumps deoxygenated blood to the lungs to take in oxygen, and the other circuit, powered by the left ventricle, pumps oxygenated blood to the rest of the body.

cont...

- [ ] That the four chambers of the mammalian heart are the right atrium, right ventricle, left atrium and left ventricle, that the thickness of a chamber wall is related to the chamber's function, and that the chambers have valves to prevent backflow.
- [ ] That the vena cava, pulmonary artery, aorta and pulmonary vein are the four major blood vessels connected to the heart.
- [ ] How to calculate heart rate, stroke volume and cardiac output, using the equation:
cardiac output = stroke volume × heart rate.

Respiration

- [ ] That respiration is an exothermic reaction, which releases energy for things such as metabolic processes, muscle contraction and maintaining body temperature, and that it occurs continuously in every cell of living organisms.
- [ ] That aerobic respiration is the process of transferring energy from glucose using oxygen in the reaction: glucose + oxygen → carbon dioxide + water, and that it occurs continuously in living cells.
- [ ] That muscles will start to respire anaerobically (without oxygen) if they can't get enough oxygen to respire aerobically, and that this involves the incomplete breakdown of glucose, which forms lactic acid: glucose → lactic acid. Anaerobic respiration transfers less energy than aerobic respiration.
- [ ] The word equation for anaerobic respiration in plants: glucose → ethanol + carbon dioxide.

Investigating Respiration

- [ ] How to investigate the rate of respiration in living organisms. (Core Practical)

Exam-style Questions

1   **Figure 1** represents the heart.

Figure 1

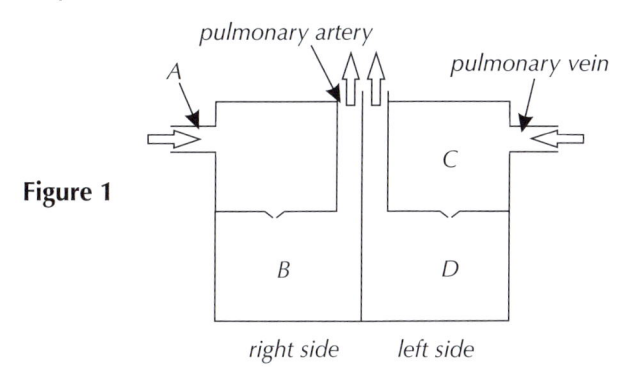

pulmonary artery, pulmonary vein, A, B, C, D, right side, left side

(a)   Name each of the structures labelled **A-C** on the diagram.

(3 marks)

(b)   Explain why structure **D** has a thicker wall than structure **B**.

(2 marks)

Figure 2 shows cross-sections through the pulmonary artery and the pulmonary vein.

Figure 2   X   Y

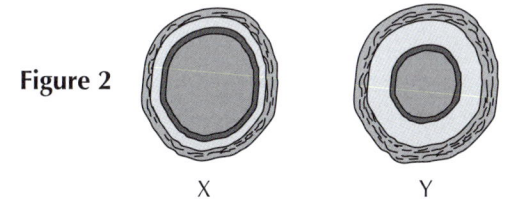

(c)   Which diagram (**X** or **Y**) shows the pulmonary vein? Explain your answer.

(1 mark)

2   A doctor is looking at the blood test results for two patients. Their results, along with the normal range for each of the blood components tested, are shown in **Figure 3**:

Figure 3

	Red Blood Cells (10^{12}/L)	White Blood Cells (10^9/L)	Platelets (10^9/L)	Urea (mmol/L)
Normal Range	3.9-5.6	4.0-11.0	150-400	3.0-7.0
Patient A	4.2	3.2	250	3.2
Patient B	3.7	10.2	315	5.4

(a)   Explain which patient (**A** or **B**) is most at risk of getting an infection.

(2 marks)

(b) **Figure 4** shows a group of blood cells.

Figure 4

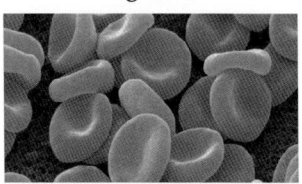

Identify the blood cells shown in **Figure 4** and explain **three** ways in which they are adapted to their function.

(4 marks)

3 Methods of exchanging substances with the environment vary between organisms. Some organisms contain specialised exchange surfaces for this purpose.

Figure 5 shows a rod-shaped bacterium, with its approximate dimensions.

Figure 5

0.6 µm
3.0 µm
0.6 µm

(a) Calculate the surface area to volume ratio of this bacterium.

(3 marks)

(b) Explain why this bacterium doesn't need any specialised surfaces for exchanging substances with the environment.

(3 marks)

4 A scientist is investigating the reactions of aerobic and anaerobic respiration.

(a) State the word equation for aerobic respiration.

(2 marks)

(b) In a cell, energy is stored in a molecule called ATP.
The scientist conducts an experiment to find out how much ATP each type of respiration forms per glucose molecule.

His results are shown in **Figure 6**:

Figure 6

Type of respiration	Number of ATP molecules released per glucose molecule
Aerobic	32
Anaerobic	2

Using the table, describe and explain the difference in the amount of energy transferred by aerobic and anaerobic respiration.

(2 marks)

Topic 9a — Ecosystems and Biodiversity

1. Ecosystems and Interactions Between Organisms

Learning Objectives:
- Be able to describe the different levels of organisation from individual organisms, populations and communities, to the whole ecosystem.
- Be able to describe the importance of interdependence in a community.
- Be able to describe how the survival of some organisms is dependent on other species, including parasitism and mutualism.

Specification References 9.1, 9.3, 9.4

Organisms live together in ecosystems. They depend on other organisms in their ecosystem for survival.

Important definitions
Topic 9 will make a lot more sense if you become familiar with these terms:

Habitat	The place where an organism lives, e.g. a field.
Population	All the organisms of one species living in a habitat.
Community	All the organisms of different species living in a habitat.
Abiotic factors	Non-living factors of the environment, e.g. temperature.
Biotic factors	Living factors of the environment, e.g. food.
Ecosystem	A community of organisms along with all the non-living (abiotic) parts of their environment.

Levels of organisation

There are different levels of organisation in an ecosystem (see Figure 1). The first and smallest level is an individual organism. Individual organisms make up a population (the next level of organisation) and several populations make up a community. The final and biggest level of organisation is the ecosystem itself.

individual → population → community → ecosystem

Figure 1: Flow chart to show the levels of organisation in an ecosystem.

Example

A fox is an individual organism. It may belong to a population of foxes living in a woodland habitat. The foxes are part of the community of other animals, birds, plants, trees and insects living in the same habitat. This community, along with abiotic factors such as the soil type, rainfall and light intensity in the woodland make up the ecosystem.

Tip: There's more on abiotic factors in ecosystems on p.212.

Interdependence

Organisms depend on each other for things like food and shelter in order to survive and reproduce. This is known as interdependence. It means that a change in the population of one species can have huge knock on effects for other species in the same community.

> **Example**
>
> Figure 2 shows part of a food web (a diagram of what eats what) from a stream.
>
> **Tip:** Imagine the arrows here mean 'is eaten by'. So the stonefly larvae is eaten by the diving beetle, the water boatman and the water spider.
>
> **Figure 2:** Diagram to show part of a food web in a stream.
>
> Stonefly larvae are particularly sensitive to pollution. Suppose pollution killed them in this stream. The table below shows some of the effects this might have on some of the other organisms in the food web.
>
> | Organism | Effect of loss of stonefly larvae | Effect on population |
> |---|---|---|
> | Blackfly larvae | Less competition for algae | Increase |
> | Blackfly larvae | More likely to be eaten by predators | Decrease |
> | Water spider | Less food | Decrease |
> | Stickleback | Less food (if water spider or mayfly larvae numbers decrease) | Decrease |

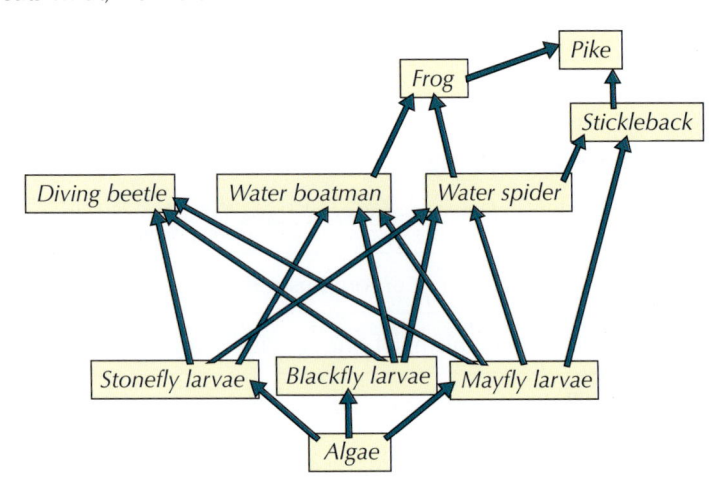

Mutualism

Mutualism is an example of interdependence in ecosystems. It is a relationship between two organisms, from which both organisms benefit.

> **Examples**
>
> - Bees and flowering plants have a mutualistic relationship. Bees visit flowers to get nectar (a sugary liquid, which the bees eat). As they do so, pollen is transferred to the bees' bodies. The bees then spread the pollen to other plants when they land on their flowers. The bees get food and the plants get help reproducing — so both types of organism benefit.

Figure 3: A honeybee visiting a chrysanthemum flower. The yellow blob on the bee is pollen.

Topic 9a Ecosystems and Biodiversity

- 'Cleaner fish' (such as cleaner wrasse) feed on dead skin and parasites on the surface of larger fish — the cleaner fish get a meal and the larger fish are helped to stay healthy.

Parasitism

Parasitism is another example of interdependence. Parasites live very closely with a host species (e.g. in or on them). The parasite takes what it needs to survive, but the host doesn't benefit.

Examples

- Fleas are parasites of mammals such as dogs. Fleas feed on their host's blood, but don't offer anything in return.
- The plant mistletoe is a parasite. It grows on the branches of trees (see Figure 4) such as apple and hawthorn, and depends on them for water and mineral ions. The trees themselves don't benefit and can be killed if too much mistletoe grows on them (especially during dry weather, when there's not enough water to be shared).

Figure 4: Mistletoe (dense green ball) growing on the branches of a tree.

Practice Questions — Fact Recall

Q1 What's the difference between a population of organisms and a community of organisms?

Q2 What is the smallest level of organisation in an ecosystem?

Practice Questions — Application

Q1 Which of the following is an example of an ecosystem?

　　A The water in a stream.

　　B The trout that live in a stream.

　　C All the fish, insects, aquatic mammals, birds and amphibians that live in a stream.

　　D All the fish, insects, aquatic mammals, birds and amphibians that live in a stream, along with factors such as the pH, temperature and oxygen content of the water.

Q2 Spider crabs live on the sea bed. Algae grow on the crabs' backs, making the crabs blend in with their surroundings. The algae make their own food through photosynthesis and don't take anything from the crabs. Is this an example of a mutualistic or a parasitic relationship? Explain your answer.

Learning Objective:
- Be able to explain how communities can be affected by abiotic and biotic factors, including:
  - temperature, light, water and pollutants;
  - competition and predation.

Specification Reference 9.2

2. Abiotic and Biotic Factors

Ecosystems contain abiotic (non-living) and biotic (living) factors.

Changes in ecosystems

Ecosystems change all the time. These changes are caused by both abiotic and biotic factors and they affect communities in different ways. For example, a change might cause the population size of one species to increase and the population size of another species to decrease. Alternatively, the distribution of populations (where they live) may change.

Abiotic factors

Some changes to ecosystems are caused by abiotic factors. These include things like temperature, light intensity, the availability of water or the presence of pollutants. They can all affect communities in different ways:

> **Examples**
> - Temperature — the distribution of some bird species is probably changing because of a rise in average temperature. For instance, the European bee-eater bird is a Mediterranean species but it's now present in parts of Germany.
> - Light intensity — as trees grow and develop more branches, the ground below them becomes more shaded. This might stop grasses from growing underneath the trees because grasses need plenty of light to grow. The grasses may be replaced by fungi (or mosses, etc.) which are better able to cope with the lower light intensity.
> - Amount of water — all organisms need water to live, so a change in the availability of water usually has a big effect on communities. E.g. daisies grow best in soils that are slightly damp. If the soil becomes waterlogged or too dry, the population of daisies in that area will decrease.
> - Levels of pollutants — lichens are unable to survive if the concentration of sulfur dioxide (an air pollutant) is too high. So an increase in sulfur dioxide concentration might reduce the population size of the lichens in an area.

Tip: Plants need light for photosynthesis (see page 146). Most plants need lots of light but some are adapted to living in areas of low light intensity.

Tip: Animals and fungi don't photosynthesise, so they don't need light to grow. This means they're not usually directly affected by changes to light intensity.

Biotic factors

Biotic factors also change ecosystems. Biotic factors relate to living organisms, so they include things like competition and predation.

Competition

Organisms need things from their environment and from other organisms in order to survive and reproduce. Plants need light and space, as well as water and mineral ions (nutrients) from the soil. Animals need space (territory), food, water and mates. Organisms compete with other species (and members of their own species) for the same resources.

> **Examples**
>
> - Weeds compete with crop plants for light and nutrients. Farmers use weedkillers to kill weeds so there is less competition and the crops get all the light and nutrients, which enables them to grow better.
> - Lions and hyenas share the same habitat in Africa. They compete with each other for food, water and territory, which results in frequent aggression between the two species.
> - Male peacocks compete with each other for mates by displaying their eye-catching tail feathers to females during mating season.

Predation

Animals that hunt and kill other animals are called predators, and the animals they eat are called prey. In a community containing prey and predators (as most of them do), the population of any species is usually limited by the amount of food available. If the population of the prey increases, then so will the population of the predators. However as the population of predators increases, the number of prey will decrease.

Tip: Disease (caused by pathogens) is another biotic factor that affects communities.

> **Example**
>
> Lions are predators. They have a number of different prey species, including gazelles. An increase in the number of gazelles might lead to an increase in the number of lions, because there'll be more food for the lions to eat. However, the increase in the number of lions might in turn lead to a decrease in the number of gazelles, as more of them will be eaten by lions.

Practice Questions — Fact Recall

Q1 Give three examples of abiotic factors.

Q2 Give two examples of biotic factors.

Practice Question — Application

Q1 An environmental study was done on a lake over a number of years. Over the course of the study, the concentration of oxygen in the lake gradually decreased due to the effect of pollution. A certain species of fish found in the lake cannot survive in water with a low oxygen concentration. Herons feed on these fish.

   a) The population size of the fish changed during the study.

   i) Suggest how the population size changed.

   ii) Was this change due to a biotic or abiotic factor?

   b) The population size of the herons also changed during the study. Suggest how and why the population size changed.

Learning Objectives:
- Be able to investigate the relationship between organisms and their environment using field-work techniques, including quadrats and belt transects. (Core Practical)
- Be able to explain how to determine the number of organisms in a given area using raw data from field-work techniques, including quadrats and belt transects.

Specification References 9.5, 9.6

3. Investigating Ecosystems

CORE PRACTICAL

You don't just need to learn the facts about ecosystems — you need to be able to investigate them too.

Distribution of organisms

You might remember from page 209, that an ecosystem is a community of organisms, along with all the abiotic parts of their environment. The distribution of an organism is where that organism is found, either in the whole ecosystem or a particular part. The abiotic factors in an ecosystem affect the distribution of the organisms that live there.

> **Examples**
> - In a field ecosystem, you might find that daisies are more common in the open than under trees, because there's more light available in the open and daisies need light to survive (they use it for photosynthesis — see p.146).
> - Some types of mayfly are more common in colder parts of a stream, as they can't tolerate the warmer temperatures in other parts of the stream.

There are a couple of ways to study the distribution of an organism:

1. You can measure how common an organism is in two or more sample areas (e.g. using **quadrats** — see below) and compare them.
2. You can study how the distribution changes across an area, e.g. by placing quadrats along a **transect** (see pages 215-216).

Both of these methods give quantitative data (numbers) about the distribution.

Quadrats

A quadrat is a square frame enclosing a known area, e.g. 1 m² (see Figure 1).

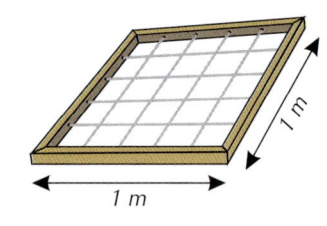

Figure 1: A diagram of a 1 m² quadrat.

Investigating distribution

You can use quadrats to study the distribution of small organisms that are slow moving or that don't move around. You can investigate the effect of a factor on the distribution of a species by comparing how common an organism is in two sample areas (e.g. shady and sunny spots in a playing field). Just follow these simple steps:

1. Place a 1 m² quadrat on the ground at a random point within the first sample area. E.g. divide the area into a grid and use a random number generator to pick coordinates (see page 238).
2. Count all the organisms that you're interested in within the quadrat.
3. Repeat steps 1 and 2 as many times as you can.
4. Work out the mean number of organisms per quadrat within the first sample area.

Tip: You might not be in the lab, but fieldwork still has hazards. Make sure you do a full risk assessment before you start investigating any ecosystem.

Tip: It's really important that the quadrats are placed <u>randomly</u> within the sample area. Taking random samples will make sure the results you get are representative of the whole sample area. This improves the validity of the study.

WORKING SCIENTIFICALLY

Topic 9a Ecosystems and Biodiversity

Example

Anna counted the number of daisies in 7 quadrats within her first sample area and recorded the following results:

Quadrat	1	2	3	4	5	6	7
Number of Daisies	18	22	20	23	23	25	23

Here the mean is: $\dfrac{\text{total number of organisms}}{\text{number of quadrats}} = \dfrac{154}{7} =$ **22 daisies per quadrat**

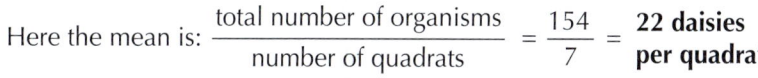

Figure 2: A student using a quadrat to gather data on the distribution of organisms.

5. Repeat steps 1 to 4 in the second sample area.
6. Finally compare the two means. E.g. you might find 2 daisies per m^2 in the shade, and 22 daisies per m^2 (lots more) in the open field.

You might want to find and compare the mode and median of your data too.

Tip: If you're counting flowering plants in your quadrat, make sure you count the number of actual plants, not the number of flowers. Some plants will have more than one flower, and some might not currently have any flowers on them.

Example

1. The mode is the number that appears most often in the data. For Anna's data above, the mode is **23 daisies per quadrat**.
2. To find the median, you first need to put your data in numerical order. The median is the middle value in your data.

    18, 20, 22, (23), 23, 23, 25

    The median of Anna's data is **23 daisies per quadrat**.

Tip: There's more on different types of averages on p.14.

Estimating population size

You can also use quadrats to work out the population size of an organism in one area.

Example

Students used 0.25 m^2 quadrats to randomly sample daisies in an open field. The students found a mean of 10.5 daisies per quadrat. The field had an area of 800 m^2. Estimate the population of daisies in the field.

1. Work out the mean number of organisms per m^2.

    $1 \div 0.25 = 4$ ← *Because the quadrat is only 0.25 m^2, first you need to work out how many quadrats make up 1 m^2.*

    $4 \times 10.5 = 42$ daisies per m^2

2. Then multiply the mean by the total area (in m^2) of the habitat.

    $42 \times 800 =$ **33 600 daisies in the open field**

Tip: If your quadrat has an area of 1 m^2, the mean number of organisms per m^2 is just the same as the mean number per quadrat.

Transects

Sometimes abiotic factors change gradually across a habitat. This change is known as an **environmental gradient**. You can use lines called transects (see Figure 3 on the next page) to help find out how organisms (like plants) are distributed along a gradient — for example, if a species becomes more or less common as you move from an area of shade (near a hedge at the edge of a field) towards an area of full sun (in the middle of the field).

Tip: Transects can be used in any type of habitat, not just fields. For example, along a beach or in a stream.

There are different types of transects. A **belt transect** is where quadrats are laid out along the line. You need to know how to collect data along a belt transect.

Figure 3: *Students using a quadrat along a transect.*

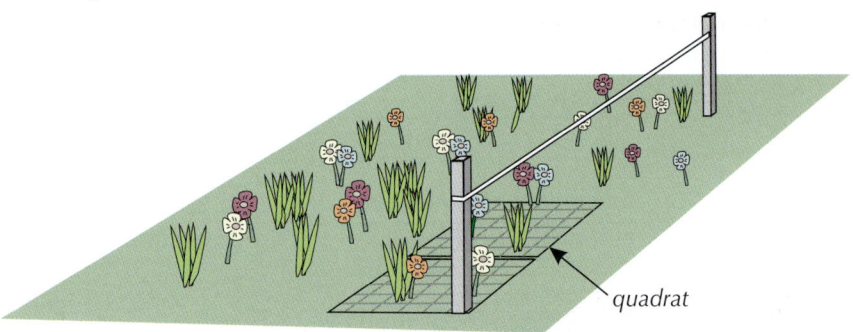

Figure 4: *A diagram showing a belt transect.*

Here's what to do:

1. Mark out a line in the area you want to study using a tape measure, for example from the hedge to the middle of the field.

2. Then collect data along the line using quadrats placed next to each other. If your transect is quite long, you could place the quadrats at regular intervals (e.g. every 2 metres) instead.

3. Collect data by counting all the organisms of the species you're interested in, or by estimating percentage cover. This means estimating the percentage area of a quadrat covered by a particular type of organism.

4. You could also record other data, such as the abiotic factors in each quadrat (e.g. you could use a light meter to measure the light intensity).

5. Repeat steps 1 to 4 several times, then find the mean number of organisms (or mean percentage cover) for each quadrat and a mean value for the abiotic factor you measured at each quadrat.

Once you've collected your data, you could use it to plot graphs. This could help you to see if the changing abiotic factor is correlated with a change in the distribution of the species you're studying.

Tip: If you've got a long transect, placing quadrats at intervals will be quicker.

Tip: If your quadrat is divided up into smaller squares, you can estimate the percentage cover of an organism by counting the number of squares more than half covered by that organism. E.g. if 55 out of 100 squares are more than half covered by grass, the percentage coverage of the grass is 55%. This is a useful technique when individual organisms are hard to count.

Tip: Make sure you can correctly identify the organisms you are investigating. If necessary, use books or information from the internet to help you.

Tip: There's more on drawing graphs on pages 16-18.

> **Example**
>
> The graph below shows the data collected along a belt transect. You can see that the number of daisies and the light intensity at each distance are positively correlated (see p.18) — as the light intensity increases, so does the number of daisies.

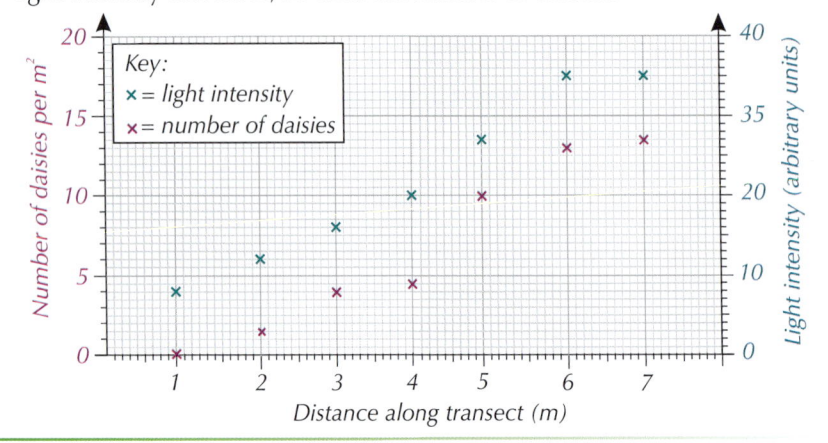

Topic 9a **Ecosystems and Biodiversity**

Practice Questions — Fact Recall

Q1 Describe how you would use random sampling with a quadrat to compare the distribution of organisms in two sample areas.

Q2 Describe how you would use a belt transect to measure the distribution of organisms across an area.

Practice Questions — Application

Q1 Joanne read that bulrushes grow best in moist soil or in shallow water. She wanted to find out whether this is true, so she investigated the distribution of bulrushes in her garden. She used a transect (as shown in the diagram) and recorded the number of bulrushes in each 1 m² quadrat as shown in the table.

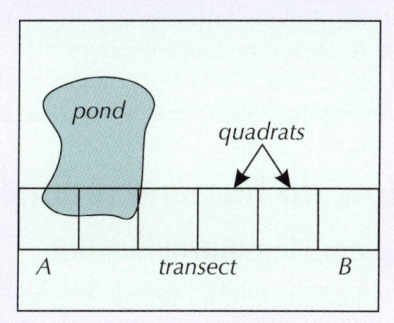

Quadrat	1	2	3	4	5	6
Number of Bulrushes	1	5	5	20	43	37

a) Calculate the mean number of bulrushes per quadrat.

b) Joanne started counting at quadrat 1 and moved along the transect in order, to quadrat 6. Assuming that the information Joanne read was correct, do you think quadrat 1 is at end A or end B of the transect? Explain your answer.

Q2 An area of the Lake District was sampled for the presence of a species of slug. Conservationists used 0.25 m² quadrats placed randomly in the landscape. The mean number of the slugs found in a quadrat was 2.5 and the area under investigation was 2000 m².

Estimate the total population of the slugs in the area.

Learning Objectives:
- Be able to explain the positive and negative human interactions within ecosystems and their impacts on biodiversity, including: eutrophication, fish farming, and the introduction of non-indigenous species.
- Be able to explain the benefits of maintaining local and global biodiversity, including the impact of reforestation and the conservation of animal species.

Specification References 9.9, 9.10

4. Human Impacts on Biodiversity

Humans have a big effect on the Earth's ecosystems — sometimes that effect is positive, but more often than not, it's negative.

What is biodiversity?

Biodiversity is the variety of living organisms in an ecosystem. The greater the biodiversity in an ecosystem, the healthier that ecosystem is.

Human interactions within ecosystems often affect biodiversity. Sometimes we have a positive impact — in other words, we increase the number and variety of living organisms in an area. This can be done through things like reforestation (see next page) or conservation schemes (see page 220). However, we often have a negative effect. Anything that reduces the number of living organisms in an ecosystem has a negative effect on biodiversity.

How do humans reduce biodiversity?

By causing eutrophication

Humans put nitrates onto fields as fertilisers (see p.230). If too much fertiliser is applied and it rains afterwards, nitrates easily find their way into rivers and lakes. The result is eutrophication (an excess of nutrients in water) which can lead to the death of many of the species present in the water, reducing the biodiversity of the habitat. This is what happens:

1. Fertilisers enter the water, adding excess nitrates (more than plants in the water can take in).
2. The excess nitrates cause algae to grow fast and block out the light.
3. Plants can't photosynthesise due to lack of light and start to die and decompose. With more food available, microorganisms that feed on decomposing plants increase in number and use up oxygen in the water.
4. Organisms that need oxygen for aerobic respiration (e.g. fish) die.

These steps are illustrated in Figure 2.

Tip: Pollution by sewage can cause eutrophication in the same way that fertilisers do — by adding excess nitrates to the water.

Figure 1: Water covered by an algal 'bloom' (a sudden increase in the amount of algae).

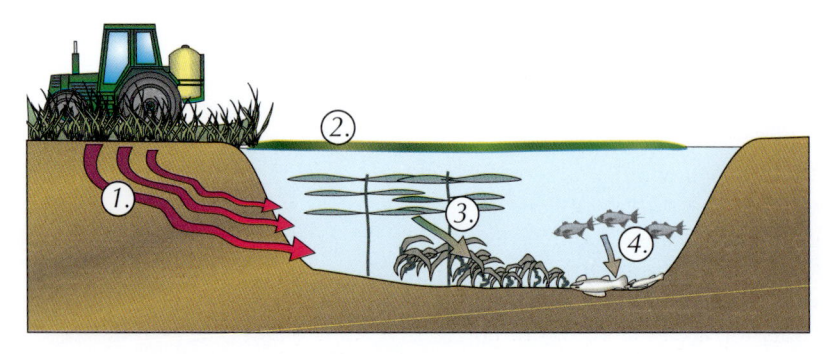

Figure 2: Diagram to show how eutrophication occurs.

Through fish farming

Fish can be farmed in holding nets in open water (e.g. lakes or the sea) — see Figure 3 on the next page. These farms can reduce biodiversity in the surrounding area. There are several different reasons for this.

One reason is that food is added to the nets to feed the fish, and the fish produce huge amounts of waste. Both the food and the waste can leak into the open water, causing eutrophication and the death of wild species.

Fish farms in open water also often act as a breeding ground for large numbers of parasites. These parasites can get out of the farm and infect wild animals, sometimes killing them. Predators (e.g. sea lions) are attracted to the nets and can become trapped in them and die. Finally, farmed fish sometimes escape into the wild, causing problems for wild populations of indigenous species (see below).

Fish can also be farmed in large tanks rather than in open water nets. These farms are low in biodiversity because often only one species is farmed, the tanks are often kept free of plants and predators, and any parasites and microorganisms are usually killed.

Figure 3: Fish being farmed in open water nets (top) and fish being farmed in tanks (bottom).

Through the introduction of non-indigenous species

A non-indigenous species is one that doesn't naturally occur in an area. They can be introduced intentionally (e.g. for food or hunting) or unintentionally (e.g. as a stowaway in international cargo). The introduction of a non-indigenous species may cause problems for indigenous (native) species.

Non-indigenous species compete with indigenous species for resources like food and shelter. Sometimes, they are better at getting these resources and out-compete the indigenous species, which decrease in number and eventually die out. Non-indigenous species sometimes also bring new diseases to a habitat. These often infect and kill lots of indigenous species, reducing the habitat's biodiversity.

> **Example**
>
> Signal crayfish were introduced to the UK for food, but they prey on and out-compete many indigenous river species, reducing biodiversity. They also carry a disease that kills indigenous crayfish.

Figure 4: An American signal crayfish.

How can humans maintain biodiversity?

While lots of human activities reduce biodiversity, there are plenty of things that we can do to increase biodiversity or help to maintain it.

Reforestation

Reforestation is when land where a forest previously stood is replanted to form a new forest (or a new forest is allowed to regrow naturally). Forests generally have a high biodiversity because they contain a wide variety of trees and plants, and these provide food and shelter for lots of different animal species. Deforestation reduces this biodiversity by removing the trees (either by chopping them down or burning them). Reforestation helps to restore it.

Reforestation programmes need to be carefully planned to maximise positive effects and minimise negative ones. For example, replanting a forest with a variety of tree species will result in a higher biodiversity than replanting using only a single type of tree.

Figure 5: Seedlings (in plastic protective sleeves) planted to reforest an area cleared by logging.

Topic 9a Ecosystems and Biodiversity

Tip: Zoos can be used as safe areas for the protection of animals. Some zoos run captive breeding programmes.

Tip: Seed banks can also be used to store and distribute the seeds of rare and endangered plants.

Conservation schemes

Conservation schemes can help to protect biodiversity by preventing species from dying out. Conservation methods include protecting a species' natural habitat (so that individuals have a place to live) and protecting species in safe areas outside of their natural habitat. Captive breeding programmes can be introduced in safe areas to increase numbers.

The benefits of maintaining biodiversity

There are lots of benefits to both wildlife and humans of maintaining biodiversity on a local and global scale.

> **Examples**
>
> - Protecting the human food supply — e.g. over-fishing has greatly reduced fish stocks in the world's oceans. Conservation programmes can ensure that future generations will have fish to eat.
>
> - Ensuring minimal damage to food chains — if one species becomes extinct it will affect all the organisms that feed on and are eaten by that species, so the whole food chain is affected. This means conserving one species may help others to survive.
>
> - Providing future medicines — many of the medicines we use today come from plants. Undiscovered plant species may contain new medicinal chemicals. If these plants are allowed to become extinct, e.g. through rainforest destruction, we could miss out on valuable medicines.
>
> - Cultural aspects — individual species may be important in a nation's or an area's cultural heritage, e.g. the bald eagle is being conserved in the USA as it is regarded as a national symbol.
>
> - Ecotourism — people are drawn to visit beautiful, unspoilt landscapes with a variety of animal and plant species. Ecotourism (environmentally-friendly tourism) helps bring money into biodiverse areas where conservation work is taking place.
>
> - Providing new jobs — things such as ecotourism, conservation schemes and reforestation schemes can provide employment for local people.

Practice Questions — Application

Q1 Thousands of years ago, huge areas of Scotland were covered in forests. Many of these forests have now been lost — some of this loss is due to deforestation by humans. Campaigns are underway to restore some of Scotland's lost forests.

   a) Explain how reforestation could increase biodiversity in Scotland.

   b) Suggest two benefits to humans of reforestation in Scotland.

Q2 A scientist carries out regular surveys to monitor the biodiversity along a stretch of river. The scientist finds that biodiversity is lower in the part of the river that runs through a farmer's wheat fields. Suggest and explain a reason for this.

Topic 9a Checklist — Make sure you know...

Ecosystems and Interactions Between Organisms

- [ ] That ecosystems are organised into different levels — from individual organisms to populations (all the organisms of one species) to communities (all the organisms of different species) to the ecosystem itself (the community of organisms, plus all of the abiotic conditions).
- [ ] That organisms depend on each other for survival and that this is known as interdependence.
- [ ] That mutualism (an example of interdependence) is a relationship between two organisms, where both organisms benefit.
- [ ] That parasitism (also an example of interdependence) is a relationship between two organisms, where one organism (the parasite) takes what it needs to survive but the other organism (the host) doesn't benefit.

Abiotic and Biotic Factors

- [ ] How communities can be affected by abiotic (non-living) factors, including temperature, light intensity, availability of water and the level of pollution.
- [ ] How communities can be affected by biotic (living) factors, such as competition and predation.

Investigating Ecosystems

- [ ] How to use quadrats and belt transects to investigate how abiotic factors affect the population sizes or distribution of organisms in an ecosystem. (Core Practical)
- [ ] How to determine the number of organisms in an area using data from quadrats and belt transects.

Human Impacts on Biodiversity

- [ ] That biodiversity is the variety of living organisms in an area.
- [ ] How humans can negatively impact biodiversity in ecosystems through: eutrophication (an excess of nutrients in water leading to increased algal growth and the death of other organisms in the water), fish farming and the introduction of non-indigenous species to an area.
- [ ] How humans can positively impact biodiversity through reforestation and conservation schemes.
- [ ] Some of the benefits of maintaining biodiversity in an area.

Exam-style Questions

1 A biology class were studying the distribution of organisms on a rocky shore line. Three students each set up a transect which ran from the water's edge up the shore, as shown in **Figure 1**. All three students counted the number of limpets in each of the 50 cm × 50 cm quadrats. The number of limpets counted by each student are shown in **Figure 2**.

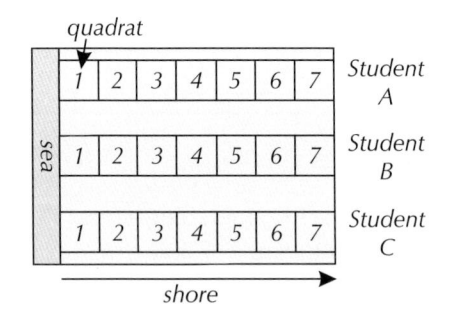

Quadrat number	1	2	3	4	5	6	7
Student A No. of Limpets	18	65	70	55	30	10	0
Student B No. of Limpets	6	72	76	41	21	18	3
Student C No. of Limpets	14	83	84	57	26	16	1

Figure 1   **Figure 2**

(a) Calculate the mean number of limpets found in quadrat 4.

(2 marks)

(b) Limpets need to stay moist in order to survive, but they are able to survive for a period of time without water by clamping down onto the surface of rocks — this helps to prevent them from drying out. Close to the water's edge, limpets have lots of competition from other species for space.

Use this information and the data in **Figure 2** to describe the distribution of limpets along the shore line and suggest reasons for it.

(3 marks)

(c) During the class study, another group of students investigated the distribution of a type of starfish. They placed 20 quadrats at random in each sample area of shoreline that they were interested in studying.

Explain why the students placed their quadrats randomly.

(2 marks)

2 Salmon are often farmed in holding nets at sea. Salmon farmers must keep the nets in good repair, in case the farmed salmon escape and mix with populations of wild salmon.

(a) Suggest **one** way in which the escaped farmed salmon could have a negative effect on wild salmon populations.

(1 mark)

(b) Describe **one** additional way in which salmon farming could negatively effect the biodiversity of local waters, even if fish do not escape from the farm.

(1 mark)

3   Scientists have been studying a species of wolf. The wolf lives in rocky mountains where the temperature at night can drop as low as –15 °C. The wolf has adaptations such as thick fur, which allow it to survive in this environment. Its main source of prey is rodents that live in burrows beneath the ground.

Scientists have been recording the total population size of the wolf over a number of years. Their findings and some other data are shown in **Figure 3**.

Year	Total population size of wolf	Total population size of one type of prey (million)	Rabies outbreak in this year
2007	401	1.96	No
2008	327	2.01	Yes
2009	330	2.09	No
2010	341	2.06	No
2011	265	2.01	Yes
2012	269	1.99	No

Figure 3

(a) Describe the overall trend in the total population size of the wolf species studied.

(1 mark)

(b) Suggest the biotic factor that's responsible for this trend.
Use data from the table to support your answer.

(3 marks)

Figure 4 shows the average height above sea level where the wolves are found.

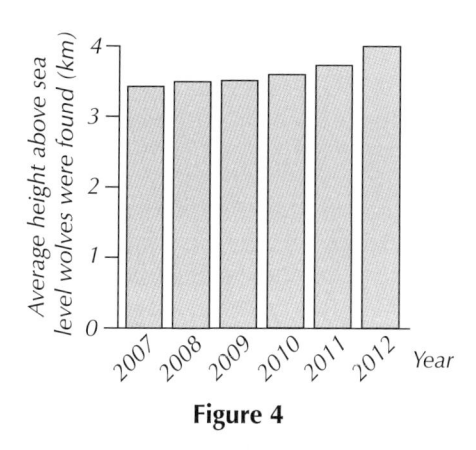

Figure 4

(c) Since 2007, the average temperature at 3.5 km above sea level has been increasing. Use data from **Figure 4** to suggest how this has affected the distribution of the wolf population.

(2 marks)

Topic 9b — Material Cycles

Learning Objectives:
- Be able to describe how different materials cycle through the biotic and abiotic components of an ecosystem.
- Be able to explain the importance of the carbon cycle, including the processes involved and the role of microorganisms as decomposers.

Specification References 9.12, 9.13

1. The Carbon Cycle

Materials such as carbon are being constantly recycled on Earth. It's really important that this happens. For example, it means that there's always enough material to make new organisms when old organisms die.

Recycling of materials

You might remember from page 209 that an ecosystem is all of the organisms living in an area, as well as all of the non-living conditions, e.g. soil type, availability of water and temperature. Materials are constantly recycled through both the living (biotic) and non-living (abiotic) components of ecosystems.

Living things are made of elements they take from the environment, e.g. plants take in carbon and oxygen from the air and nitrogen from the soil. They turn these elements into the complex compounds (carbohydrates, proteins and fats) that make up living organisms. Elements are passed along food chains when animals eat the plants and each other.

When waste products and dead organisms are broken down by decomposers (usually microorganisms such as bacteria and fungi) the elements in them are returned to the soil or air, ready to be taken in by new plants and put back into the food chain — the elements are recycled.

Tip: Decomposition of materials means that habitats can be maintained for the organisms that live there, e.g. nutrients are returned to the soil, and waste material (such as dead leaves) doesn't just pile up.

The carbon cycle

All living things contain carbon — so it's a pretty important element. However, there's only a fixed amount of carbon in the world. This means that carbon is constantly being cycled — from the air, through food chains and eventually back out into the air again. The carbon cycle shows how carbon is recycled — see Figure 1.

Tip: Fossil fuels are made of decayed animal and plant matter.

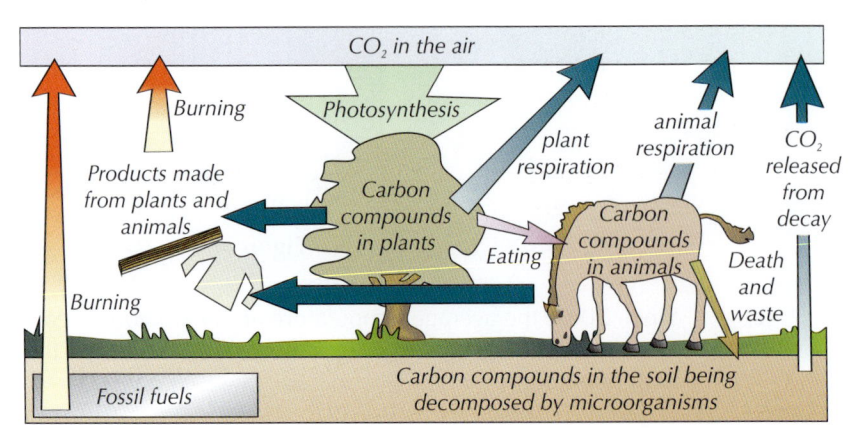

Figure 1: Diagram showing the carbon cycle.

Carbon is taken out of the air

The whole carbon cycle is "powered" by **photosynthesis**. CO_2 (carbon dioxide) is removed from the atmosphere by green plants and algae, and the carbon is used to make glucose, which can be turned into carbohydrates, fats and proteins that make up the bodies of the plants and algae.

Carbon moves through food chains

Some of the carbon becomes part of the fats and proteins in animals when the plants and algae are eaten. The carbon then moves through the food chain. The energy that green plants and algae get from photosynthesis is transferred up the food chain.

Plants, algae and animals eventually die and **decompose** (they're broken down by microorganisms and other decomposers). Animals also produce waste, and this too is broken down by decomposers.

Tip: The term decomposers usually refers to microorganisms. However, 'detritus feeders' such as earthworms and woodlice are also decomposers.

Carbon is returned to the air

Some carbon is returned to the atmosphere as CO_2 when the plants, algae and animals **respire**. It's returned to the atmosphere in the same way when decomposers such as microorganisms respire. CO_2 is also released back into the air when some useful plant and animal products, e.g. wood and fossil fuels, are burnt (combustion).

Tip: Respiration is the process of releasing energy from glucose. It also releases CO_2. There's more on respiration on pages 199-201.

Practice Questions — Fact Recall

Q1 How does CO_2 from the atmosphere first enter the food chain?

Q2 How does carbon move through food chains?

Q3 How is carbon returned to the atmosphere from dead leaves?

Practice Question — Application

Q1 The shells of many marine organisms are made from calcium carbonate (a compound containing calcium, carbon and oxygen). When these organisms die, their shells fall to the ocean floor and eventually form limestone rocks. The carbon inside the rocks returns to the atmosphere during volcanic eruptions or when the rocks are weathered down.

Explain how this example shows carbon moving between the abiotic and biotic parts of a marine ecosystem.

Learning Objective:
- Be able to explain the importance of the water cycle, including the processes involved and the production of potable water in areas of drought (including desalination).

Specification Reference 9.14

2. The Water Cycle

The water cycle is key to the survival of all living organisms. If it wasn't for the water cycle constantly recycling the water on Earth — we'd quickly run out of water to drink (and so would other animals and plants).

What is the water cycle?

The water here on planet Earth is constantly recycled. Energy from the Sun makes water **evaporate** from the land and sea, turning it into water vapour. Water also evaporates from plants — this is known as **transpiration** (see p.156). The warm water vapour is carried upwards (as warm air rises). When it gets higher up it cools and **condenses** to form clouds. Water falls from the clouds as **precipitation** (usually rain, but sometimes snow or hail) onto land, where it provides fresh water for plants and animals. Water not taken up by plants or animals drains into the sea, before the whole process starts again (see Figure 2).

Figure 1: Rain (precipitation) is a key part of the water cycle, providing plants (and other organisms) with fresh water.

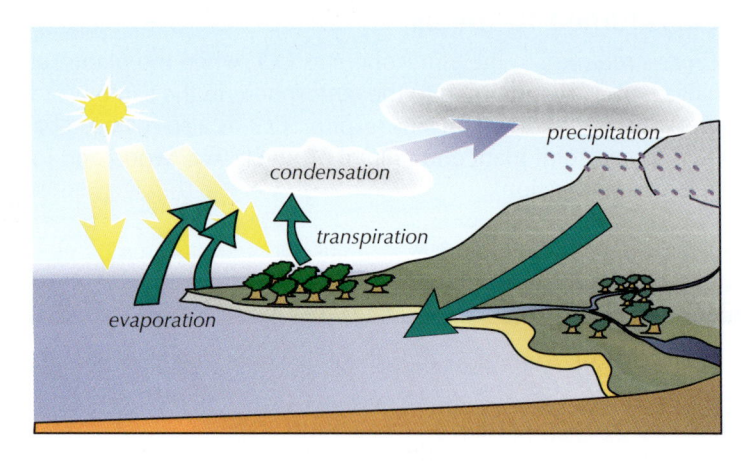

Figure 2: Diagram showing the steps in the water cycle.

The production of potable water

Potable water is water that's suitable for drinking. This means it must be clean and not too salty. In areas where there's a **drought** (in other words, there's not enough precipitation) it can be difficult to find potable water. That's partly because we rely on precipitation to get fresh water for drinking.

Tip: Drinking salt water will make you sick.

Luckily, in times of drought, there are methods we can use to produce potable water. One of these methods is called desalination.

Desalination

Desalination removes salts (mineral ions) from salt water (e.g. sea water). There are a few different methods of desalination.

Thermal desalination

Tip: Thermal desalination is also known as distillation.

Thermal desalination is very simple. Salt water is boiled in a large enclosed vessel, so that the water evaporates. The steam rises to the top of the vessel, but the salts stay at the bottom. The steam then travels down a pipe from the top of the vessel and condenses back into pure water — see Figure 3.

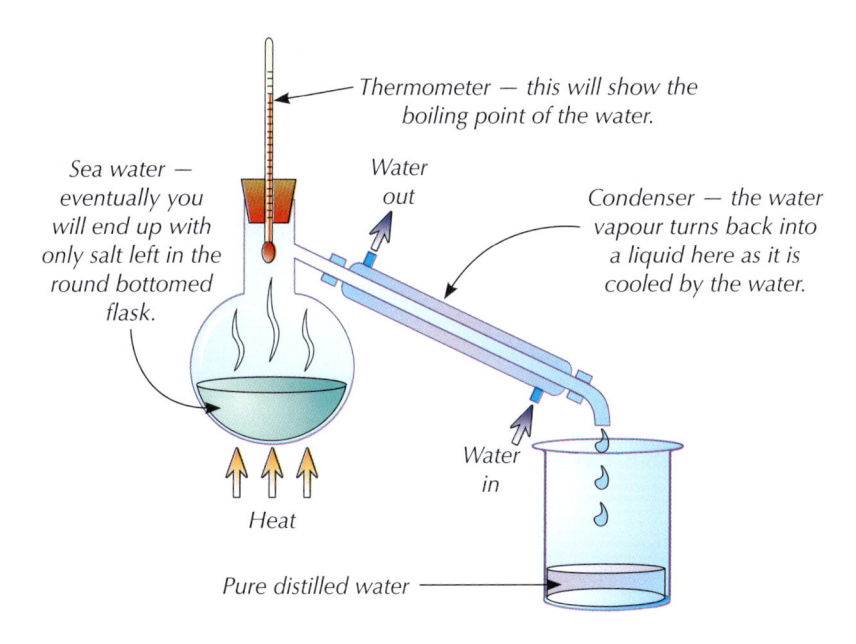

Figure 3: The thermal desalination of salt water.

Reverse osmosis

Osmosis is the net movement of water across a partially permeable membrane, from an area of higher water concentration to an area of lower water concentration (see pages 44-45). The higher the salt concentration in a solution, the lower the water concentration, so you could also say that osmosis is the net movement of water from an area of lower salt concentration to an area of higher salt concentration. Reverse osmosis reverses this process to get rid of impurities in water. Here's how:

1. Salt water is first treated to remove solids, before being fed at a very high pressure into a vessel containing a partially permeable membrane.

2. The pressure causes the water molecules to move in the opposite direction to osmosis — from a higher salt concentration to a lower salt concentration.

3. As the water is forced through the membrane, the salts are left behind, removing them from the water.

Tip: The partially permeable membrane allows water molecules through, but the large salts can't fit through the holes and are trapped.

Figure 4: Diagram to show how reverse osmosis works.

Figure 5: An engineer inspecting reverse osmosis filters at a facility in Israel. The facility produces 127 million m³ of fresh water from salt water per year.

Topic 9b Material Cycles

Practice Questions — Fact Recall

Q1 How does water vapour in the atmosphere form clouds?

Q2 Name three types of precipitation.

Q3 What is potable water?

Q4 What is a drought?

Practice Questions — Application

Q1 A student said, "Some of the water in trees eventually ends up in the sea." Do you agree with this statement? Explain your answer.

Q2 The photograph below shows a desalination plant off the coast of a Greek island. During the summer months, the Greek islands are typically hot and sunny with very little rainfall. They are visited by thousands of tourists every year.

Tip: A solar panel absorbs energy from the Sun. The energy can then be used for heating or to generate electricity.

a) Suggest and explain why the Greek islands may benefit from desalination plants such as this.

b) The desalination plant has several solar panels. Suggest why these are needed.

3. The Nitrogen Cycle

Like carbon and water, the nitrogen on Earth is constantly being recycled. Humans are able to influence this cycle for our own benefit.

Learning Objective:
- Be able to explain how nitrates are made available for plant uptake, including the role of bacteria in the nitrogen cycle, crop rotation and the use of fertilisers.

Specification Reference 9.15

The nitrogen cycle

The atmosphere contains 78% nitrogen gas, N_2. This is very unreactive and so it can't be used directly by plants or animals. Nitrogen is needed for making proteins for growth, so living organisms have to get it somehow. This is where the nitrogen cycle comes in — see Figure 1.

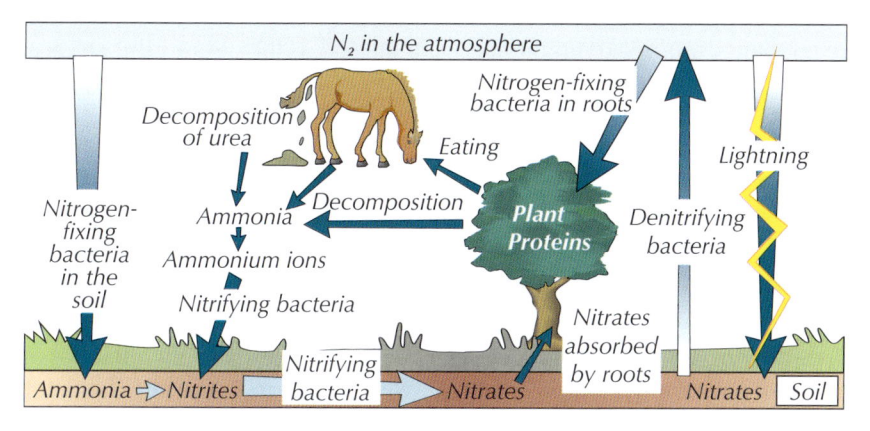

Figure 1: Diagram showing the nitrogen cycle.

Nitrogen is taken out of the air

Nitrogen in the air has to be turned into mineral ions (such as **nitrates**) in the soil before plants can use it. The process of turning N_2 from the air into nitrogen-containing ions that plants can use is called nitrogen fixation.

Nitrogen fixation happens in two main ways. The first involves lightning. There's so much energy in a bolt of lightning that it's enough to make nitrogen react with oxygen in the air to produce nitrates.

The second way involves **nitrogen-fixing bacteria** — these turn atmospheric N_2 into ammonia. Ammonia forms ammonium ions in solution that plants can use. Some nitrogen-fixing bacteria live in the soil. Others live in nodules (swellings) on the roots of legume plants, e.g. peas and beans. When legume plants decompose, the nitrogen stored in them and in their nodules is returned to the soil (see next page). Nitrogen ions can also leak out of the nodules during plant growth. The bacteria have a **mutualistic** relationship (see page 210) with the plants — the bacteria get food (sugars) from the plants, and the plants get nitrogen ions from the bacteria to make into proteins.

Tip: Nitrates have the formula NO_3^-. Ammonia has the formula NH_3 and ammonium ions have the formula NH_4^+.

Nitrogen moves through food chains

Plants absorb nitrogen-containing ions from the soil (or from their root nodules in the case of legumes) and use the nitrogen in them to make proteins. Nitrogen is then passed along food chains in the form of proteins, as animals eat plants (and each other).

Figure 2: Photo showing pea plant root nodules. The nodules contain nitrogen-fixing bacteria.

Topic 9b **Material Cycles**

Tip: Nitrites are NO_2^- ions.

Tip: Different species of nitrifying bacteria are responsible for producing nitrites and nitrates. Both nitrites and nitrates can be taken up and used by plants.

Exam Tip
Make sure you learn the different types of bacteria involved in the nitrogen cycle (nitrogen-fixing, decomposers, nitrifying and denitrifying) and what each type does.

Tip: As part of crop rotation, fields can also be left 'fallow' (not sown with a crop) for a year. In 'improved fallow' systems, the fallow field is planted with a fast-growing legume that isn't a crop.

Decomposers (bacteria and fungi in the soil) break down proteins in rotting plants and animals, and urea in animal waste, and turn them into ammonia. **Nitrifying bacteria** turn ammonia in decaying matter into nitrites or nitrites into nitrates. These processes return nitrogen to the soil (in the form of ions that can be taken up by plants) so the nitrogen in the organisms is recycled.

Nitrogen is returned to the air
Denitrifying bacteria turn nitrates back into N_2 gas. This is of no benefit to living organisms. Denitrifying bacteria are often found in waterlogged soils.

Increasing the soil nitrate content
Like all plants, crops take up nitrates from the soil as they grow. But crops are harvested, rather than being left to die and decompose, so the nitrogen they contain isn't returned to the soil. Over time, the nitrogen content of the soil decreases, leading to poor crop growth and deficiency diseases. So farmers have ways of increasing the amount of nitrates in the soil to help their crops grow better. For example:

Crop rotation
This is where, instead of growing the same crop in a field year after year, different crops are grown each year in a cycle. The cycle usually includes a nitrogen-fixing crop (e.g. peas or beans), which helps to put nitrates back into the soil for another crop to use the following year.

Fertilisers
Spreading animal manure or compost on fields recycles the nutrients left in plant and animal waste and returns them to the soil through decomposition. Artificial fertilisers containing nitrates (and other mineral ions needed by plants) can also be used, but these can be expensive.

Practice Questions — Fact Recall
Q1 a) Describe the role of nitrifying bacteria in the nitrogen cycle.
   b) How are the roles of decomposers and nitrifying bacteria linked?
Q2 What type of bacteria are responsible for turning nitrates in the soil back into nitrogen gas?

Practice Question — Application
Q1 A gardener grows vegetables in raised beds. She grows the same vegetables in each bed every year for three years. Although she uses fertilisers, she finds that she is unable to harvest as many vegetables from the beds each year. Suggest and explain one thing the gardener could do differently to increase the size of her harvest.

Topic 9b Checklist — Make sure you know...

The Carbon Cycle

- [ ] How materials cycle through both the biotic (living) and abiotic (non-living) parts of an ecosystem.
- [ ] That the carbon cycle constantly recycles carbon between the air and living organisms (in food chains) through the processes of photosynthesis, eating, decomposition, respiration and combustion.
- [ ] That decomposers such as microorganisms are important in the carbon cycle because they release carbon (as carbon dioxide) from dead matter and organic waste.

The Water Cycle

- [ ] The importance of the water cycle in making water available for living organisms and the processes involved in this, including: evaporation, transpiration, condensation and precipitation.
- [ ] How potable water (water that's suitable for drinking) can be produced in areas of drought through desalination (the removal of salt from salt water).
- [ ] Methods of desalination, e.g. thermal desalination and reverse osmosis.

The Nitrogen Cycle

- [ ] How nitrogen from the air is turned into mineral ions (e.g. nitrates) in the soil that can be taken up by plants.
- [ ] How bacteria are involved in the nitrogen cycle — including the roles of nitrogen-fixing bacteria, decomposers, nitrifying bacteria and denitrifying bacteria.
- [ ] How crop rotation and fertilisers can be used to increase the amount of nitrates available for uptake by plants.

Exam-style Questions

1. Bacteria play an important role in the nitrogen cycle.

   (a) Which of the following describes the role of nitrogen-fixing bacteria in the nitrogen cycle?

   - A Converting ammonia in decaying matter into nitrates.
   - B Converting nitrogen in the air into ammonia.
   - C Converting nitrates in the soil back into nitrogen gas.
   - D Breaking down nitrogen compounds in decaying matter into ammonia.

   (1 mark)

   (b) Some nitrogen-fixing bacteria live in the root nodules of legume plants, such as peas and beans.

   Describe the relationship between the nitrogen-fixing bacteria and the legume plants.

   (2 marks)

2* **Figure 1** shows how a particular food chain is part of the carbon cycle.

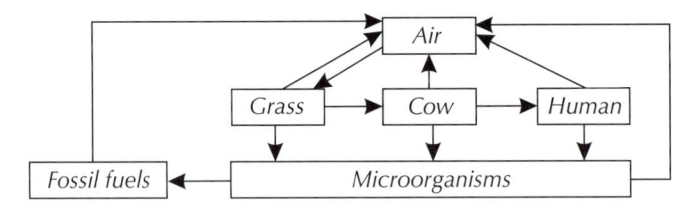

   Figure 1

   Use the information in **Figure 1** and your own knowledge to describe the processes in which carbon is cycled between this food chain, other living organisms and the air.

   (6 marks)

3. Reverse osmosis uses high pressures to move water molecules in the opposite direction to ordinary osmosis. It is a method of desalination.

   (a) Explain what is meant by the term desalination.

   (1 mark)

   (b) (i) Use your knowledge of osmosis to explain how reverse osmosis can be used to produce pure water from sea water.

   (2 marks)

   (ii) Explain how fresh water is produced from sea water in the water cycle.

   (3 marks)

Practical Skills

1. Measuring Substances

For the biology part of GCSE Combined Science, you'll have to carry out six 'Core Practicals'. You could also be asked about them in your exams. Luckily, all the biology Core Practicals are covered in this book, and the next few pages cover some of the apparatus and techniques that you'll need to know about.

Measuring the mass of a solid

To weigh a solid, start by putting the container you are weighing your substance into on a balance. Set the balance to exactly zero and then weigh out the correct amount of your substance. Easy peasy.

Measuring temperature

You can use a thermometer to measure temperature. Make sure that the bulb of the thermometer is completely submerged in the substance you're measuring and that you wait for the temperature to stabilise before you take your initial reading. Read off the scale on the thermometer at eye level to make sure it's correct.

Measuring length

Length can be measured in different units (e.g. mm, cm, m). Smaller units have a higher degree of accuracy, e.g. it's more accurate to measure the length of a potato cylinder to the nearest mm than the nearest cm. You'll need to decide on the appropriate level of accuracy for your experiment. It's also important to choose the right equipment — e.g. a ruler's probably best for small things, but a tape measure might be better for larger distances.

Measuring the volume of a liquid

There's more than one way to measure the volume of a liquid. Whichever method you use, always read the volume from the bottom of the meniscus (the curved upper surface of the liquid) when it's at eye level.

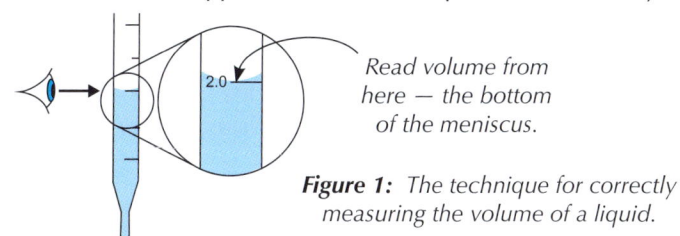

Figure 1: *The technique for correctly measuring the volume of a liquid.*

Read volume from here — the bottom of the meniscus.

Figure 2: *The meniscus of a fluid in a measuring cylinder, viewed at eye level.*

Measuring cylinders

Measuring cylinders come in all different sizes. Make sure you choose one that's the right size for the measurement you want to make. It's no good using a huge 1 dm^3 cylinder to measure out 2 cm^3 of a liquid — the graduations will be too big, and you'll end up with massive errors. It'd be much better to use one that measures up to 10 cm^3.

Tip: The Core Practicals in this book are marked with a big stamp like this...

The practicals that you do in class might be slightly different to the ones in this book (as it's up to your teacher exactly what method you use), but they'll cover the same principles and techniques.

Tip: When you're reading off a scale, write down the value of the graduation that the amount is closest to. If it's exactly halfway between two values, round up.

Tip: You need to be able to calculate areas as well as length. See page 187 for more.

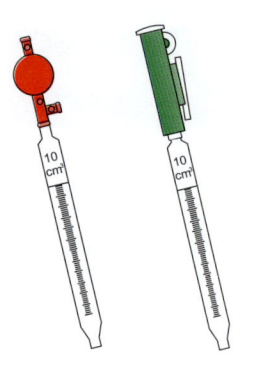

Figure 3: Graduated pipettes with two different types of pipette filler attached.

Tip: You could use a dropping pipette if you just wanted to transfer a couple of drops of liquid and didn't need it to be particularly accurate, for example, if you were adding an indicator to a mixture (see below).

Figure 5: A set of test tubes containing liquids at a range of pH levels with universal indicator added.

Tip: Blue litmus paper turns red in acidic conditions and red litmus paper turns blue in alkaline conditions.

Tip: It's a good idea to get the same person to do the timing for repeat experiments, so the results are precise.

Pipettes

Pipettes are used to suck up and transfer volumes of liquid between containers. Dropping pipettes are used to transfer drops of liquid. Graduated pipettes are used to transfer accurate volumes. A pipette filler (see Figure 3) is attached to the end of a graduated pipette, to control the amount of liquid being drawn up.

Measuring the volume of a gas

There are a few different ways of measuring the volume of a gas. However you do it, it's key that you make sure that the equipment is set up so that none of the gas can escape, otherwise your results won't be accurate.

Gas syringes

To accurately measure the volume of gas, you should use a gas syringe (see Figure 4).

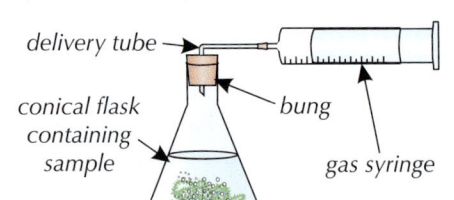

Figure 4: A gas syringe attached to a conical flask.

Displacement of water

As an alternative to using a gas syringe, you can use an upturned measuring cylinder filled with water. The gas will displace the water so you can read the volume off the scale.

Counting the bubbles

You could also count the number of bubbles produced. This method is less accurate because the bubbles could be different sizes and, if they're produced quickly, you might miss some. But it will give you relative amounts of gas to compare results.

Measuring the pH of a substance

The method you should use to measure pH depends on your experiment:

Indicator dyes

Indicators are dyes that change colour depending on whether they're in an acid or an alkali. You use them by adding a couple of drops of the indicator to the solution you're interested in. Universal indicator is a mixture of indicators that changes colour gradually as pH changes — see Figure 5. It's useful for estimating the pH of a solution based on its colour.

Indicator paper

Indicator paper is useful if you don't want to colour the entire solution that you're testing. It changes colour depending on the pH of the solution it touches. You can also hold a piece of damp indicator paper in a gas sample to test its pH.

pH meters

pH meters have a digital display that gives an accurate value for the pH of a solution.

Measuring time

You should use a stopwatch to time experiments. These measure to the nearest 0.1 s, so are pretty sensitive. Make sure you start and stop the stopwatch at exactly the right time.

2. Heating Substances and Using Potometers

Lots of scientific experiments involve heating one or more of the substances involved. The method of heating used depends on the substance being heated and what temperature it needs to be heated to. Potometers are handy pieces of apparatus that are used to measure how much water a plant takes up.

Bunsen burners

Bunsen burners are good for heating things quickly. You can easily adjust how strongly they're heating. But you need to be careful not to use them if you're heating flammable substances as the flame means the substance would be at risk of catching fire.

To use a Bunsen burner, you should first connect it to a gas tap, and check that the hole is closed. Place it on a heat-proof mat. Next, light a splint and hold it over the Bunsen burner. Now, turn on the gas. The Bunsen burner should light with a yellow flame. The more open the hole is, the more strongly the Bunsen burner will heat your substance. Open the hole to the amount you want. As you open the hole more, the flame should turn more blue.

Tip: Some things take a long time to cool down, and you can't necessarily tell by looking whether they're hot or cold. So, after heating equipment, you should always handle it with tongs so you don't get burnt.

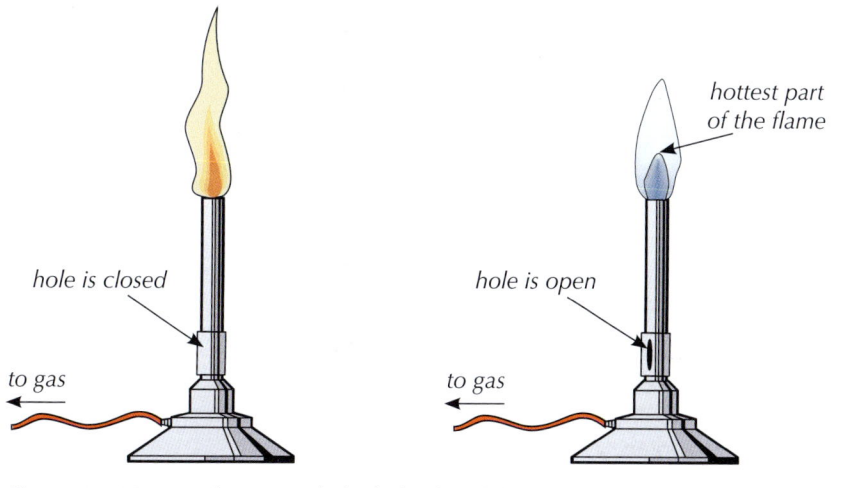

Figure 1: *A Bunsen burner with the hole closed (left) and the hole open (right).*

Tip: Whenever you use a Bunsen burner, you should wear safety goggles to protect your eyes.

If your Bunsen burner is alight but not heating anything, make sure you close the hole so that the flame becomes yellow and clearly visible. Use the blue flame to heat things. If you're heating a vessel in the flame, hold it at the top (e.g. with tongs) and point the opening away from yourself (and others). If you're heating something over the flame (e.g. a beaker of water), you should put a tripod and gauze over the Bunsen burner before you light it, and place the vessel on this.

Electric heaters

Electric heaters are often made up of a metal plate that can be heated to a specified temperature. The vessel containing the substance you want to heat is placed on top of the hot plate. The vessel is only heated from below, so you'll usually have to stir the substance inside to make sure it's heated evenly.

Figure 2: *An electric heater.*

Practical Skills 235

Water baths

A water bath is a container filled with water that can be heated to a specific temperature. A simple water bath can be made by heating a beaker of water over a Bunsen burner and monitoring the temperature with a thermometer. However, it is difficult to keep the temperature of the water constant.

An electric water bath will monitor and adjust the temperature for you. To use one, start by setting the temperature on the water bath, and allow the water to heat up. To make sure it has reached the right temperature, use a thermometer. Place the vessel containing your substance in the water bath using a pair of tongs. The level of the water outside the vessel should be just above the level of the substance inside the vessel. The substance will then be warmed to the same temperature as the water.

As the substance in the vessel is surrounded by water, the heating is very even. Water boils at 100 °C though, so you can't use a water bath to heat something to a higher temperature than this — the water won't get hot enough.

Figure 3: *A typical water bath.*

Measuring water uptake with a potometer

A potometer is a special piece of apparatus used to measure the water uptake of a plant. Here's how to set one up:

Tip: If there are air bubbles in the apparatus or the plant's xylem, it will affect your results. That's why the whole process of setting up a potometer is done underwater.

Tip: There are different types of potometer available. They won't all look like the one shown in Figure 4.

1. Cut a shoot underwater to prevent air from entering the xylem. Cut it at a slant to increase the surface area available for water uptake.

2. Assemble the potometer in water and insert the shoot under water, so no air can enter.

3. Remove the apparatus from the water but keep the end of the capillary tube submerged in a beaker of water.

4. Check that the apparatus is watertight and airtight.

5. Dry the leaves, allow time for the shoot to acclimatise and then shut the tap.

6. Remove the end of the capillary tube from the beaker of water until one air bubble has formed, then put the end of the tube back into the water.

7. As the shoot takes up water, the air bubble will move along the capillary tube. So a potometer can be used to estimate the transpiration rate of a plant. There's more about this on page 159.

Figure 4: *A potometer set up and ready to use.*

Figure 5: *Students using a potometer.*

3. Calculating Fields of View and Scientific Drawings of Equipment

A couple more practical techniques for you...

Calculating fields of view

When you look down a microscope, the circular area that's visible is called the 'field of view' (FOV). If you know the size of the field of view, you can estimate the size of your specimen. Here's how you measure the field of view:

- Position a clear ruler on the microscope stage.
- Select the lowest-powered objective lens and follow the steps on page 29 to bring the ruler into focus.
- Measure the diameter of the field of view using the ruler.

You can now remove the ruler and refocus the microscope (using the same objective lens) on a slide containing your specimen. You can estimate the size of the specimen by estimating how many times it fits into the field of view.

Example

The field of view in Figure 1 measures 5 mm in diameter. Around 7 'cells' fit across it. So each 'cell' measures approximately: 5 ÷ 7 = **0.7 mm** in diameter.

Figure 1: *Using the field of view to estimate the size of a specimen.*

Tip: The 'cells' in Figure 1 are a lot bigger than real cells. That's just so you can see what's going on easily.

Tip: To get the diameter of the FOV or the cells in μm, divide the diameter in mm by 1000.

If you need to look at the specimen under a higher magnification, you'll need to recalculate the field of view using this formula:

$$\text{FOV at higher magnification} = \frac{\text{low power magnification}}{\text{higher power magnification}} \times \text{FOV at low magnification}$$

So if your FOV is 5 mm under a magnification of × 40, at a magnification of × 100 it would be: (40 ÷ 100) × 5 = 2 mm.

Tip: The magnification here is not just the objective lens magnification — it's the objective lens magnification × the eyepiece lens magnification (see p.30).

Drawing equipment

When you're writing out a method for an experiment, it's always a good idea to draw a labelled diagram showing how your apparatus will be set up. The easiest way is to use a scientific drawing, where each piece of apparatus is drawn as if you're looking at its cross-section (with no shading or colouring).

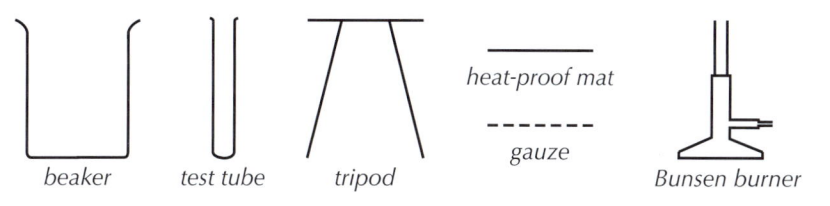

beaker   test tube   tripod   heat-proof mat   gauze   Bunsen burner

Figure 2: *Scientific diagrams of some basic laboratory equipment.*

Tip: The pieces of glassware are drawn without tops, so they aren't sealed. If you want to draw a closed system, remember to draw a bung in the top.

4. Sampling

When you're investigating the population size of a certain organism, or its distribution in an area, using sampling can save you an awful lot of time and effort. Read on for more...

What is sampling?

When you're investigating a population, it's generally not possible to count every single organism in the population. This means that you need to take samples of the population you're interested in. The sample data will be used to draw conclusions about the whole population, so it's important that it accurately represents the whole population. To make sure a sample represents a population, it should be random.

Tip: If a sample doesn't represent the population as a whole, it's said to be biased.

If you're interested in the distribution of an organism in an area, or its population size, you can take population samples in the area you're interested in using quadrats or transects (see pages 214-216).

If you only take samples from one part of the area, your results will be biased — they may not give an accurate representation of the whole area. To make sure that your sampling isn't biased, you need to use a method of choosing sampling sites in which every site has an equal chance of being chosen. For example:

Example

If you're looking at the distribution of plant species in a field...

1. Divide the field into a grid.
2. Label the grid along the bottom and up the side with numbers or letters.
3. Use a random number generator (on a computer or calculator) to select coordinates, e.g. (2,6).
4. Take your samples at these coordinates.

Non-random sampling
Only looks at a small part of the field.

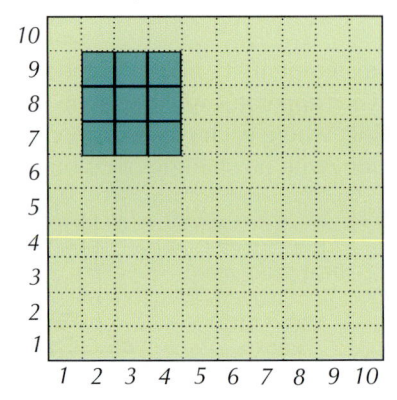

Random sampling
Randomly selects squares from all over the field.

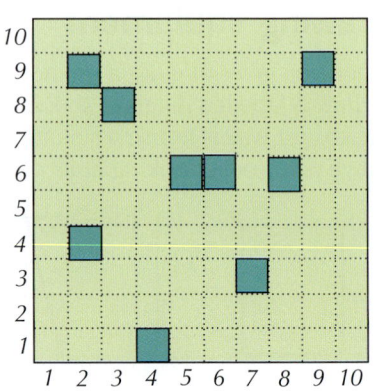

Figure 1: Many scientific calculators have a handy random number generator built in.

Collecting health data using sampling

As mentioned on the previous page, it's not practical (or even possible) to study an entire human population. You need to use random sampling to choose members of the population you're interested in.

Example

A health professional is investigating how many people diagnosed with type 2 diabetes in a particular country also have heart disease.

1. All the people who have been diagnosed with type 2 diabetes in the country of interest are identified by hospital records. In total, there are 270 196 people.
2. These people are assigned a number between 1 and 270 196.
3. The sample size is decided — e.g. 4250 people.
4. Then a random number generator is used to choose the sample group (e.g. it selects the individuals #72 063, #11 822, #193 123, etc.)
5. The proportion of people in the sample that have heart disease can be used to estimate the total number of people with type 2 diabetes that also have heart disease:

   - Find the number of people in the sample that have heart disease too — here it's 935 people.
   - Work out what proportion of the sample that number is — you can calculate it as a percentage.

$$\text{proportion (\%)} = \frac{\text{number of people sampled with heart disease}}{\text{total number of people sampled}}$$

$$= \frac{935}{4250} \times 100$$

$$= 22\%$$

   - Then use your proportion to estimate the total number of people in the population with both type 2 diabetes and heart disease.

$$= \frac{\text{total population size}}{100} \times \text{proportion (\%)}$$

$$= \frac{270\ 196}{100} \times 22$$

$$= 59\ 443 \text{ people}$$

Tip: See page 11 for more on sample size.

Tip: See page 243 for more on percentages.

Tip: Some calculators have a percentage button, which you can use instead of doing this second calculation.

Continuous sampling

Continuous sampling is when lots of samples are taken in a laboratory experiment at regular intervals over a particular time period. This means you can see what is happening during the experiment, not just the outcome of it. Using a data logger connected to a computer is an example of continuous sampling. Data loggers can be used to measure a range of variables, including temperature, pH and O_2 concentration.

5. Safety and Ethics

Science can be quite dangerous at times, so it's really important that you keep yourself (and others) safe in the lab. Some experiments can also involve ethical issues that you must deal with respectfully and responsibly.

Working safely

Make sure you're working safely in the lab. Before you start any experiment, make sure you know about any safety precautions to do with your method or the chemicals you're using. You need to follow any instructions that your teacher gives you carefully. The chemicals you're using may be hazardous — for example, they might be flammable (catch fire easily), or they might irritate or burn your skin if it comes into contact with them.

Make sure that you're wearing sensible clothing when you're in the lab (e.g. open shoes won't protect your feet from spillages). When you're doing an experiment, you should wear a lab coat to protect your skin and clothing. Depending on the experiment, you may need to also wear safety goggles and gloves.

Figure 1: *You'll often see hazard labels on bottles of chemicals. These tell you in what way a chemical is dangerous.*

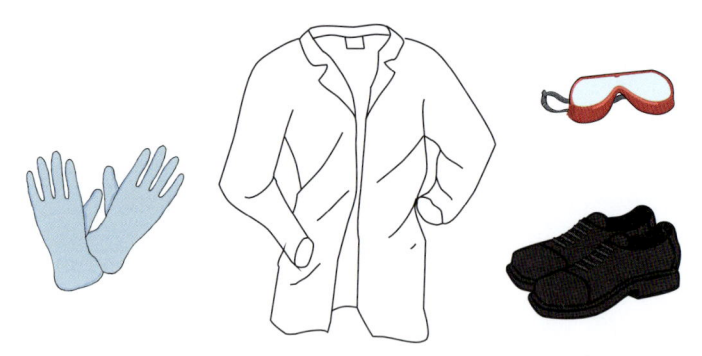

Figure 2: *Diagram showing lab safety gear.*

You also need to be aware of general safety in the lab, e.g. keep anything flammable away from lit Bunsen burners, don't directly touch any hot equipment, handle glassware carefully so it doesn't break, etc. You should also always wash your hands before and after handling living material.

Working ethically

You need to think about ethical issues in your experiments.

Any organisms involved in your investigations need to be treated safely and ethically. Animals need to be treated humanely — they should be handled carefully and any wild animals captured for studying (e.g. during an investigation of the distribution of an organism) should be returned to their original habitat. Any animals kept in the lab should also be cared for in a humane way, e.g. they should not be kept in overcrowded conditions.

If you are carrying out an experiment involving other students (e.g. if you were investigating reaction times in response to a stimulus), they should not be forced to participate against their will or feel pressured to take part.

Maths Skills

Maths skills for GCSE Combined Science

Maths crops up quite a lot in GCSE Combined Science, so it's really important that you've mastered all the maths skills you'll need before sitting your exams. Maths skills are covered throughout this book but here's an extra little section, just on maths, to help you out with the biology exams.

Exam Tip
Around 20% of the marks for GCSE Combined Science will test mathematical skills. That's a lot of marks so it's definitely worth making sure you're up to speed.

1. Calculations

Calculations are the cornerstone of maths in science. So being able to carry them out carefully is pretty important.

Standard form

You need to be able to work with numbers that are written in **standard form**. Standard form is used for writing very big or very small numbers with lots of zeros in a more convenient way. Standard form must always look like this:

$$A \times 10^n$$

This number must always be between 1 and 10. — *A*

This number is the number of places the decimal point moves. — *n*

Examples

- 1 000 000 can be written as 1×10^6.
- 0.017 can be written as 1.7×10^{-2}.

You can write numbers in standard form by moving the decimal point. Which direction the decimal point moves, and how many places it moves, is described by '*n*'. If the decimal point has moved to the left, '*n*' is positive. If the decimal point has moved to the right, '*n*' is negative.

Tip: When you're writing a measurement in standard form, make sure you keep the same number of significant figures (see page 15). E.g. 0.00400 cm³ = 4.00×10^{-3} cm³. This'll make sure that you don't lose any accuracy.

Example

Here's how to write out 0.000056 in standard form.

1. Move the decimal point to give the smallest number you can between 1 and 10 — this is '*A*'.

   $$0.00005\,6 \rightarrow 5.6$$
   (decimal point moved 1 2 3 4 5 places)

2. Count the number of places the decimal point has moved. In this example, the decimal point has moved five places to the right.

3. Write that number in the place of '*n*'. Remember, if the decimal point has moved to the left, '*n*' is positive. If the decimal point has moved to the right (like in this example), '*n*' is negative.

4. So 0.000056 is the same as 5.6×10^{-5}.

Tip: Double check you've got it right by doing the multiplication — you should end up with the number you started with. So for this example, you'd check $5.6 \times 10^{-5} = 0.000056$. It's easy to do this on your calculator — see the next page for how to type it in.

The key things to remember with numbers in standard form are...

- When 'n' is positive, the number is big. The bigger 'n' is, the bigger the number is.
- When 'n' is negative, the number is small. The smaller 'n' is (the more negative), the smaller the number is.
- When 'n' is the same for two or more numbers, you need to look at the start of each number to work out which is bigger. For example, 4.5 is bigger than 3.0, so 4.5×10^5 is bigger than 3.0×10^5.

There's a special button on your calculator for using standard form in a calculation — it's the 'Exp' button. So if, for example, you wanted to type in 2×10^7, you'd only need to type in: '2' 'Exp' '7'. Some calculators may have a different button that does the same job, for example it could say 'EE' or '×10^x' instead of 'Exp' — see Figure 1.

Figure 1: The 'Exp' or '×10^x' button is used to input standard form on calculators.

Using ratios

Ratios can be used to compare quantities.

> **Example**
>
> An organism with a surface area to volume ratio of 2 : 1 would theoretically have a surface area twice as large as its volume.

Ratios are usually written like this:

A colon separates one quantity from the other. $x : y$ x and y stand for the quantities that you want to compare.

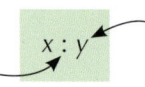

Ratios are usually most useful in their simplest (smallest) form. To simplify a ratio, divide each side by the same number. It's in its simplest form when there's nothing left you can divide by to give a whole number ratio.

Tip: When you divide one side of a ratio by an amount, you have to divide the other side by the same number for the ratio to keep the same proportions.

> **Example**
>
> To simplify the ratio 28 : 36, divide both sides by 4.
>
> You get **7 : 9**. ← You can't divide 7 and 9 by the same number to get two whole numbers, so this must be the ratio's simplest form.

To compare two ratios, it's best to get the number on the right-hand side of each ratio to be 1. Then you can easily see which ratio is the largest. To get a ratio of x : y in the form n : 1, divide both sides by y.

Tip: If you're not sure what number to divide by to simplify a ratio, start by trying to divide both sides by a small number, e.g. 2 or 3, then check to see if you can simplify your answer further. E.g. you could simplify 28 : 36 by dividing each side by 2 to get 14 : 18. But you could simplify it further by dividing by 2 again to get 7 : 9. You can't simplify the ratio any further, so it's in its simplest form.

> **Example**
>
> Organism A has a surface area to volume ratio of 6 : 1.
> Organism B has a surface area to volume ratio of 30 : 9.
>
> To compare the two ratios, you need to write the ratio 30 : 9 in the form of n : 1. To do this, just divide both sides by 9:
>
> $30 \div 9 = 3.3...$ 30 : 9 $9 \div 9 = 1$
> $= 3.3$ 3.3 : 1
>
> So the ratio of Organism B is equal to **3.3 : 1**. 3.3 is smaller than 6, so Organism A has the larger surface area to volume ratio.

Calculating percentages

Percentages are another way of comparing quantities. They come in handy when you want to compare amounts from different-sized samples.

To give the amount X as a percentage of total amount Y, you need to divide X by Y, then multiply by 100.

Example

Out of 240 patients receiving a drug in a clinical trial, 36 experienced no change to their symptoms. What percentage of patients experienced no change to their symptoms?

1. You want to give 36 as a percentage of 240, so divide 36 by 240:

    $$36 \div 240 = 0.15$$

2. Multiply this amount by 100:

    $$0.15 \times 100 = \mathbf{15\%}$$

Exam Tip
Rather than having to calculate a percentage, you might be asked to give your answer as a fraction, i.e. X/Y. To simplify a fraction, divide the top and bottom of the fraction by the same number. E.g. 36/240 = (36 ÷ 12)/(240 ÷ 12) = 3/20. To get the fraction as simple as possible, you might have to do this more than once.

Calculating percentage change

When investigating the change in a variable, you may want to compare results that didn't have the same initial value. For example, you may want to compare the change in mass of potato cylinders left in different concentrations of sugar solution, when the cylinders had different initial masses (see p.48). One way to do this is to calculate the percentage change.

To calculate it you use this equation:

$$\text{percentage (\%) change} = \frac{\text{final value} - \text{original value}}{\text{original value}} \times 100$$

Tip: A positive value for percentage change indicates an increase and a negative value indicates a decrease.

Example

A student is investigating the effect of the concentration of sugar solution on potato cells. She records the mass of potato cylinders before and after placing them in sugar solutions of different concentrations. The table below shows some of her results.

Potato cylinder	Concentration (mol/dm³)	Mass at start (g)	Mass at end (g)
1	0.0	7.5	8.7
2	1.0	8.0	6.8

Which potato cylinder had the largest percentage change?

Maths Skills

Tip: The mass at the start is the original value and the mass at the end is the final value.

Tip: A decrease in mass gives a negative value for the percentage change.

1. Stick each set of results into the equation:

$$\% \text{ change} = \frac{\text{final value} - \text{original value}}{\text{original value}} \times 100$$

potato cylinder 1: $\frac{8.7 - 7.5}{7.5} \times 100 = 16\%$

potato cylinder 2: $\frac{6.8 - 8.0}{8.0} \times 100 = -15\%$

2. Compare the results.

16% is greater than 15%, so potato cylinder 1 had the largest percentage change.

Estimating values

Estimating can help you to check your answer is roughly correct. To estimate the answer to a calculation, just round everything off to nice, convenient numbers so that you get a simple calculation that you can do in your head.

Most of the time, you should round the numbers to just one significant figure.

Example

A student calculated the number of stomata per mm^2 on ten different leaves.

The results are shown in the table below.

Leaf	1	2	3	4	5	6	7	8	9	10
Number of stomata/mm^2	245	287	322	185	316	299	178	250	332	420

The student calculates that the mean number of stomata per mm^2 is 283. You could estimate the mean of the data like this:

1. Round the numbers to one significant figure.

   200 300 300 200 300 300 200 300 300 400

2. Do the calculation with the rounded numbers.

   $(200 + 300 + 300 + 200 + 300 + 300 + 200 + 300 + 300 + 400) \div 10$

   $= 2800 \div 10 = \mathbf{280}$

From the estimated calculation, 283 is a sensible answer. If your answer was massively different, you would know that your calculation had gone wrong somewhere.

Exam Tip
By working out an estimate in the exam, you can check that you haven't made any silly mistakes while calculating your answer (like missing out a decimal place along the way) and it could be a lot quicker than typing the whole thing into your calculator again.

2. Algebra

Every so often, biology can involve a bit of rearranging equations and substituting values into equations. It can be easy to make simple mistakes though, so here are a few things to remember...

Algebra symbols

Here's a reminder of some of the symbols that you will come across:

Symbol	Meaning
=	equal to
<	less than
<<	much less than
>	greater than
>>	much greater than
∝	proportional to
~	roughly equal to

Tip: An example of using 'proportional to' can be found on p.154. There are two types of proportion — direct and inverse. When two values are directly proportional to each other, if one increases, the other increases at the same rate. When two values are inversely proportional to each other, if one increases, the other decreases at the same rate.

Using equations

Equations can show relationships between variables. To rearrange an equation, make sure that whatever you do to one side of the equation you also do to the other side.

Tip: The word formula is sometimes used instead of the word equation.

Example

You can find the magnification of something using the equation:
magnification = image size ÷ real size

You can rearrange this equation to find the image size by multiplying each side by the real size: image size = magnification × real size.

Tip: There's more about this equation for magnification on pages 30-31.

To use an equation, you need to know the values of all but one of the variables. Substitute the values you do know into the equation, and do the calculation to work out the final variable. Always make sure the values you put into an equation have the right units.

Example

3.2 cm^3 of blood passes through part of a vein in 30 seconds. Calculate the rate of blood flow through the vein in $cm^3 \, min^{-1}$. Use the equation:

$$\text{rate of blood flow } (cm^3 \, min^{-1}) = \frac{\text{volume of blood } (cm^3)}{\text{time (min)}}$$

1. You want to know the rate per minute so convert 30 seconds into minutes: 30 ÷ 60 = 0.50
2. Substitute the values into the equation:

   3.2 cm^3 ÷ 0.50 min = **6.4 $cm^3 \, min^{-1}$**

Tip: Converting all the values into the correct units <u>before</u> putting them into the equation stops you making silly mistakes.

To make sure your units are correct, it can help to write down the units on each line of your calculation.

3. Graphs

Results are often presented using graphs. They make it easier to see relationships between variables and can be used to calculate other quantities.

Finding the intercept of a graph

The y-intercept of a graph is the point at which the line of best fit crosses the y-axis. Meanwhile, the x-intercept is the point at which the line of best fit crosses the x-axis.

Tip: See pages 47-49 for more on how to carry out this experiment and analyse the results.

Example

A graph can be plotted to show the percentage change in mass of several pieces of potato against the different concentrations of sucrose solution that they were left in overnight.

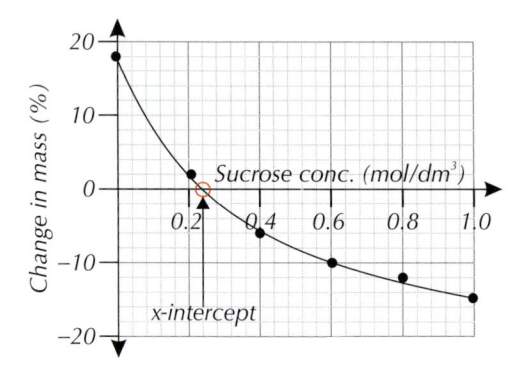

The approximate concentration of the solution in the potato cells, which is equal to the x-intercept, is **0.24 mol/dm³**.

Linear graphs

A linear graph is a straight line graph. This means that one of the variables plotted on the axes increases or decreases in relation to the other, which is shown by a straight line. An example of a linear graph is shown in Figure 1.

Tip: If one variable increases in proportion with the other (so if x is doubled, y is doubled, etc.), the graph shows a directly proportional relationship.

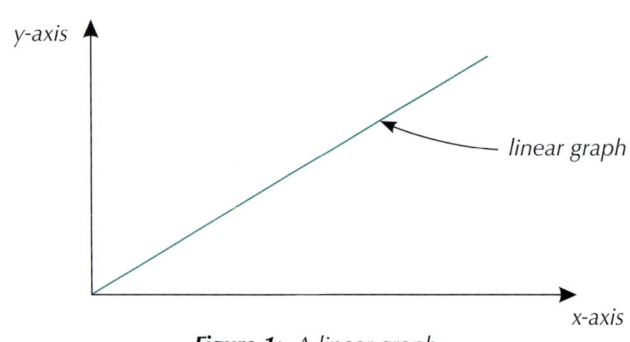

Figure 1: A linear graph.

Finding the rate

Rate is a measure of how much something is changing over time. Calculating a rate can be useful when analysing your data, e.g. you might want to the find the rate of a reaction. You can find the rate from a graph that shows a variable changing over time by finding the **gradient** (how steep it is).

For a linear graph, you can calculate the rate by finding the gradient of the line, using the equation:

$$\text{Gradient} = \frac{\text{Change in } y}{\text{Change in } x}$$

Change in y is the change in value on the y-axis and **change in x** is the change in value on the x-axis.

Tip: The gradient of a graph tells you how quickly the dependent variable changes if you change the independent variable.

Tip: When using this equation to find a rate, x should always be the time.

Example

To find the rate at which oxygen is produced in the graph below:

1. Pick two points on the line that are easy to read and a good distance apart.
2. Draw a vertical line down from one point and a horizontal line across from the other to make a triangle.

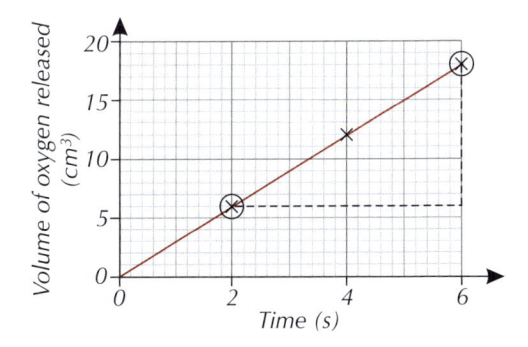

3. Use the scales on the axes to work out the length of each line. The vertical side of the triangle is the change in y and the horizontal side of the triangle is the change in x.

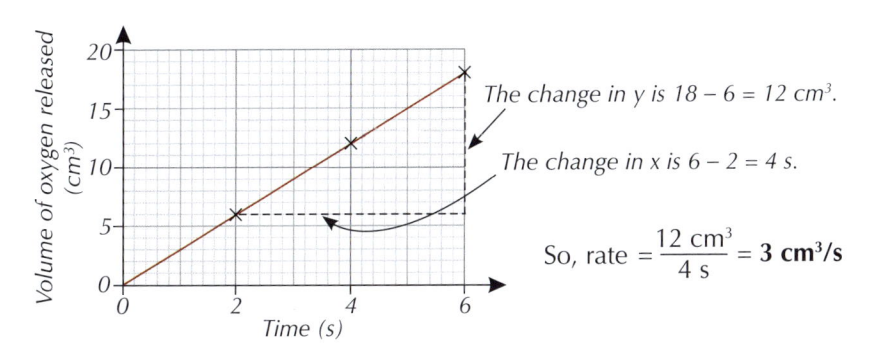

The change in y is $18 - 6 = 12$ cm^3.

The change in x is $6 - 2 = 4$ s.

So, rate $= \dfrac{12 \text{ cm}^3}{4 \text{ s}} = $ **3 cm^3/s**

Tip: The units for the gradient are the units for y divided by the units for x.

Maths Skills

$y = mx + c$

The y-intercept and the gradient of a linear graph can be used to work out the equation of the graph line. The equation of a straight line is given by:

y = y-axis value
m = gradient
$$y = mx + c$$
c = y-intercept
x = x-axis value

The equation of the line shows the relationship between the two variables. To work out the equation, you just need to plug in the values for m and c.

Tip: mx is just the same as writing '$m \times x$'.

Tip: If the straight line passes through the origin of the graph (the point at which the x-axis and y-axis meet), then the y-intercept is just zero.

Tip: You can check your equation is correct using the values of x and y from a point on the graph. Just pop the value for x into the equation and it should give you the value of y.

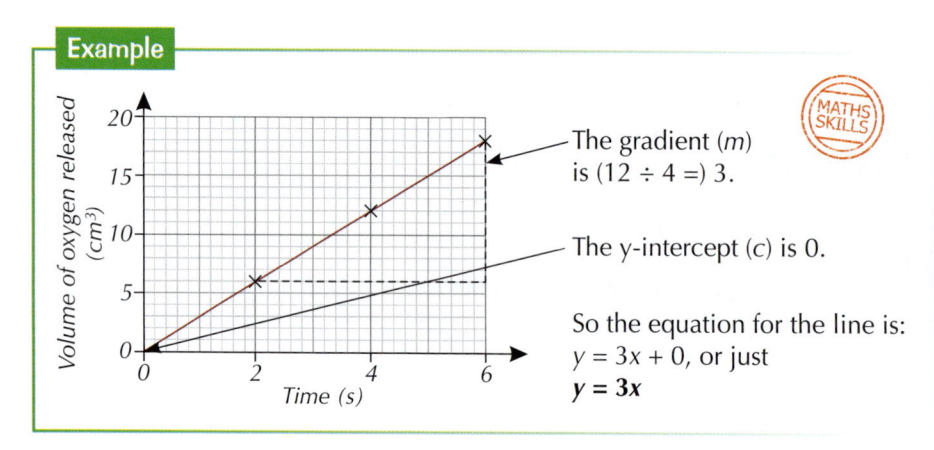

Example

The gradient (m) is ($12 \div 4 =$) 3.

The y-intercept (c) is 0.

So the equation for the line is:
$y = 3x + 0$, or just
$y = 3x$

Exam Help

1. The Exams

Unfortunately, to get your GCSE you'll need to sit some exams. And that's what this page is about — what to expect in your exams.

Assessment for GCSE Combined Science

To get your GCSE Combined Science qualification, you'll have to do some exams that test your science knowledge, your understanding of the Core Practical experiments and how comfortable you are with Working Scientifically. You'll also be tested on your maths skills.

All the biology content that you need to know is in this book. All the biology Core Practicals are covered in detail and clearly labelled, examples that use maths skills are marked up, and there are even dedicated sections on Working Scientifically (pages 2-22), Maths Skills (pages 241-248) and Practical Skills (pages 233-240). You'll also need to know all the chemistry and physics content, which isn't covered in this book.

The exams

You'll sit six separate exams at the end of Year 11 — two for each of biology, chemistry and physics. Remember, you could be asked about Working Scientifically in any of them.

Biology Exams

Paper 1

Topics assessed:
- Topic 1: Key Concepts in Biology (p.23-52)
- Topic 2: Cells and Control (p.53-71)
- Topic 3: Genetics (p.72-96)
- Topic 4: Natural Selection and Genetic Modification (p.97-114)
- Topic 5: Health, Disease and the Development of Medicines (p.115-145)

Length: 1 hour 10 minutes
Marks: 60
Worth: 16.7% of qualification

Paper 2

Topics assessed:
- Topic 1: Key Concepts in Biology (p.23-52)
- Topic 6: Plant Structures and Their Functions (p.146-164)
- Topic 7: Animal Coordination, Control and Homeostasis (p.165-185)
- Topic 8: Exchange and Transport in Animals (p.186-208)
- Topic 9: Ecosystems and Material Cycles (p.209-232)

Length: 1 hour 10 minutes
Marks: 60
Worth: 16.7% of qualification

Exam Tip
Make sure you have a good read through these pages. It might not seem all that important now, but you don't want to get any surprises just before an exam.

Exam Tip
Besides the Core Practicals, there are other practical experiments described in the specification, which you could be tested on. They're also covered in this book.

Exam Tip
You're allowed to use a calculator in all of your GCSE Combined Science exams, so make sure you've got one. You should also have a pen, spare pen, pencil and a ruler.

2. Exam Technique

Knowing the science is vitally important when it comes to passing your exams. But having good exam technique will help too...

Time management

Good time management is one of the most important exam skills to have — you need to think about how much time to spend on each question. Check out the length of your exams (you'll find them on the previous page and on the front of your exam papers). These timings give you about 1 minute per mark. Try to stick to this to give yourself the best chance to get as many marks as possible. Don't spend ages struggling with a question if you're finding it hard to answer — move on. You can come back to it later when you've bagged loads of other marks elsewhere.

> **Exam Tip**
> You shouldn't really be spending more time on a 1 mark question than on a 4 mark question. Use the marks available as a rough guide for how long each question should take to answer.

Reading the question

Make sure you always read the whole question carefully. It can be easy to look at a question and read what you're expecting to see, rather than what it's actually asking you. Read it through before you start answering, and read it once again when you've finished, to make sure your answer is sensible and matches up to what the question is asking.

Remember to pay attention to the marks available too. If it's just a one or two mark question, it'll often only need a single word or phrase as an answer, or a very simple calculation. Questions worth more marks are likely to be longer questions, which need to be clearly structured and will involve writing a short paragraph or a more complicated calculation.

> **Exam Tip**
> Don't forget to go back and do any questions that you left the first time round — you don't want to miss out on marks because you forgot to do the question.

Making educated guesses

Make sure you answer all the questions that you can — don't leave any blank if you can avoid it. If a question asks you to tick a box, circle something or draw lines between boxes, you should never, ever leave it blank, even if you're short on time. It only takes a second or two to answer these questions, and even if you're not certain what the answer is you can have a good guess.

> **Exam Tip**
> The amount of space given for your answer should also give you an idea about how much you need to write.

> **Example — Higher**
> Look at the question below.
>
> 1   Which **one** of these hormones is involved in the menstrual cycle?
>
>   **A** Insulin ☐   **B** LH ☐   **C** Testosterone ☐   **D** Glucagon ☐
>
>   *(1 mark)*
>
> Say you knew that insulin and glucagon help to regulate blood sugar level, but weren't sure about the roles of the other two hormones.
>
> You know the answer isn't insulin or glucagon, so you can ignore those two options. That leaves you with testosterone and LH. If you're not absolutely sure which is involved in the menstrual cycle and which isn't, just have a guess. You won't lose any marks if you get it wrong and there's a 50% chance that you'll get it right.

Exam Help

3. Question Types

If all questions were the same, exams would be mightily boring. So really, it's quite handy that there are lots of different question types. Here are just a few...

Command words

Command words are just the bits of a question that tell you what to do. You'll find answering exam questions much easier if you understand exactly what they mean, so here's a brief summary of the most common ones:

Command word:	What to do:
Give / Name / State	Give a brief one or two word answer, or a short sentence.
Complete	Write your answer in the space given. This could be a gap in an equation or table, or you might have to finish a diagram.
Describe	Write about what something's like, e.g. describe the trend in a set of results.
Explain	Make something clear, or give the reasons why something happens. The points in your answer need to be linked together, so you should include words like because, so, therefore, due to, etc.
Calculate	Use the numbers in the question to work out an answer.
Suggest	Use your scientific knowledge to work out what the answer might be.
Compare	Give the similarities <u>or</u> differences between two things.
Compare and contrast	Give the similarities <u>and</u> differences between two things.
Devise	Come up with or plan an experimental procedure using your existing scientific knowledge.
Estimate	Use rounded numbers to work out an approximate answer.
Evaluate	Review some information or data and use your findings to draw a conclusion about something — this usually involves, e.g. weighing up advantages and disadvantages.

> **Exam Tip**
> When you're reading an exam question, you might find it helpful to underline the command words. It can help you work out what type of answer to give.

> **Exam Tip**
> It's easy to get <u>describe</u> and <u>explain</u> mixed up, but they're quite different. For example, if you're asked to describe some data, just state the overall pattern or trend. If you're asked to explain data, you'll need to <u>give reasons</u> for the trend.

> **Exam Tip**
> Some questions will ask you to 'Use Figure X' to answer them. If so, you must refer to the Figure or you won't get the marks.

Core Practicals

For the biology bit of your qualification, you'll need to cover 6 Core Practical experiments in your lessons. At least 15% of the total marks in your exams will be for questions that test your understanding of these experiments and the techniques involved in them. Here are some basic areas you might be asked about:

- Carrying out the experiment — e.g. planning or describing a method, describing how to take measurements or use apparatus.

> **Exam Tip**
> The Core Practical questions are likely to have some overlap with Working Scientifically, so make sure you've brushed up on pages 2-22.

- Risk assessment — e.g. describing or explaining dangers which can arise from the experiment, or safety precautions which should be taken.

- Understanding variables — e.g. identifying control, dependent and independent variables.

- Data handling — e.g. plotting graphs or doing calculations using some sample results provided.

- Analysing results — e.g. making conclusions based on sample results.

- Evaluating the experiment — e.g. making judgements on the quality of results, identifying where mistakes have been made in the method, suggesting improvements to the experiment.

Core Practical questions won't be pointed out to you in the exam, so you'll need to make sure you know the practicals inside out, and can recognise them easily. For an example of a question testing your understanding of a Core Practical, see page 222.

Levels of response questions

Some questions are designed to assess your ability to present and explain scientific ideas in a logical and coherent way, as well as your scientific knowledge. These questions often link together different topics and are worth 6 marks each. These questions will be marked in your exam papers with an asterisk (*).

This type of question is marked using a 'levels of response' mark scheme. Your answer is given a level depending on the number of marks available and its overall quality and scientific content. Here's an idea of how the levels may work out for a 6 mark question:

Example

- An answer that has no relevant information and makes no attempt to answer the question receives no marks.

- A Level 1 answer usually makes one or two correct statements, but does not fully answer the question. For instance, when asked to explain how the features of an organism make it adapted to its environment, it might state one or two correct facts about the organism's features, but not attempt to link them to the environment. These answers receive 1 or 2 marks.

- A Level 2 answer usually makes a number of correct statements, with explanation, but falls short of fully answering the question. It may miss a step, leave out an important fact, or not be organised as logically as it should be. These answers receive 3 or 4 marks.

- A Level 3 answer will answer the question fully, in a logical fashion. It will make a number of points that are explained and related back to the question. Any conclusions it makes will be supported by evidence in the answer. These answers receive 5 or 6 marks.

Exam Tip
It might be useful to write a quick plan of your answer in the spare space of your paper. This can help you get your thoughts in order, so you can write a logical, coherent answer. But remember to cross your plan out after you've written your answer so it doesn't get marked.

Exam Tip
Make sure your writing is legible — you don't want to lose marks just because the examiner couldn't read your handwriting.

Make sure you answer the question fully, and cover all points indicated in the question. You also need to organise your answer clearly — the points you make need to be in a logical order. Use specialist scientific vocabulary whenever you can. For example, if you're describing cell division, you'd need to use scientific terms like mitosis and chromosomes. Obviously you need to use these terms correctly — it's no good knowing the words if you don't know what they actually mean.

There are some exam-style questions that use this type of mark scheme in this book (marked up with an asterisk, *, as in the real exams). You can use them to practise writing logical and coherent answers. Use the worked answers given at the back of this book to mark what you've written. The answers will tell you the relevant points you could've included, but it'll be down to you to put everything together into a full, well-structured answer.

Exam Tip
Make sure your writing style is appropriate for an exam. You need to write in full sentences and use fairly formal language.

Calculations

In GCSE Combined Science, around 20% of the total marks will come from questions that test your maths skills. Questions that involve a calculation can seem a bit scary. But they're really not that bad. Here are some tips to help you out...

- Show your working — this is the most important thing to remember. It only takes a few seconds more to write down what's in your head and it might stop you from making silly errors and losing out on easy marks. You won't get a mark for a wrong answer, but you could get marks for the method you used to work out the answer.

- Check your answer — a good way to do this is to work backwards through your calculation. You should also think about whether your answer seems sensible — if it's a much bigger or smaller number than you were expecting, you might have gone wrong somewhere.

> **Example**
>
> A potato chip weighs 10.2 g at the start of the experiment. At the end of the experiment it weighs 11.6 g. To calculate the change in mass, you'd subtract 10.2 g from 11.6 g — which works out as 1.4 g. You'd expect the answer to be around 1 g, so this seems sensible. To check it though, just add 1.4 to 10.2 — you should end up with 11.6.

- Sometimes you'll be asked to pick some numbers out of a table or read values off a graph to use in your calculation. If so, always read the question carefully so you know exactly what figures you need to use. Make sure you read the headings in the table carefully too (or the axes on the graph) to make sure you understand what's being shown.

In the exams, you should be prepared to do things like estimate a value, calculate a percentage or a mean, put numbers into equations that you've been given, and recall and use relevant equations.

Figure 1: A calculator. Under the pressure of an exam it's easy to make mistakes in calculations, even if they're really simple ones. So don't be afraid to put every calculation into the calculator.

Exam Tip
These aren't the only calculations you could be asked to do in an exam — they're just examples of the sort of thing that's likely to come up.

Exam Help

Answers

Topic 1 — Key Concepts in Biology

Topic 1a — Cells and Microscopy

1. Cell Structure

Page 25 — Fact Recall Questions
Q1 the genetic material / the nucleus
Q2 In the mitochondria.
Q3 protein synthesis
Q4 a) A cell wall, a large vacuole and chloroplasts.
b) A cell wall — supports and strengthens the cell.
A vacuole — maintains the internal pressure to support the cell.
Chloroplasts — contain chlorophyll, which absorbs light for photosynthesis.
Q5 A small loop of DNA (that is not part of the main chromosome).
Q6 a) A long hair-like structure, which rotates to make a bacterium move.
b) To move away from harmful substances.
To move towards nutrients/oxygen.

Page 25 — Application Question
Q1 a) It doesn't contain chloroplasts.
b) It has a cell wall.

2. Specialised Cells

Page 27 — Fact Recall Questions
Q1 acrosome
Q2 To carry the female DNA. To nourish the developing embryo in its early stages.
Q3 It has a haploid nucleus. Its membrane changes structure straight after fertilisation to stop any more sperm getting in.

Page 27 — Application Question
Q1 E.g. to supply enough energy (through aerobic respiration) to move/beat the cilia.

3. Microscopy

Page 33 — Fact Recall Questions
Q1 An electron microscope has a higher magnification and resolution than a light microscope, so it can be used to look at smaller objects.
Q2 To add colour to objects in a cell, making them easier to see.
Q3 Clip the slide to a microscope stage. Select the lowest-powered objective lens. Use the coarse adjustment knob to move the stage up to just below the objective lens. Look down the eyepiece. Use the coarse adjustment knob to move the stage downwards until the image is roughly in focus. Adjust the focus with the fine adjustment knob, until you get a clear image of what's on the slide.
Q4 $1 \text{ nm} = 1 \times 10^{-9} \text{ m}$

Page 33 — Application Questions
Q1 magnification = eyepiece lens magnification × objective lens magnification
$= 15 \times 40 =$ **× 600**
Q2 magnification = image size ÷ real size
$= 18 \div 0.002 =$ **× 9000**
Q3 image size = magnification × real size
$= 400 \times 0.08 =$ **32 mm**
Q4 real size = image size ÷ magnification
$= 10.5 \div 1500 = 0.007 \text{ mm}$
$0.007 \text{ mm} \times 1000 =$ **7 μm**
The question asks for the answer to be in μm, so to convert mm to μm you need to multiply by 1000.
Q5 magnification = image size ÷ real size
image size = 900 μm ÷ 1000 = 0.9 mm
$= 0.9 \div (2 \times 10^{-5}) = 0.9 \div 0.00002 =$ **× 45000**
You need both the image size and the real size to be in the same units here, but it doesn't matter whether they're both in mm or both in μm. You could have also done 900 ÷ 0.02 and got the right answer.

Page 35 — Cells and Microscopy Exam-style Questions
1 a) C *(1 mark)*
b) A eukaryotic cell, e.g. because it has a nucleus/mitochondria/chloroplasts / it doesn't have plasmids/a circular strand of DNA in the cytoplasm *(1 mark)*.
c) chloroplasts *(1 mark)*
2 a) The tail allows the sperm to swim to the egg *(1 mark)*.
b) A/image width = 33 mm
real width = 55 μm ÷ 1000 = 0.055 mm
magnification = image width ÷ real width
$= 33 \div 0.055 =$ **× 600**
(3 marks for correct answer, otherwise 1 mark for 33 mm and 1 mark for correctly converting both measurements into the same units.)
If you got the correct answer of × 600 by converting 33 mm into μm (33 × 1000 = 33000 μm) you would still get the marks here.

c) The real length of the sperm cell is 55 µm. The head is approximately one fifth of the length of the entire cell. 55 µm ÷ 5 = **11 µm** (accept answers between 9.2 and 13.75 µm) *(2 marks for correct answer, otherwise 1 mark for correctly estimating the head to be between one quarter and one sixth of the size of the whole cell.)*

Topic 1b — Biological Molecules and Transport in Cells

1. Enzymes
Page 38 — Fact Recall Questions
Q1 Because they increase the speed of a biological reaction without being changed or used up in the reaction.
Q2 active site
Q3 false
Different enzymes work best at different pHs.

Page 38 — Application Question
Q1 It should slow down the rate of reaction. This is because heating hexokinase up to a high temperature/50 °C will probably cause the bonds in hexokinase to break and the active site to lose its shape / the enzyme to denature. This would mean that glucose will no longer be able to fit into the active site and the reaction won't be catalysed. *For questions like this you just need to apply your own knowledge — e.g. that enzymes lose their shape at high temperatures and that enzymes need their unique shape to work — to the specific enzyme named in the question.*

2. Investigating Enzymatic Reactions
Page 40 — Application Question
Q1 a) a buffer solution
b) The iodine solution would remain browny-orange rather than changing to blue-black.
c) E.g.
Rate = $\frac{1000}{\text{time}} = \frac{1000}{120}$
= **8.3 s^{-1}** (2 s.f.)
If you used 1/time here and got the answer 0.0083 s^{-1}, then you'd still get the marks in an exam.

3. Enzymes in Breakdown and Synthesis
Page 42 — Fact Recall Questions
Q1 false
Digestive enzymes catalyse the breakdown of big molecules into smaller molecules.
Q2 a) lipases
b) glycerol, fatty acids

Page 42 — Application Question
Q1 The protease will break the protein down into amino acids. The amino acids will then react with the ninhydrin, turning the samples from a yellowish colour to a deep-purple colour.

4. Transport in Cells
Page 46 — Fact Recall Questions
Q1 The net movement of water molecules across a partially permeable membrane from a region of higher water concentration to a region of lower water concentration. / The net movement of water molecules across a partially permeable membrane from a region of lower solute concentration to a region of higher solute concentration.
Q2 Cells can absorb ions from very dilute solutions using active transport. The energy transferred from respiration is used to move ions from an area of lower concentration to an area of higher concentration / against a concentration gradient.

Page 46 — Application Question
Q1 B
The glucose molecules move by diffusion from an area of higher concentration inside the cell to an area of lower concentration outside the cell.

5. Investigating Osmosis in Plant Cells
Page 49 — Application Question
Q1 a) i) The (mean) length of the potato cylinders.
The dependent variable is the variable you measure — in this case the length of the potato cylinders.
ii) The concentration of the sugar solution.
The independent variable is the variable you change.
b) Any two from: e.g. the volume of the sucrose solutions / the age/type of potatoes used / the length of time the potato cylinders are left for.
c) percentage change in length = $\frac{\text{final length} - \text{initial length}}{\text{initial length}} \times 100$
= $\frac{8.5 - 9.6}{9.6} \times 100$ = **–11.5%** (3 s.f.)

Pages 51-52 — Biological Molecules and Transport in Cells Exam-style Questions
1 a) Inside respiring cells. The carbon dioxide molecules must be diffusing from an area of higher concentration (inside respiring cells) to an area of lower concentration (in the bloodstream) *(1 mark)*.
b) When the concentration of glucose molecules in the small intestine is lower than the concentration of glucose molecules in the blood *(1 mark)*, glucose will need to be absorbed into the blood via active transport, which requires energy *(1 mark)*.

2 a) Because every enzyme has an active site with a unique shape that usually only fits the substrate involved in a single reaction *(1 mark)*. If the substrate doesn't match the enzyme's active site, then the reaction won't be catalysed *(1 mark)*.
   b) Line A. The line for A shows a faster rate than the line for B *(1 mark)*. Higher temperatures increase the rate of a reaction, so line A must represent the experiment at the higher temperature of 25 °C *(1 mark)*.
   c) Increasing the temperature to 50 °C caused the shape of enzyme X's active site to change / denatured the enzyme *(1 mark)*, so the enzyme could no longer catalyse the reaction *(1 mark)*.
3 The photograph shows that in the test tubes with hydrochloric acid only and pepsin only (test tubes 1 and 2), the meat hasn't been fully digested *(1 mark)*.
   However, in the test tube with both pepsin and hydrochloric acid (test tube 3) the meat sample has been completely digested *(1 mark)*. This suggests that pepsin requires acidic conditions/low pH to function at its best *(1 mark)*.
4 a) Water moves by osmosis from a region of higher water concentration to region of a lower water concentration *(1 mark)*. The potato has a lower water concentration than the water in the dish, so water moves from the dish into the potato cells *(1 mark)*. The potato has a higher water concentration than the sugar/well, so water moves from the potato into the well and dissolves the sugar/creates a sugar solution *(1 mark)*.
   b) There's no sugar in the well in the potato in experiment B, so no water is drawn out of the potato into the well at the top *(1 mark)*. This means the difference in the concentration of the solution in the potato cells and in the dish is smaller *(1 mark)*, so the movement of water molecules by osmosis is reduced *(1 mark)*.

Topic 2 — Cells and Control

Topic 2a — Cell Division and Stem Cells

1. Mitosis

Page 56 — Fact Recall Questions
Q1 The DNA is copied and forms X-shaped chromosomes. (Each 'arm' of the chromosome is an exact duplicate of the other.)
Q2 Cell fibres pull the chromosomes apart and the two arms of each chromosome go to opposite ends of the cell.
Q3 cytokinesis
Q4 Any two from: e.g. growth / replacing damaged cells / asexual reproduction.

Page 56 — Application Questions
Q1 a) genetically identical
   b) two
   If a cell has two sets of chromosomes it means that it will have two copies of each chromosome.
   c) Membranes are forming around each of the sets of chromosomes, forming the nuclei of the two new cells. The cell membrane and cytoplasm are dividing.
   This photograph is showing the final stage of mitosis (telophase). Cytokinesis (division of the cytoplasm) happens alongside telophase.
Q2 number of cells = 2^{10}
   = 2 × 2 × 2 × 2 × 2 × 2 × 2 × 2 × 2 × 2 = **1024**

2. Cell Division and Growth

Page 58 — Fact Recall Questions
Q1 Cell differentiation is the process by which a cell changes to become specialised for its job.
Q2 A change in one of the genes that controls cell division can cause the cell to start dividing uncontrollably. This can result in a mass of abnormal cells called a tumour. If the tumour invades and destroys surrounding tissue, it's a cancer.

Page 58 — Application Question
Q1 60%

3. Stem Cells

Page 61 — Fact Recall Questions
Q1 An undifferentiated cell that has the potential to differentiate into different types of cell.
Q2 Early embryonic stem cells can divide and produce any type of cell at all. Adult stem cells can only produce certain types of cells.
Q3 Any two from: e.g. the transplanted cells may form a tumour if they divide too fast. / The transplanted cells could be carrying a virus that would then be passed on to the patient. / The transplanted cells may be rejected by the patient's body.
Q4 meristem

Page 61 — Application Questions
Q1 E.g. to replace damaged skin cells / repair the skin at the site of a wound.
Q2 a) Stem cells could be made to differentiate into neurones, which could replace the damaged/dead neurones.
   b) E.g. producing nerve cells to replace damaged tissue in people with paralysis. / Producing insulin-producing cells for people with diabetes.
Q3 E.g. because the embryos left over from fertility clinics will be destroyed anyway if they are not used for fertility treatment, so it's better to use these rather than creating new embryos to use in research.

Page 63 — Cell Division and Stem Cells
Exam-style Questions
1. a) chromosome *(1 mark)*
   b) D *(1 mark)*
   c) 3 *(1 mark)* e.g. because it shows the membrane around the nucleus breaking down / the chromosomes have condensed but are still in the nucleus *(1 mark)*.
   d) Mitosis produces two new daughter cells *(1 mark)*. The daughter cells are diploid *(1 mark)* and are genetically identical to each other and the parent cell *(1 mark)*.
2. a) 2nd percentile *(1 mark)*
   b) 7.9 kg (accept answers between 7.8 and 8.0 kg) *(1 mark)*
   c) E.g. It is used to assess a child's growth over time *(1 mark)*, so that an overall pattern in development can be seen / any problems can be spotted *(1 mark)*.

Topic 2b — Nervous Control
1. The Nervous System
Page 66 — Fact Recall Questions
Q1 It carries impulses away from the cell body.
Q2 To speed up nervous impulses.

Page 66 — Application Question
Q1 a) i) The stimulus is the sound of the cat moving. It will be detected by (sound) receptors in the dog's ears.
      ii) sensory neurone
   b) i) motor neurone
      ii) They will contract.

2. Synapses and Reflexes
Page 69 — Fact Recall Questions
Q1 Neurotransmitters diffuse across the gap between the two neurones, which sets off an electrical impulse in the next neurone.
Q2 A reflex is a fast, automatic response to a stimulus.
Q3 No
   Reflexes are automatic — you don't have to think about them, so they don't pass through conscious parts of the brain.
Q4 a relay neurone
Q5 The gland will secrete a hormone.

Page 69 — Application Question
Q1 a) pain
   b) A muscle in the leg. It contracts, moving the foot away from the source of the pain (the pin).
   c) Stimulus → Receptor → Sensory neurone → Relay neurone → Motor neurone → Effector/Muscle → Response

Page 71 — Nervous Control
Exam-style Questions
1. a) In the skin on the subject's fingertip *(1 mark)*.
   b) sensory neurone *(1 mark)*
   c) It would get faster *(1 mark)*. The presence of the drug increases the amount of neurotransmitter released at the synapses, so it would take less time for an impulse to be triggered in the next neurone *(1 mark)*.
   d) E.g. reflexes are fast *(1 mark)*, so we quickly respond to danger, decreasing our chances of injury *(1 mark)*. Reflexes are automatic *(1 mark)*, so we don't have to waste time thinking about our response, which reduces our chance of injury *(1 mark)*.

Topic 3 — Genetics

Topic 3a — Reproduction, DNA and Protein Synthesis
1. Sexual Reproduction and Meiosis
Page 74 — Fact Recall Questions
Q1 one
Q2 In the reproductive organs.
Q3 two
Q4 four
Q5 False
   The chromosomes from the mother and father are mixed during the first division of meiosis, then each gamete only gets half of the chromosomes during the second division.

Page 74 — Application Questions
Q1 a) 39
   b) 38
   c) 32
Q2 Before the first division, the cell duplicates its DNA. So when the first division happens, cells will have one full set of chromosomes again.
   Duplicating the DNA creates X-shaped chromosomes, where each 'arm' of the chromosome has the same DNA.

2. DNA
Page 77 — Fact Recall Questions
Q1 Two strands of DNA twisted together in a double helix shape/double stranded spiral.
Q2 gene
Q3 genome

Pages 77-78 — Application Questions
Q1 A G A T G C T T A C T T
   In DNA, A always pairs with T, and C always pairs with G.
Q2 a) The washing-up liquid is a detergent. It will break down the cell membranes of the kiwi cells so that the DNA is released.
   b) salt
   c) A stringy white precipitate/solid.

Page 79 — Reproduction, DNA and Protein Synthesis Exam-style Questions

1. a) Sexual, because it involves the joining of male and female gametes / it involves two parents *(1 mark)*.
   b) They have received genetic material/chromosomes from both the male pig and the female pig *(1 mark)* and it is this genetic material/the chromosomes that control the offspring's characteristics *(1 mark)*.
   c) i) So that when two gametes join at fertilisation, the full number of chromosomes is reached (two copies of each) *(1 mark)*.
      ii) meiosis *(1 mark)*

2. a) None of the base pairs that contain adenine contain cytosine (A always pairs with T). So 100 − 46 = 54% of the base pairs contain cytosine.
   54% of $2.16 \times 10^6 = ((2.16 \times 10^6) \div 100) \times 54$
   $= 1\,166\,400$
   (2 marks for the correct answer, otherwise 1 mark for showing that cytosine is in 54% of the base pairs)
   This question is marked as higher only because it involves a calculation using standard form (which is a higher only maths requirement).
   b) hydrogen bonds *(1 mark)*
   c) E.g. by adding ice-cold alcohol to the solution *(1 mark)*.

Topic 3b — Genetic Diagrams and Inheritance

1. Genes and Alleles

Page 80 — Fact Recall Question
Q1 a) Different versions of the same gene.
   b) When an organism has two alleles for a particular gene that are the same.
   c) The allele for the characteristic that's shown even if two different alleles for the same gene are present.
   d) The characteristics you have.

2. Genetic Diagrams and Family Pedigrees

Page 86 — Application Questions
Q1 a)
Parents' characteristics: female smooth coat / male rough coat
Parents' alleles: rr / RR
Gametes' alleles: r, r / R, R
Possible alleles of offspring: Rr, Rr, Rr, Rr
   b) a rough coat

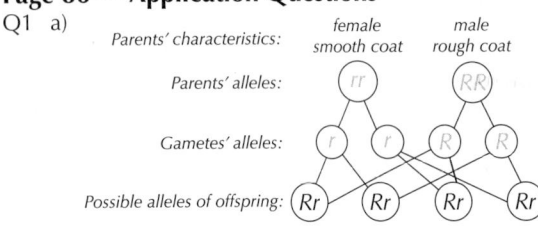

Q2 a) Because there are no carriers of the disorder.
   b) a purple circle
   c) i) dd
      ii) Dd
   You know from the diagram that Kate has polydactyly, so she must have at least one copy of the dominant allele 'D'. You also know that she doesn't have two copies of the dominant allele, as her father Clark doesn't have polydactyly, so she couldn't have inherited a second 'D' allele from him. Therefore her genotype must be Dd.
   d) Kate's alleles

	D	d
d	Dd	dd
d	Dd	dd

Aden's alleles

Probability of new baby having polydactyly = 0.5 or 50% or 1:1 or 1 in 2 or ½

3. Sex Determination

Page 88 — Fact Recall Questions
Q1 one
Q2 false
Half carry X chromosomes, and half carry Y chromosomes.

Page 88 — Application Questions
Q1 Rachael (XX) and Luca (XY) → gametes X, X / X, Y → offspring XX, XX, XY, XY (female, female, male, male)

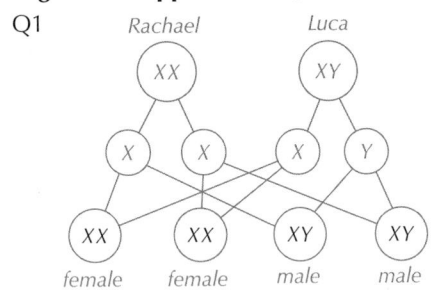

Q2 0.5 or 50% or 1:1 or 1 in 2 or ½.
Q3 Rachael's gametes

	X	X
X	XX	XX
Y	XY	XY

Luca's gametes

4. Variation

Page 91 — Fact Recall Questions
Q1 False
Variation within a population can also be caused by environmental conditions.
Q2 a) A change to the sequence of bases in DNA.
   b) Most mutations have no effect on the protein the gene codes for, so most mutations have no effect on the organism's phenotype.

Page 91 — Application Questions
Q1 a) both
b) environment only
Q2 The results from Study 1 suggest that genes must influence IQ because identical twins have the same genes and non-identical twins have different genes.
The results from Study 2 suggest that environment also influences IQ. This is because identical twins have exactly the same genes, which means that differences in their IQs must be down to differences in their environment/the way they were brought up.

5. The Human Genome Project
Page 93 — Application Questions
Q1 E.g. Sarah can get tailored advice on lifestyle factors to reduce the likelihood of developing breast cancer / doctors may be able to prescribe a more effective drug for her if she develops breast cancer / she can have regular checks to ensure early treatment if she develops breast cancer.
Q2 Any two from: e.g. Sarah could be discriminated against by life insurers / she could be discriminated against by employers / she could be put under pressure not to have children so that the gene is not passed on / she could have increased stress levels from worrying about potentially developing breast cancer.

Pages 95-96 — Genetic Diagrams and Inheritance Exam-style Questions
1 a) HH or Hh *(1 mark)*
b) A *(1 mark)*
c) mother's alleles

	H	h
H	HH	Hh
h	Hh	hh

father's alleles

HH and Hh offspring have Huntington's disease. So the probability is 3 in 4 or 75%.
(1 mark for a correct Punnett square, plus 1 mark for 75%.)

2 a) They have both inherited the same alleles for hair colour from their parents, but different alleles for eye colour *(1 mark)*. This genetic variation is the result of alleles being combined in different ways during sexual reproduction *(1 mark)*.
b) E.g. how often they train / how hard they train / how well they are coached / how good the facilities they train at are / how good their diet is *(1 mark)*.
You're not expected to know the answer to this question, just to make sensible suggestions.

3 a) 0.5 / 50% / 1 in 2 / ½ chance *(1 mark)*
b) E.g.
Kaye's alleles

	D	d
d	Dd	dd
d	Dd	dd

Mark's alleles

Kaye and Mark are likely to have a 50:50 / 1:1 ratio of dimpled to undimpled offspring.
(1 mark for correct a Punnett square, plus 1 mark for a correct ratio.)
c) Y chromosome *(1 mark)*

4 a) Homozygous, because he has a recessive disorder / cystic fibrosis *(1 mark)*.
There are carriers in the family tree, so cystic fibrosis must be a recessive disorder.
b) Ff *(1 mark)*. For a child to have cystic fibrosis, both parents must carry the cystic fibrosis allele *(1 mark)*.
Tony is a carrier so his alleles must be Ff. As their child has cystic fibrosis (ff) it must have inherited a cystic fibrosis allele from both Tony and Bex, as it's a recessive disorder. Bex doesn't have cystic fibrosis, so she must be a carrier (Ff).
c) E.g. Ivana's alleles

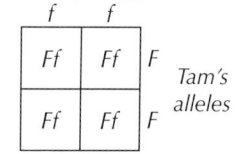

	f	f
F	Ff	Ff
F	Ff	Ff

Tam's alleles

No, because to have cystic fibrosis you need the genotype ff. None of the offspring are ff. / Tam is FF so all his offspring must inherit one healthy allele.
(1 mark for a correct Punnett square, plus 1 mark for a correct conclusion.)

Topic 4 — Natural Selection and Genetic Modification

Topic 4a — Natural Selection and Evolution

1. Natural Selection and Evidence for Evolution
Page 98 — Fact Recall Questions
Q1 Through mutation.
Q2 Something that affects an organism's chance of surviving and reproducing.
Q3 False
Organisms that are better adapted to the selection pressures in their environment are better able to compete.

Page 99 — Application Questions

Q1 E.g. the weeds in a population show variation — some are resistant to glyphosate, others aren't / a new allele arises (due to a mutation) which makes some weeds resistant to glyphosate. The glyphosate-resistant weeds are better suited to an environment where glyphosate-containing weedkillers (a selection pressure) are used, so they are more likely to survive and reproduce than weeds that aren't glyphosate-resistant. This means that the allele for glyphosate resistance is more likely to be passed on to the next generation, making glyphosate resistance more common in the population.

You could get asked to explain the selection of pretty much any characteristic in the exam — make sure you can apply the key points of Darwin's theory to any context.

Q2 a) By around 3.5 – 2.1 = **1.4 cm** (accept any answer between 1.3 and 1.5 cm).
   b) E.g. the reindeer population in 1810 would have shown variation — some would have had shorter fur and some longer fur (due to a mix of alleles in the population). The temperature of the new environment would have acted as a selection pressure. Reindeer with shorter fur would have been better suited to the new, warmer environment (as they would have been less likely to overheat), so they would have been more likely to survive and breed successfully than the reindeer with long fur. This meant that the allele for short fur was more likely to be passed on to the next generation. This allele became more common in the population, eventually reducing the average fur length.

2. Evidence for Human Evolution — Fossils

Page 102 — Fact Recall Questions

Q1 They have characteristics in between apes and humans. When arranged in chronological order, they show how hominids gradually became less ape-like and more human-like.

Q2 False
Ardi is older than Lucy by 1.2 million years.

Q3 "Turkana Boy" is a 1.6 million year old fossil skeleton of the species *Homo erectus*. He has a mixture of human and ape-like features, but is more human-like than older hominid fossils.

Page 102 — Application Questions

Q1 A = Lucy, B = Ardi, C = Turkana Boy
Q2 B (Ardi), A (Lucy), C (Turkana Boy)
Q3 You would expect the fossil to have shorter arms and longer legs than Lucy.
As the fossil is more recent than Lucy, you would expect it to have features that are more like a modern human.

3. Evidence for Human Evolution — Stone Tools

Page 104 — Application Question

Q1 a) C, A, B
   b) C is the least sculpted, least complex tool, so it is likely to be the oldest. B is the most sculpted, most complex tool, so it is likely to be the most recent. A is somewhere in between the two.
   c) B
   B is the most complex, most recent tool, so it's most likely to have been made by a Homo sapiens (modern human).
   d) Supports the answer — newer layers of rock tend to be found above older layers of rock. C is a more recent tool than A and more recently made tools are more likely to be found in newer layers of rock.

4. Classification

Page 106 — Fact Recall Questions

Q1 C
Q2 Differences in RNA sequences suggested that some members of the Prokaryote kingdom (used in the five kingdom classification method) were not as closely related as first thought. So it was suggested that this kingdom should be split into two groups, which became two of the domains in the three domain classification system.
Q3 Archaea, Bacteria and Eukarya

Page 108 — Natural Selection and Evolution Exam-style Questions

1 a) E.g. they could have used stratigraphy/looked at the depth of the rock layer the tool was found in. / They could have used radiometric dating to date the layer of rock that the tool was found in. *(1 mark)*
   b) i) C *(1 mark)*
   You should remember that Lucy is 3.2 million years old. The tool is 1.5 million years old. 3.2 – 1.5 = 1.7.
      ii) The tool is too complex *(1 mark)* and Lucy had not evolved enough to have a brain large enough to make/use it *(1 mark)*.

2 How to grade your answer:
   Level 0: There is no relevant information.
      (No marks)
   Level 1: There is some information about natural selection. The points made are basic and not linked together.
      (1 to 2 marks)
   Level 2: There is some explanation of how the milk snake may have evolved via natural selection to have a similar colouring to the coral snake. Some of the points made are linked together.
      (3 to 4 marks)

Level 3: There is a clear and detailed explanation of how the milk snake may have evolved via natural selection to have a similar colouring to the coral snake. The points made are well-linked and the answer has a clear and logical structure. *(5 to 6 marks)*

Here are some points your answer may include:

The original milk snake population showed variation — some had similar colouring to the coral snake, others didn't. / A mutation produced an allele, which caused some milk snakes to have similar colouring to the coral snake.
Predation is a selection pressure.
Milk snakes that looked like the coral snake were less likely to be eaten by predators and so more likely to survive and reproduce, than milk snakes that didn't look like coral snakes.
This means that the allele that causes coral snake colouring was more likely to be passed on to the next generation of milk snakes.
This is how it spread and became more common in the population.

Topic 4b — Genetic Modification

1. Selective Breeding

Page 110 — Fact Recall Questions

Q1 From your existing stock, select the ones which have the characteristics you want. (Individuals will have different characteristics due to genetic variation.) Breed your chosen individuals together. Select the best of the offspring and breed them together. Continue for several generations.

Q2 E.g. it can lead to inbreeding. This can cause health problems because there's more chance of organisms inheriting harmful genetic defects when the gene pool is limited. / If a new disease appears, there's less chance of resistance alleles being present, making it more likely that the whole population will be wiped out by the disease.

2. Genetic Engineering

Page 113 — Fact Recall Questions

Q1 The transfer of a gene from one organism's genome to another organism's genome in order to introduce a desirable characteristic.

Q2 a) To recognise specific sequences of DNA and cut the DNA at these points. / To cut out the desired gene and cut open the vector DNA.
   b) To join two pieces of DNA together (via their sticky ends).
   c) To transfer DNA into a cell.

Page 113 — Application Question

Q1 a) Any two from: e.g. the corn-based vaccine may be cheaper than the normal vaccine to transport and store because it does not need refrigerating. This may be particularly important in developing countries that don't have a lot of money to spend on healthcare. / The corn-based vaccine may be easier to safely administer than the normal vaccine, because it avoids the use of needles, which need sterilising. This might be particularly beneficial in developing countries where healthcare facilities might be limited. / The corn-based vaccine may increase uptake of the vaccine because it avoids the use of needles, which some people may not like. This might be particularly important in areas where hepatitis B is common.

Any sensible suggestion that links back to the information given in the question would be fine here.

   b) E.g. the transplanted gene that enables the corn to produce the vaccine may get out into the environment and be picked up by wild plants. / The GM corn might adversely affect food chains/human health.

Page 114 — Genetic Modification Exam-style Questions

1 C *(1 mark)*
2 a) i) E.g. it means more of his wheat crop will survive/the wheat crop is less likely to get damaged by the disease so the wheat yield will increase *(1 mark)*.
      ii) E.g. it may be cheaper *(1 mark)* because the farmer can selectively breed the wheat himself, rather than paying a scientist/technology company to do it *(1 mark)*.

You get one mark here for coming up with any sensible advantage to the farmer of using selective breeding and one mark for explaining it.

   b) When exposed to the disease, some of the farmer's wheat plants will be resistant to it *(1 mark)*. The farmer should select these resistant plants and breed them together *(1 mark)*. He should then select the most disease-resistant offspring and breed them together *(1 mark)*. After several generations of doing this, all/most of the wheat plants will be disease-resistant *(1 mark)*.
   c) E.g. the gene pool would be reduced, so there's less chance of alleles for resistance for a new disease being present *(1 mark)*. This means that if a new disease appears, all the farmer's wheat plants are likely to be wiped out *(1 mark)*.

3   a) E.g. the human gene for factor VIII could be cut out using restriction enzymes *(1 mark)*. The same restriction enzymes could be used to cut open the DNA of a vector *(1 mark)*. The factor VIII gene could then be joined to the vector DNA using ligase *(1 mark)*. The recombinant DNA/vector containing the factor VIII gene could then be inserted into the animal cells, which can then produce the human factor VIII protein *(1 mark)*.
    b) E.g. it avoids the creation of genetically modified embryos that do not survive. / It avoids creating genetically modified animals that may suffer from health problems. / It is easier/faster and cheaper to grow cells than it is to rear whole animals. *(1 mark)*

Topic 5 — Health, Disease and the Development of Medicines

Topic 5a — Health and Disease

1. Introduction to Health and Disease

Page 115 — Fact Recall Questions
Q1 Health is a state of complete physical, mental and social well-being.
Q2 Communicable diseases can be spread between individuals, whereas non-communicable diseases cannot.

2. Communicable Diseases

Page 120 — Fact Recall Questions
Q1 a) E.g. coughing and lung damage.
    b) The pathogen is spread through the air in droplets produced when people infected with tuberculosis cough and sneeze.
Q2 E.g. it can be reduced by making sure that people have access to clean water.
Q3 a) ash trees
    b) E.g. leaf loss and bark lesions.
Q4 Mosquito nets can prevent people from being bitten by mosquitoes when they're asleep, meaning that the protist that causes malaria isn't passed on.
Q5 An infection that is spread through sexual contact, such as genital contact and sexual intercourse.
Q6 E.g. by wearing a condom during sex or avoiding sexual contact.
Q7 HIV kills white blood cells. Eventually, the immune system of the infected individual becomes so weak that it fails. This makes the body much more susceptible to other diseases.

Page 120 — Application Questions
Q1 E.g. by wearing a condom during sex / by avoiding sexual contact / through screening people for gonorrhea and treating infected individuals.

Q2 The nurse may come into contact with pathogens for many diseases. By washing his hands, this will prevent pathogens being passed on to other people that he comes into contact with.

Page 122 — Health and Disease
Exam-style Questions
1 a) i) An organism that causes disease *(1 mark)*
       ii) protist *(1 mark)*
   b) i) E.g. damage to red blood cells *(1 mark)*.
       ii) The malarial protist is transferred between people/between people and animals by a mosquito vector *(1 mark)*. The mosquito is not present in the hospital, so the protist cannot be transferred from the patient with malaria to the other patients *(1 mark)*.
   c) E.g. they should spray exposed skin with insect repellant. They should sleep under a mosquito net. *(2 marks — 1 mark for each correct answer)*
   d) The patient may be suffering from mental/social health issues, despite being disease free *(1 mark)*.
2 a) i) The virus is spread through exchanging infected bodily fluids *(1 mark)*.
       ii) Any two from: e.g. by using a condom during sexual intercourse. / Taking medication which reduces the chance of the infection being passed on during sexual intercourse. / By drug users avoiding sharing needles.
           (1 mark for each correct answer.)
   b) A disease that can spread between individuals *(1 mark)*.
   c) HIV kills white blood cells in the body *(1 mark)*. Over time, the virus destroys enough white blood cells to cause the immune system to fail *(1 mark)*. This means that the body is less able to defend itself against pathogens, and the risk of an infection is increased *(1 mark)*.

Topic 5b — Fighting Disease

1. Defences Against Disease

Page 124 — Fact Recall Questions
Q1 E.g. the skin, mucus and cilia.
Q2 E.g. they engulf pathogens using phagocytosis. They produce antibodies.

Page 124 — Application Question
Q1 E.g. hairs and mucus in your nose trap particles that could contain the SARS-CoV. / The trachea and bronchi secrete mucus to trap the SARS-CoV. / The trachea and bronchi are lined with cilia. These waft mucus containing the SARS-CoV up to the back of the throat where it can be swallowed.

2. Memory Lymphocytes and Immunisation
Page 126 — Application Questions
Q1 E.g. the vaccination will involve injecting a small amount of dead or inactive whooping cough pathogen. The pathogen will carry antigens which will trigger the B-lymphocytes to produce antibodies to target the pathogen. It will also trigger the production of memory lymphocytes which 'remember' the antigen. If the vaccinated person is infected with the whooping cough pathogen at a later date, the memory lymphocytes should be able to rapidly mass-produce antibodies to kill off the pathogen.

Q2 Following the first exposure to the chickenpox virus, memory lymphocytes were produced that were specific to an antigen on the chickenpox virus. When the child was exposed to the chickenpox virus again, the memory lymphocytes recognised the antigens and quickly mass-produced antibodies. The chickenpox virus was then removed by the immune system before symptoms were able to develop.

3. Developing Drugs
Page 129 — Fact Recall Questions
Q1 Human cells, human tissues and live animals.
Q2 Any two from: e.g. to find out whether the drug works. / To find out about the drug's toxicity. / To find out the optimum/best dose of the drug.
Q3 a) healthy volunteers
    b) It is very low.
Q4 A placebo is a substance that looks like the drug being tested but doesn't do anything.
Q5 A blind trial is a clinical trial where the patient does not know whether they are receiving the drug or the placebo. In a double-blind trial, neither the doctor nor the patients know who has been given the drug and who has been given the placebo, until the results of the trial have been gathered.
   It's helpful to remember that 'double' means 'two' — so in a double-blind trial, there are two groups of people (doctors and patients) who don't know who receives the drug and who receives the placebo.

Pages 129-130 — Application Questions
Q1 a) E.g. a capsule without paracetamol.
    b) E.g. an inhaler without steroids.
    c) E.g. an injection without cortisone.
Q2 a) i) No, because it was a double-blind trial.
        ii) E.g. a pill without any weight-loss drug.
    b) E.g. Group 2 was included in the trial to make sure that the new drug, Drug Y, worked as well as/better than other, similar weight-loss drugs already available on the market (like Drug Z). / To see how Drug Y compared to Drug Z.
    c) E.g. that, on average, people taking Drug Y in this trial lost 4 lbs more than those taking the placebo, but 3 lbs less than those taking Drug Z.

4. Antibiotics
Page 131 — Fact Recall Questions
Q1 Antibiotics are drugs that kill or prevent the growth of bacteria.
Q2 Different antibiotics kill different types of bacteria.
Q3 Viruses aren't cells, they reproduce using a host organism's cells. Antibiotics selectively target bacterial cells, so antibiotics have no effect on the virus or the host cell.

Pages 133-134 — Fighting Disease Exam-style Questions
1 a) It produces hydrochloric acid which kills pathogens *(1 mark)*.
   b) The trachea and bronchi secrete mucus to trap pathogens *(1 mark)*. They are also lined with cilia *(1 mark)*. These waft the mucus up to the back of the throat where it can be swallowed *(1 mark)*.
   c) Lysozyme is an enzyme present in several secretions which kills bacteria *(1 mark)*.
   d) Antibodies only bind to specific antigens on the outside of specific pathogens *(1 mark)*. These pathogens bound to antibodies can then be found by white blood cells and destroyed *(1 mark)*.

2 a) In 1980, there were just over 4 million reported measles cases *(1 mark)*. Between 1980 and 2014 the number of reported measles cases dropped to around 0.3 million (after rising to a peak of 4.5 million in around 1981) *(1 mark)*. The estimated immunisation coverage was around 15% of the population in 1980 *(1 mark)*. Between 1980 and 2014 it increased to around 85% *(1 mark)*.
   The question asks you to use data from the graph to support your answer — so you must include some figures to get the marks. The graph has three different axes, which can make things a bit tricky. Take your time and work out what each one shows before answering the question.
   b) E.g. the data suggests that as the estimated percentage immunisation coverage increased, the number of reported measles cases decreased — this supports the case for immunising people against measles *(1 mark)*. However it doesn't prove that the increase in immunisation coverage definitely caused the decrease in measles cases, since other factors may have been at work *(1 mark)*.
   c) The pathogens in the vaccine are dead/inactive *(1 mark)*.

3 a) Using knowledge about how a particular disease works allows scientists to find molecules which could fight the disease *(1 mark)*.

Answers 263

b) Because live animals have an intact small intestine and circulatory system *(1 mark)*. Testing on just cells or tissues wouldn't show whether the drug has the desired effect on the absorption of nutrients from the small intestine to the bloodstream, because these body systems would not be intact *(1 mark)*.
c) How to grade your answer:
Level 0:   There is no relevant information.
(No marks)
Level 1:   There is a brief explanation of what happens during a clinical trial, but no information about placebos or double-blind testing.
(1 to 2 marks)
Level 2:   There is some explanation of what happens during a clinical trial, including some information about placebos or double-blind testing.
(3 to 4 marks)
Level 3:   There is a clear and detailed explanation of what happens during a clinical trial, including clear and detailed information about placebos and double-blind testing.
(5 to 6 marks)

Here are some points your answer may include:
The drug is first tested on healthy volunteers. This is to make sure that it doesn't have any harmful side effects when the body is working normally.
A very low dose of the drug is given at first, and this is gradually increased.
If the results of the tests on healthy volunteers are good, the drug is tested on people suffering from the illness.
The optimum dose is found — this is the dose of drug that is the most effective and has few side effects.
To test how well the drug works, a placebo may be used.
A placebo is a substance that looks like the drug being tested but doesn't do anything. Patients are randomly put into two groups — one is given the new drug, the other is given a placebo. This is so the doctor can see the actual difference the drug makes — it allows for the placebo effect.
Clinical trials are often double-blind — neither the doctor nor the patients in the study know who is getting the drug or the placebo. This is so the doctors monitoring the patients and analysing the results aren't subconsciously influenced by their knowledge.

Q4 a) B *(1 mark)*
b) E.g. When a pathogen first enters the body (point A), there aren't many B-lymphocytes that can produce the antibody required to bind to the new antigen, so the response is slow *(1 mark)*. Memory lymphocytes are produced in response to the new antigen, and they 'remember' the antigen *(1 mark)*. So at point C, when the pathogen enters the body for the second time, the memory lymphocytes can mass-produce the required antibody faster *(1 mark)*.

Topic 5c — Non-Communicable Diseases

1. Risk Factors for Non-Communicable Diseases

Page 137 — Fact Recall Questions
Q1   Something linked to an increase in the likelihood that a person will develop a certain disease during their lifetime.
Q2   Any two from: e.g. smoking / drinking alcohol / diet / low levels of exercise.
Q3   E.g. cardiovascular disease, (lung) cancer.
Q4   E.g. obesity
Q5   E.g. they are costly because the National Health Service provides the resources for the treatment of patients all over the UK. / Sometimes, people suffering from a non-communicable disease may not be able to work. A reduction in the number of people able to work can affect a country's economy.

2. Measures of Obesity

Page 139 — Application Question
Q1   a) Robyn's BMI = $77.0 \div (1.78^2)$ = 24.302...
= **24.3 kg m^{-2} (3 s.f.)**
Lauren's BMI = $75.0 \div (1.55^2)$ = 31.217...
= **31.2 kg m^{-2} (3 s.f.)**
Remember, the BMI formula uses height in m. To convert cm to m, you divide by 100, so 178 cm = 1.78 m.
b) Robyn is in the normal weight category. Lauren is in the moderately obese category. Lauren may be recommended to lose weight by a doctor.

3. Treating Cardiovascular Disease

Page 143 — Fact Recall Questions
Q1   Disease of the heart or blood vessels.
Q2   A reduction in blood pressure helps to prevent damage to blood vessels. This reduces the risk of fatty deposits forming, which restrict blood flow.
Q3   E.g. it could cause a heart attack / bleeding / clotting / infection / stroke.

Page 143 — Application Questions

Q1 Smoking is a lifestyle factor which increases the risk of cardiovascular disease. By stopping smoking, Clifford will reduce the risk of further development of the disease and help to prevent a heart attack or stroke.

Q2 The time the surgery takes is shorter for having a stent compared to having coronary bypass surgery. The patient is also likely to spend less time in hospital and recover faster if they have a stent inserted (compared to having coronary bypass surgery). Although there is a higher chance of needing repeat surgery with a stent, the benefits may outweigh this risk.

Page 145 — Non-Communicable Diseases Exam-style Questions

1 a) E.g. waist circumference = 0.72 m = 72 cm
waist-to-hip ratio =
waist circumference ÷ hip circumference
= 72 ÷ 89 = 0.8089... = **0.81 (2 s.f.)**
OR
hip circumference = 89 cm = 0.89 m
0.72 ÷ 0.89 = 0.8089... = **0.81 (2 s.f.)**
(2 marks for the correct answer to 2 significant figures or 1 mark for converting measurements to the same units.)

b) Nadira is more at risk because she has a higher waist-to-hip ratio than Moira so she carries more weight around her middle *(1 mark)*. This means she is at higher risk of developing obesity-related diseases such as type 2 diabetes *(1 mark)*.

c) E.g. liver disease / liver cancer *(1 mark)*. Drinking too much alcohol causes damage to liver cells which leads to disease *(1 mark)*.

2 a) (3 ÷ 154) × 100 = 1.948... = **1.9%** *(1 mark)*

b) By keeping the artery open, stents can help to increase blood flow *(1 mark)*. People who have had a heart attack are likely to have narrowed coronary arteries, so putting stents in these arteries can prevent another heart attack *(1 mark)*.

c) E.g. yes, because the results show that patients are less likely to die after having a drug-eluting stent inserted compared to a bare-metal stent *(1 mark)*. Also renarrowing of the artery is much less likely in patients treated with a drug-eluting stent (9%) compared to those treated with a bare-metal stent (21%) *(1 mark)*. The trial was fairly large (307 patients) which means the results are likely to be representative of the whole population *(1 mark)*.

Topic 6 — Plant Structures and Their Functions

1. Photosynthesis

Page 147 — Fact Recall Questions
Q1 glucose
Q2 carbon dioxide
Q3 oxygen
Q4 a) chloroplasts
   b) It absorbs light.
Q5 endothermic
Q6 carbon dioxide + water → glucose + oxygen
Q7 glucose

Page 147 — Application Question
Q1 Plant C. It received the most hours of sunlight, so it will have photosynthesised for longer. As photosynthesis produces glucose, it will have produced the most glucose.

2. Limiting Factors in Photosynthesis

Page 150 — Fact Recall Question
Q1 a) A factor which stops photosynthesis from happening any faster.
b) E.g. carbon dioxide concentration and temperature.
c) Increasing the light intensity increases the rate of photosynthesis (up to a point).

Page 151 — Application Questions

Q1

Environmental conditions	Most likely limiting factor
Outside on a cold winter's day.	temperature
In an unlit garden at 1:30 am, in the UK, in summer.	light
On a windowsill on a warm, bright day.	carbon dioxide concentration

Q2 a) Before point X, increasing the light intensity increases the rate of photosynthesis.
b) Flask A levels off at a lower point than Flask B because at this point, carbon dioxide concentration becomes the factor limiting the rate of photosynthesis in Flask A. Flask A has a lower carbon dioxide concentration than Flask B. All the other variables that affect the rate of photosynthesis are the same for both flasks.

3. Investigating the Rate of Photosynthesis

Page 153 — Application Question
Q1 $0.5 \text{ cm}^3 \div 3 \text{ min} = 0.166... = \mathbf{0.2 \text{ cm}^3 \text{ min}^{-1}}$ (to 1 s.f.)

4. The Inverse Square Law
Page 154 — Application Question
Q1 a) light intensity = $1 \div d^2$,
$1 \div 15^2 = 0.004444... =$ **0.0044 a.u.**
b) light intensity = $1 \div d^2$,
$1 \div 30^2 = 0.001111... =$ **0.0011 a.u.**

5. Transport in Plants
Page 157 — Fact Recall Questions
Q1 food substances / dissolved sugars/sucrose
Q2 Phloem tubes are made up of columns of elongated living cells. There are small pores (holes) in the end walls of the cells.
Q3 water and mineral ions
Q4 Water escapes from the leaves by evaporation and diffusion through the stomata. This creates a slight shortage of water in the leaves, which causes more water to be drawn up the xylem and into the leaves. This in turn causes more water to be drawn up the xylem from the roots.
Remember, the transpiration stream only goes on in the xylem — it doesn't involve the phloem.
Q5 Root hair cells have projections ("hairs") that give the roots a large surface area for absorbing water and mineral ions from the soil.

6. Transpiration and Stomata
Page 160 — Fact Recall Questions
Q1 The transpiration rate increases.
Q2 The uptake of water by a plant.
Q3 a) guard cells
b) When the plant is short of water, the guard cells lose water and become flaccid, making the stomata close.

Page 160 — Application Question
Q1 a) i) 26 mm $\div$ 30 min = 0.866... = **0.87 mm min^{-1}**
ii) 31 mm $\div$ 30 min = 1.03... = **1.0 mm min^{-1}**
b) E.g. A higher temperature means that more water is lost from the surface of the leaves by transpiration / the rate of transpiration is higher. This causes the plant to take up more water, so the bubble moves more.

Pages 163-164 — Plant Structures and Their Functions Exam-style Questions
1 a) chloroplasts *(1 mark)*
b) carbon dioxide + water → glucose + oxygen *(1 mark)*
c) Light intensity B. At this light intensity, it took the shortest time for all of the discs to float *(1 mark)*. This suggests that photosynthesis was happening the fastest at light intensity B *(1 mark)*. The rate of photosynthesis increases with increasing light intensity *(1 mark)*.

d) No. Increasing the light intensity will increase the rate of photosynthesis up to a certain point *(1 mark)*. However, past this point increasing the light intensity will not increase the rate of photosynthesis *(1 mark)* as another factor (such as carbon dioxide concentration or temperature) will start to limit the rate *(1 mark)*.
e) You would expect it to take more than 11 minutes, because the carbon dioxide concentration will be lower *(1 mark)* so the rate of photosynthesis will be slower/will be limited to a lower level than in the first experiment *(1 mark)*.
With so little carbon dioxide present in the second experiment, you would expect carbon dioxide concentration to be the limiting factor rather than light intensity.
2 a) phloem *(1 mark)*
b) Xylem tubes are made up of dead cells joined end to end *(1 mark)*. They have no cell walls in between them *(1 mark)*. Xylem tubes are also strengthened by lignin *(1 mark)*.
c) Root hair cell *(1 mark)*. This role of this cell is to absorb water and mineral ions from the soil *(1 mark)*.
3 a) 10 minutes = 10 × 60 = 600 seconds
Rate of transpiration = 0.84 ÷ 600
= **0.0014 cm^3 s^{-1}**
(2 marks for correct answer, otherwise 1 mark for correctly converting 10 minutes to 600 seconds.)
b) i) To open and close the stomata *(1 mark)*.
ii) They would lose water and become flaccid *(1 mark)*. In the dark, the stomata don't need to be open to allow carbon dioxide into the leaf for photosynthesis *(1 mark)*, so they close to reduce water loss *(1 mark)*. In order to close the stomata, the guard cells must become flaccid *(1 mark)*.

Topic 7 — Animal Coordination, Control and Homeostasis

Topic 7a — Hormones and Fertility

1. Hormones
Page 167 — Fact Recall Questions
Q1 By the blood (plasma).
Q2 false
A particular hormone will only affect certain organs, called target organs.
Q3 endocrine glands
Q4 E.g. testosterone
Q5 nerves

2. Adrenaline and Thyroxine

Page 169 — Fact Recall Questions
Q1 the adrenal glands
Q2 E.g. it helps to regulate (basal) metabolic rate.

Page 169 — Application Question
Q1 a) adrenaline
   b) It increases blood flow to the muscles, so the cells receive more oxygen and glucose for increased respiration. This gives the muscles the extra energy they need for increased contraction. This will allow Pierre to 'fight' or to run away if necessary.

3. The Menstrual Cycle

Page 172 — Fact Recall Questions
Q1 The lining of the uterus breaks down and is released from the body.
Q2 Oestrogen and progesterone.
Q3 It causes the follicles to mature.
Q4 It stimulates the release of an egg/ovulation at around the middle (day 14) of the menstrual cycle. / It stimulates the remains of the ruptured follicle to develop into a corpus luteum.
Q5 progesterone
Q6 The pituitary gland and the ovaries.

Page 173 — Application Question
Q1 a) LH (luteinising hormone). LH is the hormone responsible for stimulating the release of an egg. The concentration of the hormone on the graph increases just before the middle of the cycle (day 14) — the time at which an egg is normally released.
   b) the pituitary gland
   c) LH is needed to stimulate the release of an egg. This woman's LH level peaks at a much lower level than the other woman's, suggesting that she may not be releasing an egg during her menstrual cycle. This could be the reason why she's struggling to have children.

4. Controlling Fertility

Page 175 — Fact Recall Questions
Q1 To stimulate the production of multiple eggs (so that more than one egg can be collected).
Q2 It inhibits FSH production, and so prevents egg maturation and therefore release.
Q3 Barrier methods are designed to put a barrier between the sperm and egg so they don't meet.

Page 177 — Hormones and Fertility Exam-style Questions
1 a) i) E.g. hormonal contraceptives are more effective than barrier contraceptives. / If using hormonal contraceptives correctly, a couple doesn't need to think about contraceptives each time they have intercourse, unlike with barrier methods of contraception *(1 mark)*.
      ii) E.g. hormonal contraceptives don't protect against sexually transmitted infections (STIs) whereas some barrier methods/condoms do protect against STIs *(1 mark)*.
   b) E.g. progesterone stimulates the production of thick cervical mucus which prevents sperm getting through the cervix and reaching the egg. / Progesterone can inhibit egg maturation and therefore the release of an egg *(1 mark)*.
   c) i) E.g. clomifene therapy *(1 mark)*
      ii) The drug clomifene causes more FSH and LH to be released by the body *(1 mark)*. This stimulates egg maturation and ovulation *(1 mark)*. By knowing when the woman will be ovulating, a couple can have intercourse during this time to improve the chance of becoming pregnant *(1 mark)*.
   d) progesterone *(1 mark)*
2 a) C *(1 mark)*
   b) When the level of thyroxine in the blood is lower than normal, the hypothalamus is stimulated to release thyrotropin releasing hormone/TRH *(1 mark)*. TRH stimulates the secretion of thyroid stimulating hormone/TSH from the pituitary gland *(1 mark)*. TSH stimulates the thyroid gland to release thyroxine, so the level of thyroxine in the blood rises back to normal *(1 mark)*.
   c) 1 day = 24 hours
      1860 ÷ 24 = 77.5
      77.5 × 6 = **465 kcal**
      (2 marks for correct answer, otherwise 1 mark for correct working.)

Topic 7b — Homeostasis

1. Homeostasis

Page 178 — Fact Recall Questions
Q1 Homeostasis is the regulation of the conditions inside your body (and cells) to maintain a constant internal environment, in response to changes in both internal and external conditions.
Q2 Any two from: e.g. temperature / blood glucose content / water content of the body.

2. Controlling Blood Glucose

Page 183 — Fact Recall Questions
Q1 the pancreas
Q2 Insulin makes body cells take up more glucose from the blood.
Q3 the pancreas
Q4 It causes glycogen to be converted into glucose which then enters the blood.
Q5 A condition where the pancreas produces little or no insulin, which means blood glucose can rise to a dangerous level.
Q6 Any two from: e.g. eating a healthy diet / exercising regularly / losing weight if necessary / medication/insulin injections if necessary.

Page 183 — Application Question
Q1 a) Glucagon, because the subject's blood glucose level rises following the injection. Glucagon causes glycogen to be converted back into glucose, which enters the blood, causing the blood glucose level to rise.
   b) i) insulin
      ii) The blood glucose level would fall following the injection, as insulin causes body cells to take up more glucose from the blood, causing the blood glucose level to fall.

Page 185 — Homeostasis
Exam-style Questions
1 a) B *(1 mark)*
   b) insulin *(1 mark)*
   c) People with type 1 diabetes produce little or no insulin *(1 mark)*. Injecting insulin stops their blood glucose level from rising to a dangerous level *(1 mark)* as insulin causes the body's cells to take up glucose from the blood *(1 mark)*.
   d) E.g. because homeostasis is the regulation of conditions inside the body to maintain a constant internal environment *(1 mark)* and in people with diabetes, the blood sugar level (an internal condition) cannot be properly regulated / cannot be kept constant *(1 mark)*.
2 a) E.g. more adults with type 2 diabetes are overweight or obese than are a healthy weight or underweight *(1 mark)*. A higher percentage of adults with type 2 diabetes in the 16-54 age group are obese than in the 55 and over age group *(1 mark)*.
   b) BMI = weight ÷ (height)^2
      BMI = 80 kg ÷ (1.89 m)^2 = 22.395...
      = **22.4 kg m^{-2}** (3 s.f.)
      (2 marks for the correct answer, otherwise 1 mark for the correct BMI equation)

Topic 8 — Exchange and Transport in Animals

1. Exchange of Materials

Page 188 — Application Question
Q1 a) Cell A:
      SA = 2 × (0.2 × 0.4) + 2 × (1 × 0.4) + 2 × (1 × 0.2)
      = 0.16 + 0.8 + 0.4 = 1.36 µm^2
      V = 1 × 0.4 × 0.2 = 0.08 µm^3
      SA : V = 1.36 : 0.08
              1.36 ÷ 0.08 = 17, 0.08 ÷ 0.08 = 1
      so ratio is **17 : 1**
      Cell B:
      SA = 2 × (0.5 × 0.5) + 4 × (2 × 0.5) = 0.5 + 4
      = 4.5 µm^2
      V = 2 × 0.5 × 0.5 = 0.5 µm^3
      SA : V = 4.5 : 0.5
              4.5 ÷ 0.5 = 9, 0.5 ÷ 0.5 = 1
      so ratio is **9 : 1**
   b) Cell A, because it has the largest surface area to volume ratio.

2. The Alveoli

Page 190 — Fact Recall Questions
Q1 alveoli
Q2 B. The concentration of oxygen is higher in the air in the alveoli than in the blood in the capillaries. Diffusion takes place from an area of higher concentration to an area of lower concentration.
Q3 Any three from: a large surface area / a moist lining for dissolving gases / very thin walls / a good blood supply to maintain the concentration gradients of oxygen and carbon dioxide.

Page 190 — Application Question
Q1 The destruction of the alveolar walls will reduce the surface area of the alveoli in the lungs. This will result in a decrease in gas exchange.

3. Circulatory System — The Blood

Page 192 — Fact Recall Questions
Q1 a) haemoglobin
   b) It carries oxygen.
Q2 To defend against microorganisms that cause disease.
Q3 To help blood to clot at a wound to prevent excessive blood loss and entrance of microorganisms.
Q4 plasma

4. Circulatory System — The Blood Vessels

Page 194 — Fact Recall Question
Q1 capillaries

Page 194 — Application Question

Q1 A. Arteries carry blood at a higher pressure than veins and their walls are more muscular as a result. Blood vessel A carries blood at a higher pressure than blood vessel B, and so is more likely to be an artery and have more muscle in its walls.

5. Circulatory System — The Heart

Page 198 — Fact Recall Questions

Q1 One circuit pumps deoxygenated blood from the heart to the lungs, and then oxygenated blood from the lungs back to the heart. The other circuit pumps oxygenated blood from the heart to the rest of the body, and then deoxygenated blood from the rest of the body back to the heart.

Q2 right atrium, right ventricle, left atrium, left ventricle

Q3 a) vena cava and pulmonary vein
b) pulmonary artery and aorta

Page 198 — Application Questions

Q1 vena cava
Q2 $6.46 \text{ dm}^3 \text{ min}^{-1} = 6460 \text{ cm}^3 \text{ min}^{-1}$
stroke volume = cardiac output ÷ heart rate
$= 6460 \text{ cm}^3 \text{ min}^{-1} ÷ 85 \text{ bpm}$
= 76 cm³

To convert dm^3 into cm^3, you multiply by 1000.

6. Respiration

Page 201 — Fact Recall Questions

Q1 E.g. mammals use energy for building larger molecules from smaller ones, to contract muscles and to keep warm.
Q2 Respiration using oxygen. / The process of transferring energy from glucose using oxygen.
Q3 It transfers energy to the environment.
Q4 The body uses anaerobic respiration when it can't get enough oxygen to the muscles for aerobic respiration, e.g. during vigorous exercise.
Q5 glucose → lactic acid

Page 201 — Application Questions

Q1 a) oxygen
b) water
Q2 The limited availability of oxygen in the soil means that the root cells of rice plants will have to respire anaerobically. Anaerobic respiration in plants produces ethanol, so the concentration of ethanol will build up in the plant root cells. The root cells will need a high tolerance for ethanol so that they are not killed by it.

7. Investigating Respiration

Page 204 — Application Question

Q1 a) The cotton wool ensures that the maggots don't come into contact with the harmful soda lime granules.
b) To absorb the carbon dioxide produced by the maggots during respiration and stop it from affecting the results of the experiment.

c) A. The maggots will be taking in oxygen during respiration, which decreases the volume of air in their test tube. This reduces the pressure in their test tube, which causes the coloured fluid to move towards it.
d) The further the liquid moves, the more oxygen has been taken up by the maggots, and so the higher the rate of respiration. Since the liquid moved further at 20 °C, it suggests that an increase in temperature increases the rate of respiration.

Pages 207-208 — Exchange and Transport in Animals Exam-style Questions

1 a) A — vena cava *(1 mark)*, B — right ventricle *(1 mark)*, C — left atrium *(1 mark)*.
b) Structure D/the left ventricle has a thicker wall because it needs to pump blood around the whole body at a high pressure *(1 mark)*, whereas structure B/the right ventricle only has to pump blood to the lungs *(1 mark)*.
c) X, because veins have thinner walls than arteries *(1 mark)*.

2 a) Patient A, because the number of white blood cells in their blood is below the normal range / lower than the number of white blood cells in Patient B's blood *(1 mark)*. White blood cells help to defend the body against microorganisms that cause disease, so with fewer white blood cells in their blood, Patient A is more likely to get an infection *(1 mark)*.
b) Red blood cells *(1 mark)*. They have a biconcave shape to give them a large surface area for absorbing oxygen *(1 mark)*. They contain a red pigment called haemoglobin, which carries the oxygen *(1 mark)*. They don't have a nucleus, allowing for more room for haemoglobin, meaning that they can carry more oxygen *(1 mark)*.

3 a) surface area:
$0.6 \times 0.6 = 0.36$
$3.0 \times 0.6 = 1.8$
$(2 \times 0.36) + (4 \times 1.8) = 7.92 \text{ μm}^2$
volume:
$0.6 \times 0.6 \times 3.0 = 1.08 \text{ μm}^3$
ratio:
$7.92 ÷ 1.08 = 7.3333... = 7$
so the ratio is **7 : 1** *(3 marks for correct answer, otherwise 1 mark for correct surface area and 1 mark for correct volume.)*
b) Because it is a single-celled organism *(1 mark)*, so it has a large surface area to volume ratio *(1 mark)*. This means it can exchange enough substances across its cell membrane/outer surface to meet its needs *(1 mark)*.

4 a) glucose + oxygen → carbon dioxide + water *(1 mark for glucose and oxygen on the left-hand side of the equation, 1 mark for carbon dioxide and water on the right.)*

b) Anaerobic respiration forms less ATP than aerobic respiration, which shows that it transfers less energy *(1 mark)*. This is because glucose is not completely broken down in anaerobic respiration *(1 mark)*.

Topic 9 — Ecosystems and Material Cycles

Topic 9a — Ecosystems and Biodiversity

1. Ecosystems and Interactions Between Organisms

Page 211 — Fact Recall Questions
Q1 A population is a group containing only one species, whereas a community is a group containing different species.
Q2 an individual organism

Page 211 — Application Questions
Q1 D
Q2 A mutualistic relationship because both organisms benefit from it. The crabs are camouflaged by the algae, so they are less likely to be spotted by predators and eaten, and the algae get a place to live.

2. Abiotic and Biotic Factors

Page 213 — Fact Recall Questions
Q1 Any three from, e.g. temperature, light intensity, water availability, pollution.
Q2 E.g. competition, predation.

Page 213 — Application Question
Q1 a) i) It decreased.
    ii) an abiotic factor
    Remember, it's the oxygen concentration that changed, and oxygen isn't alive — making it an abiotic factor.
  b) The population size of the herons is likely to have decreased because there were fewer fish to eat.
    Here the environmental change was caused by a biotic factor — the availability of food.

3. Investigating Ecosystems

Page 217 — Fact Recall Questions
Q1 E.g. you would place the quadrat on the ground at a random position in the first sample area and count the number of the organisms within the quadrat. You would then repeat this many times. Next you would repeat this whole process in the second sample area. Finally you would work out the mean number of organisms per quadrat or the population size in each sample area and compare the results.

Q2 You would mark out a line across the area you want to study using a tape measure. You would then place quadrats next to each other/at regular intervals along the line. Next you would collect data by counting all of the organisms of the species you're interested in each quadrat/estimating the percentage cover. Finally, you would repeat the process and find the mean number of organisms (or mean percentage cover) for each quadrat.

Page 217 — Application Questions
Q1 a) $1 + 5 + 5 + 20 + 43 + 37 = 111$
       $111 \div 6 = \mathbf{18.5}$
    Remember the mean is the average you get by adding together all the values in the data and dividing it by the number of values that you have.
  b) End B, as the amount of bulrushes is lower here and you would expect there to be fewer bulrushes further away from the pond as they prefer moist soil or shallow water.
Q2 First calculate how many of the quadrats used by the conservationists would fit in 1 m²: $1 \div 0.25 = 4$
   Then work out how many slugs there would be in 1 m²: $4 \times 2.5 = 10$
   Finally, work out how many slugs there would be in 2000 m²: $10 \times 2000 = \mathbf{20\,000\ slugs\ in\ the\ area}$

4. Human Impacts on Biodiversity

Page 220 — Application Questions
Q1 a) Reforestation could increase biodiversity in Scotland, by increasing the number and variety of tree species. This, in turn, could increase the number and variety of animal species by providing them with food and shelter.
  b) E.g. it could increase ecotourism, bringing money into the country. It could provide new jobs through reforestation schemes/tourism.
Q2 E.g. the lower biodiversity could be because excess fertilisers are running off the fields into the water, causing eutrophication. Eutrophication is an excess of nutrients in the water, which causes increased algal growth followed by the death of other organisms in the water (such as plants and fish) due to lack of oxygen.

Pages 222-223 — Ecosystems and Biodiversity Exam-style Questions

1. a) 55 + 41 + 57 = 153
   153 ÷ 3 = **51**
   (2 marks for correct answer, otherwise 1 mark for correct working.)
   b) The number of limpets increases as you move away from the water's edge, and then begins to decrease after the position of quadrat 3 *(1 mark)*. The low number of limpets in quadrats closest to the water's edge could be due to competition for space from other organisms *(1 mark)*. The decrease in the number of limpets after quadrat 3 could be due to there being less water available further from the water's edge, which increases the limpets' chance of drying out *(1 mark)*.
   c) To make sure their samples were representative of the whole shore line *(1 mark)* and therefore to increase the validity of their results *(1 mark)*.
2. a) E.g. they could carry parasites which could infect wild salmon, making them ill/killing them. / They could out-compete the wild salmon for resources such as food. *(1 mark)*
   b) E.g. the food/waste from the farm could leak into the surrounding water, causing eutrophication, which could result in the death of aquatic organisms. / Wild predators could be attracted to the nets, become trapped and die. *(1 mark)*
3. a) It is decreasing *(1 mark)*.
   b) The outbreak of rabies is responsible for the trend *(1 mark)*. In the years when there were rabies outbreaks the population size fell *(1 mark)*. For example, the numbers fell from 401 to 327 in 2008 / 341 to 265 in 2011 when there was a rabies outbreak *(1 mark)*.

   There's a lot of data to look at in the table so think carefully about what you're looking for. The numbers of prey don't really change much throughout the study so that's unlikely to have caused the change in the number of wolves, so it's sensible to look at the outbreaks of rabies.

   c) It has made the wolf population move to higher ground *(1 mark)* from an average height of 3.4 km above sea level in 2007 to an average height of 4 km above sea level in 2012 *(1 mark)*.

Topic 9b — Material Cycles

1. The Carbon Cycle

Page 225 — Fact Recall Questions
Q1 CO_2 is removed from the atmosphere by green plants and algae during photosynthesis, and the carbon is used to make glucose. The glucose can be turned into carbohydrates, fats and proteins that make up the bodies of the plants and algae.
Q2 By animals eating plants or other animals.
Q3 E.g. dead leaves are fed on by decomposers. These organisms release CO_2 when they respire.

Page 225 — Application Question
Q1 The carbon in the marine organisms' shells is in a biotic part of the marine ecosystem. When these shells eventually form limestone rocks, it becomes an abiotic component of the ecosystem. The carbon moves to another abiotic component of the ecosystem when it is released into the air.

2. The Water Cycle

Page 228 — Fact Recall Questions
Q1 It cools and condenses.
Q2 E.g. rain, snow, hail.
Q3 Water that is suitable for drinking.
Q4 Not having enough precipitation / a shortage of fresh water.

Page 228 — Application Questions
Q1 Yes. Water evaporates from plants in transpiration and cools and condenses to form clouds as it gets higher up. Water falls from the clouds as precipitation onto land. Some of this water then drains into the sea.
Q2 a) E.g. because they have very little rainfall/droughts during the summer months, which will limit the amount of potable water available. There will be added pressure on potable water supplies due to the large numbers of tourists visiting the islands. Desalination plants will remove the salt from sea water (which the islands have easy access to) making it suitable for drinking. This will help the islands to produce enough potable water for everyone.
   b) E.g. the solar panels will capture energy from the Sun and use it to heat the sea water. This is part of the thermal distillation process — heat causes the water to evaporate, leaving the salt behind. The pure water can then be condensed and collected for drinking.

3. The Nitrogen Cycle

Page 230 — Fact Recall Questions
Q1 a) Nitrifying bacteria turn ammonia in decaying matter into nitrites or nitrites into nitrates, which can be taken up by plants from the soil.
   b) Decomposers break down dead organisms and waste matter to produce ammonia, which nitrifying bacteria then act upon.
Q2 denitrifying bacteria

Page 230 — Application Question
Q1 E.g. she could grow a different crop in each vegetable bed each year, in a cycle that includes a nitrogen-fixing crop (e.g. peas or beans) in one of the years. The nitrogen-fixing crop will help to put nitrates back into the soil for the next crop to use the following year. This will help the crops to grow better and should help to increase the yield of vegetables.

Page 232 — Material Cycles
Exam-Style Questions
1   a) B *(1 mark)*
    It's easy to get the different types of bacteria in the nitrogen cycle mixed up — make sure you learn what each type does.
    b) It is a mutualistic relationship (from which both organisms benefit) *(1 mark)*. The bacteria provide the plants with nitrates and obtain sugars in return *(1 mark)*.
2   How to grade your answer:
    Level 0: There is no relevant information. *(No marks)*
    Level 1: There is a brief description of one or two steps in the carbon cycle. The points made are basic and not linked together. *(1 to 2 marks)*
    Level 2: There is a description of three or four steps in the carbon cycle. Some of the points made are linked together. *(3 to 4 marks)*
    Level 3: There is a detailed description of five or six steps in the carbon cycle with named processes. The points made are well-linked and the answer has a clear and logical structure. *(5 to 6 marks)*
    Here are some points your answer may include:
    The grass absorbs carbon dioxide from the air in photosynthesis.
    The grass uses this carbon to make glucose/carbohydrates/fats/proteins.
    This carbon is passed onto the cows when the cows eat the grass, and onto humans when the humans eat the cows, so it moves through the food chain.
    Dead organisms/waste materials are broken down/decayed by decomposers/microorganisms.
    All the organisms/the grass/cows/humans/microorganisms respire and release carbon dioxide into the atmosphere.
    Some decayed organisms go on to eventually form fossil fuels.
    Combustion/burning of fossil fuels also releases carbon dioxide into the air.

3   a) The removal of salts/mineral ions from salt water *(1 mark)*.
    b) i) In reverse osmosis, the water molecules are forced to move from an area of lower water concentration / higher salt concentration to an area of higher water concentration / lower salt concentration *(1 mark)* across a partially permeable membrane. The membrane prevents the movement of the dissolved salts, so pure water is produced *(1 mark)*.
       ii) Energy from the Sun makes water evaporate from the sea, turning it into water vapour *(1 mark)*. The water vapour is carried upwards, until it cools and condenses to form clouds *(1 mark)*. Fresh water then falls to Earth as precipitation/rain *(1 mark)*.

Glossary

A

Abiotic factor
A non-living factor of the environment.

Accurate result
A result that is very close to the true answer.

Acquired characteristic
A characteristic that an organism gets during its lifetime due to environmental effects.

Acrosome
A subcellular structure in the head of a sperm cell, which stores enzymes needed by the sperm to digest through the egg cell membrane.

Active site
The part of an enzyme where a substrate molecule binds.

Active transport
The movement of particles against a concentration gradient (i.e. from an area of lower concentration to an area of higher concentration) using energy transferred during respiration.

Adrenal gland
A gland that produces the hormone adrenaline.

Adrenaline
A hormone secreted by the adrenal glands that is released in response to stressful situations in order to prepare the body for 'fight or flight'.

Aerobic respiration
The reactions involved in breaking down glucose using oxygen, to transfer energy.

Allele
An alternative version of a gene.

Alveolus
A tiny air sac in the lungs, where gas exchange occurs.

Amylase
The enzyme amylase catalyses the breakdown of starch to maltose.

Anaerobic respiration
The incomplete breakdown of glucose, which takes place in the absence of oxygen.

Anomalous result
A result that doesn't seem to fit with the rest of the data.

Antibiotic
A drug used to kill or prevent the growth of bacteria inside of the body.

Antibiotic resistance
When bacteria aren't killed by an antibiotic.

Antibody
A protein produced by white blood cells in response to the presence of an antigen (e.g. on the surface of a pathogen).

Anticoagulant
A drug taken to reduce likelihood of blood clot formation.

Antigen
A molecule (often found on the surface of a cell) that triggers an immune response.

Antihypertensive
A drug taken to lower blood pressure.

Aorta
A blood vessel (artery) which transports blood from the heart to the rest of the body (excluding the lungs).

Artery
A blood vessel that carries blood away from the heart.

Asexual reproduction
Where organisms reproduce by mitosis to produce genetically identical offspring.

Atrium
A chamber of the heart into which blood enters from either the pulmonary vein or the vena cava.

Axon
An extension of a neurone, which carries nervous impulses away from the cell body.

B

Bacterium
A single-celled microorganism without a 'true' nucleus. Some bacteria are able to cause disease.

Belt transect
A transect along which quadrats are placed.

Bias
Prejudice towards or against something.

Biodiversity
The variety of different species of organisms on Earth or within an ecosystem.

Biological catalyst
A substance that increases the speed of a chemical reaction both inside and outside living cells.

Biomass
The mass of living material.

Biotic factor
A living factor of the environment.

Blind trial
A clinical trial where the patients don't know whether they have received the drug or the placebo.

Blood
A tissue which transports substances around the body in the circulatory system.

B-lymphocyte
A type of white blood cell involved in the specific immune response that produces antibodies.

C

Cancer
A disease caused by a mass of abnormal cells, which divide uncontrollably and invade and destroy surrounding tissue.

Capillary
A type of blood vessel involved in the exchange of materials at tissues.

Carbohydrase
A type of enzyme that converts carbohydrates into simple sugars.

Carbohydrate
A large biological molecule made up of long chains of sugar molecules.

Cardiac output
The total volume of blood pumped by a ventricle every minute.

Cardiovascular disease
Disease of the heart or blood vessels.

Carrier
A person who carries the allele for an inherited disorder, but who doesn't have any symptoms of the disorder.

Catalyst
A substance which increases the speed of a reaction, without being changed or used up in the reaction.

Categoric data
Data that comes in distinct categories (e.g. sex — male and female, etc.).

Causation
When a change in one variable causes a change in another.

Cell cycle
The process that all body cells from multicellular organisms use to grow and divide.

Cell differentiation
The process by which a cell becomes specialised for its job.

Cell elongation
The process by which a plant cell expands, so that the plant grows.

Cell membrane
A membrane surrounding a cell, which holds it all together and controls what goes in and out.

Cell wall
A structure surrounding some cell types, which gives strength and support.

Central Nervous System (CNS)
The brain and spinal cord. It's where reflexes and actions are coordinated.

Chlorophyll
A green substance found in chloroplasts which absorbs light for photosynthesis.

Chloroplast
A structure found in plant cells and algae, which contains chlorophyll. Chloroplasts are the site of photosynthesis.

Chromosome
A long, coiled-up molecule of DNA, which carries genes.

Ciliated epithelial cell
A cell lining the surface of an organ that has cilia (tiny hair-like structures used to move substances along) covering its upper surface.

Circulatory system
A system which uses blood to transport materials around the body.

Clinical trial
A set of drug tests on human volunteers.

Communicable disease
A disease that can spread between individuals.

Community
All the organisms of different species living in a habitat.

Competition (in ecosystems)
When organisms strive against other organisms to win resources such as food, water, mates, etc.

Complementary base pairing
Hydrogen bonding between specific pairs of bases on opposite DNA (or DNA and RNA) strands.

Concentration gradient
The gradual change in the concentration of a substance from one area to another. Diffusion occurs down a concentration gradient.

Condensation
The process by which a gas turns into a liquid.

Continuous data
Numerical data that can have any value within a range (e.g. length, volume or temperature).

Contraceptive
A method of preventing pregnancy that can be hormonal or non-hormonal.

Control experiment
An experiment that's kept under the same conditions as the rest of the investigation, but doesn't have anything done to it.

Control group
A group that matches the one being studied, but the independent variable isn't altered. It's kept under the same conditions as the group in the experiment.

Control variable
A variable in an experiment that is kept the same.

Coronary bypass surgery
Surgery that takes a healthy piece of blood vessel and uses it to bypass a blocked coronary artery (an artery supplying the heart).

Corpus luteum
A structure developed from the remainder of a ruptured follicle following the release of an egg during ovulation. It produces progesterone.

Correlation
A relationship between two variables.

Crop rotation
A method of growing different crops in the same area each year in a cycle to prevent the soil from being depleted of nutrients.

Cytokinesis
The process by which the cell membrane and cytoplasm divide to form two separate cells.

Cytoplasm
A gel-like substance in a cell where most of the chemical reactions take place.

D

Decomposer
An organism (e.g. a microorganism such as a bacterium or a fungus) that breaks down dead organisms and organic matter.

Decomposition
The breakdown of dead organisms and organic matter.

Denatured (enzymes)
The point at which an enzyme no longer functions as a catalyst due to the altered shape of its active site.

Dendron
An extension of a neurone, which carries nervous impulses towards the cell body.

Denitrifying bacterium
A bacterium that turns nitrates (nitrogen-containing ions) in the soil into nitrogen gas.

Dependent variable
The variable in an experiment that is measured.

Desalination
The removal of salts (mineral ions) from salt water.

Diffusion
The spreading out of particles from an area of higher concentration to an area of lower concentration.

Diploid
When a cell contains two copies of each chromosome (one from each parent).

Discrete data
Numerical data that can only take certain values with no in-between value (e.g. number of people).

DNA (deoxyribonucleic acid)
The molecule in cells that stores genetic information.

Dominant allele
The allele for the characteristic that's shown by an organism if two different alleles are present for that characteristic.

Double-blind trial
A clinical trial where neither the doctors nor the patients know who has received the drug and who has received the placebo until all the results have been gathered.

Drought
A lack of fresh water in an area due to a lack of precipitation (i.e. not enough rain).

E

Ecosystem
A community of living organisms with the abiotic parts of their environment.

Effector
Either a muscle or gland which responds to nervous impulses.

Egg cell
A gamete (reproductive cell) that carries the female DNA for sexual reproduction.

Endocrine gland
A gland that secretes hormones into the bloodstream.

Endothermic reaction
A reaction where energy is taken in from the environment.

Environmental gradient
A gradual change in an abiotic factor (e.g. light intensity) across a habitat.

Environmental variation
The differences between individuals of the same species caused by environmental factors.

Enzyme
A large protein that acts as a biological catalyst.

Erythrocyte
Another name for a red blood cell.

Eukaryotic cell
A complex cell containing a nucleus, such as a plant or animal cell.

Eutrophication
An excess of nutrients in water, which leads to increased algal growth, oxygen depletion and the eventual death of organisms living in the water.

Evaporation
The process by which a liquid turns into a gas.

Evolution
The changing of the inherited characteristics of a population over time.

Exchange surface
A specialised surface in an organism used for the exchange of materials, e.g. gases and dissolved substances.

Exothermic reaction
A reaction which transfers energy to the environment (usually via heat).

F

Fair test
A controlled experiment where the only thing that changes is the independent variable.

Family pedigree
A diagram which shows how a characteristic (or disorder) is inherited in a group of related people.

Fertilisation
The fusion of male and female gametes during sexual reproduction.

Fertiliser
A substance added to soil to increase the soil's nutrient content.

Flagellum
A long-hair like structure present on some bacterial cells, which rotates to make the cell move.

Follicle (ovaries)
An egg and its surrounding cells.

Follicle-stimulating hormone (FSH)
A hormone produced by the pituitary gland involved in the menstrual cycle. It causes eggs to mature in the ovaries.

Fungus
A type of eukaryotic organism that includes mushrooms, yeasts and mould. Some fungi are able to cause disease.

G

Gamete
A sex cell, e.g. an egg cell or a sperm cell in animals.

Gene
A short section of DNA, which contains the instructions needed to make a specific protein (and so controls the development of a characteristic).

Gene pool
The number of different alleles in a population.

Genetically modified (GM) organism
An organism which has had its genome altered through genetic engineering.

Genetic engineering
The process of transferring a useful gene from one organism's genome to another organism's genome.

Genetic variation
The differences between individuals of the same species caused by differences in their genes.

Genome
All of the genetic material in an organism.

Genotype
What alleles you have, e.g. Tt.

Glucagon
A hormone produced and secreted by the pancreas when the blood glucose level is too low. It causes glycogen to be converted back into glucose, increasing the blood glucose level.

Glycogen
A molecule that acts as a store of glucose in liver and muscle cells.

Guard cell
A cell found on either side of a stoma, which controls the stoma's size.

H

Habitat
The place where an organism lives.

Haemoglobin
A red pigment found in red blood cells which carries oxygen.

Haploid
Containing half the number of chromosomes that's in a normal body cell.

Hazard
Something that has the potential to cause harm (e.g. fire, electricity, etc.).

Health
A state of complete physical, mental and social well-being and not merely the absence of disease or infirmity.

Heart rate
The number of times a heart beats per minute.

Heterozygous
Where an organism has two alleles for a particular gene that are different.

Homeostasis
The regulation of conditions inside your body (and cells) to maintain a constant internal environment, in response to changes in both internal and external conditions.

Hominid
A member of the classification family containing humans and their ancestors.

Homozygous
Where an organism has two alleles for a particular gene that are the same.

Hormone
A chemical messenger which travels in the blood to activate target cells.

Hypothesis
A possible explanation for a scientific observation.

I

Immune system
The structures and processes that protect the body against disease.

Immunisation
The process of giving a patient immunity to a certain pathogen through the injection of a small amount of the dead or inactive pathogen.

Immunity
The ability of the white blood cells to respond quickly to a pathogen.

Inbreeding
When closely related animals or plants are bred together.

Independent variable
The variable in an experiment that is changed.

Insulin
A hormone produced and secreted by the pancreas when the blood glucose level is too high. It causes the body's cells to take up more glucose from the blood, reducing the blood glucose level.

Interdependence
The dependence of organisms on each other in order to survive and reproduce.

Interphase
The stage in the cell cycle when the cell grows, the amount of subcellular structures increases and the DNA is copied.

L

Lactic acid
The product of anaerobic respiration that builds up in muscle cells.

Ligase
An enzyme that joins pieces of DNA together.

Limiting factor
A factor which prevents a reaction from going any faster.

Lipase
A type of enzyme that catalyses the conversion of lipids into glycerol and fatty acids.

Lipid
A large biological molecule made up of fatty acids and glycerol.

Luteinising hormone (LH)
A hormone produced by the pituitary gland, which stimulates egg release (ovulation).

Lymphocyte
A type of white blood cell which can produce antibodies or antitoxins against microorganisms.

M

Magnification
How much bigger an image is than the real object that you're looking at.

Malnutrition
A condition where a person doesn't have the right balance of nutrients to stay healthy.

Mean (average)
A measure of average found by adding up all the data and dividing by the number of values there are.

Median (average)
The middle value in a set of data when the values are in order of size.

Meiosis
A type of cell division where a cell divides twice to produce four genetically different haploid gametes. It occurs in the reproductive organs.

Memory lymphocyte
A type of white blood cell that remains in the body for a long time and has the ability to 'remember' and recognise a specific antigen.

Menstrual cycle
The monthly sequence of events in which the female body releases an egg and prepares the uterus (womb) in case it receives a fertilised egg.

Menstruation
The bleeding that occurs during the first stage of the menstrual cycle as the uterus lining is shed.

Meristem tissue
Tissue found at the growing tips of plant shoots and roots, which is made up of cells that are able to differentiate.

Mitochondria
Structures in a cell which are the site of most of the reactions for aerobic respiration.

Mitosis
A type of cell division where a cell reproduces itself by splitting to form two genetically identical offspring.

Mode (average)
The most common value in a set of data.

Model
A representation of an object or system that is used to describe or display how that object or system behaves in reality.

Monohybrid cross
The study of the inheritance of one gene.

Motor neurone
A nerve cell that carries electrical impulses from the CNS to effectors.

Mutualism
A relationship between two organisms, from which both organisms benefit.

Myelin sheath
A fatty layer surrounding the axon of some neurones, which acts as an electrical insulator and speeds up nervous impulses.

N

Natural selection
The process by which species evolve.

Negative feedback
A mechanism that restores a level back to normal in a system.

Neurone
A nerve cell. Neurones transmit information around the body, including to and from the CNS.

Neurotransmitter
A chemical that transmits a nerve impulse across a synapse.

Nitrate
A nitrogen-containing ion with the formula NO_3^-.

Nitrifying bacterium
A bacterium that turns ammonia from decomposing matter into nitrites or nitrites into nitrates (nitrogen-containing ions).

Nitrogen-fixing bacterium
A bacterium that turns nitrogen gas in the air into nitrogen-containing ammonia.

Non-communicable disease
A disease that cannot spread between individuals.

Non-indigenous species
A species that does not naturally occur in an area.

Nucleus (of a cell)
A structure found in eukaryotic cells (e.g. animal and plant cells) which contains genetic material that controls the activities of the cell.

O

Obesity
A condition were a person is very overweight and has too much body fat.

Oestrogen
A hormone produced by the ovaries which is involved in the menstrual cycle.

Osmosis
The movement of water molecules across a partially permeable membrane from a region of higher water concentration to a region of lower water concentration.

Ovary
An organ in the female body which stores and releases eggs. It is also a gland and secretes the hormone oestrogen.

Ovulation
The release of an egg from an ovary.

P

Pancreas
An organ (and gland) in the mammalian digestive system. It produces insulin and glucagon to control blood sugar level.

Parasitism
A relationship between two organisms, where one organism (the parasite) takes what it needs to survive but the other organism (the host) doesn't benefit.

Partially permeable membrane
A membrane with tiny holes in it, which lets some molecules through it but not others.

Pathogen
An organism that causes disease, e.g. a bacterium, virus, protist or fungus.

Phagocyte
A type of white blood cell which engulfs foreign cells.

Phagocytosis
The process by which white blood cells engulf and digest foreign cells.

Phenotype
The characteristics you have, e.g. blue eyes.

Phloem
A type of plant tissue which transports dissolved sugars around the plant.

Photosynthesis
The process by which plants use light energy to convert carbon dioxide and water into glucose and oxygen.

Pituitary gland
A gland located in the brain that is responsible for secreting various hormones.

Placebo (in drug testing)
A substance that looks like the drug being tested but doesn't do anything.

Plasma
The liquid component of blood, which transports the contents of the blood around the body.

Plasmid
A small loop of DNA, present in some bacterial cells, which is not part of the main chromosome.

Platelet
A small fragment of a cell, which helps blood to clot at a wound.

Population
All the organisms of one species living in a habitat.

Potable water
Water that is suitable for drinking.

Precipitation
Any water that falls to the Earth from clouds, e.g. rain, snow or hail.

Preclinical trial
A set of drug tests on human cells, human tissues and live animals that occurs before clinical trials.

Predation
Where an organism (the predator) hunts and kills another organism (the prey) for food.

Prediction
A statement based on a hypothesis that can be tested.

Producer
An organism at the start of a food chain that makes its own food using energy from the Sun.

Progesterone
A hormone produced by the ovaries, which is involved in the menstrual cycle.

Prokaryotic cell
A small, simple cell, without a nucleus, e.g. a bacterium.

Protease
A type of enzyme that catalyses the conversion of proteins into amino acids.

Protein
A large biological molecule made up of long chains of amino acids.

Protist
A eukaryotic, single-celled organism. Some protists are able to cause disease.

Pulmonary artery
A blood vessel which transports deoxygenated blood from the heart to the lungs.

Pulmonary vein
A blood vessel which transports oxygenated blood from the lungs to the heart.

Q

Quadrat
A square frame enclosing a known area which can be used to study the distribution of organisms.

R

Random error
A difference in the results of an experiment caused by things like human error in measuring.

Range
The difference between the smallest and largest values in a set of data.

Reaction time
The time it takes to respond to a stimulus.

Recessive allele
An allele whose characteristic only appears in an organism if there are two copies present.

Red blood cell
A cell, which forms part of the blood, that transports oxygen around the body.

Reflex
A fast, automatic response to a stimulus.

Reflex arc
The passage of information in a reflex.

Reforestation
The replanting or regrowth of forests in areas where they have been removed.

Relay neurone
A nerve cell in the CNS that carries electrical impulses from sensory neurones to motor neurones.

Repeatable result
A result that will come out the same if the experiment is repeated by the same person using the same method and equipment.

Reproducible result
A result that will come out the same if someone different does the experiment, or a slightly different method or piece of equipment is used.

Resolution (instruments)
The smallest change a measuring instrument can detect.

Resolution (microscopes)
The ability to distinguish between two parts. A higher resolution gives a sharper image.

Respiration
An exothermic reaction which releases energy for metabolic processes and occurs continuously in every cell of living organisms.

Restriction enzyme
An enzyme that recognises specific DNA sequences and cuts the DNA at that point.

Ribosome
A structure in a cell, where proteins are made.

Risk
The chance that a hazard will cause harm.

Risk factor
Something that is linked to an increased likelihood that a person will develop a certain disease.

S

Sampling
Taking a number of organisms from a population to study.

Selection pressure
Something in an organism's environment that affects its chance of surviving and reproducing, e.g. competition, predation, disease.

Selective breeding
When humans artificially select the plants or animals that are going to breed so that the genes for particular characteristics remain in the population.

Sensory neurone
A nerve cell that carries electrical impulses from sensory receptors to the CNS.

Sensory receptor
A group of cells which are sensitive to a stimulus and initiate a response to that stimulus. E.g. light receptor cells in the eye are sensitive to light.

Sex chromosome (humans)
One of the 23rd pair of chromosomes, X and Y — together they determine whether an individual is male or female.

Sexually transmitted infection (STI)
An infection caused by a pathogen that is transmitted through sexual contact.

Sexual reproduction
Where two gametes combine at fertilisation to produce a genetically different new individual.

SI unit
A unit of measurement recognised as standard by scientists worldwide.

Specialised cell
A cell which performs a specific function.

Sperm cell
A gamete (reproductive cell) that carries the male DNA for sexual reproduction.

Statins
A group of drugs that can reduce the amount of 'bad' cholesterol in the bloodstream to help slow the rate of fatty deposits forming in blood vessels.

Stem cell
An undifferentiated cell which has the ability to become one of many different types of cell or more stem cells.

Stent
A wire mesh tube that's inserted inside an artery to help keep it open.

Sticky end
A section of unpaired bases at the end of a DNA molecule, which allows two pieces of DNA to be joined together.

Stimulus
A change in the environment.

Stoma
A tiny hole in the surface of a leaf.

Stratigraphy
The study of rock layers.

Stroke volume
The volume of blood pumped by one ventricle each time it contracts.

Subcellular structure
A part of a cell, e.g. the nucleus, a chloroplast.

Synapse
The connection between two neurones.

Systematic error
An error that is consistently made every time throughout an experiment.

T

Target organ
A particular organ on which a hormone acts.

Testis
A gland in the male body which secretes the hormone testosterone.

Testosterone
The main male reproductive hormone, produced by the testes.

Theory
A hypothesis which has been accepted by the scientific community because there is good evidence to back it up.

Thyroid gland
A gland which produces the hormone thyroxine.

Thyroxine
A hormone secreted by the thyroid gland that controls metabolic rate.

Transect
A line which can be used to study the distribution of organisms along an environmental gradient.

Translocation
The movement of food substances (i.e. dissolved sugars) around a plant.

Transpiration stream
The movement of water from a plant's roots, up through the xylem and out of the leaves.

Trial run
A quick version of an experiment that can be used to work out the range of variables and the interval between the variables that will be used in the proper experiment.

Tumour
A growth of abnormal cells.

Type 1 diabetes
A condition where the pancreas produces little or no insulin, which means blood glucose can rise to a dangerous level.

Type 2 diabetes
A condition where the pancreas doesn't produce enough insulin, or when a person becomes resistant to their own insulin, which means blood glucose can rise to a dangerous level.

U

Uncertainty
The amount of error your results might have.

Urea
A waste product produced from the breakdown of amino acids in the liver.

Uterus
The main female reproductive organ and where the embryo develops during pregnancy. (Another word for the womb.)

V

Vacuole (plant cells)
A structure in plant cells that contains cell sap and maintains the internal pressure of the cell.

Valid result
A result that is repeatable, reproducible and answers the original question.

Valve (in the circulatory system)
A structure within the heart or a vein which prevents blood from flowing in the wrong direction.

Variable
A factor in an investigation that can change or be changed (e.g. temperature or concentration).

Variation
The differences that exist between individuals within a species.

Vector (in disease)
An organism that carries and transmits a pathogen from one host to another, but does not suffer from the disease that the pathogen causes.

Vector (in genetic engineering)
Something used to transfer DNA into a cell, e.g. a virus or a bacterial plasmid.

Vein
A blood vessel that carries blood to the heart.

Vena cava
A blood vessel (vein) which transports blood into the heart from the rest of the body (excluding the lungs).

Ventricle
A chamber of the heart which pumps blood out of the heart through either the pulmonary artery or the aorta.

Virus
A disease-causing agent which lives and replicates within host cells.

W

White blood cell
A cell which forms part of the blood and part of the immune system, helping to defend the body against disease.

X

Xylem
A type of plant tissue which transports water and mineral ions around the plant.

Z

Zero error
A type of systematic error caused by using a piece of equipment that isn't zeroed properly.

Zygote
The diploid cell formed when two gametes fuse at fertilisation.

Acknowledgements

Data acknowledgements

Edexcel specification reference points reproduced by permission of Edexcel and Pearson Education.

Percentile growth chart on pages 58 and 63 Copyright © 2009 Royal College of Paediatrics and Child Health.

Definition of health on pages 115 and 275 From: Preamble to the Constitution of the World Health Organization as adopted by the International Health Conference, New York, 19 June – 22 July 1946; signed on 22 July 1946 by the representatives of 61 States (Official Records of the World Health Organization, no. 2, p. 100) and entered into force on 7 April 1948.

Data used to construct the measles graph on page 133 from: Immunisations, Vaccine and Biologicals. Measles Global Annual Reported Cases 1980-2014. Measles Graph: http://www.who.int/immunization/monitoring_surveillance/burden/vpd/surveillance_type/active/measles/en/

Data used to construct the table on the use of stents on page 145 reprinted from the Journal of the American College of Cardiology, Vol 49/19. H Vernon Anderson et al. Drug-Eluting Stents for Acute Myocardial Infarction, pgs 1931-1933. © 2007, with permission from Elsevier.

Data used to construct the graph on page 185 taken from the National Diabetes Audit Executive Summary 2009-2010.

Photograph acknowledgements

p 3 Science Photo Library, p 6 **Tony Craddock**/Science Photo Library, p 8 **Tony McConnell**/Science Photo Library, p 9 **Tek Image**/Science Photo Library, p 21 **Adam Hart-Davis**/Science Photo Library, p 23 **Alfred Pasieka**/Science Photo Library, p 24 **Dr. Martha Powell, Visuals Unlimited**/Science Photo Library, p 26 **Steve Gschmeissner**/Science Photo Library, p 27 **Steve Gschmeissner**/Science Photo Library, p 30 **Kevin & Betty Collins, Visuals Unlimited**/Science Photo Library, p 37 **Clive Freeman, The Royal Institution**/Science Photo Library, p 43 **Andrew Lambert Photography**/Science Photo Library, p 52 **Martyn F. Chillmaid**/Science Photo Library, p 53 **Power And Syred**/Science Photo Library, p 55 (Fig. 7) **Steve Gschmeissner**/Science Photo Library, p 56 **Herve Conge, ISM**/Science Photo Library, p 59 **Pascal Goetgheluck**/Science Photo Library, p 66 **Dr Keith Wheeler**/Science Photo Library, p 67 **Thomas Deerinck, NCMIR**/Science Photo Library, p 73 **Adrian T Sumner**/Science Photo Library, p 77 **Voisin/Phanie**/Science Photo Library, p 81 **Wally Eberhart, Visuals Unlimited**/Science Photo Library, p 87 Science Photo Library, p 89 (centre) **Coneyl Jay**/Science Photo Library, p 89 (Fig. 1) **Kate Jacobs**/Science Photo Library, p 92 **Lawrence Berkeley National Laboratory**/Science Photo Library, p 100 (Fig. 1) **Pascal Goetgheluck**/Science Photo Library, p 100 (Fig. 2) **Mauricio Anton**/Science Photo Library, p 101 (Fig. 3) **John Reader**/Science Photo Library, p 101 (Fig. 4) **Elisabeth Daynes**/Science Photo Library, p 101 (Fig. 5) **S. Entressangle/E. Daynes**/Science Photo Library, p 108 (Fig. 1) **Phil Degginger**/Science Photo Library, p 108 (Fig. 2) **Ken M. Highfill**/Science Photo Library, p 112 **Sputnik**/Science Photo Library, p 117 **Dennis Kunkel Microscopy**/Science Photo Library, p 118 **UK Crown Copyright Courtesy of Fera**/Science Photo Library, p 119 (Fig. 4) **AMI Images**/Science Photo Library, p 123 **Juergen Berger**/Science Photo Library, p 124 **Biology Media**/Science Photo Library, p 126 **Saturn Stills**/Science Photo Library, p 127 **James King-Holmes**/Science Photo Library, p 129 **St. Bartholomew's Hospital**/Science Photo Library, p 136 **Arthur Glauberman**/Science Photo Library, p 146 **Biophoto Associates**/Science Photo Library, p 149 Science Photo Library, p 152 **E. R. Degginger**/Science Photo Library, p 155 (Fig. 2) **Dr. Richard Kessel & Dr. Gene Shih/Visuals Unlimited, Inc.**/Science Photo Library, p 155 (Fig. 4) **Biophoto Associates**/Science Photo Library, p 159 (Fig. 3 top and bottom) **Dr Jeremy Burgess**/Science Photo Library, p 165 **Scott Camazine**/Science Photo Library, p 172 **Professors P. M. Motta & J. Van Blerkom**/Science Photo Library, p 175 **Cordelia Molloy**/Science Photo Library, p 180 **Coneyl Jay**/Science Photo Library, p 190 **Biophoto Associates**/Science Photo Library, p 191 **Steve Gschmeissner**/Science Photo Library, p 192 (Fig. 3) **Biophoto Associates**/Science Photo Library, p 192 (Fig. 4) **Power And Syred**/Science Photo Library, p 192 (Fig. 5) **Susumu Nishinaga**/Science Photo Library, p 192 (Fig. 6) **Antonia Reeve**/Science Photo Library, p 193 **Steve Gschmeissner**/Science Photo Library, p 194 **CNRI**/Science Photo Library, p 199 **Samuel Ashfield**/Science Photo Library, p 208 **Power And Syred**/Science Photo Library, p 215 **Martyn F. Chillmaid**/Science Photo Library, p 216 **Martyn F. Chillmaid**/Science Photo Library, p 227 **Photostock-Israel**/Science Photo Library, p 229 **Wally Eberhart, Visuals Unlimited**/Science Photo Library, p 233 **GIPhotoStock**/Science Photo Library, p 234 **Andrew Lambert Photography**/Science Photo Library, p 235 **Martyn F. Chillmaid**/Science Photo Library, p 236 Science Photo Library, p 240 **Martyn F. Chillmaid**/Science Photo Library, p 253 **Photostock-Israel**/Science Photo Library.

Every effort has been made to locate copyright holders and obtain permission to reproduce sources. For those sources where it has been difficult to trace the originator of the work, we would be grateful for information. If any copyright holder would like us to make an amendment to the acknowledgements, please notify us and we will gladly update the book at the next reprint. Thank you.

Index

A

abiotic factors 209, 212
accurate results 12
acquired characteristics 89
active sites 36
active transport 46
adrenal glands 165, 168
adrenaline 165, 168
adult stem cells 59
aerobic respiration 199-201
AIDS 119
alcohol 136
algebra symbols 245
alleles 80
alveoli 189, 190
amino acids 41
amylase 39, 41
anaerobic respiration 200, 201
animal cells 23
anomalous results 13
antibiotic resistance 97, 98
antibiotics 131
antibodies 124-126, 192
antigens 124-126
Archaea (domain) 106
Ardi (fossil) 100
ART (Assisted Reproductive Technology) 174
arteries 193
asexual reproduction 55
axons 65, 66

B

bacteria 24, 116-119, 224, 229, 230
Bacteria (domain) 106
bacterial cells 24
bar charts 16
barrier contraceptives 175
bases (DNA) 76
belt transects 216
biodiversity 218-220
biological catalysts 36
biological molecules 41, 42
biomass 146
biotic factors 209, 212, 213

blood 191, 192
   glucose level 179-182
   vessels 193, 194
B-lymphocytes 124, 125
BMI (Body Mass Index) 138, 139, 181
Bunsen burners 235

C

cancer 57, 135
capillaries 193
carbohydrases 41
carbohydrates 41
carbon-14 dating 104
carbon cycle 224, 225
cardiac output 198
cardiovascular disease 135, 136, 140-143
causation 21, 22
cell
   cycle 54
   differentiation 57
   division 54-57
   elongation 57
   membranes 23, 24, 43, 44
   structure 23, 24
   walls 24
Chalara ash dieback 118
Chlamydia 119
chloroplasts 24, 146
cholera 117, 118
chromosomes 53, 75
ciliated epithelial cells 27
circulatory system 191-198
classification 105, 106
clinical testing 128, 129
clomifene therapy 174
CNS (central nervous system) 64, 65, 68
command words 251
communicable diseases 115-119
communicating results 4
communities 209, 210, 212, 213
competition 212, 213
complementary base pairing 76
conclusions 21, 22

conservation schemes 220
continuous sampling 39, 239
contraceptives 174, 175
controls 10
control variables 10
converting units 19, 20, 32
Core Practicals 233, 249, 251, 252
coronary bypass surgery 142
correlations 18, 21, 22
crop rotation 230
cytokinesis 54, 55
cytoplasm 23

D

Darwin, Charles 97
decomposers 224, 225, 230
decomposition 224, 225, 230
defences against disease 123, 124
denaturation (enzymes) 37, 38
dendrites 65, 66
dendrons 65
denitrifying bacteria 230
dependent variables 10
desalination 226, 227
diabetes 180, 181, 182
diffusion 43, 44
diploid cells 53, 72
diseases 115-119, 135-137
distribution of organisms 214-216
DNA 53, 75-77
   extracting from fruit 76, 77
   structure 76
dominant alleles 80
droughts 226
drug development and testing 127-129

E

ecosystems 209-213
   investigating 214-216
   levels of organisation 209
effectors 64, 68
egg cells 26, 27, 72
electric heaters 235

electron microscopes 28
embryonic stem cells 59, 60
endocrine glands 165, 166
endothermic reactions 146
environmental variation 89, 90
enzymes 36-42
   investigating activity 39, 40
equations 245
errors 13
erythrocytes 191
estimating
   size of cell structures 32, 33
   values 244
ethics 6, 240
Eukarya (domain) 106
eukaryotic cells 23, 24
eutrophication 218
evaluations 22
evolution 97-104
   of humans 100-104
exams 249
exam technique 250
exchange surfaces 188-190
exothermic reactions 199

F

fair tests 10
family pedigrees 85, 86
fatty acids 42
fertilisation 72
fertilisers 230
fields of view 237
fight or flight response 168
fish farming 218, 219
five kingdom classification 105
flagella 24
food webs 210
fossils 98, 100, 101, 104
frequency tables 17
FSH (follicle-stimulating hormone)
   170, 171, 174
fungi 116, 118, 224, 230

G

gametes 72, 73
gas exchange
   mammals 189, 190
   plants 159, 160
gas syringes 234
gene pools 110
genes 75

genetic diagrams 81-84, 87, 88
genetic engineering 111, 112
genetic variation 89-91
genomes 75
genotypes 80
glucagon 180
glucose 146, 147, 179-182,
   199, 200
glycerol 42
glycogen 179, 180
GM organisms 111
gradient (of a graph) 247
graphs 18, 246-248
growth 57
growth charts 58
guard cells 159, 160

H

haploid cells 27, 72, 73
hazards 7, 8
health 115
heart attacks 140
heart (structure of) 196, 197
heart transplants 143
heterozygous organisms 80
histograms 16, 17
HIV 119
homeostasis 178
hominids 100, 101
homozygous organisms 80
hormonal contraceptives
   174, 175
hormones 165-175, 179, 180
human evolution 100-104
Human Genome Project 92, 93
hypothalamus 169
hypotheses 2, 9

I

immune system 123-125
immunisation 125, 126
inbreeding 110
independent variables 10
insulin 179-182
intercepts (graphs) 246
interdependence 210, 211
interphase 54
inverse square law 154
iodine test (for starch) 39
IVF 174

L

Leakey's fossils 101
levels of response questions 252
LH (luteinising hormone)
   170, 171, 174
ligases 111, 112
light microscopes 28, 29
limitations of science 6
limiting factors 148-150
lines of best fit 18
lipases 42
lipids 42
liver disease 136
lock and key model 37
Lucy (fossil) 101
lungs 189
lymphocytes 124-126, 192
lysozymes 123

M

magnification 28
   calculations 30, 31
malaria 118
malnutrition 136
mean (average) 14
measuring
   length 233
   mass 233
   pH 234
   temperature 233
   time 234
   volume 233, 234
median (average) 14
meiosis 73
memory lymphocytes 125, 126
menstrual cycle 170-172
meristems 57, 60, 61
metabolic rate 168, 169
microscopes 28, 29
mitochondria 23
mitosis 54-56
mode (average) 14
models 3, 4
monohybrid inheritance 81-84
motor neurones 64-66, 68
mutations 90, 91
mutualism 210
myelin sheaths 65, 66

N

natural selection 97, 98
negative feedback 168, 169, 178
nervous system 64-66
neurones 64-68
neurotransmitters 67, 68
nitrifying bacteria 230
nitrogen cycle 229, 230
nitrogen-fixing bacteria 229
non-communicable diseases 115, 135-137
non-indigenous species 219
nuclei 23, 53

O

obesity 136, 138, 139, 181
oestrogen 170, 171, 174, 175
osmosis 44, 45
   investigating 47-49
ovaries 166, 170, 171

P

pancreas 165, 179, 180
parasitism 211
partially permeable membranes 43, 44
pathogens 116-119
   defences against 123, 124
peer-review 2
percentage change 48, 243
percentages 243
percentile charts 58
phagocytes 192
phenotypes 89-91
pH indicators 234
phloem 155
photosynthesis 146-150, 154, 225
   investigating rate 152, 153
pituitary gland 165, 169, 171
plant cells 24
plasma 192
plasmids 24, 111, 112
platelets 192
pollution 212
populations 209
population sizes 215
potable water 226, 227
potometers 158, 159, 236

precise results 12
preclinical testing 127
predation 213
predictions 2, 9
progesterone 170, 171, 174, 175
prokaryotic cells 23, 24
proteases 41
proteins 41
protists 116, 118
Punnett squares 81-84, 87

Q

quadrats 214-216
question types (exams) 251-253

R

radiometric dating 104
random errors 13
random sampling 214, 238, 239
range (of data) 14
rate calculations 40, 153, 159, 203, 247
ratios 186-188, 242
reaction times 65
receptors 64, 68
recessive alleles 80
red blood cells 191
reflex arcs 68
reflexes 67-69
reforestation 219
relay neurones 65, 66, 68
repeatable results 9, 12
reproducible results 9, 12
resistant organisms 97, 98
resolution
   of instruments 12
   of microscopes 28
respiration 199-201, 225
   investigating 202, 203
restriction enzymes 111, 112
reverse osmosis 227
ribosomes 23, 24
risk factors for disease 135, 136
risks 7, 8
root hair cells 157

S

safety in experiments 8, 240
sample size 11
sampling 238, 239
scientific developments 5
scientific drawings 30, 237
secondary immune response 125, 126
selection pressures 97
selective breeding 109, 110
sensory neurones 64-66, 68
sensory receptors 64, 68
sex determination 87, 88
sexual reproduction 26, 72, 73
significant figures 15
SI units 19
slides (microscopes) 28, 29
smoking 135
specialised cells 26
specific immune response 124
sperm cells 26, 27, 72
stains (microscopy) 28
standard form 31, 241, 242
starch 39, 41
statins 141
stem cells 59-61
stents 142
sticky ends 111, 112
stimuli 64, 68
STIs (sexually transmitted infections) 119
stomata 159, 160
stone tools 103, 104
stratigraphy 104
subcellular structures 23, 24
surface area to volume ratios 186-188
synapses 67, 68
systematic errors 13

T

tables (of data) 14
testes 166
theories 2, 3
three domain classification 105, 106
thyroid gland 165, 168, 169
thyroxine 168, 169
transects 215, 216
translocation 155

transpiration 155, 156, 158, 159
trial runs 11
tuberculosis 117
tumours 57
Turkana Boy (fossil) 101
type 1 diabetes 180, 182
type 2 diabetes 181

U
uncertainty 15
units 19, 20
urea 186

V
vacuoles 24
valid results 9
valves 194, 196
variables 10
variation 89-91
vectors
   in disease 117, 118
   in genetic engineering 111
veins 194
viruses 116, 119

W
waist-to-hip ratios 139, 181
water baths 236
water cycle 226
water uptake (plants) 158, 159

white blood cells 123-126, 192

X
X and Y chromosomes 87, 88
xylem 155

Z
zero errors 13
zygotes 72